RICHARD OLNEY:

Evolution of a Statesman

RICHARD OLNEY

Evolution of a Statesman

Gerald G. Eggert

The Pennsylvania State University Press

University Park and London

Library of Congress Cataloging in Publication Data

Eggert, Gerald G
  Richard Olney: evolution of a statesman.

  Bibliography: p. 377
  1. Olney, Richard, 1835-1917. I. Title.
E664.045E33   973.8'7'0924 [B]   73-6878
ISBN 0-271-01162-9

Printed in the United States of America
Manufactured by The Maple Press Co. Inc.

TO MY TEACHERS:

Adrian D. Davis
Robert R. Russel
Robert Friedmann
Sidney Fine

Contents

Acknowledgments

The scholarly debts that I have incurred in researching and writing this biography are many. For proposing the project, guiding the initial stages of research, and for reading and commenting most helpfully on various drafts, I am under deep obligation to my mentor and friend, Professor Sidney Fine of the University of Michigan. I wish to thank Professor Fine and other readers of the manuscript for their appropriate—though agonizing—advice, "Reduce!" "Cut!" "Boil down!" Numerous students and colleagues have served (and not always voluntarily) as sounding boards for my thoughts about Olney; their questions and suggestions have considerably improved the book. Most patient and helpful has been my colleague, Robert James Maddox.

Two of Richard Olney's grandchildren, Francis Minot, Sr., and Agnes Abbot, and a niece, Catherine Olney, generously supplied me with family stories and reminiscences that made possible the portrayal of Olney's private life as a husband and father. With permission of the Baker Library at Harvard University I have used and quoted from the Henry Lee Higginson Papers. The Massachusetts Historical Society kindly granted me use of materials from its Richard Olney and William Endicott Collections. I am especially grateful to the Burlington Northern for allowing me to use and quote from the Burlington Railroad Archives on deposit at the Newberry Library, Chicago, and to Professor Richard C. Overton for making available to me a microfilm copy of the personal papers of Charles E. Perkins which have subsequently been deposited in the Burlington Archives. The University of North Carolina Press permitted me to quote from *The Cabinet Diary of William L. Wilson*, edited by Festus P. Summers, and Professor Joseph J. Mathews generously provided me with information from the papers of Lord Salisbury and Joseph Chamberlain. The conclusions that I have drawn from all these sources are my own and do not necessarily reflect the views of the persons or institutions who made the materials available.

I wish to thank the many staff members of the Manuscript Division of the Library of Congress and the National Archives, where the great bulk of the research was done, for their courteous assistance. For providing financial assistance I am most grateful to the University of

Michigan (which awarded me an Orla B. Taylor Fellowship) and the Central Fund for Research of the Pennsylvania State University.

Chapter VII originally appeared in slightly different form in the June 1961 issue of the *Mississippi Valley Historical Review* and is used here with permission of the *Journal of American History*.

To my ever-patient wife Jean and to my children Michael, Susan, and Christine, who have lived with Mr. Olney for a long time, I can only say, "it's done!"

Gerald G. Eggert
State College, Pennsylvania

Making His Mark

Richard Olney died in Boston on the eighth of April 1917. That same week, leaving its "age of innocence" behind, the United States entered World War I. The coincidence of the two events was not inappropriate. As secretary of state, Olney had done much to arouse the nation from its post-Civil War isolationism and to hurry it onto the stage of world affairs. Of his eighty-one years, Olney spent only four in high public office: two as attorney general of the United States and two as secretary of state. He dominated the second-term cabinet of President Grover Cleveland, his hand helping to shape every major act of the administration. As attorney general during the depressed years that followed the Panic of 1893, Olney fought in the battles to preserve the gold standard, to halt the march of Coxey's Army, and to suppress the Pullman Strike. Promoted to head the Department of State, he wrestled with the difficult Venezuela boundary dispute, the Cuban revolution, and the rising tide of American expansionism.

By the time of his death, Olney was no longer a well-known public figure. The war crowded his obituaries off the front pages of most newspapers, even in Boston. Twenty years had passed since his return from Washington to a quiet law practice, and except for a brief flurry in 1904, when Massachusetts Democrats boomed him for president, his name appeared in few headlines. Occasionally, leading Democrats sought him out for advice as an elder statesman, and from time to time he published thoughtful articles or made public addresses on questions that interested him. For the most part, however, he shunned popular attention.

Those who still remembered Olney probably associated him with the war scare over the Venezuelan boundary in 1895. Although his brash note to Great Britain at the time stirred deep feelings of patriotism, his anti-British stance aroused suspicions in 1917 when everything was being measured by a rigid scale of loyalty to the war effort. Nathan Matthews, who prepared the principal memorial address for Olney before the Supreme Judicial Court of Massachusetts, found that some people believed Olney to have been pro-German. In reaching this conclusion they had linked together his Venezuela note, the long residence of one of his daughters in Germany, and his refusal in 1913 to serve as ambassador to Great Britain. In his attempt to put the absurd charge to rest, Matthews went too far, portraying Olney as sinking into his final coma, cheered by Wilson's war message, and regretting only that he would not live to see the final victory of the Allies over the Central Powers.[1]

The pro-German allegation was the last of several petty antagonisms that marked Olney's long relationship with his fellow Bostonians. Obituary notices and graveside appraisals of his career, though containing the usual tributes evoked by the death of a successful and once-prominent citizen, unintentionally touched on several of the frictions that had persisted through the years.

For example, Olney's acumen as a lawyer had brought him into constant contact with the best families, the so-called Proper Bostonians. He had lived and moved among them, joined their clubs, summered with them on Cape Cod, read their newspaper (the *Evening Transcript*), and lived in general according to their precepts. He was even buried among them in Mount Auburn cemetery. In serving them he amassed a fortune of over a million dollars, was recognized as a corporation lawyer of unusual caliber, and had distinguished himself in high public office more than any other son of Massachusetts between Charles Sumner and Oliver Wendell Holmes, Jr. Nonetheless, Olney did not and could not have become one of them. Though he lived in the Hub for over sixty years, obituary writers were careful to point out that he was an outlander, neither born in Boston nor nurtured at Harvard College. An editorial in the *Evening Transcript*, written with the correct restraint expected and appreciated by Boston Brahmins, observed that Mr. Olney was "a man whom [Massachusetts] might *almost* call its first citizen."[2]

The *Boston Herald* unwittingly referred to another point that separated Olney from the Brahmins—his politics. His personal conservatism and elite clientele bespoke solid Republicanism. But Olney was a Democrat. This peculiarity was frequently explained away by the story that he, like a number of other eminent Bostonians, had bolted the Grand Old Party during the Mugwump revolt against Blaine in 1884. But stubbornly independent, Olney had come to Boston a Democrat and a Democrat he had remained. The *Herald* recalled that he had not deserted his party even in 1896 when many conservative

Democrats shifted to McKinley or to the Gold Democrat rather than vote for William Jennings Bryan. Olney said at the time that "he had been a Democrat in Boston when it cost a man something in social and professional lines to avow such a political affiliation" and he did not propose "to turn away from it on the mere rising of a spectre of free silver."[3] Olney did not vote in that election.

Another factor in Olney's standing apart was his celebrated bad temper. His pugnacity was legend, his brusque manner and lack of camaraderie notorious. Little of this appeared in his obituaries, of course, but it was hinted at in a eulogy delivered before the Massachusetts Historical Society. Olney, though a most agreeable companion to the few who knew him well, "was so little responsive in manner that he did not make friends easily. . . . "[4]

But Boston Brahmins, however petty and snobbish they could be about outsiders, were also frequently shrewd appraisers of men. Bishop William Lawrence, shepherd of souls of Massachusetts Episcopalians and a Proper Bostonian of impeccable standing, after officiating at Olney's funeral, noted in his diary, "As Attorney General and Sec. of State of U.S. very strong: had elements of a great man. . . . "[5]

Many eminent American statesmen have sprung from families more obscure than Richard Olney's and from villages more remote than Oxford, Massachusetts. Even so, little in Olney's background hinted at the distinguished career that would follow. His parents, Wilson and Eliza Butler Olney, represented a blending of three traditional New England strains: Massachusetts puritan, Rhode Island independent, and French Huguenot. Both families had come to the Bay Colony during the Great Migration out of England—Thomas Olney landing at Salem in 1635, Stephen Butler at Boston in 1640. The Butlers remained in Boston for four generations. Then in 1779, James Butler moved to Oxford, in Worcester County, to operate an inn that eventually passed to his son, Peter (Richard Olney's grandfather). James's wife, Mary Sigourney, had ties to Oxford that dated from 1686 when a band of French Protestants, including her grandfather, Andrew Sigourney (André Séjourné), settled in the village. Soon driven out by hostile Indians, many of the Frenchmen took refuge in Boston. Over the years some drifted back to leave their marks on Oxford in the form of family and place names.[6]

As for the Olneys, Massachusetts officials in 1638 expelled Thomas (a man of "stern and decided opinions who did not hesitate to advance his views among his neighbors") for espousing the doctrines of Roger

Williams. Moving to Rhode Island, Thomas became one of the thirteen proprietors of Providence, a founder of the Baptist Church in America, and the progenitor of a large and prominent Rhode Island family.[7]

Richard Olney, a direct descendant of Thomas and the father of Wilson Olney, settled permanently in Oxford in 1819. Some of his wealth might have been inherited; the rest he accumulated as profits from a combination tavern-inn that he operated just outside Providence, and from investments in the West Indies trade. Driven from shipping by the Napoleonic Wars and by "Mr. Jefferson's Embargo," Olney invested in a small cotton mill at East Douglas, Massachusetts, in 1811. Not long after his removal to Oxford, he helped organize the Oxford Woolen Manufacturing Company and became its president. The firm quickly acquired a national reputation for its product and paid a regular ten per cent dividend on its stock until the Panic of 1837. Refusing to tie himself to a single venture, Olney became the chief stockholder, a director, and president of the Oxford Bank; he loaned money privately to residents of the area, and he operated a 170-acre farm. Wealth brought him instant status. Less than a year after he had moved to Oxford, the town elected Olney to represent it at the state constitutional convention. Subsequently he served two terms in the Massachusetts General Assembly and held a number of elective posts in Oxford.[8] A stubborn, domineering man, Richard Olney ruled his brood of eleven children "with an iron hand as long as he could"; with some he quarrelled and parted.[9] Several daughters married young to escape his rule and two sons migrated West, one never to be heard from again.

Wilson, Richard's oldest son, failed ever to win full independence from his father. At fifteen he started work in his father's cotton mill. Then, after teaching school for one winter, he clerked for a few years in the combination store and inn that his father opened at Oxford. At twenty-one, Wilson struck out on his own, clerking in stores in Rhode Island, New York, and New Jersey. After six years, at his father's request, he returned to a stool in the counting house of the Oxford Woolen Company.[10] Easy-going, unassuming, and somewhat ineffective, Wilson did not marry till the age of thirty. Eliza Butler, a woman of "abrupt and commanding manner," seems to have supplied some of the ambition and strength of personality that her husband lacked.[11] The couple had been married four years before their first child, Richard, named after his grandfather Olney, was born on 15 September 1835. Within a few years three more sons, George, Peter, and Frederick, and a daughter, Gertrude, were added to the family.

About the time of his marriage, Wilson once more left his father's employ, this time setting up a dry goods store in Oxford with two partners. Business was dull, however, and the three decided to leave New England for Louisville, Kentucky, in the bustling Ohio River Valley. There they operated a dry goods store for five years. If Wilson and Eliza hoped for a fresh start on their own, away from the overbearing influence of Grandfather Olney, their years in the West were disappointing. The Panic of 1837 struck the year after they arrived and Wilson was obliged time and again to turn to his father for loans.

The elder Richard Olney died in 1841, leaving property inventoried at nearly $140,000. Wilson immediately wound up his affairs in Louisville and returned with his family to Oxford to help administer his father's estate. Grandfather Olney continued to dictate to his children from beyond the grave. In his will he decreed that the money left to his daughters was not to fall into the hands of their husbands. As a special bequest to Wilson, he forgave $2,000 in unpaid loans, but imposed a final lesson in financial responsibility. To collect his inheritance, Wilson first must account for and pay in to the estate everything owed to his father "on notes or otherwise, whether barred by statute or not."[12] By not allowing Wilson to charge off his obligations against his share of the estate, the father put his son to the embarrassment of having to raise a considerable sum of money, probably by borrowing.

Wilson spent four years in settling his father's affairs, after which he drifted first into a small flannel-making business and then into a two-man shoe-making venture. Finally, in 1855, Wilson was named cashier of the Oxford Bank founded by his father. His personal traits did not augur favorably for great success in that business. Wilson was "a money-earner but not a money maker"; his "nature was kindly, his impulses generous, and his judgments of others most charitable."[13] Although he never rose above the position of cashier, he lived the last twenty years of his life in modest comfort.

Upon the return from Kentucky, young Richard Olney began his formal education at a small school in the "woolen village" near his grandfather's factory. Classmates remembered him as a bright, intelligent scholar, but one who memorized his lessons at home and spent much of his time at school playing tricks on those who were trying to study. Once through common school, Richard and a few boys from the village prepared for the academy at a "dame's school" kept by the wife of a local clergyman.[14]

When he was twelve, Richard entered the distinguished academy at nearby Leicester. Founded in 1784, the school differed from most others of the time in that it was coeducational and nonsectarian. Religious training was not neglected: students attended daily morning and evening devotions, observed all public days of fasting and thanksgiving, and went to services twice on Sundays in one of the village churches.

Many of the students at Leicester Academy were from the village and lived at home. Others, including some from as far away as Louisiana or Illinois, took quarters in the academy building itself. Olney, who arrived too late to find space at the academy, roomed at the Congregational Church parsonage during the week and returned to Oxford on weekends and holidays. Instruction at Leicester Academy stressed Greek and Latin, but the modern languages, French and German, were also offered. Smatterings of mathematics, science, history, and philosophy rounded out the curriculum. Olney did well scholastically, receiving "excellent" in every subject. He also found time for football-kicking and marble-snapping in the schoolyard and for spruce beer and cookies at "Uncle" Evi Chilson's store in the village.[15]

Olney, who was the first in his family to go to college, enrolled at Brown University in Providence in September 1851. His schooling was made possible by the economizing of his father "whose early opportunities had been small and whose resources were always slender."[16] Of Wilson Olney's four sons, only Richard and Peter went to college and on into the practice of law. George, following the example of Grandfather Olney, became a small-scale textile manufacturer while Frederick went into the hardware business—a pursuit taken up earlier by uncles James and Peter Butler. Quite possibly Uncle Peter Butler, who had amassed a considerable fortune from hardware in Boston, helped with Richard's and Peter's college expenses.[17] Certainly both boys became closely attached to their uncle and his family. Peter married Butler's daughter Mary, while Richard became the mentor and champion of Butler's son, Sigourney. Although Sigourney was seventeen years younger than his cousin, he became Richard Olney's closest friend and confidant over the years.

Olney initially enrolled in Brown's new three-year bachelor of arts program. "[D]esigned especially for those who desire to prepare for the different professions, and yet, from unavoidable circumstances, are unable to pursue a complete course of liberal education," it required one less year than the usual master of arts program.[18] Except for election into the school's foremost literary and debating club, the Philermenian Society, Olney was unsuccessful in his first term at Brown and he dropped out for a full year. Eye trouble has been given as the reason and Olney's low grades and the withdrawal of only two books from the college library seem to support this explanation. But another family tradition holds that Olney was suspended for beating a fellow student. Whatever the case, there were changes when he returned in February 1853. He enrolled in the four-year program, he took a room in the town rather than in a dormitory, and his grades improved markedly.[19]

By the start of his junior year in September 1854, financial problems seem once more to have arisen. Wilson Olney, not yet cashier of the Oxford Bank, had temporarily gone into the shoe-making business. Richard moved back to the less expensive rooms on campus and that winter taught school for twelve weeks in nearby Foxboro, Massachusetts. For teaching forty-seven children he received $105. Otherwise the experience was unrewarding, as the succinct report in the town records show:

> During the winter season, this school was under the charge of Mr. Olney, a gentleman from Brown University. This term was his first experience in teaching, and [as] is apt to be the case with tyro teachers he expected to find his pupils more advanced in their studies than they were. This led him to undervalue their talents and discouraged his efforts to improve them. Early in the term there was some considerable lack of order, but towards its close, the school manifestly improved in this respect. During the term there was a complaint entered before your committee that the teacher had exercised undue severity towards one of the pupils, we thereupon made a thorough investigation of the matter, hearing the evidence on both sides, and came to the unanimous decision, that, although it was evident that the boy had been cruelly beaten by some one, yet, by his own statement repeated at several different times during the examination, it was proved not to have been inflicted by the teacher.[20]

At Brown, Olney met with considerably greater success. His oratorical skills were recognized when he was chosen to speak at the Junior Exhibition in the fall of 1854. Ranking sixth in his class academically, he served as marshal at the Junior Burials in July—an annual event marking the class's completion of rhetoric, when the texts for the unpopular course were dumped into the river following elaborate mock-funeral services.[21] Olney's academic standing came from determined effort rather than brilliance. His classmates later described him as serious and "always brimful of study." His reputation was that of a "plodder and a pusher." One wrote that Olney was "an early riser and a close student after the shades of night had fallen. He was a bookworm at spells and a hard student all the time." There was little nonsense about Olney and little college conviviality. The commonest adjectives used to describe him were "quiet," "aloof," "unostentatious," and "reticent." To fellow students he appeared a man "always up on the hill . . . working like one possessed to get higher still."[22]

Few got to know young Olney intimately. One freshman who roomed in the same dormitory when Olney was a "gray and reverend Senior," held his breath in anticipation at what would befall even seniors who presumed to address Olney as "Dick." Back in Oxford, some people regarded Olney as a snob. A young schoolteacher who roomed at his parents' home thought "that Richard had pretty high notions. Those times when he came home from college he held his head up well and seemed to think a good deal of aristocracy. I got that idea from remarks he would make."[23]

His stand-offishness and lack of camaraderie nearly blocked his election to Phi Beta Kappa. At a meeting to vote on new members, the society skipped over both the third-ranked man (regarded as "an informing sneak") and sixth-ranked Olney. When William Dearth (who did call Olney "Dick") nominated him, after the election of the seventh-ranked junior, some members protested. They had *"no objection to the man,"* but did not wish to admit too many juniors at once. Incensed by the "hypocrisy" of this obvious stratagem, Dearth did some politicking and succeeded in pushing through Olney's name at the next meeting.[24]

In no essential way did Brown University differ greatly from Leicester Academy. Olney pursued much the same course of study: Greek and Latin, French, mathematics, chemistry, geology, physiology, philosophy (natural, intellectual, and moral), rhetoric, political economy, and history. Olney did his best work in history, political economy, and rhetoric, his poorest in the sciences. Recreation was no more organized than at Leicester. Physical education was unknown and there were neither intramural nor intercollegiate sports. Elaborate pranks provided outlets for the energies of some, spontaneous ball games for those of others. Olney played both baseball and football, but his classmates noticed that "even when ball was played by him the game apparently was clothed in a garb of seriousness. Athletics were indulged in by Mr. Olney more for the health of the thing than for anything else."[25] If health rather than pleasure were the goal, Olney was successful. He developed a broad set of shoulders and a large, well-muscled frame by the time he reached maturity, and suffered no serious illness until his mid-seventies.

Brown, closely affiliated with the Baptist Church, required its students to attend chapel twice each day and to listen to sermons and prayers. None of this seems to have had much impact on Olney's religious outlook. His adult life was all but void of religion. He attended church rarely and his extensive correspondence in later years with the Episcopal bishop of Massachusetts reveals more of the bishop's responsibilities for matters of this world than of Olney's concern for the next.[26]

Olney graduated in 1856, already possessing some of the characteristics of his adult life. The joking, playful boy of the Oxford school had given way to a serious, determined, and ambitious young man. Life was a grim business in which even recreation must serve some practical end. Although respected for his hard work and scholastic abilities, Olney made no close friends and was never popular. His austere outlook, his quick temper and sharp tongue, and his unwillingness or inability to share in the give-and-take of real friendship, isolated him and made of him a loner. A loner he remained throughout his life.

At some point, Olney decided upon a career in law. Instead of simply reading in the office of a practicing attorney, as was the rule, he chose to take formal training at the Harvard Law School. Standards at the nation's leading law school in September 1856, when Olney entered, were not exacting. Because there were no admission requirements, as many as half of the students had no previous college training. Attendance at lectures and moot court sessions and reading the textbooks were all voluntary. The school conferred a law degree automatically, without examination, on anyone who enrolled for three terms and paid the stipulated fees.

Even those who faithfully attended lectures (and apparently most students did), were not given a complete introduction to the mysteries of the law. The course of study, taught by three professors who maintained important private practices, was designed to cover two full years. Since only half of the subjects were offered each year, it was the rare student who stayed four terms and completed the whole program. Free to join or leave classes at any time, students frequently enrolled after the series of lectures was under way, completed eighteen months of study, received a bachelor of laws degree, and were gone before the professors had finished their round of lectures.[27]

Having earned his degree and passed his bar examination, in April 1859 Olney applied for his first position, in the office of Judge Benjamin F. Thomas of Boston. Theophilus Parsons, one of Olney's law professors, wrote a glowing letter of recommendation for his "friend" Richard Olney. "He is among the best men we have ever had here;— best I mean, for industry, intelligence, and devotion to duty. . . . He needs nothing but opportunity. If he can get *that*, I know no one more sure of success."[28]

Other factors may have influenced Judge Thomas's decision in favor of Olney. Although he came from an old Boston family, Thomas, like Olney, had attended both Leicester Academy and Brown University. For twenty years he had practiced law in Olney's native county and was judge of probate for Worcester County when Grandfather Olney's estate was settled in the 1840s.[29] Quite possibly he knew the Olneys long before Richard applied for a position. Of greater consequence, his daughter Agnes, an attractive young lady in her early twenties, had met and fallen in love with Richard Olney. A young friend of the judge, hearing that he had resigned from the Supreme Judicial Court of Massachusetts to go into private practice, asked for a place in his office. Thomas replied that the request came too late; his daughter had "engaged herself to a young lawyer," and the place was to go to him.[30] Olney served nearly two years in the judge's office, however, before he and Agnes Thomas were married on 6 March 1861.

To many young men of Olney's age, the outbreak of the Civil War in April 1861 meant suspension of their private careers while they fought to preserve the nation. Olney, however, had no sympathy with the policy of holding the union together with bayonets. A lifelong, states' rights Democrat, he believed that the Southern states had the right to secede peacefully if they chose. Furthermore, by the time of President Lincoln's call for volunteers after the fall of Fort Sumter, the Olneys were expecting a child. A daughter, Agnes, was born in December 1861. Four years later a second daughter, Mary, was born. The young attorney, opposed to coercing the seceded states, with a growing family to support and a career to launch, decided against marching off to war. Instead, he hired a substitute.[31]

For seventeen years, Olney's practice was closely interwoven with that of Judge Thomas. He became Thomas's junior associate, they shared a common office, and their names appeared jointly on briefs throughout the period. Like Thomas, Olney specialized in wills and trust estates, and though he did not become wealthy, the association provided a comfortable living. He admired and respected the judge

and the relationship between the two was always cordial.[32] Nevertheless, during those years, Olney fretted in the shadow of his eminent
father-in-law. He also experienced frustration and envy as he watched
classmates and finally his younger brother, Peter, open law offices
in New York City and meet with almost immediate success. "It is
a great mistake for a young lawyer to start in Boston," he complained
to a friend in the sixties. "I ought to have gone to New York."[33]

The standing to which Olney aspired meant, in Boston, building
up a clientele among the Proper Bostonians, the small group of wealthy,
inbred aristocrats who dominated the social and business life of the
city and of New England in the second half of the nineteenth century.
From the point of view of his intended clients, Olney had several
handicaps. By birth, social standing, and education he was an outsider.
Not until he entered Harvard Law School had he had contacts with
sons of the right families. The merchant princes of Boston, nonetheless,
were quick to recognize legal and business acumen, and when a man
possessed such talents—even an outlander—he was pressed into their
service if not to their bosoms.[34]

Olney's early cases did not win the attention of the general public,
and were of no lasting significance because of either the persons
involved or the legal principles at stake. For the most part they
concerned bankruptcy proceedings, property rights, and technical con-
structions to be given wills, contracts, and devices of trusteeship. Frequently members of the Boston elite called upon him to handle small
matters in these areas, and, apparently satisfied with his work, increasingly gave him more of their business to conduct.[35] Then, in 1876,
the problems of the Eastern Railroad Company brought Olney the
opportunity to make his mark as a lawyer.

For years, the officers of the Eastern had squandered the company's
resources, lavishing funds on unprofitable feeder lines in which some
of them held financial interests, buying up unfinished projects and
completing them at unjustifiably high costs, and engaging in spurious
stock and real estate deals never formally authorized by the board
of directors. Great sums also were wasted trying to tap into the traffic
of the Eastern's arch-rival, the Boston & Maine, which operated a
parallel line between Boston and Portsmouth, New Hampshire. Most
costly of all, the Eastern leased lines at inflated prices in a futile attempt
to block the Boston & Maine from the "down east" traffic out of
Maine and the Maritime Provinces of Canada.

By December 1875, the Eastern's debts exceeded $15,000,000 and
receipts no longer covered interest payments.[36] Since much of the
debt was not secured by mortgage, some creditors stood to lose all.

Uniting in adversity, the creditors and shareholders formed a committee to save the company. Their plan was simple: All existing debts were to be exchanged for new low-interest-bearing "Certificates of Indebtedness," and control of the company was to be vested in nine trustees—three representing the stock and six the creditors. When the debt was reduced to under $10,000,000, control would revert to the stockholders.[37]

After investigating the Eastern's affairs, the General Assembly of Massachusetts passed a law enabling the committee to put its plan into effect. Whether Olney had any part in formulating the scheme or pushing it through the legislature is uncertain. The trustees, however, promptly hired him as their legal counsel and he remained as attorney for the trustees and the company until the Eastern worked itself out of its difficulties.[38] His greatest challenge was to meet the barrage of litigation arising out of the reorganization of the company. Because the Eastern was separately incorporated in Massachusetts and New Hampshire, the constitutionality of the enabling act, its scope, the meaning of its various provisions, and the determination of debts to be included or excluded under the plan, had to be tested in the courts of both states.[39]

More conservative, responsible leadership, coupled with the new scheme's reduced interest burden, and the general business recovery that marked the end of the Panic of 1873, halted the deterioration of the Eastern's financial standing. Beginning in 1878, the company each year realized a small income above expenses. The market value of its certificates, which had fallen to below 50 in 1876, reached 112 by 1883, and Eastern stock, which stood at an all-time low of 2½ in 1877, rose to 55 by 1881 and to 129 by 1886.[40] These spectacular gains were not due solely to the wisdom of the reorganization plan or to the skill of the men administering it. Of greater importance were rumors of consolidation with the Boston & Maine which repeatedly touched off speculative buying of the securities of both lines.

From the first, Olney sided with those favoring such a union. It was their expectation that in the long run consolidation would prove to be more profitable than continued competition. Many of the Eastern's stockholders, however, saw the improved conditions as heralding a new era of prosperity for the company and had no wish to share that prosperity with the ancient foe. Various proposals for consolidation were blocked by the Eastern's stockholders, much to the disgust of the major creditors of the company. On one occasion a representative of Baring Brothers of London suggested ("probably not seriously") that the trustees should consider defaulting on the certificates of indebtedness, allow foreclosure of the mortgage (which would wipe out the stock), and then effect the desired lease with the Boston & Maine.[41] Finally, in 1884, under terms most favorable to the Boston & Maine, that company leased the Eastern for fifty-five years.[42]

By 1879 Olney had successfully disposed of the litigation growing out of the reorganization plan and was rewarded with the general counselship of the Eastern and election to its board of directors. After the lease to the Boston & Maine in 1884, Olney became the attorney for that company and sat on its board of directors as a representative of Eastern interests. It was not that Olney had won all of the Eastern's cases—he had not. His friend, Judge Caleb W. Loring, put it well when he said that it was Olney's "carrying thru [sic] an important matter that brot [sic] him into prominence rather than a singularly brilliant piece of work from the legal point of view."[43] Success had been neither swift nor easy. Olney was forty-four in 1879 when at last he emerged as one of Boston's leading authorities on railroad law.

2

Railroad Lawyer

During the 1880s and 1890s, Richard Olney devoted himself to two of railroading's major legal problems—consolidation and regulation. He helped transform the Boston & Maine from a simple Boston-to-Portland line into a system that controlled all rail transportation northeast, north, and northwest of Boston. At the same time, he worked to check efforts of reformers to bring railroads under state and federal regulation. In neither struggle did he pursue long-range, carefully planned objectives or adhere to a consistent philosophy regarding the proper relationship of railroads and the public interest. A skillful tactician rather than a strategist, Olney concentrated on winning each skirmish for his clients as it arose. Only by looking back over a string of small victories could the outlines of his accomplishments be discerned.

When Olney went on to the board of directors of the Boston & Maine in 1884, two other representatives of Eastern Railroad interests—Samuel C. Lawrence and Frank Jones—joined him. The trio had worked together in saving the Eastern and arranging for the lease to the Boston & Maine. Now they moved to take over leadership of the Boston & Maine. Olney would serve as general counsel and director of the line for thirty years, Lawrence would sit on the board of directors for twenty-four. Jones, who had a streak of piracy in his make-up, played a briefer but more spectacular role. Assisted by a group of New Hampshire adventurers that included his son-in-law, Charles A. Sinclair, he at first dominated the Boston & Maine from behind the scenes. Then in 1889 he became president of the line and controlled it openly.

The Boston & Maine system expanded rapidly during the decade that Jones and his crew were in charge. Their rule, however, was characterized by spurious deals and stock-watering episodes as well as by growth. Quite possibly Lawrence and Olney did not sympathize with Jones or his methods even at first, and certainly they were frequently at odds with him after 1890. Nonetheless, Olney, as counsel of the corporation, drew up the leases and drafted the legislation needed for Jones's operations. He also argued on behalf of those proposals before legislative committees and defended them in the courts. To that extent, at least, Olney was an accomplice of the Jones gang.[1]

Jones and his associates chose the Worcester, Nashua & Rochester Railroad (WN&R), a potentially valuable link in a Worcester-to-Portland route around Boston, as their first victim. Forming a syndicate, Jones, Sinclair, and the others began buying WN&R stock in 1884 when it stood at 60 and paid only three per cent dividends. In 1885 the syndicate took over the board of directors, elected Sinclair president, and announced that the WN&R was up for lease to the highest bidder. As the Boston & Maine, the Boston & Lowell, and other lines became interested, WN&R stock rose. The Boston & Maine won by paying the WN&R an annual rental equal to a five and one-half per cent dividend on its stock. Sinclair and his associates promptly voted a generous stock dividend and watched their shares skyrocket to 135 by 17 December 1885. Olney drafted legislative authorization for the lease and defended it in committee.[2]

The chief opposition to the WN&R lease came from officials of the Boston & Lowell. They wanted the Boston & Maine neither to cross their line nor to enter the territory north and west of Boston that they had staked out as their own. As early as 1880 the Boston & Lowell started leasing other lines, aiming ultimately at forging a Boston-to-Montreal route via Lowell, Massachusetts, and Nashua, Manchester, and Concord, New Hampshire. By 1884 it controlled track as far as Nashua. The Concord Railroad, connecting Nashua with Concord, however, firmly rejected all Boston & Lowell offers for a lease.

To put pressure on the Concord, the Boston & Lowell skipped north and leased lines stretching from Concord to the Canadian boundary. At that point minority stockholders in one of the northern companies brought suit in the New Hampshire courts to invalidate the Boston & Lowell's lease. Making much of the fact that the Boston & Lowell was a foreign corporation, the New Hampshire Supreme Court in March 1887 set the lease aside. Boston & Lowell officials saw their plans dashed and envisioned the massive new depot they had built in Boston standing half-used. To salvage what they could, they leased their line and all of the companies under their control to the Boston & Maine because that company held charters from both New Hampshire and Massachusetts.[3]

Jones and his lieutenants promptly undertook to lease the Concord Railroad and complete the route to Montreal. To validate the Boston & Lowell leases they also supported a bill in the New Hampshire legislature to give out-of-state corporations the same powers and privileges as in-state corporations with regard to the leasing of New Hampshire railroads. Fighting for its life, the Concord backed a counter-measure forbidding any railroad company to lease noncontiguous lines—such as the Boston & Lowell had done in northern New Hampshire. In the celebrated railroad war that followed, Jones and his forces won, only to have their bill vetoed by the governor on grounds of alleged improprieties by both sides during the session.

With charges of bribery rife, the legislature investigated the affair. It found that none of the people's representatives had sinned, although various offers had been made and a few legislators had indiscreetly accepted free passes for themselves and their families to vacation resorts. Frank Jones, denying that he had tried to bribe anyone, told the committee that he did find men to be a good deal like hogs. "If I were to undertake to drive a lot of hogs," he observed, "I should take a little corn along."[4]

In the aftermath of the 1887 battle, the Concord merged with another company to form the Concord & Montreal. Jones and Sinclair at once bought stock in that company and launched a series of harassing minority-stockholder suits against its management. Winning a $650,000 judgment in one instance for one of their small railroad properties, the two became chief beneficiaries of the "extra dividend" which that company immediately declared.[5]

By 1893 Jones was weighing the advisability of seeking authorization from the Massachusetts legislature to lease the Concord & Montreal. Olney regarded the move as untimely. Because the measure would be special legislation rather than general, it could come to a vote only after all parties in opposition had been notified and given an opportunity to organize. The resulting lobby, unless paid (and "the price is likely to be large"), would fight vigorously. Possibly the Concord & Montreal's directors and certainly its stockholders would resist the bill. At the same time no other company could be expected to assist the Boston & Maine. More crucial, the Democrats had just won the election of 1892. With political feelings running high, the bill would not be considered on "its railroad merits," but as part of a scheme to put New Hampshire into the hands of the Democrats. A year later, Olney suggested, political passions in Massachusetts would have cooled and the New Hampshire legislature would not be in session

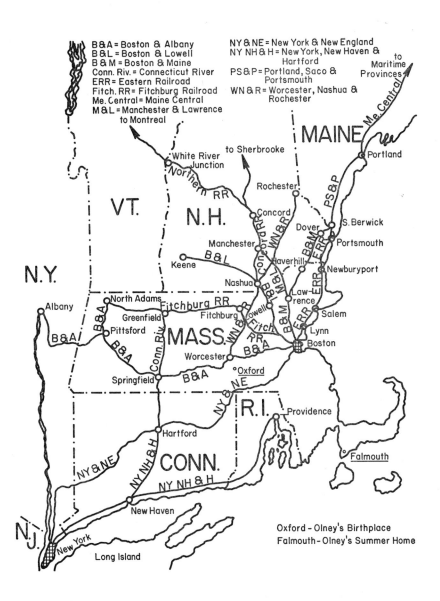

B&A = Boston & Albany
B&L = Boston & Lowell
B&M = Boston & Maine
Conn. Riv. = Connecticut River
ERR = Eastern Railroad
Fitch. RR = Fitchburg Railroad
Me. Central = Maine Central
M&L = Manchester & Lawrence

NY&NE = New York & New England
NY NH & H = New York, New Haven &
    Hartford
PS&P = Portland, Saco &
    Portsmouth
WN&R = Worcester, Nashua &
    Rochester

to Montreal
to Maritime Provinces
to Sherbrooke

MAINE
MASS.
VT.
N.H.
N.Y.
R.I.
CONN.
N.J.

White River Junction
Rochester
Concord
Manchester
Keene
Nashua
Haverhill
Dover
S. Berwick
Portsmouth
Newburyport
Lawrence
Salem
Lynn
Boston
North Adams
Albany
Greenfield
Pittsford
Fitchburg
Worcester
Oxford
Springfield
Providence
Hartford
Falmouth
New Haven
New York
Long Island
Portland

Northern RR
Conn. RR
WN&R
PS&P
B&M
ERR
B&L
Me. Central
Fitchburg RR
Fitch. RR
Lowell
B&A
Conn. Riv.
B&A
NY&NE
NY NH&H

Oxford - Olney's Birthplace
Falmouth - Olney's Summer Home

The Boston & Maine Railroad: Its Subsidiaries and Rivals

to inflame the issue.[6] Olney's advice prevailed. The lease was put off until 1895.

Throughout the New Hampshire struggles, Olney kept out of public view, leaving to Jones and the politicos the more open debate of public policy. In the same quiet way, Olney helped to bring about the amalgamation of the Eastern and Boston & Maine railroads. Despite the lease of 1884, many Eastern security-holders continued to favor independence for their company. At the annual meeting in December 1885, these forces ran a slate of directors that won out over the pro-lease directors who were seeking reelection. Olney was the only person whose name appeared on both slates—a tribute to his fairness and talents, or perhaps to his ability at concealing his true position.

The triumph of the "wrong" side forced Olney to take steps to undo the election. He challenged two blocks of votes: a number of undistributed bonds that the trustees of the Eastern mortgage had cast for the rebels, and bonds held by Harvard University that had been voted by the anti-lease faction under a proxy signed by Harvard President Charles Eliot. Because the trustees held the undistributed bonds in trust for all bondholders, Olney argued, they could not vote them against the interest of even one bondholder. Unless all bond-holders were in agreement, the undistributed bonds simply could not be voted. As for the Harvard bonds, only the treasurer of the university was empowered to sign proxies, so the one signed by President Eliot was invalid. At a second annual meeting a few days later, the pro-lease directors, including Olney, were declared the victors.[7]

Early in January 1888, Olney suggested action to unite the Eastern and the Boston & Maine. "I want to say to you—as being the power behind the throne—," he wrote to Henry Lee Higginson, one of Boston's leading investment bankers, "that if it is desired by those at present interested in the Eastern Railroad, to take any steps towards a consolidation with the Boston & Maine Railroad, it is time proceedings were initiated." He confided that the Boston & Maine would undoubtedly cooperate in putting through the necessary legislation so long as the bill did not specify the terms of the amalgamation. Such matters should be left to the two corporations to work out. "Please think of it," he concluded, "consult your friends on the Eastern Board, and, if anything is to be done, have them instruct me as counsel to file the proper petition and take such other steps as may be necessary to set the consolidation ball rolling."[8]

Consummation of the union did not take place until 1890 despite passage of enabling legislation in 1888. The matter was delayed in part by a dispute between Olney and Jones as to how much capital stock the Boston & Maine should issue when it bought up the Eastern. Olney argued for only enough to cover the purchase price. Jones and his followers, intent on stock-watering, proposed a larger issue, some of which was to be distributed gratuitously to stockholders.

Outvoted, Olney set forth his position in a letter of resignation. Should the measure fail before the legislature, as seemed "tolerably sure," the credit and prestige of the Boston & Maine would be hurt, and if the intended beneficiaries of the plan were revealed in the process, a "seriously damaging" scandal would ensue. On the other hand, if the measure succeeded, injury to the company would be postponed only until such time as the terms of the transaction became public. "It will be believed, no matter what the truth may be, that the Boston & Maine has fallen into the hands of men who are using it and its property for their own private benefit." Finally, he suggested, it would be "unwise, to say nothing more," to seek such legislation in the face of a warning from "the most competent authority" that it could not be obtained without "a lavish expenditure of money."[9] Olney's arguments rested wholly on expediency rather than principle. It may be that other grounds would not have reached Jones.

In the end, Olney won and his resignation was rejected. Once victorious, he spared no effort on behalf of the project. He drafted a bill authorizing sufficient new stock to finance the purchase. He testified on behalf of the measure before the railway committee. He inspired a favorable editorial in the *Boston Journal*.[10] He even twisted the arm of one lawmaker who stood in the way of the bill. Olney's letter was a model of brevity and directness: "Dear Sir:—You asked me a question before election to which I gave you an answer, and I now wish to put a similar question to you, hoping for an equally explicit answer. I am told that you are opposing and making an organization to oppose the legislation proposed to the present legislature by the Boston & Maine Railroad. Is it so?" The next day Olney reported that the legislator might vote for and even possibly speak for the bill. If not, he would stand neutral.[11] The measure soon passed and the Boston & Maine and Eastern became one.

In thwarting the stock-watering scheme, Olney wrought no permanent improvement in the conduct of Jones and his associates. For example, Asa P. Potter, a member of the Jones syndicate, was president of the Maverick National Bank of Boston. There Jones deposited part of his personal funds as well as considerable sums belonging to the Boston & Maine. In June 1890, the Maverick suddenly closed its doors, unable to pay off its depositors, including the Boston & Maine. Although Potter was indicted for a number of irregularities in connection with the bank's failure, he never lost favor with the Jones gang. Potter resigned from the board of the Boston & Maine in December 1891, but immediately was elected to serve with Sinclair, Jones, and Lawrence as remnant director to wind up the affairs of the Eastern.[12]

The collapse of the Maverick seems to have driven Jones and his associates to Wall Street for loans to run the Boston & Maine. Concluding that too much of the company's earnings went to dividends and too little to line maintenance, the House of Morgan would lend only at very high interest. And so Jones turned to other New Yorkers who, in exchange for $500,000, asked that two of their number be elected to the Boston & Maine's board. William C. Whitney and George G. Haven thus became the first non-New Englanders to sit on the board of the Boston & Maine.[13] To many the line looked like a plum, ripe and ready for picking, and others too would soon move in for the harvest.

At the meeting that elected Whitney and Haven to the board, disgruntled stockholders called for a committee to investigate why large amounts of the company's moneys were on deposit at the Maverick bank and why they had not been withdrawn prior to the failure. That the group's target was Jones became evident when they asked that the committee also determine who owned stock in the Worcester, Nashua & Rochester and other small lines when they were leased by the Boston & Maine.

Olney promptly took charge. He disarmed the dissidents by agreeing that their questions should be answered and he seconded their motion for a committee of investigation. The three-man committee, headed by Whitney—whom Olney unblushingly described as "neutral"—reported back one year later. Its findings were a complete whitewash: the collapse of the Maverick had come too quickly to save the Boston & Maine's funds, and Sinclair, who prior to the leasing of the various small railroads had purchased large blocks of their stock for himself and Jones, had not been a director of the Boston & Maine at the particular times they were leased and so could not be accused of any impropriety.[14]

By the time of the report, such matters were of little consequence. Dazzled by dramatic events during the preceding three months, and buoyed up by promises of future earnings, the stockholders no longer much cared about the past indiscretions of Jones and his friends. Late in October 1892, Jones had suddenly stepped down to the vice-presidency of the Boston & Maine to make room for a new president, A. A. McLeod. McLeod was one of the rising stars of railroading.

In 1890, backed by J. P. Morgan, George M. Pullman, John Wanamaker, and others, he had become president of the impoverished Philadelphia & Reading Railroad. At once, McLeod embarked on an expansion program, leasing anthracite coal lines so as to gain greater influence over the hard-coal market. The success of McLeod's scheme hinged on reducing anthracite prices enough to increase substantially the traffic over the Reading and thus restore its prosperity.[15]

A search for new outlets for anthracite led McLeod to acquire interests in the New York & New England (NY & NE) and other lines connecting the Reading with the Boston & Maine. McLeod's resources were too limited for him to purchase outright control of the Boston & Maine, but through the agency of a Boston financier, Frederick H. Prince, he acquired enough shares to gain standing among the shareholders. According to Prince, bringing the Boston & Maine, the NY & NE, and the Reading together was the first step on the part of a syndicate to create a coast-to-coast system that eventually would be headed by James J. Hill of the Great Northern. Prince claimed that he paid Olney $10,000 to persuade McLeod to accept the presidency of the Boston & Maine. In any event, at the October meeting of the Boston & Maine board, it was Olney who moved McLeod's election as president.[16]

Winning Jones, Sinclair, and their allies to McLeod was not easy. Prior to 1892, members of that group had already appeared on the board of the NY & NE, a good indication that they had plans of their own for expanding the Boston & Maine westward, perhaps beyond the Hudson. And, in October, the Jones faction tried to postpone McLeod's election, urging delay at least until the annual meeting in December. McLeod's large block of stock and the backing of board members such as Olney, however, forced them to yield.[17]

Once in power, McLeod worked easily with Jones. In December 1892, they snatched the Connecticut River Railroad from the very fingertips of J. P. Morgan and his New York, New Haven & Hartford line. The New Haven had already signed a lease to take over the conservatively managed little company that for thirty years had paid generous dividends and had on hand an accumulated surplus of nearly $1,000,000. Only ratification by Connecticut River shareholders remained to make the lease effective. At this juncture, McLeod and Jones made a bold move to gain control of enough Connecticut River shares to block ratification. Buying up as much stock as possible—most of it within a forty-eight-hour period at inflated prices—they succeeded in their scheme. Within a few weeks the Boston & Maine offered to lease the Connecticut River line and rumors spread that a stock dividend could be expected.[18]

Olney regarded the whole affair as overly hurried and unbusiness-like. No stock dividend should be considered, he suggested, until a good justification had been formulated and the books and general accounts of the Connecticut River company examined to see if a dividend was warranted. "No one that I have yet seen has such knowledge of the affairs of the Conn. River as to state what its outlying property is," he complained. "For instance, one of the directors stated to me yesterday that the road owned 6000 shares of Conn. & Pass. [Connecticut & Passumpsic Rivers Railroad] stock. To-day another director is authority for the statement that the Conn. River has an option at par of 8000 shares of Conn. & Pass. stock. The exact facts as to the Conn. & Pass. stock and any other convertible assets of the Conn. River ought to be got before any scrip dividend is declared or any lease is made."[19]

Such cautions did not long delay McLeod or Jones. A lease running for ninety-nine years and guaranteeing the Connecticut River shareholders an annual dividend of ten per cent was signed. This offer, little better than that of the New Haven, was sweetened by a special fifty per cent dividend, paid in the form of ten-year, four per cent bonds. In effect, Connecticut River stockholders received a twelve per cent per annum dividend, McLeod, Jones, and other recent stock purchasers were partially reimbursed for their outlays, and the million-dollar surplus was converted into a quarter-million-dollar debt. The Massachusetts Railway Commission commented that "no more unconscionable transaction has occurred in the railroad history of the state."[20]

Seizure of the Connecticut River line served only to widen an already growing gulf between McLeod and his one-time supporter, Morgan. By the time of the "steal," Morgan had trained his guns on Mc-Leod's jerry-built empire. McLeod, who had purchased his initial New England railroad shares on margin, putting up personal securities as collateral, was extremely vulnerable. In October 1892, without authorization from the Reading board of directors, he used company securities for collateral in acquiring Boston & Maine stock. Learning officially of the transaction in December, the board ratified McLeod's arrangements and indemnified him for advances made on his own account to the sum of $400,000.

The Reading, however, faced mounting expenses of its own. The rentals on the recently leased anthracite lines ran higher than the incomes the lines produced. Severe winter weather added to mining costs in early 1893, thereby forcing anthracite prices up rather than down as had been planned. In response to the rising prices, the attorney general of New Jersey brought action to invalidate the leases, charging that they were part of a conspiracy to raise the cost of anthracite to customers. To save its long-range projects—expected someday to bring in profits—the Reading resorted to short-term loans at high interest rates. The crisis came in February 1893, when McLeod attempted to float Reading bonds. Although Speyer & Company of New York accepted the issue, Drexel, Morgan & Company refused and began dumping their Reading securities on the open market for whatever they would bring. On 15 February, McLeod transferred all his stock accounts to the Reading. Between the seventeenth and the twentieth, Reading stock fell from 46¾ to 28, and on the twentieth the company passed into receivership with McLeod named one of the receivers. Morgan and his associates kept up their attack, determined to drive McLeod from both the Reading receivership and the presidency of the Boston & Maine.[21]

Collapse of the Reading dumbfounded McLeod's New England backers and they soon were at his throat. "Mr. McLeod has acted very foolishly," declared Prince, "he ought to be spanked. . . . He neglected to sell bonds when he could. . . . I had no more thought of the Reading failing than I had of the Bank of England." Olney, representing the interests of Prince and of a Boston merchant, Benjamin P. Cheney, was the first board member to turn on McLeod. Jones and his pack joined in, however, sensing an opportunity to regain control of the property.[22]

Although McLeod temporarily held on as president, the Boston & Maine hastened to end its feud with the New Haven. At Morgan's suggestion, representatives of the two companies met and settled the New England railroad situation by dividing the region into two provinces along the line of the Boston & Albany Railroad. All railroads south of and including the Boston & Albany became the property of the New Haven; everything north of the line fell to the Boston & Maine.[23] The settlement stood until an attempt was made to merge the two monopolies a decade and a half later.

Just as affairs reached their most complex and delicate stage, Olney entered upon his duties as attorney general of the United States. So far as he could from Washington, he worked to prevent Jones and his associates from resuming control of the Boston & Maine. This meant keeping McLeod on as president until a suitable successor could be found. In the meantime, McLeod installed a man of his own as a vice-president, giving him powers that overlapped those of Vice-President Jones.[24] "Things are quite as mixed up at the Station as ever," Sigourney Butler wrote from Boston. "Sundry of the officials come to me to ask me from whom they are to take orders. I say the same thing to all: Take yr orders from everybody & do what they say! . . . I see little of Jones, & he is suspicious & non-commital."[25]

When Prince and other former backers disposed of their Boston & Maine holdings, McLeod's position became untenable. Butler, commenting to Olney about McLeod's resignation on 23 May, confided that it looked as if "the old N.H. crowd in again."[26] In the meantime, however, Olney had joined with a group of New Yorkers, represented by Lewis Cass Ledyard, their attorney, who were buying into the Boston & Maine. "Shall not be at Saturday meeting," he wired one director on 31 May. "New purchasers do not want Jones." Jones was reelected, nonetheless. Allegedly for health reasons, however, he agreed to serve out only the balance of McLeod's term, which ended in October.[27]

A committee made up of Jones, George M. Pullman (who had joined the board in October 1892), and Lawrence began the search for a permanent president. In the end they selected Lucius Tuttle, an experienced New England railroad official. "My impression," Olney wrote Ledyard, "is that a very good result has been reached. It is certain that Mr. Tuttle would come to the office with the good wishes of everybody and with considerable confidence on the part of everybody in his ability as an operating man."[28]

In the final jockeying before the annual meeting in October 1893, Jones and his allies tried to salvage seats on the board for both Jones and Sinclair. Lawrence with 20,000 shares, Pullman and another director with 10,000, and the American Express Company with 24,000 shares once controlled by McLeod, offered the New Hampshire men but one seat. When that offer was declined, a committee headed by Olney drew up a slate of directors that for the first time since 1884 did not include Jones or any of his friends. Speaking for the committee, Olney told the assembled stockholders that the omission of Jones's name was not only with Jones's consent, but was "against the wishes and consent of the directors who had repeatedly and strongly urged him to consent to a re-election."[29] With the fall of the Jones regime and the installation of Tuttle, the Boston & Maine entered upon an era of conservative, businesslike management. In the years that followed, President Tuttle, assisted by General Counsel Olney and the new owners of the line, solidified the system that Jones and his associates had so haphazardly thrown together.

Early in the twentieth century, the eminent railroad scholar, William Z. Ripley, offered an elaborate justification for the monopolistic character of the New Haven and Boston & Maine railroads. New England's relatively isolated position, he wrote, somewhat removed it from the main currents of the nation's commerce. Its remoteness from sources of vital raw materials and from markets for its finished products made the region particularly dependent upon railroads. Small, competing companies, however, could never have met on equal terms the great systems of the west, which transported bulky farm and mine products over vast distances. Costs and rates were lower beyond the Hudson than in New England, where passengers and small, compact shipments of manufactured goods made up most of the traffic, where distances between population centers were not great, and where street railways between urban centers were a threat to steam railways. Only by merging into large, efficient systems and by reducing competition and costs could New England's railways hope to serve their section well and profitably.[30] There is, however, little evidence that Jones, McLeod, Olney, or any of the other builders of the Boston & Maine gave much thought to such considerations. Their objectives were simpler and shorter-ranged. They took over the Eastern primarily to eliminate competition that was proving too costly; the Worcester, Nashua & Rochester to make a financial killing; the Concord & Montreal to complete a profitable line to Canada; and the Connecticut River line to divide up that company's million-dollar surplus and to steal a march on the rival New Haven.

In his more recent account of the development of New England's railways, Edward C. Kirkland, after graphically relating swindles, plots, schemes, and promotions of all sorts in the building of New England's railroads, concludes that the "dreamers, promoters, investors, builders, workers, and politicians" who made the railroads "served Boston and New England well."[31] But if the history of the Boston & Maine—particularly that part with which Olney was connected between 1876 and 1895—proves anything, it would seem to be that the men responsible for promoting the railroads served not so much Boston or New England as themselves. That their work incidentally benefited the region too, might better be offered as proof of Adam Smith's contention that each man, pursuing his own self-interest and intending only his own gain, is led by an invisible hand to promote ends which were not part of his intention.

After 1886 the Boston & Maine increasingly shared Olney with another major railroad, the Boston-dominated Chicago, Burlington & Quincy. In March 1889, Olney became general counsel of the Burlington and was elected to its board of directors. The Burlington operated between Denver and Chicago, running through the heart of the "granger country" where agitation for government supervision of railroads was particularly strong. Much of Olney's work for his railroad clients between 1886 and 1893—and especially for the Burlington—involved protecting them from various forms of public regulation. He interpreted regulatory statutes for his clients, advised them as to bills they should promote or oppose, and sketched outlines of attack for testing regulatory laws in the courts. He also drafted legislation, lobbied for their interests in both Boston and Washington, and, in a few instances, argued cases for them before the courts and the Interstate Commerce Commission (ICC).

The advice Olney gave tended to be pragmatic and realistic. He rarely recommended fighting battles for principle's sake or counseled resistance to accomplished fact. Instead, he gave his clients shrewd analyses of the situations they faced and offered suggestions as how best to turn those situations to advantage. He skillfully detected loopholes in laws, unerringly spotting the flaw in a piece of legislation by which it could be evaded or rendered innocuous. He also had a gift for wringing favorable interpretations from laws that were supposed to restrict the railroads. Occasionally Olney recommended simply staying out of the public eye. "Corporations are to the ordinary legislator like a red rag to a bull," he observed, "and ought not to display themselves any oftener or any earlier than is necessary."[32]

Some of Olney's earliest work for the Burlington consisted of advising its officials how to meet state laws that fixed the rates that its branch lines could charge. In the Wabash decision of 1886, the United States Supreme Court had invalidated all state regulation of interstate railroads.[33] It had left intact, however, the absolute power of state governments over wholly intrastate railways. As a consequence, Iowa, in 1888, empowered its railway commission to fix a schedule of rates for all lines operating within the state. As a practical matter, Olney recommended that the Burlington open negotiations with the commission to secure the best possible rates. After all, it had to "live or fail to live" on the rates allowed by the commission. At the same time he urged bringing a case to test the matter in the federal courts. The Supreme Court, he observed, had never had an opportunity to reconsider its ruling in the Munn Case of 1877 that had held state powers over railroad rates to be final. Olney perceived that the high court was moving in the direction of judicial review of such rates; at least, recent intimations of several justices indicated a growing belief that state-fixed rates must allow a railroad "reasonable remuneration for the work done and services rendered."[34]

In 1890, Iowa again interfered with railroad rates by authorizing its railway commission to draw up a schedule of maximum joint rates that connecting lines could charge between points within the state. Olney saw little to be gained from contesting the law; the Supreme Court repeatedly had upheld the right of states to fix such standards. To evade the measure, however, he suggested that the Burlington not publish joint rates with other lines, thereby giving the commission nothing to measure against its schedules. That Olney's advice in both instances was sound became evident when late in 1890 the Supreme Court ruled that the reasonableness of any rate set by state governments could be tested in the federal courts.[35]

As matters turned out, the struggle against state regulation was but the prelude to efforts by the railroad community to avoid and circumvent federal regulation.[36] Both the Burlington and the Santa Fe had hired Olney to lobby at Washington in a futile campaign to prevent enactment of the Interstate Commerce Act of 1887. As soon as the measure became law, Olney and other Burlington lawyers prepared a memorandum for the guidance of the company's president, Charles E. Perkins. Construing most provisions of the act as narrowly as possible, the attorneys suggested that their interpretations be followed only until the many "obscure" provisions of the law could be carried to the courts for authoritative rulings.[37]

Olney realized that effective regulation would be difficult if not impossible without reliable and complete data from the railroads themselves. With this in mind, he consistently advised his clients to supply the Interstate Commerce Commission with the absolute minimum of information required by law. He also recommended that whenever possible they decline to go before the ICC. "[T]he carrier who does not appear before the commission," he told Perkins, "is likely to be in a better and stronger position to contest [an ICC] order than a carrier who does so appear."[38]

In 1891 Olney found it necessary to defend the Boston & Maine before the ICC in the so-called Free Pass Case. Republican Senator William E. Chandler of New Hampshire had complained that officials of the Boston & Maine were using the influence and power of their company to overthrow Republican rule in the Granite State. Their chief weapon, he charged, was the lavish issuing of free passes to state legislators, judges, lawyers, clergymen, newspaper editors, and anyone else who helped to shape legislation, litigation, or public opinion.[39]

At the request of the ICC, the Boston & Maine revealed the names of all persons to whom it issued passes, classifying them into various groups such as charity cases, agents of firms with whom the line did business, public officials, railroad employees, and the like. Olney defended the company's pass policy by an ingenious twisting of the Interstate Commerce Act. That law, he argued, did not prohibit free passes, except for the classes of persons listed in section 22 of the act, as was widely believed. Rather, the law prohibited discriminatory rates when a charge was made, excepting for those categories listed in section 22. In its "true meaning" section 22 permitted a railroad company to allow one clergyman, for example, to travel at a special rate over its line while another clergyman making the same trip the same day could be denied the special rate. Otherwise, although a railroad could not charge passengers different rates, it could give anyone a free pass anytime within the limits prescribed by the common-law test of reasonableness. Under that common-law rule, the Boston & Maine currently issued free passes "whenever its interests have seemed to demand it," just as it had before enactment of the Interstate Commerce Act. That congressmen and other public officials continued to accept and use free passes—apparently without feeling that they were violating the law—seemed to support the contention that they had not intended the law to bar free passes.

Olney objected to the manner by which the ICC initiated the Free Pass Case against the Boston & Maine. If the commission intended a "new departure" with regard to passes, it should have given reasonable notice, its ruling should have been prospective in operation, and it should have applied to all railroads, not just to the Boston & Maine. Further, the ICC should not have permitted itself to be worked by Senator Chandler in his own favor simply because of his assertion that the Boston & Maine was operating a political machine against him.[40]

Rejecting Olney's arguments, including his novel interpretation of section 22, the ICC issued a cease-and-desist order limiting free passes to those categories of person listed in section 22. Olney sent a copy of the order to President Perkins of the Burlington. "Personally and unofficially," he said, he agreed with Perkins that the Burlington should go on issuing passes if that would promote its pecuniary interests. At the same time, as counsel he could not advise such a course because the penalties for violating the law were severe and fell upon both the companies and their agents. "How can the C., B. & Q. indemnify an officer or employee against the risks or consequences of a sentence to the penitentiary?" he asked.[41]

From the moment that the Interstate Commerce Act became law, Perkins had hoped to find some way to get rid of the ICC. At first he argued that strict compliance with the law would reveal the weakness of "political" regulation of private business and lead to a quick repeal of the act. He soon abandoned that tactic, however, and wrote to Olney asking how best to test the constitutionality of the commission. No case was brought because at best it was a desperate move. Olney on another occasion put the matter well: "in a criminal case when everything else fails, the plea of insanity is set up—in a civil case, unconstitutionality serves the same end."[42]

On the eve of Olney's appointment as attorney general of the United States, he and Perkins discussed the wisdom of trying to get Congress to abolish the ICC. Perkins hoped to persuade the public of the "uselessness" of the commission. It was "of no earthly account to anybody; and as it costs a good deal of money, it ought to be abolished."[43] Olney's response was shrewd. "[L]ooking at the matter from a railroad point of view exclusively," such an attempt would not be wise because it would probably fail. If the move did not succeed, after having been made on the grounds that the ICC was inefficient and useless, the probable result would be new legislation giving the commission the powers it lacked. "The Commission, as its functions have now been limited by the Courts, is, or can be made of great use to the railroads," Olney pointed out. "It satisfies the popular clamor for a government supervision of railroads, at the same time that that supervision is almost entirely nominal. Further, the older such a commission gets to be, the more inclined it will be found to take the business and railroad view of things. It thus becomes a sort of barrier between the railroad corporations and the people and a sort of protection against hasty and crude legislation hostile to railroad interests." The Commission cost something, to be sure, Olney admitted, but so long as its powers were "advisory merely," it seemed well worth the expense. "The part of wisdom," he concluded, "is not to destroy the Commission, but to utilize it."[44]

Perkins did not agree. If the ICC were not abolished it surely would be given additional power, "and the power in the hands of the Commission, whether it can be constitutionally exercised or not, is exceedingly troublesome, if not dangerous." The Commission, Perkins argued, was "foreign to our system of government." For Congress to "pick out one class of law-breakers to be practically tried and punished, not in the constitutional manner, through the courts, but by an irresponsible commission," was bound to fail. If regular courts were incompetent to handle railroad offenders, Congress had the power to set up special courts. "In courts, railroads would have some chance of getting justice; but before a political commission, there is no chance of it whatever."

Perkins doubted that a commission would mellow with use. The Massachusetts commission was an exception, perhaps, but Iowa's was not; "so far from having the business view, as it has grown older, and so far from having become a barrier between popular clamor and the railroads," it had "taken more and more the granger view of things," and has become an added weapon in the hands of the confiscators, instead of a barrier of protection to railroad property." Perkins feared that any commission appointed for the country at large would drift the same way.[45]

Each saw much truth in the position of the other. Perkins refused to give up hope of getting rid of the ICC, but from its creation onward repeatedly tried to utilize it as Olney suggested. Between 1890 and 1894, for example, Perkins recommended a number of men for appointment to the ICC: John H. Gear, the ex-governor of Iowa (a man with "good business sense"), J. Sterling Morton of Nebraska (a long-time lobbyist and paid propagandist of the Burlington), William P. Hepburn (who in the 1870s and 1880s had handled much of the company's legal business in Iowa), and James Wilson McDill. Of the four, McDill was appointed but died without completing his term.[46]

Perkins tried to influence the choice of McDill's successor, working through Morton who meanwhile had become secretary of agriculture in the second Cleveland administration. Perkins proposed a man named Mallory, but then withdrew the suggestion. "It did not occur to me," he wrote, that Mallory was president of a small line controlled by the Burlington. Finding the "proper man" for the ICC was difficult, Perkins found, because most businessmen fitted for the position did not want it. Moreover, since it was a "quasi-court," nonlawyers, even if good men, would have trouble "keeping up" with the other commissioners who were lawyers "accustomed to writing legal opinions and drawing fine lines." That, of course, was one of the objections to having lawyers on the commission—they were "very apt to draw their lines too fine, and to think statutes come first and the laws of nature afterwards."[47]

For his part, Olney regarded the ICC as a permanent factor in railroad affairs. He was always willing to promote legislation, however, to weaken or abolish it and to oppose measures designed to give it additional power. At Perkins's suggestion, for example, Olney drafted a bill to substitute circuit courts of interstate commerce in each of the federal judicial circuits, and an appeals court of interstate commerce, for the ICC. All cases arising under the interstate commerce act would be tried in these special courts. The bill made its way to Congress and was introduced, referred to committee, and then dropped. Through the years, however, Olney's bill or variations of it repeatedly popped up. Eventually, in 1910, Congress created a Court of Commerce to hear appeals from the ICC.[48]

At each session of Congress during the late 1880s and 1890s, bills were introduced to bring the railroads under greater public control, usually by strengthening the ICC. Most of these were spotted by the friends of railroads, and pressure was put upon congressional committees to prevent action from being taken. On occasion, however, a bill would slip through and be adopted by one house or the other. In such instances the railroads made special efforts to prevent the legislation from getting through the other house. One such measure passed the House of Representatives in January 1893. The correspondence between Olney and his clients with respect to blocking the bill in the Senate is suggestive of the tactics by which the railroads bottled up troublesome bills.

The proposal, introduced by Representative David B. Culberson of Texas, would have made railroads and other corporations, for purposes of court jurisdiction, "residents" of each state in which they did business. Under existing law, when a citizen of Iowa, for example, brought suit in an Iowa court against the Burlington Railroad, that company, if to its advantage, could have the case removed to federal court because the company was chartered in Illinois and therefore was a "citizen" of that state. Under Culberson's bill, the Burlington, for litigative purposes, would be treated as a citizen of Iowa, and removal to federal court solely on grounds of citizenship of the litigants would be impossible. Perkins urged Olney to write to members of the Senate Judiciary Committee to "stop its passage."[49]

Olney prepared a letter setting forth the objections to the bill. He found, however, that the only member of the Judiciary Committee whom he knew was Senator George F. Hoar of Massachusetts. "Mr. Hoar is a good lawyer and I have no personal quarrel with him . . . " Olney wrote, but "we have always been on opposite sides of the political fence—Mr. Hoar is a pronounced partisan—and anything I might write to him on the subject would simply be pigeon-holed."[50] Olney suggested that the letter be addressed to Perkins as if in answer to an inquiry on the scope, operation, and general validity of the act. Perkins could then pass it on to some senator to use in building opposition to Culberson's bill. Perkins agreed. The letter was sent and Perkins gave it to Senator Edward O. Wolcott of Colorado, for many years general counsel of the Denver & Rio Grande Railroad and a long-time friend of Perkins.[51]

In the meantime, George R. Peck, general solicitor of the Santa

Fe, wrote to Olney calling attention to the Culberson bill and asking him to bring influence to bear on Senator Hoar. "The necessity for immediate action is imperative," Peck declared, "and I should be greatly obliged if you would do what you can to have some Boston influence brought to bear. All the great corporate interests there are vitally interested." Olney informed Peck of the steps already taken. "My first inclination had been to write Senator Hoar," he said, "but he is so much more partisan than lawyer, or, indeed, than anything else, that I feared a letter to him from a Democrat would simply prejudice the case instead of doing it any good."

Peck appreciated Olney's point and replied that perhaps Hoar's partisanship could be put to good use. "As the bill was introduced by Mr. Culbertson [*sic*] of Texas," he suggested, "I think it may be assumed that it is another attempt to overthrow the government, to re-establish the Confederacy or at the least to pay the rebel debt. This ought to powerfully appeal to Senator Hoar's patriotism."[52] Olney, however, proposed to Perkins yet another line of attack. Perhaps "Col. Fairchild" of Lee, Higginson & Company could be induced to write to Hoar. "No very long letter is necessary," Olney said. "It would be better for him not to undertake to state any legal objections to the bill. Let him simply say that, if the bill passes, it will be a great blow to all the great western railroad companies in which capitalists in Boston are so very largely interested. . . . Col. Fairchild is a particularly good man to communicate with Senator Hoar," Olney added. "He is a shining light in the Republican party and one of the large contributors to campaign expenses."[53] Whatever influences were ultimately used, the Culberson bill did not get out of committee.

Sometimes bills were introduced in Congress offering railroads something they wanted in exchange for increased authority for the ICC. This tactic frequently divided the railroad community. In 1894–95, Olney's two major clients split over such a bill. The measure would have permitted railroad pooling, but, at the discretion of the court, findings of the ICC would be treated as conclusive in certain equity cases. President Tuttle of the Boston & Maine opposed the bill. His company, with almost no competition within its realm, stood to profit little from pooling but might be adversely affected by a stronger ICC. Perkins, president of the Burlington, favored the bill—much to Olney's surprise because he had opposed a similar piece of legislation in 1892.[54] "The Eastern roads do not feel the want of it," Olney, who was now attorney general, wrote to Sigourney Butler. "The Western roads seem to think it almost essential to their salvation." Olney personally thought the eastern roads should give in to the western roads on pooling since the measure might help the western lines without harming the eastern roads. There was, however, the matter of enlarged powers for the ICC. That stick frightened him as much as the carrot, pooling, lured him. Olney understood that sixty senators favored the bill and it seemed certain of passage if brought to a vote. "It is very easy, however," he noted, "for a few determined opponents to prevent action on the bill, so that its fate is very uncertain."[55] This measure, too, failed to get out of committee.

Certainly Olney's efforts to protect the railroads from regulation did not end when he became attorney general. Indeed, that struggle was to engage a part of his energies for the rest of his life. As head of the Justice Department, however, Olney would protect the railroads in many ways, not merely from regulatory legislation.

3

The Measure of Success—1893

The seventeen years between 1876 and 1893 brought Olney far toward realization of the success he had craved as a young attorney in the sixties. During these years he acquired a large and important practice, his work interested and satisfied him, and the rewards of his labors were adequate for his mode of living. For the most part his achievements were the result of his own hard work and talent. But in any fair assessment of a man it is necessary to look beyond his professional attainments to the successes and failures of his personal life. To varying degrees, Olney sacrificed personality, family, friends, even recreation and pleasure, to feed his ambition.

By 1893 Olney's clientele included many of Boston's prominent businessmen and financiers, some of the nation's major railroad companies, and a number of other large corporations. Among his individual clients were such eminent businessmen and social leaders as John Murray Forbes, Charles Eliot Perkins, Benjamin P. Cheney, and William Lawrence, the Episcopal bishop of Massachusetts. Frequently he worked with Boston bankers: Henry Lee Higginson, Frederick H. Prince, and T. Jefferson Coolidge. Counsel and director of the Eastern (1879–1884), the Boston & Maine (1884–1914), and the Burlington (1889–1901) railroads, he also served many smaller railroads briefly as counsel, or director, or both. As counsel to Cheney, who was a director of the Atchison, Topeka & Santa Fe Railroad, Olney became involved in the affairs of that company and occasionally served it as counsel. According to a member of the New York Stock Exchange, Cheney used to take Olney as his attorney to every meeting of the Santa Fe's directors and consult him in an anteroom about every vote that was taken.[1]

From the time of its incorporation in 1890, Olney was a director of the Old Colony Trust Company, and between 1890 and 1893 he helped in the organization of the General Electric Company and in the reorganization of the Union Stock Yards Company of Chicago. With the passage of the Sherman Antitrust law in 1890 he was called upon frequently to advise corporations on antitrust matters and in this connection served as a defender of Joseph Greenhut in the whiskey trust prosecutions in Boston in 1892. A significant part of his practice consisted of counseling other lawyers, particularly with reference to matters concerning wills and trust property.[2]

Olney was an "insatiate worker," but once his reputation was established he found himself unable to handle all the business offered him. Under the circumstances he was able to choose both cases and clients with considerable discretion and rarely had to argue against his own beliefs. Though the size and importance of his practice would have warranted partners or junior associates, Olney, after the death of Judge Thomas, practiced alone. His only assistants were an extremely efficient clerk-stenographer-secretary, Miss Antoinette M. Straw, who served him for thirty-one years, and a succession of office boys. Because he was alone there were, of course, no quarrels over the conduct of his practice, and clients whose causes he undertook had the benefit of the personal attention and wide experience of their attorney rather than the work of law students or junior associates as was usual in the larger law offices.[3] But these advantages were somewhat offset by certain disadvantages. A major drawback to his wholly personal practice, Olney once observed to his brother Peter, who had invited him to go on a fishing trip, was "the impossibility of leaving your work without discommoding & perhaps seriously offending more or less of your clientele."[4] As a result, until 1893, except for a few weeks' walking vacation in the British Isles and a business trip to London and Paris and another to Cuba, Olney was rarely farther from Boston than New York City, where he went on business, or Falmouth on Cape Cod, where he spent his summers.[5]

Through most of his career Olney operated from the same three-room suite of offices (in the Adams Building at 23 Court Street) that he had first shared with Judge Thomas at the time of the Civil War. Visitors to the office noted few changes through the decades in either its physical appearance or the office procedures used. "It is doubtful," an editor of the *Boston Herald* mused at the time of Olney's death in 1917, "if any other lawyer in Boston, of the practice and influence of Mr. Olney, has worked in a law office of such simple arrangements and furnishings."[6] Olney occupied a long, narrow room at the inner end of the suite. It contained two roll-top desks, a long consultation table, and shelves of law books. There were no carpets on the hard-wood floors or other adornments. Olney's telephone, which the Boston & Maine had originally installed in his office by stealth one night, stood on his desk and was answered by Olney in person. Its unlisted number was known to only a few intimates.

Miss Straw sat at a desk in the office located between Olney's and the anteroom, filing correspondence or typing. A boy in the outer office delivered messages and took the cards of callers. Most of the time Olney worked alone at his desk, preparing his briefs and arguments by writing them out in his own illegible hand. Occasionally he called Miss Straw in to take dictation at a little table behind his roll-top desk. When he dictated seated at his desk, she was completely hidden from him. Much of the time, however, Olney paced the room or stood before the open fireplace, arms folded behind his back, while dictating.[7]

The letters that Olney wrote were models of clarity, brevity, and directness. Usually each was devoted to a single topic which was discussed in a logical progression from point to point. His economy of phrase was remarkable. Though he always spoke and wrote with absolute conviction of the rightness of his position, he never put on the mantle of a champion of goodness battling the forces of evil. He wrote in a style notably free of sentiment, cant, and self-righteousness. He was never obliged to complain that he had been "misunderstood" or "misinterpreted," nor was he ever apologetic for anything he wrote or said. Olney's legal briefs were similar to his letters—concise, orderly, logical, penetrating, and directly to the point.

In serving his clients, Olney spent little time in trial courts, not that he was an ineffective pleader, but rather because of the nature of his clients' business. The railroads used him to advantage at directors' meetings, in the appellate courts, and before legislative committees and regulatory commissions. The Boston & Maine, to free Olney for such work, hired other counsel to handle the company's trial work. Olney's individual clients were also less expensively and better served by the avoidance of trials, and he became noted for his ability to win out-of-court settlements. It was once said of Olney that his preparation of cases was so complete and thorough, his honesty and fairness so well recognized, and his judicial temperament so thoroughly appreciated by both opposing counsel and all parties to disputes that his ultimata were generally accepted and his clients satisfied that they had gotten all they were fairly entitled to.[8] On occasion, however, he was blunt in forcing a settlement. "My Dear Sir:—" he wrote one attorney. "Shall I bring suit on behalf of F. H. Prince & Company against the administrator of the Haskell estate? Or are you going to make me some proposition which I can decently and reasonably advise my clients to accept?"[9]

As had been true of his academic successes at Brown, Olney's success at the law seems to have been due more to his hard work and plodding thoroughness than to any unusual mental capacity. "He is a solid lawyer," said Solomon Lincoln, the Boston & Maine's trial lawyer. "I think that is a more fitting term than brilliant."[10] But Olney's philosophy of life and his attitude toward the law and lawyers may also help to account for his success.

So far as he ever expressed it, Olney's outlook on life was essentially based on the Social Darwinist thought of the era in which he lived. "Man is by nature a fighting animal," he once told a graduating class of lawyers, "and whether you look to the lives of individuals or the histories of nations, it is the fighters preeminently to whom is due the progress of the race. Collision, attrition, friction, are as necessary to bring out the best qualities of a man as to develop the lustre and beauty of the mahogany block or the gold or silver nugget. It follows . . . " he continued, that "if there be failure, the fault will not be in your stars but in yourselves."

In the practice of law, he told the young men, they would find unusual opportunities for growth because in the legal profession

> rivalry is direct, continuous, intense, and personal to the last degree, and makes the lawyer's career one life-long duel. Every cause is distinguished, of course, by its own principles and its own facts. But the prime appeal of each to the lawyer is through its personnel—through the particular man or woman concerned—through the lawyer on the other side who for that suit is an enemy to be watched, studied, and beaten by every intellectual weapon which can fairly be brought to bear. . . . in the career of the lawyer, every suit is an independent battle ground, every opposing counsel a foe to be vanquished, and every judgment a trophy and guerdon of personal prowess.[11]

In line with these views, Olney was ruthless in exploiting every possible argument to win a case. He was little concerned with consistency or principle from one case to the next. For one client he would argue in his most convincing manner for the broadest possible interpretation of a law and for another client would ask for the narrowest, most restrictive ruling on perhaps the same law. He displayed

a positive genius for making highly technical distinctions which benefited the causes of his clients.[12] In his later years, Olney once deplored
a novelette which portrayed a successful lawyer as a man who used
his legal acumen and agility "in advising how nearly the extreme
limits of the law can be approached without being overstepped; as
influencing legislation in favor of his clients' interests, and as dextrously
manipulating the issue and sale of corporate securities."[13] Yet such
might well have been a description of some of the *technically* legal
and *strictly* honest services that he had performed while working for
Frank Jones and his associates.

On the same occasion Olney wrote of the lawyer as being a sort
of "minister of justice" as well as the agent of his client and he declared
that the lawyer's code of ethics could not be compared with that
of the businessman, "whose one rule necessarily is to take care of
No. 1, and not even to know of any No. 2." The lawyer, Olney
insisted, occupied a two-fold fiduciary relationship—on the one hand
to the public and on the other to his immediate client.[14] Though Olney
frequently handled cases in which the public had a considerable interest, it was not always easy to discern his regard for the public. He
was ever careful to keep himself and his work as far from the newspapers and the public view as possible. That he faithfully served his
private clients, however, was beyond question. Trust estates in his
keeping were carefully guarded from speculative ventures. Olney once
resigned from the directory of a railroad and withdrew trust funds
in his charge from it because he thought it "moving too quickly"
for trust-fund purposes. Because he had never speculated with his
own money, he said, he had no fortune from which to reimburse
his client should the funds in his care be lost in the venture.[15]

Olney approached each new case with considerable zest. His preparations were careful and exhaustive whether the point at issue was
great or small and whether his client was important or insignificant.
The case that best illustrated this, perhaps, was one assigned to him
by the court. A man named Peter Larachelles, a heavy-drinking, impoverished immigrant who resided in the dock area of Boston, was
accused of the murder of John Barters, a common drunk. The police
on 18 March 1875 had picked Barters off the street in very bad condition and the next day he died. It was charged that on St. Patrick's
day Larachelles and Barters had been drinking at the former's home
and that Barters had become ill and vomited on the floor. Larachelles,
in a rage, allegedly beat the man severely and threw him from the
house. Although the immediate cause of Barters's death was erysipelas,
a disease brought on by his intemperate way of life, the sudden and

fatal eruption of the disease, it was charged, had been precipitated by the beating he had received. Hence Larachelles was indicted for murder in the second degree.

Under the circumstances Olney, who had never engaged in criminal practice, could have contented himself with a perfunctory defense of his assigned client. No one of importance would care whether Larachelles was found innocent or guilty. There were no fees to be collected for his work, and victory in such a case would do little to enhance Olney's reputation as a corporation lawyer. For the personnel involved in the case—Larachelles, his wife, the victim Barters, and the host of miserables brought from the slums to testify for one side or the other—Olney had nothing but disdain. Nevertheless his defense of Larachelles was masterful and must have been given careful preparation. Olney skillfully discredited the testimony of the prosecution's witnesses and then paraded before the jury an impressive group of witnesses of his own who raised doubts as to whether the beating had been the cause of Barters's fatal attack and as to whether the beating had actually been given him by Larachelles in the first place. A number of witnesses were hunted out to testify that they had seen Barters, or someone resembling him, beaten on the streets by a mob of boys on St. Patrick's day.

In his summation Olney played most deftly upon the jury's emotions. He did not want the jurymen to waste any sympathy on Larachelles, who was beneath their contempt, he said. He only sought absolute justice for his client. The police tactic of placing Larachelles's wife in a cell opposite him and then taking down their conversation as testimony, Olney deplored. He heaped scorn upon the witnesses for the prosecution whom he had already demonstrated to be liars and incompetents. The testimony of his own medical witnesses, that the beating might not have been connected with the final onset of erysipelas, he pointedly drove home to the jury. The acquittal of Larachelles, according to contemporary lawyers, was one of the few won from a Suffolk County jury in a murder indictment within a half-century.[16]

When Olney found it necessary to go into court, his presentation, as in the Larachelles case, was able. He was not given to the oratorical or florid type of delivery common in his day. Rather he spoke clearly, logically, briefly, and directly to the point.[17] Olney prepared his oral presentations by writing them out in full. He did not stop work on an argument but continued changing and polishing sentences till almost the last moment. Though he spoke from brief notes as if extemporaneously, his remarks were virtually memorized. Speaking of the fidelity with which he followed his prepared text, Miss Straw commented, "it was the remarkable way in which he followed 'phraseology' which seemed to me so surprising."[18]

Businessmen and attorneys of Boston ranked Olney high on the list of New England lawyers by the end of the eighties. "Mr. Olney is not a mere lawyer," John Murray Forbes once wrote, "but is a first rate business man—bound up in the lawyer—a great combination."[19] In 1889 upon the death of Sidney Bartlett, the ninety-year-old Nestor of the Boston bar who for years had been counsel and a director of the Burlington Railroad, Forbes wrote to Charles E. Perkins, "We lost Brother Bartlett last night about 10 o'clock, peacefully departing . . . We had some discussion today as to Mr. Bartlett's successor. If a lawyer, the first choice seemed to be Olney. . . . " Perkins agreed that Olney should become counsel though he preferred having some businessman rather than a lawyer on the board. "I suppose," he wrote, "we can get almost as much good out of Olney for $10,000 a year off the Board as on—tho not quite." When Olney was elected a few weeks later, however, Perkins wrote that the directors had felt the need for a lawyer and he thought their choice of Olney wise. "Olney's as good, I judge, as any one here."[20]

That the lawyers of Boston thought well of Olney is testified to by the fact that they chose him to head the Boston Bar Association in October 1892. On at least two occasions he was offered a place on the bench of the Supreme Judicial Court of Massachusetts.[21] In February 1893, when Olney accepted the position of attorney general of the United States, the more discerning comments of his colleagues at the bar indicated further his standing with the legal profession. "There was no stronger lawyer at the Bar, and he was excelled by none in the conduct of railroad business," declared the clerk of the Massachusetts Supreme Court. Another attorney, W. H. Coolidge, pointed to the fact that Olney had succeeded to the greater part of Sidney Bartlett's practice. "[W]hat greater honor or higher certificate can a man ask than that?" he exclaimed.[22]

Olney, it would appear, was generally pleased with the success he met in life. In his view he had earned his place in the American tradition of the self-made man. "Eminence at the bar in this country," he once asserted, "is never the result of luck, nor of favoritism, nor of anything but sterling ability, sedulously devoted to the theory and practice of the law."[23] Certainly such was true so far as his own career was concerned. While it could be said (and it was so said on at least one occasion) that he got his start from Judge Thomas, in fairness it should be added that when the Judge took Olney into his office, Olney had already demonstrated his ability at Harvard Law School. And, while Thomas gave him his opportunity, it was Olney's own hard work and ability and not "pull" that converted that opportunity into success.[24]

Throughout his career Olney lived in a style befitting his position. Until about 1880 he resided with his wife and daughters in the comfortable "Forest Hills" section of West Roxbury, then a suburb of Boston.[25] Once established professionally he moved first to a house on Marlborough Street in Boston and finally to a large and impressive residence on the sunny side of Commonwealth Avenue, overlooking the Back Bay Fens. The Olneys' new home was four stories high and was equipped with electric lights and an elevator. Charles Follen McKim, the famous architect of many of Boston's public buildings, designed the house for them, and Olney had it built for $40,000, exclusive of the architect's fee, furnishings, and site.[26] Summers were spent by the Olneys out of Boston in accord with the custom of their class. For several years they vacationed at Quincy, near the home of Peter Butler, Olney's uncle. After 1872, however, they summered at Falmouth on Cape Cod where eventually they built a twenty-six-room residence on the shore of Martha's Vineyard Sound.[27]

As might be expected, Olney adopted many of the characteristics of the Proper Bostonians whom he served. He took on a number of their prejudices and habits as his own; he observed their customs; he read their newspaper; and he joined—but rarely frequented—one or two of their clubs. Nevertheless, Olney remained a man apart in Boston. Though he had many business and social acquaintances he had few intimates and almost no friends. Only his younger cousin, Sigourney Butler, seems to have enjoyed a genuine give-and-take relationship with him. His background might initially have been a bar to the middle and upper levels of Boston society, but it appears to have been his temperament that kept him apart through the years.[28]

To appreciate him properly, people had to view Olney from just the right perspective and distance. Those who were close enough to be invited to his home saw him at his best. To them he was a charming and attentive host and an urbane and witty conversationalist. He entertained well and served excellent food and drink.[29] Those who knew him only from afar usually respected him but had no affection for the clever attorney. Alfred Henry Lewis, writing for the *Boston Journal* in 1896, perhaps best expressed the mixed emotions of those who knew Olney a little but not well. "Richard Olney," he wrote, " . . . is hard, lucid, scintillant, . . . a man-diamond. A cold sparkle, as of frost, not of fire, goes with Olney. He is clear, frigid, wintry, and has no sympathies. Being superbly egotistical," Lewis continued, "no tale of woe moves him, being a thoroughbred, a challenge to battle brings him speedily forward. . . . By nature he is exclusive, seclusive, shields himself selfishly from common contact . . . wraps himself in his cloak, and witholds his hand. . . . A man gem . . . no influence corrodes, no fires melt; under all pressures, through all conditions, Olney is immutable."[30]

It was, however, in his home, at the dinner table, on the tennis courts, and in his everyday relationships with his immediate circle of family and servants that Olney, in many respects, was least attractive. At home Olney was a tyrant who ruled as if his family existed solely to accommodate his purposes. With rare exceptions nothing he said or did was challenged; his decrees were obeyed without question, and his whim and caprice carried the weight of law. Outward signs of warmth and affection were foreign to him and a stiff formality marked his relationship with his wife and daughters. The old custom of addressing one another as "Mr. Olney" and "Mrs. Olney" prevailed even within the intimacy of the family circle. By all accounts a delightfully sweet and charming person, Mrs. Olney deferred to her husband's wishes and seems to have lived in awe of him. At times she rebelled against him—when, for example, she believed that his orders might endanger the health of their children—and on those few occasions she won.

Daughters Agnes and Mary learned to conform rigidly to patterns of behavior pleasing to their father. When he came home from his office in the evening, all conversation was hushed, the piano stood silent, and a quiet settled over the household until his mood was ascertained. When the question, "Papa, did you have a good day today?" was asked, as often as not he did not answer, and a flaring of his nostrils gave warning that he was in a bad humor. "His nose always told me what his mood was," one member of his family declared, "and sometimes the look of it made me quake." On such an evening, dinner, which was always a dress affair, passed in absolute silence. On the other hand, when Olney himself initiated table conversation, everyone was expected to participate enthusiastically.

Evenings were given over to doing whatever pleased and refreshed Olney. After dinner he frequently gathered the family about him and read to them selected articles from the *Boston Transcript;* comments from his audience were neither expected nor volunteered. Readings from "good literature" might take up the balance of the evening or his wife and daughters might join him in part-singing or at cards. One winter Agnes and Mary were obliged to play tennis with him in the attic, where he constructed a sort of indoor court. They discovered that their father would never accept mere fatigue as an excuse for dropping out of the game.

As a young man in college, Olney, whose temper was always rather short, seems to have given vent to his feelings from time to time by physically assaulting people who angered him. Through the years his disposition did not improve, but the way in which he struck out at offending objects took on a variety of forms. For example, he disliked pets and animals, excepting horses, and when his grandson's dog strayed from its carefully defined limits, Olney would kick it mightily. A cow that broke loose one night and spoiled his tennis lawn was shot the next morning. Babies too, caused Olney annoyance. When his widowed daughter, Agnes Minot, and her infant son, Francis, came to live at the Olney household, it became a matter of course that the child be scooped up and whisked away to another part of the house at the approach of his grandfather. Nor as the boy grew older did he win favor with Olney. Francis consorted with the servants, accepted cigarettes from them, and in general fell short of the standards which his grandfather expected. By mutual agreement, as soon as practicable, Francis moved out of the main house at Falmouth to the overflow house—an outbuilding equipped to handle guests.

The most extreme example, perhaps, of Olney's unreasoning temper was the banishment of his daughter Mary from the family home. Mary, in 1886, married Charles H. Abbot, a dentist descended from an old New England family. Abbot was relatively unknown in Boston because he had for many years lived in Berlin, Germany, where his father, also a dentist, practiced his profession. It was not that Olney disliked or disapproved of the young man. He had himself encouraged Abbot to come to his home; he raised no objections when the couple announced their engagement; and at the wedding, which was in his home, he gave the bride away. While the Abbots were on their wedding trip, however, word came to them that the elder Dr. Abbot had died in Berlin. They immediately made arrangements to go to Germany, and Mary wrote to her father, probably from the boat in New York, informing him of the change in plans. When the letter arrived, Olney glanced at it, tossed it on a table, and announced to Mrs. Olney that henceforth to him Mary was dead. He gave no explanation then or later, and no one ever presumed to broach the topic with him. It has been surmised by his family that Olney resented his daughter's marriage and that her sudden departure for Europe triggered off a fit of unsuspected jealousy, resentment, and anger that had been smoldering within him.

Olney's family accepted the extraordinary decree as final. They knew that once he had made such a pronouncement he became the victim of a sort of lockjaw of the will and was constitutionally incapable of revoking an order. Mary, deeply hurt and angered by her father's unjust act, made no attempt at reconciliation, believing that any advances that she might make would be rebuffed by her father. Olney's act was regarded as unforgivable by many in the circles of Boston society where both he and his daughter were known. But Olney was immovable, and opposition—even when silent—made him more adamant.

Through the years Mrs. Olney visited Mary and her family in Potsdam, Germany, and for several summers the Abbots were at South Yarmouth on Cape Cod where they were frequently visited by Mrs. Olney and Agnes. Olney made no attempt to prevent these meetings, knowing that his wife, in this matter, would never conform to his wishes. He himself encountered Mary and her husband only once in the many years that followed the banishment. The Abbots were at the theater in Boston, and just as the curtain was going up on the first act of the play, Olney took his seat which, by accident, was on the aisle next to his daughter and her husband. Olney, though seated next to his son-in-law, made no acknowledgement whatever of the Abbots' presence, and when the curtain began to fall at the end of the first act, he bolted from the theater and did not return. If Olney regretted the break with Mary, he was never moved to relent. In his will, however, though Mary was intentionally unmentioned and unprovided for, Olney directed that upon the death of both his wife and his daughter Agnes, his estate was to be shared equally by Agnes's son, Francis, and the four children of Mary.[31]

Olney often resorted to the mails to get at people beyond his immediate reach—using sarcastic, insulting letters to set them aright. To a gentleman who made a speech to which he took exception, the imperious Bostonian wrote, "I have read your last Summer Stockbridge speech—with the admiration its bright and attractive features are calculated to inspire. Nevertheless, you must allow me to say that if your statement of the attitude of the last Cleveland administration in respect of the Monroe Doctrine is a sample of the accuracy of the statements of the speech generally, you cannot be too quick in retracting it and making a humble apology to your Stockbridge audience."[32] And, when one of his landlords in Washington pressed him too closely about renewing the lease on his house, Olney began a long letter listing complaints about the place with the statement that he and Mrs. Olney had been unable to give attention to taking the house for another term because "it has taken all our time to devise ways and means of living in it at present."³³

On at least one occasion Olney used his influence to strike a blow at the curse of "yellow journalism" when it began to menace Boston. He wrote to John H. Holmes, editor of the *Boston Herald*,

> If a newspaper ever offered anything to the Boston public more offensive & indecent than the front display page of this morning's Boston Herald, I have failed to see it. The page is practically made up of murder, rape & attempt at rape, with all the unwholesome details. What is the use of that sort of thing? The Herald can't hope to compete with Hearst . . . while its attempt to do so will forfeit the respect & patronage of the better part of the community. I had my paper burnt in the hope—I daresay a vain one—to keep the stuff from the servants. I certainly won't have it in my house if the style of today's paper is to be continued.³⁴

He followed up the letter to Holmes with notes to Henry Lee Higginson and to Robert M. Burnett, calling their attention to the offending issue of the *Herald* and asking them to protest to Holmes too if they shared his view.³⁵

The servants and other employees whose welfare Olney so carefully watched over found him a very exacting person for whom to work. A few who performed at the level he insisted upon were kept on for years and were treated well. For example, his secretary, Miss Straw, was appointed by Olney in his will as an executrix and trustee of his estate, which assured her an income. To Reuben B. Handy, his long-time boatman, Olney left his small yacht, the *Sea Robin*.³⁶ But his favors were not always restricted to those who had grown old in his service or who performed important tasks for him. He once wrote to a surgeon on behalf of an office boy in his employ who was about to undergo an operation on his throat. "I shall be glad," Olney said, "to have the operation made as painless as possible and will bear any expense that may be thus occasioned."³⁷

Other employees, however, fared less well. There were cooks who were dismissed the same day that they were hired because they neglected to close the door between the kitchen and the rest of the house while cooking cauliflower, cabbage, or onions. Olney especially liked those vegetables but detested their odor while they were cooking. His gardeners too had to be ever on the alert. Olney had a "phenomenal hatred" of dandelions, according to his grandson, and "God help the man responsible if one appeared on the lawn."[38]

One of Olney's chief pleasures was to preside over the traditional New England family Thanksgiving dinner. To this annual feast were summoned not only the immediate family but the brothers and sisters, the nieces and nephews, and the other kinsmen of both Olney and his wife. Olney also liked giving small dinner parties for groups of neighbors and family friends. Opera was his favorite form of music and, though he loathed spectator sports, he attended football games at Harvard. Bridge-whist, the singing of carols and hymns, and reading—particularly biographies and histories—were pastimes which he enjoyed at home. As a sort of hobby, Olney collected church music.

For the greater part of his recreation, Olney turned to vigorous outdoor activities: tennis, golf, fishing, yachting, horseback riding, and walking. Although he had not played the game as a youth, lawn tennis became his favorite. His form was awkward in appearance, but he developed a powerful side-swing and he used both the overhand and backhand stroke effectively; the underhand stroke he disparaged. Olney played tennis at a furious pace and with an aggressiveness, determination, and grimness that resembled his conduct of a case in court. He rarely afforded his opponents time to ready themselves before smashing his serves over their side of the net. With him a game of tennis was slam, slam, slam, from start to finish.

Olney preferred to play doubles because, according to his grandson, that way there was someone to blame for any errors which might occur on his side of the net. His partners and opponents were carefully and formally nominated and were frequently changed. A nominee who failed to appear was not accorded a second invitation. While playing, Olney did not tolerate interruptions or conversation. One distinguished visitor who accepted an invitation to a set of tennis and to luncheon made the mistake of joking while playing. Olney put down his racket, walked off the court and went fishing, leaving the offender to lunch alone with the Olney ladies.

Nearly every day Olney went for a walk, sometimes going as far as ten miles. These "walks" were not leisurely strolls but were so brisk that his shorter-legged companions were obliged to jog or trot along to keep up. Each day he walked from his home to his office, and his daughters—for their health—were forced to accompany him as far as their school. During the summer months the Olney family frequently set out at a hard and fast pace across the fields near Falmouth. On these excursions Olney was careful to have the family walk single-file across hay fields to avoid any unnecessary damage to the property of others.[39]

Through the years Olney remained strong, healthy, and vigorous, and aside from an occasional bout with colds or with the "grippe" he was never ill. Probably because of his constant exercising he never became overweight or paunchy, and he maintained the general appearance and vitality of a much younger man. Aside from streaks of gray in his dark brown hair, a deepening of the lines on his face, and his full, gray moustache, Olney looked in the 1890s much the same as in the 1860s.[40]

In February 1893, Olney reached the second major turning point of his career when President-elect Grover Cleveland asked him to become attorney general of the United States. Olney had little preparation for the job. His political experience consisted of a one-year term in the Massachusetts legislature in 1874 and an unsuccessful bid for the attorney generalship of Massachusetts in 1876. His training and temperament and his experience as a corporation lawyer, far from making a politician of him, had shaped him, as his biographer Henry James observed, into "a hard-thinking, accomplishing, ruthless being like one of those modern war-tanks which proceeds across the roughest ground, heedless of opposition, deaf alike to messages from friends and cries from the foe, able to crush every person and every obstacle that gets between it and its chosen objective."[41] In spite of this, a man of Olney's temperament, although it was uncommon in politics, might be expected to have little trouble in meeting the ordinary demands of public life during the Gay Nineties. Unfortunately, however, the second Cleveland administration would face deep-seated, difficult, and often delicate problems; and where tact, patience, and imagination were needed, Olney would bluntly, and sometimes in bad temper, respond with tank-like force.

4

Serving Two Masters

"In making up the cabinet for the new administration," Olney wrote William C. Whitney in late January 1893, "please do not forget how many people at the east—including numberless widows and orphans—are interested in railroads and require and deserve a reasonable amount of consideration." Whitney, Cleveland's campaign manager and adviser on political matters, promised to remember.[1] Olney was not seeking a position for himself; he was writing on behalf of his railroad clients who wished to block the selection of a southern congressman as postmaster general.[2] Olney did not know it at the time, but Cleveland on 4 January had already "casually mentioned" his name in connection with a cabinet position and within three weeks would be inviting him to join the new administration.[3]

By the time of Olney's letter, Cleveland's efforts to form his cabinet were running into difficulty. The men he most wanted were all declining to serve. It was not that Cleveland's standards were exacting; he required neither prominence nor great experience. Having himself been a relatively obscure lawyer in Buffalo only five years before rising to the presidency, Cleveland believed a good country lawyer was fitted for any cabinet post (except for the State and Treasury Departments where some experience might be useful), and that a "perfectly competent" attorney general could be found in almost any county seat.[4]

Six of eight cabinet positions were filled by mid-February. For secretary of state, Cleveland chose Federal Judge Walter Q. Gresham of Illinois, an anti-Harrison Republican who in 1892 had bolted his party and helped to put his state in the Democratic column. (To assuage party regulars, Cleveland named Josiah Quincy, a loyal Democrat from Massachusetts, assistant secretary and put him in charge of State Department patronage.) Senator John G. Carlisle of Kentucky, a party leader second only to Cleveland, agreed to be secretary of the treasury.

Headship of the Interior Department went to a rising young southerner, Hoke Smith of Georgia. Daniel S. Lamont, confidant and private secretary to Cleveland as governor of New York and during the first term as president, was named secretary of war. The president-elect's close friend and one-time law partner, Wilson S. Bissell, accepted the postmaster generalship, and J. Sterling Morton, a conservative editor from Nebraska, became secretary of agriculture.[5]

As for the remaining vacancies, Cleveland decided to reserve the navy portfolio for a New Englander and the attorney generalship for a southerner. Increasingly, Olney's name cropped up for one of the positions. Cleveland had met Olney in person but once in 1890 or 1891. The attorney had accompanied former Secretary of War William C. Endicott on a social call to Cleveland's summer cottage at Buzzard's Bay on Cape Cod. The president-elect knew Olney by reputation, however. In 1888 prominent New Englanders had urged him for appointment as chief justice of the Supreme Court, and Whitney, of course, spoke highly of Olney. The two had served together as directors of the Boston & Maine since 1891 and during the recent presidential campaign Olney had helped Whitney raise funds and secure the services of John Quincy Adams as a speaker on behalf of Cleveland. Another link to both Whitney and Cleveland was Olney's brother, Peter. Since the early 1870s he had worked closely with Whitney in New York politics and for services rendered in electing Cleveland governor of New York in 1883 had been rewarded with the post of district attorney of New York County.[6]

Two others played a role in bringing Olney's name to Cleveland's attention. Former Congressman John E. Russell of Massachusetts, a classmate of Olney's at Leicester Academy and a leader in the first-term tariff war, called on Cleveland at his headquarters in Lakewood, New Jersey, in late January. Declining any position for himself, he recommended Olney for attorney general and John Quincy Adams for secretary of the navy. Not long after, Sigourney Butler, a distant relative of the president-elect and second comptroller of the currency in Cleveland's first administration, wrote to propose the same two men for cabinet places, stressing their "supereminent qualifications."[7] When by mid-February Cleveland had approached neither man, Butler discussed the matter with Charles S. Hamlin, an active young Massachusetts Democrat and an admirer of Olney. The two concluded that Josiah Quincy was killing off all prominent New Englanders by telling Cleveland they would refuse positions if asked. Quincy's motive, Butler and Hamlin suspected, was to secure a place for himself by default.

Butler called on Cleveland on 15 February and assured him that, if asked, both Olney and Adams would accept cabinet appointments. When Cleveland expressed great surprise, Butler revealed his suspicions about Quincy.[8] That same day Cleveland summoned Peter Olney to Lakewood and asked him to act as his emissary to Richard Olney, offering him a place in the cabinet and urging him not to decline without first coming to Lakewood for a conference.[9]

In a hurried trip to Boston next day, Peter delivered the message. Back in New York before the best arguments for accepting occurred to him, he sent Richard a number of considerations to bear in mind. The unsought offer, which might never again be made, gave him an opportunity to increase his reputation and fame. It offered a chance to share in shaping the policy of one of the world's greatest powers at a time when major financial, economic, and legal problems demanded wise solutions. Richard could "aid in no small degree in the proper disposition of these great questions." Further, patriots and party men alike owed much to Cleveland—"the Moses of the Democratic party who has led his followers out of the Egyptian bondage to a land promising great prosperity." Finally, Peter reminded his brother, "what a source of pride and joy this would be to our dear father if he were alive and could know of it."[10]

Richard Olney's initial reaction was to decline, but to refuse to go to Lakewood, even on a useless errand, would be "discourteous," he decided.[11] Perhaps the offer appealed to him far more than he admitted, even to himself. Certainly his efforts during the next few days were aimed at accepting, not rejecting the offer. His immediate concern was the long-run pecuniary sacrifice involved. Earning perhaps $50,000 a year, Olney was engaged in a number of delicate and complicated negotiations for his employers and had no associate or firm to carry on for him while he went into public office. Unless he could continue serving his clients enough to hold his practice together, entering the cabinet would be too costly—not simply because his income would drop to $8,000 a year for several years, but because his clients in the meantime, of necessity, would have to turn to other counsel.[12] Arranging his business so as to be able to accept the post required time and through the media of Peter Olney and Lamont, Richard was given until 22 February to decide.

Two questions had to be settled: Could he continue his private law practice while in the cabinet, and would his clients accept his services on a limited basis for a few years? Peter checked on the first while Richard looked into the second. Cleveland and Lamont believed that if Olney wanted to continue his private practice, he would find it easier as secretary of the navy than as attorney general.[13]

" . . . I have thought that Mr. Olney's railroad clientage, while with such a man as he no real objection, might in the estimation of the public make him a more desirable Secretary of the Navy," Cleveland wrote Lamont. This was "in subordination" to his "main idea," however, that Olney was "so desirable a man to have in my cabinet" that he was "entirely willing to leave the choice in the two places, to him."[14] Peter learned from Benjamin H. Bristow, a former solicitor general of the United States and acting attorney general in the early 1870s, that it was "customary" for attorneys general to continue their private practices while in office. Several had even argued cases before the Supreme Court when no government interest was involved.[15]

Meanwhile, Richard Olney sounded out his major clients. Telling Charles E. Perkins, president of the Burlington, of Cleveland's offer, he added that he believed it his duty to "take time to consider." Among other things he wanted to find out where he would stand with his clients. He was "not a millionaire" and could not "take any office of the sort without a good deal of pecuniary sacrifice—just how much I should like to ascertain." He asked Perkins to do him "the personal favor" of expressing his views "with entire freedom and frankness. You will be governed, as you always are, by what is the true interest of the C., B. & Q. . . . "[16]

Perkins's reply was encouraging: " . . . I say take it by all means— there is no question—it is important to the country & of the utmost importance to the administration. It alters my opinion of Cleveland. You must accept—and it shall make no difference in our relations except as you may think it expedient to make. . . . " He wanted Olney to discuss the matter, however, with John Murray Forbes.[17] Olney did not see Forbes, but the elderly chairman of the Burlington's board of directors sent him a copy of a letter he had written to Perkins. "I hear that Olney can have the Cabinet Post of Attorney General and that it is thought this would not stand in the way of his remaining our C., B. & Q. counsel. If we had to lose him from our service I should hope he might not go into the cabinet but if the two are not incompatible it seems to me rather for our advantage to have him at Washington. I am sure it would be the best appointment that Cleveland can make from New England."[18]

Olney apparently also consulted officials of the Boston & Maine and Santa Fe railroads. All agreed that he ought to accept and that they wanted him to "continue to do for them anything he properly could do."[19] When he entered the cabinet, Olney continued to draw a regular salary of $2,500 per quarter from the Burlington. Possibly he continued on the Santa Fe's payroll.[20] The Boston & Maine, however, apparently paid him neither salary nor fees while he was in the cabinet except for one payment for work done prior to 4 March 1893.[21] Assured that acceptance of a cabinet post would not ruin his practice, Olney went to Lakewood on 21 February.

Meeting with Lamont and Whitney the previous evening, Olney listened to arguments why he should accept the post of secretary of the navy. At Lakewood Olney flatly rejected the navy portfolio, but not that of attorney general. He suggested, however, that John Quincy Adams would be the best man to represent New England in the cabinet and was sure that if asked Adams would accept the navy post. Cleveland, who did not know Adams personally, took Olney's recommendation. "If he accepts, well and good; if he does not, then you must not decline anything I tender you."[22]

Agreeing, Olney returned to Boston and delivered Cleveland's offer to Adams. To his "astonishment as well as dismay," Adams absolutely refused. Olney then wired Cleveland the agreed-upon code message, "I will go with you," meaning that Adams had declined and that Olney would serve as attorney general. The Bostonian made one final effort to escape appointment: "I confirm yesterday's telegram," he wired, "but if you can possibly excuse me I must be excused. Please wire your decision." Cleveland, who had had much trouble getting his bait taken, did not let this one get away. "Nothing will now excuse you," he wired, "but the act of God or the public enemy."[23]

Throughout January and February, newsmen, particularly in New York, had vied with one another in predicting cabinet appointments. Not content to make predictions, Joseph Pulitzer, editor of the *New York World*, urged Cleveland to name a prominent reformer as attorney general. He believed that the popular success or failure of the administration hinged on how well it enforced the newly enacted Sherman Antitrust Act.[24] The *Boston Herald*, however, first broke the news of Olney's appointment on 22 February. The next day formal announcement was made at Lakewood that the cabinet was complete with the appointment of Hilary A. Herbert of Alabama as secretary of the navy and of Richard Olney as attorney general. "Who is Mr. Olney?" a reporter asked Lamont when he issued the public statement. "Mr. Olney?" repeated Lamont, "Why one of Massachusetts' brightest and foremost lawyers. Everybody knows Richard."[25] Editorial comment on Olney's appointment for the most part was limited to generalities. Apparently Lamont's "everybody" did not include the nation's press. Even Boston newspapers knew little of their local celebrity, not even having his picture to print.

The *New York World*, learning something of Olney's clientele, gulped hard and swallowed the appointment as gracefully as possible. "Of Mr. Olney's legal abilities and his high character there is no question. But it is at least questionable whether a corporation attorney, however eminent, is adapted to fulfil the obligation of the Democratic party to enforce the laws against trusts and other monopolies, to compel delinquent railroads to pay or better secure their debts to the Government, and to restore popular confidence in the just and equal administration of the laws against the rich and powerful combinations." Unwilling to "prejudge any man," however, the *World* took comfort that Cleveland had selected him and that both old and young Democrats in Massachusetts "warmly indorsed" him.[26]

Scores of congratulatory letters poured in on the new appointee. Old school friends wrote to assure him that they had detected his potential greatness on the playing fields and in the classrooms even in those remote years. Relatives long unheard from sent letters of congratulation, and some people, presuming relationship on the basis of a common last name, did not hesitate to ask favors. Leaders of the bench and bar in New England and New York expressed their delight at Cleveland's judicious appointment.[27] The most enthusiastic note, however, came from the president of the Burlington Railroad:

> I am very glad to see by this morning's dispatches that you have accepted the Att'y. Generalship, & I am satisfied now that Cleveland not only wants to but that he will elevate politics—& it is a great thing for the country. I hear Bissell very well spoken of & they told me in Atlanta the other day that Hoke Smith was a first-rate man—Morton I know and Carlisle we all know. . . .
>
> In a certain sense of course the C., B. & Q. loses by your appointment, but in a larger sense it in common with every property interest, gains—I consider every share of my Stock worth more today than yesterday . . . [28]

Well might Perkins have regarded his property—especially railroad stocks—more valuable as he looked over the new administration. The president, for example, between his two terms had practiced law from the offices of the New York firm of Bangs, Stetson, Tracy & MacVeagh. Francis Lynde Stetson of that firm, who regularly represented the interests of J. P. Morgan, had been a friend and counselor of Cleveland since his days as governor of New York. Among the president's friends were William C. Whitney, railway and traction company manipulator; Charles S. Fairchild, banker; and Oscar S.

Straus, department-store millionaire. No one was closer, however, than E. C. Benedict, a New York financier and gas magnate. Ever accommodating, Benedict advised Cleveland on stocks and bonds and handled transactions for the president after his return to the White House. To facilitate these operations, the two shared a bank account. "I must say," Cleveland wrote shortly after leaving office, "that I like the joint account which has one careful father and an uncle who wishes it well for what he may make out of it. I as such an uncle am certainly much obliged to the Dad in this particular instance. . . ."[29]

As for the cabinet, most had close ties to the business world and none could be classified as hostile or even unfriendly to business interests. There was Olney, with his ties to the Burlington, Santa Fe, and Boston & Maine railroads, who continued to sit on the board of the Old Colony Trust Company and to serve such Boston financiers as Henry Lee Higginson, T. Jefferson Coolidge, and Frederick H. Prince.[30] Gresham, the new secretary of state, as a federal judge had long since proven himself a strong defender of railroad property by the creative use of injunctions to help break the Great Burlington Strike of 1888.[31] Secretary of War Lamont, who in league with Whitney had amassed a fortune in railway and traction companies, in March 1893 sat as a director on the boards of over a dozen large corporations including several New York City banks.[32] The incoming postmaster general, Bissell, was one of western New York's leading railroad lawyers. Formerly president of the Buffalo & Rochester and a director and counsel of several other small lines, at the time he entered upon his duties he was president of the Buffalo & Southwestern and counsel at Buffalo for the Reading Railroad.[33]

As already noted, Secretary of Agriculture Morton had long been in the hire of the Burlington as a propagandist against the Grangers in Nebraska and as a sometime lobbyist in Washington.[34] Hoke Smith, who was to head the Interior Department, had not alienated the railroad community despite his successful handling of personal damage suits against railroads and his demands as editor of the *Atlanta Journal* for stricter regulation of railroads. While in office he would find time to defend in court the interests of private clients who were railroad bondholders.[35] Although Treasury Secretary Carlisle and Navy Secretary Herbert apparently had no direct ties to railroads, banks, or other commercial interests, they were regarded as friendly. In fact neither they nor Smith represented the growing spirit of Populism then sweeping their native region. Opposed to joining with western agrarian radicals for monetary and other reforms, they favored continuing the alliance of southern Democrats with conservative eastern business-minded Democrats. Herbert, of the old "Redeemer" element, some years before had edited that group's leading apology, *Why the Solid South?*, which he dedicated to northern businessmen.[36]

In making up the cabinet for the new administration, Cleveland and his advisers had not forgotten how many people in all sections of the country—including numberless widows and orphans—were interested in railroads and other business enterprises. Insofar as cabinet appointments were concerned, those groups received consideration that should have exceeded their fondest expectations.

In his inaugural address, Cleveland set forth the basic beliefs of the new administration. To protect "a sound and stable currency," the country could no longer "defy with impunity the inexorable laws of finance and trade." "Protection for protection's sake" was no longer acceptable to the American people, and with it must go the "brood of kindred evils which are the unwholesome progeny of paternalism." "Governmental favoritism" and "wild and reckless pension expenditure" should give way to frugal and economical government. Plain honesty and good government dictated that public expenditures be controlled by public necessity. While the people should "patriotically and cheerfully support their government," the functions of government did "not include the support of the people." Americans must refuse bounties and subsidies from their government. Nodding to the growing demand for destruction of the trusts, Cleveland damned "immense aggregations . . . and combinations of business interests formed for the purpose of limiting production and fixing prices. . . . " He promised no vigorous prosecutions, however. "To the extent that they can be reached and restrained by Federal power, the General Government should relieve our citizens from their interference and exactions."[37]

To a man the cabinet accepted the precepts of sound money, tariff reform, an end to paternalism, and economy in government. All were convinced that legislation could do little to help the world and much to harm it. That they had no policy for meeting the trust problem, the labor problem, the farm problem, or the many economic problems that faced the country, did not disturb them. Had they been asked, they would proudly have disclaimed a positive program for any group—such would imply a spirit of paternalism or favoritism. Government was at its best, Cleveland Democrats believed, when it remained passive and negative.[38] Vigorous action was reserved for those rare occasions when law and order were threatened by violence.

President Cleveland met regularly with his cabinet on Tuesdays and Fridays except during the hot summer months when everyone whose duties permitted left Washington. Usually the group fell to chatting about current happenings. After a few minutes the president would introduce subjects for consideration. If he had nothing to present, he would ask the others, beginning with the secretary of state, to bring their problems before the group. No one dominated the sessions, no one rose to give formal remarks, and everyone was free to speak on any topic brought up whether it related to his department or not. Cleveland usually asked each member for his views, but took no formal vote and the final decision and full responsibility for it lay with the president.

As a matter of policy, Cleveland left most matters to the department heads. Each had his own province and was expected not to meddle in the affairs of the others. From time to time each would carry "some budget of business" to the White House to be worked over with the president.[39] So great was the discretion left to department heads that sometimes they rather than the president made major policy decisions. Occasionally only after a program—adopted and put into operation by a cabinet officer—ran into trouble was Cleveland told of it and asked for assistance. Faced with the choice of repudiating both the policy and its maker, or backing the already formulated policy, Cleveland usually supported his subordinate.

The cabinet was torn by neither power struggles nor personal quarrels; no rival cliques or bickering factions arose to divide it. Rarely did the group differ seriously over a major policy. Some healthy differences of opinion or even a split over a significant issue might have stimulated the administration beneficially. Week after week, one member recorded in his diary: "The Cabinet meeting today was unimportant"; "Cabinet meeting became this morning a very free and easy affair, and public matters, of which there were not very many . . . at times gave way to a general interchange of anecdotes . . . "; "Most of the time of the session was taken up in an informal discussion of the situation of affairs in the Indian territory"; "Nothing special at the Cabinet meeting this morning, but we sat out the usual two hours and talked on a miscellany of matters"; "Nothing worth noting at the Cabinet meeting today."[40]

Olney's cabinet colleagues found him pleasant and cordial, but remote. They respected his intelligence and ability, but most of them thought him reserved and not very companionable. Except for Judson Harmon (Olney's successor as attorney general) and Secretary Morton, few had any real affection for him. "Olney is a very serious man and seldom gives utterance to anything humorous," one wrote, "but he has a keen relish for the comic and does not object to a little joking at his expense." The same man could not imagine any real intimacy between himself and Olney, "nor is it possible to suppose that Mr. Olney will ever draw to him the affectionate reverence that the whole official family, including the President," felt for Gresham. Postmaster General Bissell, writing years afterwards, remembered Olney as "wayward." "With him, as with many," he noted, "the greater intellectuality seemed to work a displacement of a corresponding amount of good judgment." He attributed Olney's "excellent public record" to the restraining influence of Cleveland's "stronger personality."[41]

Of all the members of the cabinet, President Cleveland came to admire Judge Gresham the most. "You don't know what a comfort Gresham is to me," he wrote, "with his hard sense, his patriotism and loyalty. It is but little for me to say that I would trust my life or honor in his keeping at all times."[42] The president's reliance on Secretary Lamont was also complete: "In your Department the judgment and opinion of its Head settles all questions with me." His relationship with Carlisle he summed up in the sentence: "He knows all that I ought to know, and I can bear all that he needs to bear."[43] It was Olney, however, who came to wield the greatest influence over the president.

Neither Olney nor Cleveland ever clearly defined the relationship between them. The president apparently recognized that Olney had a greater sophistication in law than he, and a greater working knowledge of the business world. Whenever the two did not see eye to eye on a matter, Olney, who could argue legal circles around the president, usually prevailed. By January 1894, Morton was saying that the president depended on Olney more than on anyone else in his cabinet.[44] That Olney's influence grew is evidenced by his promotion to the State Department on Gresham's death in 1895.

So far as the public knew, Olney thought highly of his chief. The letters between the two, in office and after, were cordial and friendly but never intimate as between comrades-in-arms. In the privacy of his home, Olney spoke disparagingly of Cleveland. The fastidious Bostonian was disgusted at Cleveland's large brood of children (the president late in life had taken a young wife and was the father of four youngsters), and was dismayed that the president not only freely associated with the "commonest" sorts of people, but actually enjoyed their company. That the president could sleep very late in the morning or sit fishing, literally saying or doing nothing for hours at a time, was incredible to the ever-active Olney. These things all added up, in Olney's mind, to proof that Cleveland was a "second rater." "Cleveland!" Olney would snort in unmistakable tones of scorn, "small-mouthed black bass!"[45]

Although as Olney soon discovered, the administration was run by the president himself and not by some power behind the throne, Cleveland needed and eagerly accepted advice and recommendations from others. Though competent men, most of the cabinet members were not especially gifted. Aside from Carlisle, who concentrated on Treasury Department affairs, most had little of the practical knowledge the president needed. Without pushing himself on the president, Olney gradually moved in to fill the vacuum. He made it his business to be well informed on every subject that concerned the government. Because he had answers to questions and carefully worked-out arguments to defend them, Olney reached the ear of ex-lawyer Cleveland more readily than did his colleagues. Before long the two men were seeing each other almost daily.[46] Olney learned how Cleveland's mind worked and saw what types of argument most easily convinced him. Using this information, when he had a program to push he knew exactly how to tailor his presentation of data so as to win his chief's approval.

The transition from running his one-man office in Boston to heading the Justice Department in Washington required a considerable adjustment on the part of the new attorney general. By 1893 Olney had acquired the narrow, conservative, Hub-centered point of view usually attributed to the Cabots, the Lowells, and the Lodges, and did not at once grasp the full significance of his new commitment. He seems to have looked upon it much as he might have regarded being hired as counsel by another great corporation. There were differences, of course; his new client did not pay well—a fact that Olney sometimes complained of.[47] Too, since the government was not a Boston firm, he would be obliged to be out of town considerably. Initially he seems to have planned to commute between Boston and Washington, spending three or four days at a time in each place. When an acquaintance asked him whether Mrs. Olney was moving to Washington before or after Inauguration Day, he replied, "Why she is not going to move there at all!"[48]

But the Olneys did move to Washington. The attorney general's new responsibilities took up most of his time and he could scarcely ignore the traditional round of official receptions, dinners, and parties in the nation's capital. Leasing his home on Commonwealth Avenue, he rented an equivalent mansion in Washington.[49] In Boston the Olneys had entertained little outside the family and a limited circle of friends and neighbors. In Washington they blossomed out as the social leaders of the new administration. The reserved and formal Olney found himself enjoying the role of host to the brilliant assortment of foreigners and Americans who made up Washington society. While attorney general he gave a large dinner party at least once a week. "I need not have done so," he afterwards wrote, "But the recent cabinet had not been particularly strong on the entertaining side and I have felt bound to do what I reasonably could to help out in that direction." Credit for the success of these parties belonged primarily to Mrs. Olney, a woman of much charm, grace, and tact, who made all the necessary arrangements.[50]

Once in office, Olney complained of being "driven very much by all sorts of work that I am not fitted for."[51] Although he spent some time in preparing legal opinions for the president and his cabinet colleagues, he was surprised at how much of his time went to managing the Justice Department. "So far as strictly legal work is concerned," he observed, "the duties of the Attorney-General are not more exacting than those of any lawyer having a large general practice. But the truth is that the Attorney-Generalship corresponds to what is known in European countries as the 'Ministry of Justice'—that is, the duties are very largely administrative." The preparation and argument of government cases before the Supreme Court, for example, over the years had devolved on the solicitor general and the assistant attorneys general. Olney was in office nearly two years before he himself prepared and argued cases before the high tribunal.[52]

In Boston Olney had directed only his own work and that of quiet, efficient Miss Straw, an errand-running office boy, and an occasional young lawyer hired to do detail work on a specific case. In Washington he had under his immediate charge the solicitor general, three assistant attorneys general, six assistant attorneys, one pardons attorney, thirty-six clerks, eight copyists, six messengers, and twenty-two others who performed a variety of duties, mostly custodial. He was also responsible for supervising the far-flung activities of six departmental examiners and of the United States attorney and marshal in each of the nation's sixty-nine judicial districts. The sixty-four federal district judges and twenty circuit court judges were also to a degree under his jurisdiction.[53] Unwilling to leave the direction of this force in the hands of subordinates, he brought it completely under his personal supervision.[54]

In effect, Olney ruled the Justice Department much as he governed his own family. His assistants found him distant, formal, and firm; his wrath, once aroused, formidable. When an underling was absent from his post, he sent the attorney general a formal excuse; when promoted, he sent an extravagant letter of thanks; and when he offended, he received from the attorney general a reprimand generously spiced with sarcasm. Whatever the attorney general deemed to be good for his employees, they received. "I should like to make sure that all the persons in this Department who need vaccinating are in fact vaccinated and to that end should like to have some Doctor come here to do up the job," he once wrote to the secretary of war.[55] Only Solicitor General Lawrence Maxwell, a man of considerable reputation as a lawyer and one whose appointment had been made by President Cleveland himself, seems to have operated independently of the attorney general. Eventually, after a sudden dispute, Olney forced Maxwell to resign.[56]

The physical facilities of the Justice Department and the appropriations that Congress made for the government's legal arm considerably disturbed the attorney general. Although his private law office in Boston was notorious for its frugal, old-fashioned furnishings, Olney found the building on Lafayette Square that housed his department grossly inadequate. It had been purchased by the government at an auction sale, he declared, and though "wholly insufficient" could not be enlarged. There was but one "presentable" room in it and the offices were poorly lighted and ventilated. "The treatment received by the Department is not only of the most niggardly character," he observed, "but is the poorest sort of economy." Only about half enough money was appropriated each year to keep the library in a "state of efficiency," and it was already cramped for space without the addition of badly needed books.[57]

Insufficient funds also made it difficult for the department to secure satisfactory persons to do the government's legal work. There were few competent lawyers willing to leave their private practices to accept the meager salaries paid by the government. "[C]ases against the United States involving hundreds of thousands and perhaps millions of dollars," Olney complained, "are constantly [in the] trying for the defense . . . by lawyers whose salaries range from $1,500 to $2,500 per year." When a case of importance arose in any district, "neither the Treasury nor the Comptroller of the Currency nor the Interstate Commerce Commission nor any other body or party interested is willing to leave it in the hands of the regular U.S. Attorney. . . ." Application was made for appointment of a special counsel. When compensation for such counsel came to be fixed, it was "the thankless duty of the Attorney General to cut down the charge made by 50% or 75% because Congress will never appropriate, in payment of professional services, what would have to be paid for the same services by any private client."[58]

Perhaps Olney's most irksome duty was selecting marshals, attorneys, and other Justice Department personnel. Dealing with the hordes of party hacks and spoilsmen who infested Washington at the start of the new administration added to his misery. With a patrician disdain for politics, Olney warded off many of these pests, but he could not escape them all since his department had scores of positions to fill. He also had to determine which hold-overs should be retained, which promoted, and which displaced. From the beginning Olney refused to hold open house for office-seekers; most did not get beyond his receptionist's desk. Some with letters of introduction got in, but they found the attorney general cold, formal, and brusque.[59]

Although a life-long Democrat, Olney was not an extreme partisan. In making appointments he gave more attention to a candidate's supporters and past record than to party affiliation. "The present incumbent," he wrote of one office-holder, "though a Republican, is a capital officer and . . . personally I should be sorry to see him displaced." To a United States attorney in Texas he wrote that he had no desire to have the marshal in that district removed. "My anxiety is for the efficient administration of the Marshal's office and nothing else. If that would be promoted by retaining Hunter, I want him retained—if it would be promoted by removing Hunter, I want him removed." The attorney's letter seemed "non-committal" and indicated "only a personal preference for a marshal in political accord" with himself. "If that is all that is to be said in favor of a change of marshal," Olney concluded, "my inference is that he is a valuable officer and should be allowed to serve out his time."[60]

One consideration that carried weight was the support given candidates by railroad officials. A large number (but by no means a majority) of those highly recommended by railroaders were subsequently appointed to office. Olney's long-time associates in the railroad community did not hesitate to nominate candidates for Olney to appoint to office and they candidly stated their interest in such matters. "The appointment, as our Attorneys put it, is of very great importance," observed one businessman in regard to the selection of the United States marshal for Kansas. "[I]f the Populists should succeed in changing the character of the Supreme Court of the State of Kansas, it would be out of the question trying any more of our important suits before it, and we would have to get transfer of them to the United

States Court, and from their [the attorneys'] standpoint it would be equally important to have a strong and reliable man as United States Marshal, as to have a good judge on the bench." George R. Peck, counsel for the Santa Fe, in recommending two men for places as United States marshals, said that he felt "considerable interest in the appointments for the territories through which we run, for we have frequent occasions to invoke their assistance in protecting property and sometimes life."[61] Some of these railroad nominees were to serve their sponsors well during the Coxeyite and Pullman Strike troubles in 1894.

In the appointment of the United States attorney for the southern district of New York, Olney faced a delicate problem because his brother, Peter, was a serious contender. Francis C. Barlow, a New York attorney, in congratulating Olney upon becoming attorney general, expressed concern that "a false notion" might interfere with Peter's chances of being appointed. No one was more opposed to nepotism than he, Barlow said, but he thought it "absurd to say that where a family has two competent sons, the public shall not have the advantage of the services of both of them." The attorney general did not agree. "If the President should consult me on the subject," he declared, "I should have to recommend him not to make the appointment both on his own account and mine."[62]

Peter was piqued by his brother's letter to Barlow since he had been proposed for the district attorneyship long before Richard had been mentioned as cabinet material. When he wrote to ascertain what stood behind the objection, Richard replied that the reason seemed perfectly obvious to him. That Peter harbored an ambition to become the district attorney had never entered his mind, he said, at least not since he had himself accepted the attorney generalship. Following this reply, Peter wrote Cleveland asking that he not be considered for the post because "such appointment might cause unfavorable criticism because of my relationship to the Attorney General."[63]

At the very time that he was scotching the possible appointment of his brother to a district attorneyship, however, Olney was contriving to bring his closest friend and first cousin, Sigourney Butler, to Washington. But Sigourney, whose surname was not likely to attract attention or to raise the cry of nepotism, declined a judgeship on the District of Columbia Court of Appeals. His father's poor health and his belief that his law practice in Boston was improving led him to refuse the offer. In January 1894, he also refused appointment as collector of the port of Boston lest fellow-townsmen who knew well his relationship to the attorney general label Olney a nepotist.[64]

Two months after entering office, Olney learned from an examiner of the Justice Department of a conflict-of-interest problem. Clifford L. Jackson, the newly appointed United States attorney for the Indian Territory, had continued to serve as counsel to two railroad companies in the territory. He had, moreover, offered the clerk of federal court an annual pass over one of the lines in lieu of charging the line the usual fees when involved in litigation.[65] Jackson freely admitted his ties when Olney apprised him of the charges, but explained that he had hired a young lawyer to assist him. Should he ever find his work load too great, he promised to resign his position with the companies at once. As for the pass, he confessed offering one not only to the clerk but to the deputy clerks, the federal marshal, and the marshal's deputies on the same terms. He saw nothing improper in the arrangement—it had been in effect since before he became attorney for the companies in 1889.[66]

Olney promptly wired Jackson to disapprove of the pass arrangements. In a detailed letter he stated that the objections to exchanging passes for legal fees seemed to him "so obvious and cogent" that he was "surprised at the apparent necessity for stating them." To the extent that public officials profited more from passes than fees, their sympathies were "necessarily" enlisted to the railroads in litigation. In effect the railroads became "suitors to whom the Clerk and Marshal have placed themselves under pecuniary obligations." On the other hand, if officials accepted the passes only because Jackson insisted, "the embarrassments and difficulties arising from the attempt to serve at one and the same time two masters, whose interests do not necessarily coincide, are strikingly illustrated."

Further, under the arrangement the clerks and marshals would be furnishing the railroads with official services free of charge, while in return receiving free transportation for both the performance of the public duties and their private purposes. "Can there be doubt," he asked, "that this confusion of public and private relations and obligations is necessarily demoralizing in its effects upon all parties concerned?" The arrangement, he added, violated the Interstate Commerce Act. Since Jackson defended as "right and proper" what seemed to him "most objectionable," Olney called for his immediate resignation.[67]

Jackson threw himself on Olney's mercy, pleading that the "practice of giving passes to officials had become so prevalent" that he had not given it "even a passing thought" or considered "for a moment" that the officials involved "were likely to be influenced one way or the other . . . much less demoralized." If he were wrong, it was at most an error of judgment involving "no intentional personal or official turpitude or dishonorable conduct. . . . I have concealed nothing; I have acted openly and frankly; I meant no wrong; I have done no act by which any one has been harmed . . . ; I am conscious of the rectitude of my purpose and feel that I have done, at every step what seemed right and duty."[68] Whether his abject appeal for clemency or the intervention of Senator George Vest of Missouri saved him, Jackson was permitted to serve out his term. Later reports indicated that he had learned his lesson: there were complaints that he had become overzealous in taking up all free passes issued to federal officials in the territory.[69]

Occasionally subordinates asked Olney whether certain acts would be considered conflicts of interest. The federal attorney in Boston, for instance, was offered the post of counsel to the Boston chamber of commerce. Little work was involved and the position paid only $200 per year. It would give the attorney valuable contacts with about a thousand New England produce and cereal dealers, however. Olney saw no objection so long as the attorney observed his pledge to resign as chamber of commerce counsel in the event of a conflict of interest.[70] Another federal attorney from Florida asked if he could properly take on as clients the defendants in a suit brought by the receiver of a national bank under direction of the Comptroller of the Currency. Again, Olney raised no direct objections, but cautioned that it would be "embarrassing" should the defendants later be prosecuted for any federal offense. "If there was a probability or even a possibility" of such, the United States attorney "ought not to act for the parties interested."[71]

Clearly Olney understood fully the dangers inherent in permitting public officials to be under even slight obligation to private persons whose interests might conflict with those of the government. The ethical code of conduct that he insisted upon for his subordinates called for strict observance of the proprieties. He demanded that those under him avoid any confusion of their public and private duties and obligations. He urged the utmost discretion in cases where conflict of interest, though not obvious, might develop. And his censure of Jackson's offenses, while not so severe as dismissal would have been, was harsh.

Olney himself fell short of the rigid standards he imposed on others. As the newspaper columnist Alfred Henry Lewis wrote of him, "in picking up politics, Olney has not mislaid any of his connections."[72] Although his continued ties with several of his corporate clients were not illegal, they certainly involved the question of ethics. However pure Olney's intentions, he and his clients offered and sometimes accepted favors from one another.

The tone of the relationship is hinted at in remarks that Olney exchanged with Henry Lee Higginson. Olney, who usually wrote with a precision that defied misinterpretation, informed Higginson on one occasion, "Am always at your service for talk or anything else—here or in Boston." The banker, on another occasion, wrote Olney in a similar vein. After acknowledging receipt of money for deposit to the attorney general's account, Higginson added, "at any time that during your absence you either need to lend or to borrow, we are always at your service—without notice—I mean just this thing, & for any loan *to* you, your name on the receipt is enough. Give your orders."[73] The generous offer was inviting; whether Olney took advantage of it is not known.

The attorney general's protestation that granting railway passes to public officials in the Indian Territory was "demoralizing," illegal, and tended to produce a confusion of loyalties, was hypocritical given the fact that he, as a railroad official, held exchange passes over several railroad lines throughout his term in office. Once misplacing his annual pass over the New Haven line, he sent for "trip passes as before" to cover a journey from New York to Boston and back.[74] When the president of the Pennsylvania Railroad offered "to extend the courtesy of free travel to the Attorney General and his wife," Olney sent him no strictures about demoralizing a public official or violating the Interstate Commerce Act. "I return the enclosed passes," he responded, "with full appreciation of the courteous spirit which induced their being sent to me. But I already hold an exchange pass, while Mrs. Olney will travel so infrequently over your lines of road that it is hardly worth while to add another 'Deadhead' to your list on her account."[75]

The first of Olney's clients to seek favors was the Old Colony Trust Company. The firm's president, T. Jefferson Coolidge, Jr., in May 1893 asked the attorney general's assistance on a matter involving the Cartagena Terminal & Improvement Company. The government of Colombia had granted the company a concession for a coaling station on the Caribbean coast at Cartagena. "It is of considerable importance to our Company," Coolidge noted, "that both naval and merchant vessels should be informed of the fact that we shall always keep a stock of coal on hand." Coolidge did not wish to "trouble" Olney, but asked him to give a letter to the secretary of the navy requesting that the information be passed on to the proper naval officers in charge of vessels in the Caribbean.[76] Olney at once notified Secretary Herbert. "Whether or not it is a matter of public interest that they should have that information," he said, "is, of course, for you to decide. Personally, I have no knowledge on the subject and no wish except that the request of the Cartagena Company may be granted if the efficiency of the public service will be thereby promoted." The request was granted.[77]

About a year and a half later, Coolidge wrote to complain of the United States consul at Cartagena, who was charged with public drunkenness. He added that the Cartagena-Magdeline Railway in Colombia was completed. "All we want now is 'earnings'!" A week later when turbulence in the South American republic followed the sudden death of the country's president, Coolidge again wrote. "We have got, as you know, a railroad running from Cartagena to Calamar, workshops and wharves, and it would add a great deal to the security of our property if an American Man of War should put her nose, as if by accident, into the harbor of Cartagena." Coolidge had already written Herbert, and having received no reply, wanted Olney to request the dispatch of a ship to Cartagena—"if consistent with the interests of the Navy."[78] Again Olney relayed the request. Although Herbert in the meantime had advised Coolidge that no warships were available for such a mission, he now thought that one might be spared. Coolidge was grateful: "It is a wonderful port," he wrote Olney, "& ought to be oftener visited. We thank you for your cooperation in arranging this."[79]

The Boston & Maine, too, sought a small favor from Olney. President Tuttle reported a controversy in St. Johnsbury over the moving of the post office. He did not know the local politics involved, but pointed out that moving the post office from Main Street to Railroad Street, as proposed, would cost the Boston & Maine between $500 and $600 a year. At its present location the post office was so far from the railroad station that the cost of transporting mail between the two points was borne by the government. If moved to Railroad Street, the post office would be within eighty rods of the railway station and by law the cost of hauling its mail would fall to the company. "I find that the better and larger portion of the population of St. Johnsbury will be better accommodated if the office remains where it is. . . . " Tuttle realized that such matters were not the business of the Justice Department, but, he added, "I have reason to believe that a suggestion from you to the Post-Office Department will only be necessary to prevent any change in the location." Olney asked to be heard on the matter should it arise and the postmaster general agreed. The dispute, however, was prolonged beyond Olney's tenure in the cabinet.[80]

Olney entered the cabinet with the blessings of his leading clients and with assurances that he could continue to serve them. Commenting on Olney's departure for the capital, Forbes wrote Perkins, "Of course we shall lose the benefit of constant & early counsel with Olney but I think we can get more good out of him on great points for his being at head quarters, where he may have a chance to do good work for all Rail Roads against Interstate Commerce meddling and Paternalism generally. . . . It may be proper as consideration of his doing so much less work for us, to make a reduction in his salary but this *ought* to come from him when he find [*sic*] how little time his public engagements leave him to give us." " . . . I do not know what relations he wants to hold toward us while in the Cabinet," Perkins replied, "but we can afford I think to do what he wants done."[81]

These men were pleased that Olney would sit in the nation's highest councils, not only because they knew him to be capable of doing work that would redound to the credit of the Cleveland administration, but because they expected to reap direct benefits from having their attorney in Washington. The benefits they expected were not little favors to be bought with railroad passes or continuing salaries, nor did these men expect assistance only in the locating of post offices. They did not see in Olney a person who could be easily pressured into catering to their whims. They looked on him, rather, as a spokesman for their views. They knew him to be sound on those public issues that involved the rights of private property and private capital. When questions affecting those interests arose—the struggle to preserve the gold standard, the reorganization of the federally subsidized railroads, the protection of the nation's railway system from marauding bands of unemployed Coxeyites and from striking employees—Olney sought the advice of his business friends. When he did not, they freely sought him out for consultation. The policies that he adopted were frequently their policies, not because they induced him to accept their views, but because he was one of them, and his views and their views were the same. Throughout his stormy two years as attorney general, Olney would be haunted by the specter of conflicting interests. That he was guilty of gross improprieties is beyond question.

5

Panic Problems

Collapse of the Reading Railroad in February 1893 signaled the beginning of economic troubles for the nation. As the new administration settled into office in March and April, depression broke over the land. President Cleveland and Secretary Carlisle, of course, bore chief responsibility for shaping the administration's response to the Panic. Attorney General Olney, however, became involved in a number of key policy decisions.

It is now clear that the Panic of 1893 developed out of a variety of complex economic forces. At the time, however, men preferred simpler, moralistic explanations. Olney, for example, speaking at Harvard in June, saw the difficulties as the consequence "of over-trading, of reckless speculation, of wasteful expenditure, of violations of trust, of official dishonesty, [and] of the mad rush to be quickly rich."[1]

More generally it was thought that monetary policy, if not the sole cause of the depression, certainly lay at its heart. Debtor and agrarian interests, located particularly in the West and South, blamed the bad times on an alleged currency stringency. Wall Street and eastern bankers (minions of Lombard Street and the international Jewish banking conspiracy, it was said) were deliberately constricting the money supply in order to enrich themselves. To restore prosperity it was necessary to break the power of these groups and to inflate the currency supply. Eastern businessmen and bankers, on the other hand, attributed the disorders primarily to a growing, world-wide lack of confidence in the ability of the United States government to keep all of its currency on a par with gold, especially given the steady decline in the market price of silver.[2]

Two long-standing policies—the redemption of greenbacks in gold and the regular purchase of silver by the Treasury—contributed greatly to the monetary crisis of the Panic years. In 1875, Congress had directed that greenbacks (paper money issued without backing during the Civil War) should become redeemable in specie on 1 January 1879. The Treasury Department, having already adopted a policy of honoring all governmental liabilities in gold, accumulated a gold reserve in excess of $100,000,000 to meet this new obligation. Then, on the eve of redemption, Congress enacted a law requiring the secretary of the treasury, upon redeeming a greenback, to feed it back into circulation so as to maintain a constant supply of some $346,000,000 worth of greenbacks in circulation at all times. To further appease inflationists, Congress in 1878 also initiated a policy of purchasing silver. Under the Sherman Silver Purchase Act of 1890 (which superceded the 1878 law) the secretary of the treasury was ordered to buy up to 4,500,000 ounces of silver at market price each month, paying for it with treasury notes redeemable in coin. In effect the Treasury Department was required to purchase nearly the entire domestic output of silver and, in the process, to inflate the currency by approximately $4,000,000 worth of paper money each month.

Despite a proviso in the Sherman Act that it was "the established policy" of the government to maintain parity between silver and gold at the legal ratio, many bankers and businessmen both in the United States and abroad doubted the ability of the government to keep all of its obligations as good as gold. Consequently, gold began to leave the country at an alarming rate or to go into hiding in the United States. Since one of the easier ways to get gold was by redeeming greenbacks, the government's redemption policy soon became an endless chain by which gold was drained from the treasury. As the federal reserve fell, confidence in silver and paper money deteriorated even more, creating fresh demands for gold.[3]

Shortly after his election, President Cleveland let it be known that he welcomed suggestions from the financial community with respect to the monetary problem. The many new friends that he had acquired in New York banking and financial circles between his two terms responded generously. Almost to a man they agreed that repeal of the Sherman Silver Purchase Act was the first step to be taken.[4] Boston financial and business leaders, unlike their New York counterparts, had fewer direct contacts with the president. "To get as near as possible to the source of power," these men turned to their fellow townsman, Richard Olney.[5]

The attorney general received a steady flow of mail from State Street bankers and commercial leaders. His most persistent correspondent on currency matters, however, was Henry Lee Higginson. The banker's tone ranged from the imperative to the plaintive. "I sit and wonder if you gentlemen in Washington know how very uneasy the legitimate property holders and merchants of the country are about the state of the currency," he wrote in April 1893. "We all expected that this state of uncertainty would be removed with the advent of the new administration . . . but just now we are more at sea than ever." Were he managing the treasury he would at once make it clear that the gold reserve would not be allowed to fall below $100,000,000. This, Higginson was certain, would end the drain on the reserve and would restore confidence to the business community. Two days later he wrote that "only some overt act, like selling some bonds, will do any good," and he urged that $5,000,000 in bonds be sold for gold in order to reassure businessmen everywhere. In May he predicted that a panic, causing widespread misery over the entire country, was imminent unless Congress was called into special session to repeal the Sherman Silver Purchase Act.[6]

But the panic was already under way. On 22 April the gold reserve for the first time dipped below the $100,000,000 mark, and early in May the failure of the National Cordage Company presaged a general collapse of the stock market. Despite the seriousness of the situation and the insistent pleadings of bankers, commercial leaders, industrialists, chambers of commerce, and eastern newspaper editors, Cleveland waited until the last day of June before calling a special session of Congress for early August. The delay was calculated. The president wished to educate the public to the need for repeal and such education, he believed, required some fear and suffering. Southern and western congressmen, many of whom were Democrats, remained unconvinced. When Congress assembled on 7 August, they declared that they would battle vigorously to save the Sherman Act or to move in the direction of free and unlimited coinage of silver, at sixteen to one.[7]

By early July the Boston financial community was organizing to push for repeal. "Lee Higginson & Co. are very anxious to do something," Sigourney Butler wrote from the Hub. "They feel patriotic & want to show it. If you and Mr. Carlisle think of any plan which organization & money can further, let me know right away. . . . " Olney immediately informed the secretary of the treasury, asking for suggestions and a list of senators known to be doubtful on repeal "who ought to be persuaded to see the thing in the right light." Carlisle sent a list but doubted that letters from Boston would do much good. The New Englanders, however, might stir their personal friends in the South and West to bring pressure to bear on wrong-thinking legislators.[8]

As the sound-money forces girded for battle, doctors discovered that Cleveland had a small cancer in the roof of his mouth. The uneasy state of the nation's finances made it imperative that the president's condition be kept an absolute secret, even from the cabinet. Vice President Adlai E. Stevenson was a silverite and the prospect of his coming to power might precipitate panic on Wall Street or lead to a disastrous run on the treasury's gold reserve. And so the operation was performed at sea on the yacht of Cleveland's close friend, E. C. Benedict. The delay in the president's appearance at Buzzard's Bay on Cape Cod, where he was to summer, gave rise to newspaper rumors including one that accurately reported the operation. When the party landed, Secretary Lamont, who had accompanied the president, convinced reporters that Cleveland had had a slight attack of rheumatism. With time for relaxation and fishing, the president would soon be as good as ever.[9]

Olney knew nothing of Cleveland's operation until 8 July when he and his wife, en route to Falmouth for a month's vacation, stopped at Buzzard's Bay to pay their respects. The attorney general found that the president had lost weight, was much changed in appearance, and was very low in spirits. "My God, Olney, they nearly killed me," the president muttered through a mouth filled with antiseptic wads. Cleveland confided that preparation of his message to the special session of Congress had bogged down and he despaired of completing it. Olney offered his assistance and was commissioned to prepare a draft.[10]

Pressure from Boston continued. In an agonized letter to Olney on 12 July, Higginson declared, "This is the worst day in a long time—People who are rich & *sound* when asked to pay up their % cannot do it & we cannot sell their stocks. . . . The banks are drained dry—When people are in this condition, a fearful panic may quickly come. . . . I [have] never seen—nor has the oldest bank-president seen such a time. . . . Is there any use talking with Mr. Cleveland?" Maintaining secrecy about the president's condition, Olney replied that nothing could be done until Congress met in August. Higginson relented until fall.[11]

A few days later the attorney general received a lengthy communication on the monetary problem from Charles E. Perkins. " . . . a wise settlement of this money question is of the utmost importance to all of us at this time, & as Congress meets in about three weeks there is no time to lose." Perkins urged Olney to confer with John Murray Forbes, whose "good judgment and long years of business experience are worth a great deal." Since he "is near you," Perkins added, " . . . there need be no ceremony between you."[12] Forbes and Olney, despite at least a decade of business association, were not close. In this time of national peril, however, Forbes did not stand on formalities. In fact he became most attentive to his sometime attorney, the attorney general. Without waiting for Olney to make contact, he proposed that they sail up to Gray Gables in his yacht, the *Wild Duck*, and pay Cleveland a "neighborly" visit.[13]

A follow-up operation on the president's mouth prevented the visit, but the delay did not bother Forbes. "Perhaps we shall do best not to attack Gray Gables until you and I have exchanged views confidentially," he wrote Olney.[14] By 21 July, Olney had prepared a draft of the message to be used by the president. The next day he went on a cruise with Forbes and the two discussed the monetary problem and quite possibly went over Olney's draft of the president's address. Towards evening the *Wild Duck* put in briefly at Gray Gables.[15]

Within a few days Forbes and Olney were laying plans "to repeat the program" of the previous Saturday. "Let us take our sail," Forbes wrote, "and have a good lunch on board and a good time; and call at Gray Gables or not as you think best when we meet." Because his mind was "rather in a chaotic condition" on the subject of their last meeting, Forbes hoped that he and Olney might "reach a conclusion as to certain points ourselves before we say much outside of the Duck's cabin!" Both he and his yacht were at Olney's disposal for the rest of July, he said.[16]

Meanwhile, by 26 July, Olney had prepared a revised draft of the message. Two days later he again went sailing with Forbes and, as before, the *Wild Duck* dropped anchor in Buzzard's Bay towards the end of the voyage.[17] Despite two full days of consultation, Forbes and Olney apparently had not reached complete agreement on details for saving the nation's currency. "*I wish you could give me* another day—tomorrow, with a fishing pole or anything else to divert our dullness but really to quarrel or agree a little further about—the next great step which the credit of the country & the safety of large Bankers and still more of industries . . . depends . . . , " Forbes wrote. The proposed third session apparently never took place. Meanwhile, Forbes sent Olney a few letters written by some of the leading business minds of Boston, offering suggestions to the administration for ending the financial crisis. Olney promised to use the letters as "advantageously" as possible.[18]

Whether it was proper for Olney to allow one of his private employers to advise him on a major public policy, it appears that the advice made little difference in the end. To begin with, Forbes, the other Boston financiers, Olney—and Cleveland for that matter—were all in substantial agreement as to what was needed. Their differences were only over matters of tactics and detail, and the specific recommendations to Congress in the various drafts by Olney remained the same in spite of his conferences and correspondence with Forbes. The merchant's only obvious contribution to Cleveland's message (via Olney's draft) was a quotation from Daniel Webster to the effect that working men had the most to gain from sound money and the most to lose from inflation. The quotation was not new; Cleveland had previously used it in a message during his first administration.[19]

Between 31 July and 4 August, Olney, Cleveland, Carlisle, and Lamont put the message in final form. Olney's draft was used only in part, chiefly because his trenchant and often sarcastic remarks would have won the president's recommendations more enemies than friends. Olney felt no slight. Years later he reported, " . . . I went to Gray Gables with a draft of a message which was approved by Mr. Cleveland practically as drawn."[20]

The president's message was sent to Congress on 8 August. After vigorous debate, the House of Representatives, three weeks later, repealed the silver purchase act by the decisive vote of 239 to 108. Most of the opposition came from the president's own party. In the Senate the struggle was longer, running on into the autumn. In October a group of Democratic senators declared that compromise, somewhat short of complete repeal, was the only possible solution. Cleveland remained adamant.[21]

"Look out for repeal vote in the Senate about Tuesday next," Olney wrote Higginson on 27 October. "If you don't fire a salute of at least a hundred guns on Boston Common, you will demonstrate that you don't appreciate the stubbornness of the fight or the greatness of the victory." Repeal came on the thirtieth. "We fired no salute," Higginson wrote, "because we all crave quiet & would offend no one—& our joy is too deep for words—It is a great victory & an immense gain for the country—We know our grand man—& we all know very well how much we owe to our President—He has done a great thing."[22]

Olney was not deluded into thinking that the nation's economic ills had been cured. "Repeal accomplished . . . , " he wrote, "you will readily understand that it is but one & not a very long step on the road that ought to be travelled. The path of this administration, indeed," he noted, "however you look at it, & whether foreign or domestic affairs are considered, seems to me to be all the way up hill and very rocky at that."[23]

The attorney general's observation was not amiss. Despite repeal of the silver purchase act, the drain on the gold reserve continued. By 17 January 1894, it had dropped to $69,000,000, and the administration was forced to replenish it by selling $50,000,000 worth of bonds for gold. Unfortunately, nearly half of the gold came from sources that promptly redeemed greenbacks and treasury notes to get back the precious metal with which they bought the bonds. Even so, the reserve on 28 February stood at $106,000,000.[24]

Relief was temporary. By mid-November the reserve had dwindled to $61,000,000 and another $50,000,000 public bond sale for gold was negotiated. Again relief was immediate, but this time much shorter; by 24 January 1895 the reserve had fallen to $68,000,000. Barring suspension of gold payments, the Treasury apparently had no recourse but to sell more bonds. The question was whether to offer the bonds publicly a third time or to deal with a private banking syndicate. The first public subscription had given ten months' relief; the second but ten weeks'. Cleveland and Carlisle feared that a third might be exhausted even more quickly. With gold flowing from the treasury at the rate of over $3,000,000 a day, there was little time to execute a third public sale. Negotiating with a private syndicate offered two advantages: speed and the possibility that at least part of the gold could be secured in Europe. The chief drawback was political. Cleveland and Carlisle did not wish to appear to be selling out the country to Wall Street in time of national crisis. And so, despite the advice and warnings of eastern financiers, they continued to think in terms of a third public bond subscription.[25]

On 28 January, the president made one last appeal to Congress to break the endless chain by allowing greenbacks and Sherman Act notes to be cancelled when redeemed rather than fed back into circulation. He also requested authorization to collect import duties in gold so as to assure the treasury of a steady supply of that metal.[26] These measures were promptly brought before the House of Representatives in the Springer bill.

Meanwhile, treasury officials explored with August Belmont and other New York bankers the possibility of a private syndicate. On 31 January, when the reserve sank to $45,000,000, J. P. Morgan assumed control of the negotiations on behalf of the bankers. Between then and 2 February, Morgan, Belmont, and Assistant Secretary of the Treasury William A. Curtis worked out a scheme under which the bankers promised to buy $50,000,000 worth of 3¾ per cent bonds, with half of the gold to come from abroad. Secretary Carlisle rejected the proposal.

On 5 February, Morgan and Belmont, with Morgan's "attorney general," Francis Lynde Stetson, and Morgan's young associate, Robert Bacon, went to Washington to convince the president, Carlisle, and Olney of the gravity of the situation and to urge the sale of bonds to their syndicate. No agreement was reached. Cleveland and Carlisle accepted Morgan's interpretation of conditions but were not yet convinced of the futility of another public bond issue. Further, having asked for remedial legislation, they believed it unwise to undertake negotiations with a private syndicate while Congress pondered their recommendations.[27]

Two days later, Morgan, accompanied by Stetson and Bacon, once more set out for the nation's capital. Arriving two and a half hours after the House voted down the Springer bill, they were met by Lamont who informed them that the president would not see Morgan. The financier replied that he had come to see the president and would stay until he did. Going to the home of a friend, he sent Bacon, scion of an old Boston family and a one-time member of the firm of Lee, Higginson & Company, to find Olney. In Morgan's opinion, the attorney general was the only man in Washington other than Assistant Secretary Curtis who was "alive to the situation."[28]

Morgan convinced Olney that unless something was done by the next day to relieve the situation, "great financial and commercial calamities" would follow. The banker outlined his plan "by which the government could be let out of its difficulties," at least for the time being. But if the president would not even see him, Morgan said, he would go "back to New York and take his chance with the rest of the world." Olney promised that if Morgan would stay overnight, he would see that the banker had an interview with the president the next day.[29]

Morgan, Stetson, and Bacon went to the Executive Mansion in the morning, where they joined Olney and Carlisle in the president's office. A few moments later Cleveland entered, exchanged greetings all around, and went into a huddle with Olney and Carlisle. What followed resembled a half-rehearsed, half-improvised bit of stage play designed to bring the stubborn president around to the position already held by the bankers, Olney, and possibly Carlisle—namely, that the one way to keep the nation from leaving the gold standard was a private bond sale. For three hours the president discussed the subject of a public bond sale with his advisers. More used to giving orders than to waiting for others to make decisions, Morgan impatiently ground his unlighted cigar to dust between his fingers as he sat listening. Frequent telephone calls from Curtis at the Treasury Department and from the New York Sub-Treasury interrupted the discussion. Finally Carlisle received a bulletin from New York disclosing that the gold coin on hand in the government's vaults stood at nine million dollars. Morgan broke in for the first time. "Mr. President," he said, "the Secretary of the Treasury knows of one check outstanding for twelve million dollars. If this is presented to-day, it is all over." He had learned of the check the night before from Carlisle, he said. The secretary confirmed Morgan's statement. The president then turned to the New Yorker and asked what he would suggest.

Morgan quickly sketched out a plan. The administration was to abandon any public bond sale. Instead, bonds were to be issued to a syndicate of American and European banking houses in payment for a large amount of gold, at least half of which would be obtained in Europe. The president asked on what legal basis such a transaction could be made. Morgan recalled a similar instance during the Civil War when the secretary of the treasury had been authorized by an act of Congress to buy gold and to pay for it with bonds. He thought that the act was "Section four thousand and something" of the *Revised Statutes,* but was uncertain whether the law was still in force. "Is that so, Mr. Olney?" the president asked. Olney, who had "satisfied" himself beforehand that it was valid, replied that he did not know and left the room, ostensibly to check. When he returned he declared that the section in question was number 3700 and that apparently it did permit such a purchase of gold with bonds. Both the president and Carlisle then examined the statute book and decided that Section 3700 fitted the situation.[30]

Morgan's alleged "recollection" of the old law is not convincing. It was not as if Section 3700 were lost in a legal attic awaiting rediscovery by the great financier. The *Revised Statutes* was a simple codification of federal law to which any lawyer, including Cleveland and the six members of his cabinet who were lawyers, would automatically have turned. Moreover, if Morgan remembered that Congress had passed the act during the Civil War, it is unlikely that he would have recalled it by the number given it in 1876 when the *Revised Statutes* was first drawn up. Apparently someone—possibly Olney—had coached him the night before.

Whatever the reason behind the dramatics, two years earlier Cleveland and several members of his cabinet—just prior to going into office—had discussed using Section 3700 for just such a gold purchase. Writing on 19 February 1893, Cleveland asked Secretary-designate Lamont to "go to Belmont & Co and see if they can arrange for the purchase *abroad* of say fifty millions of coin bonds (but within the declaration of the Sherman Act of the intention of the government to maintain the parity between the two metals and undoubtedly as good as if declared payable in gold) with interest at 3 or 4 per cent. I want in the transaction the *actual gold* brought from abroad and put in our treasury and I want it done promptly, and in such manner that the par value of the bonds shall be forthcoming to us free from commission. Of course, we do not commit ourselves to the issuance of those bonds. . . ."[31] In February 1895, Cleveland and Morgan simply consummated the proposal outlined in 1893.

Curtis, Carlisle, Olney, and Stetson drafted the contract, which provided that the syndicate would purchase $62,317,500 worth of 4 per cent "coin bonds" for $65,317,500 in gold. At least half was to come from European members of the syndicate. So long as the contract was in force, the syndicate promised to protect the treasury against withdrawals of gold. Finally, if Congress would substitute the words "gold bonds" for "coin bonds" within ten days, interest would be reduced to 3 per cent. Later that day Cleveland sent a bare announcement of the transaction to Congress. The stunned silverites rallied a few days later. Refusing to be "bribed," they rejected the proposal that "gold" be substituted for "coin," thereby depriving the treasury of a saving of $16,000,000 in interest.[32]

Within two weeks the syndicate publicly disposed of the bonds it had purchased at 104½ for 112¼. Not long after, the bonds were selling on the open market for 119. In the West and South it was generally believed that the government had been fleeced by Wall Street and European bankers with the connivance of Cleveland and Carlisle. Even eastern newspaper editors who favored sound money complained of the terms exacted by the syndicate. But whether the bankers acted from patriotism, profit-seeking, or a combination of the two, and whether their profits were small, fair, or exorbitant, the deal restored the gold reserve to over $100,000,000 and probably prevented the nation from leaving the gold standard.[33]

The syndicate faithfully observed the terms of its contract. Until August 1895, the reserve remained healthy. In January 1896, it once more slipped to $60,000,000. Morgan offered salvation again, this time on a larger scale—$200,000,000 worth of bonds on the same terms as before. Cleveland, who had always defended the first deal as necessary, proper, and negotiated on the best terms possible, never seriously considered entering into a second such arrangement. Instead, by selling bonds to the general public, enough gold was raised to tide the treasury over to McKinley's administration, when the panic ended.[34] Despite severe criticism, Cleveland and his cabinet believed that they had saved the Republic from financial chaos and ruin.

In October 1893, in the midst of the Senate debate over repeal of the Sherman Silver Purchase Act, the Union Pacific Railroad went into receivership, another victim of the panic. Because the company was heavily in debt to the United States government, Attorney General Olney became responsible for protecting the interests of the government in the railroad. News of the receivership came as a surprise. Only two weeks earlier the annual report of the five government-appointed directors of the company had spoken in glowing terms of the excellent condition of the line. But the directors were referring to the railroad's physical condition. Only in passing did they note that the company's earnings had "quite considerably decreased." This they attributed to the bad times, giving the impression that although income was disappointing there was no particular emergency. Nowhere in the report, as the *New York World* observed, was there "the breath of a suspicion of the impending collapse of the company."[35]

Panic conditions had hastened the collapse, but overcapitalization and an enormous debt accumulated prior to 1893 had left the Union Pacific unable to weather even a minor economic crisis, much less a major panic. Controlled first by the celebrated stock manipulator, Jay Gould, and then by the conservative railroad executive, Charles Francis Adams, the Union Pacific undertook extensive building and buying of branch lines to expand business and increase profits. Instead, the projects produced a floating debt of nearly $76,000,000. To meet pressing liabilities in 1890, the company had issued over $11,000,000 worth of three-year, six per cent collateral notes. Had the Union Pacific been moderately capitalized, with normal earnings well in excess of fixed costs, and had the stock market improved between 1891 and 1894, it might have met its short-term obligations when they fell due. But neither condition obtained and the company faced the problem of raising large sums of money to meet its notes (due in 1894) at a time when its income was falling and its costs rising, and when it anticipated a deficit of $3,000,000 in its 1893 operations. To heap trouble upon trouble, the federal government's loan to the Union Pacific was scheduled to begin maturing in November 1895.[36]

To promote construction of the first transcontinental railroad, Congress, by the Pacific Railway Act of 1864, had provided extensive land grants and sizeable loans in the form of government bonds to both the federally chartered Union Pacific and a California corporation, the Central Pacific. The subsidy bonds, bearing six per cent interest and running for thirty years, were secured by a second mortgage against those portions of the two lines built with federal assistance. In all, the United States lent the Union Pacific $33,539,512, due to mature between 1 November 1895 and 1 January 1899. With accumulated interest the debt totaled approximately $52,000,000 by late 1893.[37]

When it became known that the Union Pacific had passed into receivership, the House of Representatives inquired of the attorney general whether the government's interests were affected, what steps had been taken to protect those interests, and what legislation, if any, was needed to further secure the government claim. Olney replied that the government had neither been notified nor made a party to the proceedings and that the receivership should be regarded as "tending to seriously prejudice the interests of the United States. . . . " To date his one defensive move had been to appoint George Hoadly of New York as special counsel so that the important interests of the government would receive the "continuous and almost exclusive attention of competent counsel." Special legislation would probably be needed, but he asked for time to investigate before making recommendations.[38]

In private Olney spoke of the receivership as "probably the best thing that could happen for the railroad company and for the interest of all parties concerned."[39] His quarrel was not with the receivership but with the forces that controlled it. Of the three receivers—S. H. H. Clark, president of the Union Pacific, Oliver W. Mink, comptroller, and E. Ellery Anderson, a recently appointed government director— Anderson alone represented the government. The attorney general wanted the group altered so that control would be in the hands of representatives of the United States.

The attorney general's plan for changing the receivership attracted the attention of everyone with a vital interest in the Union Pacific, including Olney's Burlington Railroad associates, Perkins and Forbes. Both men were speculators in Union Pacific stock. Of greater interest to them, however, was the relationship of the Union Pacific to the Burlington. From the Rocky Mountains to the Missouri River, the two companies were rivals. The Union Pacific terminated at Omaha, however, and its traffic between Omaha and Chicago had to be carried over one of three lines: the Chicago & Northwestern, the Chicago, Rock Island & Pacific, or the Burlington. The attitude of the Union

Pacific's management could make a considerable difference in the amount of business given to the Burlington.[40]

Accordingly, the first concern of Perkins and Forbes was the make-up of the board of receivers. On 3 November, Perkins drafted a letter to Olney. "The Union Pacific situation is a conundrum which is of considerable interest and importance," he observed. "Can you tell me anything—If so I shall be glad to hear—The property is so big & so vulnerable that it offers great temptations and opportunities to political & other pluckers—If it is run as a bankrupt affair *it may bankrupt all its neighbors;* and what it wants is an honest business management, for the present under the protection of the court, pending which an adjustment should be made of its debts including what is due to the government." Turning to the current receivers, Perkins noted that Mink was a "first rate man," but that Clark was rumored to be "going back to Gould's Missouri Pacific." Anderson he did not know. In the event of a change of personnel, Perkins suggested that Mink be retained and that Clark and Anderson be replaced by two of his acquaintances, Albert Fink and P. S. Hayes.[41]

Apparently Perkins never sent the letter. "I have been thinking of writing to Olney," he reported to John Murray Forbes the next day, "but, on the whole, I have some doubt about the expediency of it, since he is bound, as a Government official, to look only after the interest of the Government in recovering the debt due from the Union Pacific in full." On the other hand, the Union Pacific offered "such temptations and opportunities for political and other vultures," that there was danger of a "New York coterie" getting control of the system "for the purpose of lining their own pockets." Passing along his views about the three receivers, Perkins suggested that if Olney happened to be in Boston it might be well for Forbes to talk with him.[42]

The elderly merchant not only conferred with Olney, he also wrote him with regard to Union Pacific affairs.[43] "Excuse me if I seem too officious," he said in one letter, "but it does seem to me that you do not quite realize the importance of getting the *very highest possible board of receivers* seated before bringing forward any scheme of reorganization of the U.P." Clark, Forbes declared, was "under suspicion" and it was a bad move from a business point of view to retain him, no matter how unjust it might be to let him go. "[I]t is very important," Forbes continued, "that the next step taken to secure your fifty millions [the government debt], to say nothing of my fifty *cents* interest, should be well considered, for the U.P. has been kicked about so badly . . . that it *is in danger of ultimate failure and ruin* in spite of its INTRINSIC VALUE, if it makes any more mistakes;—so I do want to see Clark out, no matter how he got in or whose man he is, and some well known R.R. man who is above suspicion in his place." If men like Fink or Hayes were appointed in Clark's place, Forbes added, he would value the property at from one to five millions higher than if Clark remained even with good associates. "[I]f YOU can save a *million or two* now by such a businesslike stroke as you once used when rescuing Nat. Thayer from his perilous condition, you will make a name as the best business lawyer in this little Republic or Democracy, whichever you like to call it."[44]

Meanwhile, Henry Lee Higginson, whose banking house dealt in Union Pacific securities and frequently acted as agent for Perkins in buying and selling stock, wrote Olney urging retention of Mink as one of the receivers. "He will administer the property for the good of *all*, & if he sees anybody sinning he will stop it." Higginson's main purpose, however, was to discourage the government from taking control of the receivership. " . . . I sincerely hope that U.S. will do no such thing," he said, "for it is already very well represented, will get its dues more easily & quickly . . . & will make a great mistake in taking any responsibility as to management of this R.R.—We all wish to keep our government out of business, banking or otherwise."[45]

Olney reacted cautiously to the recommendations and blandishments from Boston. The long history of the government's relationship with the Union Pacific was marred by scandal, corruption, and conflicts of interest. Olney apparently was determined that his conduct should be above criticism. The task would not be easy. A "very prominent official of the Government," he warned Hoadly, had recently intimated to him that every move to date in Union Pacific affairs had been wrong. Receivers Clark and Mink, this source charged, were intimate friends of George Gould (Jay Gould's son), and one of Hoadly's law partners allegedly had connections with Gould interests. The insinuation was that Hoadly was not as independent or as disinterested as he ought to be. Olney mentioned the matter only because it clearly demonstrated how important it was that the "Goverment's interest should not only be looked after properly in point of fact but should appear to be so, beyond all possibility of question."[46]

Concern for appearances led Olney himself reluctantly to dispose of his personal holdings of Union Pacific stock. He sent 129 shares to Lee, Higginson & Company to be sold. "Having to do with the company & its affairs now in behalf of the government," he wrote, "I do not want to give some blackguard the chance to say that I am influenced in any course I may see fit to take by private interest." Olney complained that he had purchased the stock when it was selling above par and paying six per cent annually. Higginson sold it at a considerable loss—100 shares for 19¼, and 29 shares for 19.[47]

In spite of the recommendations of Higginson and others, Olney proceeded with his plan to put the government in control of the Union Pacific receivership. Unable to have either Clark or Mink removed to make way for a second government appointee, he and the federal judge in charge of the matter agreed that the government should be given control by adding two government receivers to the original three-man panel.[48] "[I]f you see Olney," Perkins wrote to Forbes, "you can perhaps find out what these new appointments signify." It was important to know whose men they were and what forces backed them.[49]

Forbes met with Olney but learned nothing. Perkins, for one, was at a loss to explain the attorney general's moves. He suspected that Standard Oil interests, who were speculating in Union Pacific stock, were trying to get control of the company and to enhance its value. They would settle the government's claim, refinance the first morgage debt, and put the company on a sound business footing. Accordingly, during November and December, Perkins boosted his own holdings in Union Pacific stock from one thousand to at least four thousand shares.[50]

Meanwhile, in November, the creditors of the Union Pacific formed a committee to reorganize the company. Their objectives were to prevent dismemberment of the system, to settle the debt owed to the government, and to refund all other debts so as to lower the fixed costs of the line to a reasonable amount.[51] From the first, Olney worked whole-heartedly with the committee. As he saw it, the interests of the United States and the other creditors were nearly identical. Once again playing the familiar role of broker among the interests, he hoped to settle Union Pacific affairs in a manner acceptable to all of its creditors.[52]

A scheme satisfactory to both Congress and the private creditors proved difficult to formulate. At one extreme, Populists and other anti-railroad congressmen demanded that all money due the government, including accumulated interest, be paid in full, in cash, and on time. If the Union Pacific defaulted, these legislators were prepared to have the government pay off the first mortgage and take over the ownership and operation of the railroad. At the other extreme, first-mortgage bondholders argued that the government loan should be cancelled because the Union Pacific had already more than repaid it in the form of services—reduced rates for soldiers, government supplies, and the mail. Whatever the merits of this argument, the Crédit

Mobilier scandal of the 1870s and Jay Gould's notorious manipulation of the company's stock in the 1880s had exhausted public patience with the Union Pacific. Moreover, cancellation of a just debt seemed to many a bad precedent for the government to set. Any attempt by the first-mortgage creditors to run roughshod over the government's claim was doomed to failure because the government could intervene legislatively to protect itself.[53]

Working closely with Olney and Hoadly, the reorganization committee at length hit upon a scheme for refunding the entire indebtedness of the Union Pacific—both principal and interest—with new, long-term, low-interest-bearing bonds. Olney accepted the plan in principle, then proceeded to rewrite the committee's draft when it came to him for approval. He in turn altered his draft to meet objections raised by the committee. In its final form the Olney plan provided that the government would accept one-hundred-year, two per cent Union Pacific bonds equal in value to the total amount due the government as of 1 July 1894. The bonds would be secured by a second mortgage over the entire Union Pacific system (not just over line built with federal subsidies, as in the original contract). The plan provided for refunding the first-mortgage debt at rates not exceeding five per cent and authorized a third mortgage for maintaining the physical plant and to meet emergency expenses.[54]

The reorganization committee refused to endorse Olney's draft because it gave the government claim precedence over existing second mortgages.[55] Perkins and Forbes were upset that Olney's plan did not include their suggestion that the Union Pacific by law be required to stand neutral at the Missouri River and not ally itself with any Omaha-to-Chicago railroad. At first they suspected that Olney had not included the proviso because of his close ties to the Burlington, preferring to have some neutral congressman amend the bill to that effect.[56] Perkins learned from Secretary Morton, however, that Olney opposed governmental interference with the conduct of the Union Pacific's affairs. The company was privately owned, he argued, and if it was a good thing for the Burlington and other lines to tie themselves by traffic agreements to one another, it might be a good thing for the Union Pacific too. "This does not at all meet our point," Perkins observed, "but it shows that the Administration is willing that the U.P. shd. borrow Govt money at 2 per cent & then become a tail to the Vanderbilt kite—I don't see anything to do but try to beat it in Congress—I am rather surprised at Olney—."[57]

Olney's plan—only one of several for resolving the Union Pacific's problems—never got out of the House Railroad Committee.[58] In the meantime, the House committee, aided by Olney, the Union Pacific reorganization committee, and others, framed another measure designed to refund the debts of both the Union Pacific and the Central Pacific with fifty-year, three per cent first-mortgage bonds. The reorganization committee objected to the three per cent interest rate and Olney thought inclusion of the Central Pacific only complicated matters. Even so, Olney used his influence on behalf of the bill, which, in the end, was defeated.[59] So were proposals to refund the government debt at two per cent in return for a first mortgage and to repay the principal in full while forgiving accumulated interest. Congress apparently would accept nothing less than repayment of both principal and interest in full. This the Union Pacific's creditors refused to undertake. In March 1895, the reorganization committee dissolved and Union Pacific affairs were left dangling. Finally, during the McKinley administration, the United States received payment in full of the principal and all but $6,000,000 of accumulated interest owed by the Union Pacific.[60]

Throughout the 1893–95 negotiations, Olney maintained that the Union Pacific was private property. Despite the line's peculiar relationship to the government, he was unwilling to bring it under government control or to subject it to regulation beyond what was necessary to protect the government's claim. Although he accepted responsibility for protecting public interests, he assumed that they coincided with those of private creditors. He favored refunding the government debt at low interest rates so as to protect everyone—stockholders, bondholders, and the public—rather than pressing for full payment of the debt to the government, which might embarrass the others. Olney's views apparently were the same as those of a correspondent who wrote of Union Pacific affairs: " . . . if public interests are important, private rights are sacred."[61]

The claim of the United States against the Central Pacific received a different kind of attention from the attorney general. Like the Union Pacific, the Central Pacific had received loans of nearly $28,000,000 in United States subsidy bonds to finance its construction. Unlike the Union Pacific, which had been chartered by the federal government, the Central Pacific was organized under California law. Four men, Collis P. Huntington, Mark Hopkins, Charles Crocker, and Leland Stanford, were the driving forces behind the Central Pacific, and for many years they were directors and major stockholders in the company. The four had become millionaires, but by 1893 the company was represented as too poor to meet debt payments to the government that were to begin in July 1895. Since under California law, original stockholders of California corporations were liable for the debts of a company in proportion to the amount of stock originally held by each, it was possible that if the Central Pacific defaulted, the United States could bring suit to collect the money from the individual original stockholders.[62]

In June 1893, D. H. Solomon, a St. Louis attorney, informed President Cleveland of two large debts, totalling $35,000,000, due the government from unnamed debtors. Although these debtors, now deceased, had left estates ample enough to pay their debts fully, no claim had been filed by the government. Solomon believed that at least ninety per cent could still be recovered and he asked that the president commission him to institute suits on the government's behalf to collect them. Cleveland forwarded the letter to the Justice Department and officials there wrote for details. The St. Louis lawyer refused to disclose any information until he had a contract putting him in charge of the case and/or guaranteeing him a percentage of whatever money should be recovered.[63]

Justice Department officials had no way of divining that Solomon proposed to file claims against the estates of Hopkins and Crocker (who had died in 1879 and 1888, respectively) for recovery of part of the Central Pacific's debt to the government. Solomon's hint of "new developments" after the death of Leland Stanford in June 1893 did not provide much of a clue. The attorney general, therefore, informed Solomon in October that the Justice Department could not sign the requested contract.[64]

Three weeks earlier, however, Olney's brother-in-law, William Thomas, a San Francisco lawyer, had written describing the unusual liability feature of California law and informing Olney that "time was running" for filing claims against the Stanford estate. "I do not mean to make any suggestion," Thomas declared, "but simply to post you in regard to the right of the Government to file a claim against the Stanford Estate."[65] Whether or not Olney connected this information with the Solomon letters, the communication from Thomas, who was a competent lawyer, would certainly have justified Olney in taking action to protect the government's rights. He did nothing, however, until the next spring.

On 7 April 1894, Solomon sent Olney a long letter giving full details of his plan. He revealed the names of the debtors, enclosed a legal brief that he had prepared, and urged the attorney general to act quickly. Olney at once sent a letter of inquiry to the United States attorney in St. Louis to find out what he could about Solomon. He learned that the man had once been a prominent lawyer in Iowa but had become somewhat unbalanced and was given to "extravagant ideas of business affairs."[66] When Olney still refused to commission him or to bring suit, Solomon released an account of the affair to a St. Louis newspaper.[67]

Alert congressmen picked up the story immediately and the House of Representatives sent a resolution to Olney asking for an opinion as to whether stockholders of the Central Pacific were liable for the debts of that company to the national government. Olney's tart reply that he was "not in possession of any facts bearing upon the subject" was not true. If the resolution was designed to secure an official opinion upon a legal question, he added, he was "without authority to accede to the request" because it had been "uniformly held" by his predecessors "from the beginning of the Government" that the attorney general was not permitted to give legal advice to Congress.[68]

Olney now sprang into action. On 12 May he sent a packet of Solomon's letters to Hoadly in New York. Characterizing Solomon as a crank or insane, he pledged that so long as he was attorney general, he would never retain the St. Louis lawyer. Nevertheless, he wanted Hoadly's advice as to whether there was "anything in Solomon's propositions—whether the Government has any claim on any stockholders or directors on the grounds he suggests."[69] Olney also checked with the United States attorney in San Francisco to determine the deadline for presenting claims against the Stanford estate. When he learned that the date was 27 May, he at once prepared a statement and ordered the United States attorney to file it with the court. Special counsel was retained to press the claim and Olney from time to time gave advice on handling the case. Ultimately, after Olney had left the Justice Department, the Supreme Court rejected the government's claim.[70]

The conduct of the attorney general from the first betrayed his lack of sympathy for recovering the government's money from the Stanford estate. In a personal letter to Senator Hoar, Olney made clear his feelings in the matter. "Whatever money may be due the Government, or might be collected by it at the end of a litigation," he declared "will probably be of more use to humanity at large, if applied to the charitable purposes for which Mr. Stanford designed it than if administered by the United States." He had delayed taking any steps until the last moment, he added, even though his attention had been called to the matter "'immediately after Mr. Stanford's death.'" He had hoped that enactment of a bill to refinance the Central Pacific's debt would resolve the question, but in the end he had been forced to act because he did not feel that he could allow the government's claim, "whatever it may be worth," to be embarrassed by the restrictions of the California statute of limitations.[71]

Olney's actions with respect to repeal of the Sherman Silver Purchase Act, the Morgan bond deal, the reorganization of the Union Pacific, and the claim against the Stanford estate proved him to be a staunch defender of both "sound money" and private property rights. They also revealed his penchant for getting things done by negotiating directly with the real powers in a given situation. In all these affairs, Olney's long-time associates, Forbes, Perkins, Higginson, and others, felt free to flood him with advice. But Olney, sometimes to their surprise, retained his independence. When he agreed with their specific proposals and thought them consistent with the public interest, he accepted them. When he disagreed, he did not hesitate to act in accord with his own interpretation of the public welfare, even if the interests of his friends suffered. Olney rarely found much conflict between the two.

6

Battling the Trusts

Three major decisions of the United States Supreme Court in 1895 came under attack from reform-minded citizens as backward-looking, illiberal defenses of vested property interests. Since Olney personally argued the income tax and Debs cases before the high court, he must bear, as will be seen, much of the credit or blame for their outcome.[1] His role in the third, the sugar trust case, though less direct, contributed to the ineffectiveness of antitrust policy for the next decade.

Although the Sherman Act had been in force only thirty-two months at the time he became attorney general, Olney already belonged to the select band of lawyers who had defended clients from its provisions. Harrison's attorney general, William H. H. Miller, had launched seven antitrust suits in all. Four he passed on unfinished to the Cleveland administration. Of the three completed cases, the government lost two.[2] It was in the most notable of these defeats, the whiskey trust case, that Olney first prepared a brief against the antitrust law.

The officers of the whiskey trust lived in various sections of the country. They had been indicted in the federal court in Boston, however, and in Boston they were ordered to stand trial. Their legal counsels—Elihu Root and Thomas Thatcher, of the New York bar— initiated defensive actions in New York, Cleveland, Cincinnati, and Boston, and employed eminent local lawyers to assist with the trials. In Boston, in *United States* v. *Greenhut*, the objective was to quash the original indictment. There Root handled the oral arguments, but hired Richard Olney to appear on brief.[3]

The charges against the defendants included the destruction of competition by buying up and operating the distilleries of several of their competitors and attempting to shut off the sales of the remainder by giving rebates to distributors who would handle the trust's whiskey exclusively. In his brief, Olney contended that any companies brought into the combine prior to 2 July 1890, when the Sherman Law became effective, were exempt from the suit because no law could constitutionally operate in an ex post facto manner. As for the other complaints, Olney argued that the government charged "nothing more than the lawful use of property and the exercise of lawful freedom of trade." No rule of common law or public policy prevented anyone from investing in any lawful business to any extent that he saw fit. Moreover, an owner was free to charge whatever price he could get for his property and, if it served his purposes, he might well give rebates to his customers.

Olney's main defense, however, hinged on the definition of the terms "monopoly" and "interstate commerce," and the "loose language" of the Sherman Act. Historically, monopoly meant a grant from the state legally excluding all others from a given business, Olney pointed out. More recently it had come to mean a contract that disabled one of the parties from continuing in a given business. In either event, "the true characteristic of monopoly . . . puts the party or parties against whom it is directed under a legal disability as respects to carrying on a particular trade or business." The whiskey trust, of course, had no such grant from the state and had entered into no such contracts with its competitors.

Anticipating by almost three years Chief Justice Melville W. Fuller's ruling in the sugar trust case, Olney defined interstate commerce in its narrowest and most technical sense. Manufacturing was not a part of interstate commerce even when the product was sold over state lines. Neither was the act of selling, because it occurred wholly within the bounds of a single state. Although the parties to the transaction might be from different states and the product subsequently transported over state boundaries, these facts were incidental to an intrastate transaction. Transportation of goods over state lines alone constituted interstate commerce, and only attempts to monopolize or restrict such transportation came within the scope of the Sherman Act. The government's indictment, he observed, had failed to deal in any way with transportation.

Turning to the wording of the law, Olney noted that the second section, which "purported" to create and punish a crime, was "inoperative and void because of vagueness, indefiniteness and ambiguity of its terms, whereby it is left wholly uncertain what offense is aimed at or what facts will constitute such an offense." For example, was the word "monopolize" to be interpreted in its popular meaning? Did any trader who "by good luck, superior ability, larger capital or through any other circumstance" got and kept to himself any part of the trade referred to in the Sherman Act thereby violate the law? Or did "monopolize" mean that in addition to having appropriated to himself a part of interstate commerce, the trader also had put others under a legal disability from engaging in it? The latter, Olney maintained, was sound and made the law reasonable, but was not clear from the wording of the statute.

"The thing not to be monopolized," Olney continued, was "any part of the trade or commerce among the several states or with foreign nations." Interpreted "naturally and literally," these words outlawed all interstate and international trade since "every person engaging in such trade necessarily appropriates to himself some part of it, however small, and thereby excludes from it every other trader." Again, since such an interpretation would be unreasonable, these words, too, would have to be given a construction other than that derived from their usual meanings. But writing a law properly was a legislative, not a judicial function, and the courts were not at liberty to construe the phraseology of poorly worded laws in the hope of giving them reasonable meaning.[4]

The judge who heard the case chose not to go into the meaning, scope, or constitutionality of the Sherman Act. Instead, he quashed the indictment on grounds suggested in one of Olney's lesser arguments. The indictment, he ruled, was "clearly insufficient according to the elementary rules of criminal pleading" and charged "no offense within the letter or spirit of the second section of the statute." A new indictment was subsequently entered, but the case never came to trial.[5] Meanwhile, the various habeas corpus proceedings initiated to block extradition of the defendants to Boston for trial were all successful.[6] The opinion in one, handed down by the United States Circuit Court in Cincinnati, particularly impressed Olney and was to play an important part in the later sugar trust case.

Judge Howell E. Jackson's opinion in *In re Greene* included a lengthy exposition of the scope and meaning of the Sherman Act. Jackson discussed the main points previously raised by Olney in his Greenhut brief, and reached essentially the same conclusions. The weight attached to the opinion was enhanced when President Harrison appointed Jackson to the Supreme Court, and Olney, as attorney general, hailed the Greene decision as the best interpretation yet given the Sherman Act.[7] A third person connected with the case, Lawrence Maxwell, Jr.—who had appeared on brief—became Cleveland's solicitor general.[8] It would be Olney and Maxwell, of course, who after 1893 would be responsible for enforcement of the act they both had helped to defeat.

Joseph Pulitzer, publisher of the *New York World,* who supported Cleveland, was especially anxious that the new administration proceed vigorously against the trusts. The naming of Olney to head the Justice Department had disappointed him, but the editor apparently decided to give the new attorney general a month in which to prove his intentions. When, by 3 April 1893, Olney had not moved against a single combine, the *World* began a series of articles that each day called attention to different trusts that should be prosecuted. The series began with an exposé of the sugar trust; the rubber, lead, and cordage trusts, General Electric's attempted monopoly, and the copper, whiskey, tobacco, cotton-oil, and cash register trusts were exposed in succeeding issues. Each article included the full text of the Sherman Act and quotations on the trust question from both the Democratic Platform of 1892 and Cleveland's inaugural address. In some, the *World* reported that Olney was about to begin a lively attack on the trusts; in others it pleaded with him, or commanded him, to do so.[9]

A friend from New York sent Olney a copy of the *World's* article on the cordage trust. "It may amuse you," he suggested. The friend was probably right. As late as 28 February 1893, Olney had represented the National Cordage Company in a law suit and was one of the company's creditors.[10] In April 1893, the *World* was also unaware that Olney had recently represented the whiskey trust. "The Bandits," said the *World,* referring to officials of that combine, "were too smart for incompetent Mr. Miller, but they can't fool Richard Olney."[11]

Despite Olney's scorn for the *World's* crusade, its insistent prodding may have contributed to his decision to make a test of the Sherman Act before the Supreme Court. On 20 April he inquired into the status of the sugar trust suit then pending before the federal circuit court in Philadelphia. By 5 July 1893, he and Solicitor General Maxwell had decided to push the case through the courts.[12] Attorney General Miller had ordered the prosecution in March 1892, shortly after the American Sugar Refining Company purchased the stock of four of its principal competitors. Alone, American Sugar had refined sixty-five per cent of all sugar consumed in the United States. After the merger it turned out about ninety-eight per cent, its only competition coming from a small refinery in Boston.[13]

While Harrison's solicitor general drew up the government's bill in *United States* v. *E. C. Knight Company,* the federal attorney in Philadelphia, Ellery P. Ingham, and Samuel F. Phillips, a former solicitor general, employed as special counsel in the case, gathered evidence and prepared briefs. Although testimony on both sides had been taken by the time Olney became attorney general, the case had not yet been argued. Once Olney decided to advance the suit, he continued to make inquiries and suggestions from time to time. General management of the case, however, fell to Maxwell. He in turn left the conduct of the case in both the circuit court and circuit court of appeals entirely in the hands of Ingham, his assistant, Robert Ralston, and Phillips.[14]

"The case will be an awkward one for the def'ts," Ingham wrote to Phillips in November 1893. "The more I think the case over in the light of the authorities, the more I am impressed that we have a good case. At all events we can make a respectable showing & put the other side on their metal [*sic*]." In looking over the evidence, however, special counsel Phillips at once detected what proved to be the fatal flaw in the government's case from the lowest to the highest tribunal. There was abundance of evidence and witnesses to prove a monopoly in sugar refining, but only one witness who testified to the carrying-on of interstate commerce. Ingham was unconcerned. "You will find," he assured Phillips, "that we charge in the bill that the def'ts. were engaged in the business & sold sugar in various states and that in their answers they admit it, so that point can not be one against us."[15] Phillips apparently did not again take up the matter with Ingham, though he sent Ingham's letter to the Justice Department.

If Ingham and Phillips were not alert to the importance of establishing beyond all doubt the relationship of the sugar trust's monopoly in refining to its control of interstate commerce in sugar, both Olney and Maxwell, from their experiences in the whiskey trust cases, should have been. Olney, in fact, had argued the very point: the government's case against the whiskey trust was invalid because it implied, but did not prove, restraint of interstate or international trade. But no advice on strengthening the case was sent to Ingham or Phillips by either the attorney general or the solicitor general; and when the latter was invited by Ingham to participate in the oral arguments he declined. "I am satisfied that the case will be fully and ably presented by yourself and Mr. Phillips," he wrote. "The concern of the Department is to get the case on. . . ."[16]

Meanwhile, in December 1893, Olney issued his annual report, which, among other things, set forth an interpretation of the Sherman Act that greatly reduced its scope and usefulness as a weapon against trusts. "There has been and probably still is a widespread impression," he began, "that the aim and effect of this statute are to prohibit and prevent those aggregations of capital which are so common at the present day and which are sometimes on so large a scale as to control practically all the branches of an extensive industry." The next three pages corrected that erroneous impression.

Even if it could be done, Olney doubted the value of ascertaining the "precise purposes" of the men who framed the statute. It was sufficient to note that the act was limited to any part of the trade or commerce among the states or with foreign nations. The "immense mass of contracts, dealings, and transactions" that arose and was carried on wholly within the boundaries and jurisdiction of the various states was exempted. So were interstate railroads because "special and exclusive" legislation had been enacted to regulate them. A recent court decision holding a strike by New Orleans dockworkers to be in violation of the antitrust act, Olney characterized as "strikingly illustrating the perversion of a law from the real purpose of its authors. . . . "

Summarizing part of the argument that he had previously used in his whiskey trust brief, Olney pointed out that "any literal application of the provisions of the statute" was "out of the question" because any ownership of property was in itself a monopoly and every business contract or transaction could be viewed as a combination in restraint of some part or kind of commerce. The Greene decision, he observed, was the one notable opinion dealing "thoroughly and comprehensively" with the Sherman Act, and he enumerated its main points: (1) Congress could not limit the right of state-chartered corporations or of citizens to acquire, accumulate, and control property. (2) Congress could not prescribe prices at which such property should be sold. (3) Congress could not make criminal the intentions or purposes of corporations or persons in acquiring or controlling property that were sanctioned by the states of their creation or residence. (4) The word "monopoly," as used in the Sherman Act, meant an exclusive right in one party, coupled with a legal restriction on another, limiting the latter from exercising or enjoying the same right. (5) Contracts in restraint of interstate commerce under the Sherman Act were already void at the common law, independently of any legislation. "This exposition of the statute," Olney said, "has not so far been questioned by any court and is to be accepted and acted upon until disapproved by a tribunal of last resort." Because of the gravity of the questions arising under the law and the pecuniary interests involved, he reported that he had "deemed it his duty" to push a test case to the Supreme Court, and a ruling on the Sherman Act could be expected during the current term.[17]

That Olney chose to give so detailed an exposition of his own views on the eve of a definitive court ruling was unusual if not improper. His report certainly was not designed to support or strengthen the government's suit at Philadelphia; to the contrary, it seemed better calculated to point up the deficiencies of that case. The *New York World* suggested that the sugar trust lawyers could find no more effective or authoritative arguments for their side than those provided in the attorney general's report.[18] Whether any of the judges who subsequently rendered decisions in the sugar trust case read the report is not known, but clearly Olney anticipated their decisions. He also revealed that Attorney General Richard Olney's views on the Sherman Act were identical with those of Richard Olney, whiskey trust lawyer.

Argument of the Knight case was delayed time and again between October 1893 and January 1894 at the request of the attorney for the sugar trust, John G. Johnson, who seemed unable to squeeze a court appearance into his busy schedule. Judge George M. Dallas, who indulged Johnson's procrastinations despite pleas of urgency from the government, later fell ill and a substitute judge heard the arguments. Phillips, the strongest member of the government's team, also took to his bed because of illness. "In view of the importance of the case," Ingham wrote Olney, "might it not be advisable for the solicitor general to come on and make the closing argument . . .?"[19] In court, however, Ingham faced the "formidable" Johnson, "King of the American Bar" and one of the nation's outstanding corporation lawyers, aided only by his assistant, Ralston. Reporting to Olney next day, Ingham sought to prepare his chief for the worst. "So far as indications go, I would not be surprised if Judge Butler decided the case against the government."[20]

As Ingham anticipated, Butler dismissed the government's bill. "The contracts and acts of the defendants," he ruled, related "exclusively to the acquisition of sugar refineries and the business of sugar refining, in Pennsylvania" and had no bearing on interstate or international commerce. Even if a monopoly existed in the ownership of sugar refineries, it did not constitute restriction or monopolization of interstate or international trade; "the latter is untouched, unrestrained, and open to all who choose to engage in it." The government's contention that the monopoly in refining incidentally gave the trust a monopoly in commerce was dismissed as "unsound" and "unwarranted" by Butler, though he conceded that "the alleged control of refining . . . might possibly enable the defendants to secure a monopoly in commerce."

At present, he noted, no monopoly over commerce in sugar existed, and the trust showed no disposition to establish such a monopoly. "If they have a monopoly," he said, "it is in refineries and refining alone—over which the plaintiff has no jurisdiction." The question was "not new," Butler concluded. It had been fully considered in the Greene case and that opinion was "so clear and satisfactory" that only a desire to be brief prevented him from quoting it at length.[21]

Apparently Olney and Maxwell were neither surprised nor distressed at the decision. Although Olney sent Ingham several letters on carrying the case to the circuit court of appeals, none explored the causes of the defeat or offered suggestions for perfecting the government's arguments in the hope of upsetting the lower court's finding. The only apparent concern was to get the case to the Supreme Court as quickly as possible.[22] To that end, Ingham and Phillips called on Judges Dallas and Marcus W. Acheson to "find out whether the Court would not— *quasi* informally—affirm Judge Butler's opinion,—as we were anxious to get to the Supreme Court at once." Both judges were unwilling to commit themselves, though Acheson promised an early ruling.[23]

The decision, written by Dallas and handed down on 26 March, declared that "manufacturing and commerce" were "two distinct and very different things. The latter does not include the former. Buying and selling," the judge continued, "are elements of commerce, but something more is required to constitute commerce," namely, intercourse and traffic, including navigation, and the transportation and transit of persons and property. The government, at best, had proved only that the defendants controlled sugar refining. He too referred approvingly to the Greene decision.[24]

Appeal was entered at once for a hearing before the Supreme Court. Arguments were not made, however, until 14 October 1894. Solicitor General Maxwell and the special counsel, Phillips, spoke for the government. Olney's name appeared on the brief but there is no indication that he had anything to do with its preparation.[25] Maxwell, in his oral remarks, declared that the plain intent of the sugar combine was to control the production of an important article of interstate commerce. The fact that the article ultimately entered into such commerce brought its production within the jurisdiction of Congress. He pleaded with the court to interpret the term "interstate commerce" broadly.[26]

The opinion of the court, dissented from only by Justice John Marshall Harlan, was written by Chief Justice Fuller. The fundamental issue, Fuller declared, was whether, conceding the existence of a monopoly in manufacturing, that monopoly could be suppressed under the Sherman Act "in the mode attempted" by the government. Carefully distinguishing manufacturing from commerce, the Chief Justice ruled that the federal government had full authority over interstate commerce, but that only the states were competent to regulate manufacturing within their boundaries. Neither the manufacture of a product intended for sale over state lines nor the act of selling it into interstate commerce were parts of interstate commerce per se. Such trade was in fact subsequent and incidental to manufacturing. "Contracts, combinations, or conspiracies to control domestic enterprise in manufacture, agriculture, mining, production in all its forms, or to raise or lower prices or wages, might unquestionably tend to restrain external as well as domestic trade," Fuller stated, "but the restraint would be an indirect result, however inevitable or whatever its extent, and such result would not necessarily determine the object of the contract, combination, or conspiracy."

The chief justice, though not citing it by name, pronounced the main points of the Greene decision to be "well-settled principles." That portion of his decision, indeed, appeared to be almost a paraphrase of the summary of the Greene decision that Olney had given in his 1893 annual report. In concluding, Fuller noted that since "nothing in the proofs" indicated any intent on the part of the trust to restrain interstate commerce in sugar, the decree of the lower court was affirmed.

In a lengthy dissent, Justice Harlan stated that although the court had failed to declare the Sherman Act unconstitutional, it had, nonetheless, defeated the main object for which the law had been enacted. He admitted that no proof of contracts to monopolize or restrain interstate trade had been produced, but argued that such agreements probably did not exist. "Men who form and control these combinations are too cautious and wary to make such admissions orally or in writing." As he saw it, the mere existence of a combination admittedly organized for the purpose of controlling the manufacture of a product sold in interstate commerce constituted a direct restraint upon trade.[27]

Olney regarded the Knight case decision as a vindication of his personal view of the Sherman Act. "You will have observed that the govt has been defeated in the Supreme Court on the trust question," he wrote to Miss Straw in Boston. "I always supposed it would be & have taken the responsibility of not prosecuting under a law I believed to be no good—much to the rage of the New York World." He felt entitled to apologies from "many sources" that had criticized him for not enforcing the apparently unenforceable antitrust law, but he knew that these would never be forthcoming. Instead, some newspapers only heaped more criticism on him. "The press has so abused me about the trusts," he observed to Miss Straw, "that the defeat of the govt. seems to be looked upon as my personal triumph—which ought not to be."[28]

Olney's culpability for the defeat was great, but not exclusive. Ultimately, of course, it was his responsibility that the case went to trial weak on the crucial point of interstate commerce. If the case could not have been strengthened, it could have been dropped in favor of a more promising suit; when defeated, it need not have been appealed to the Supreme Court. All too obvious was Olney's purpose of pushing the case through to a final decision with the expectation that the law, which he thought a bad one, would be struck down by the high tribunal.

Some responsibility for the defeat, however, must rest on the various federal judges who rendered decisions along the way. After all, it was they who accepted the restrictive definitions of interstate commerce and monopoly. Contemporaries, to be sure, believed that the government could easily have procured evidence that the trust was involved in interstate commerce. Fuller's statement that nothing in the proofs showed intent to monopolize interstate commerce implied that if the government had presented a better case, the decision would, perhaps, have gone the other way.[29] In the light of their decisions, however, it seems quite possible that the federal judges, including Fuller, would not have been satisfied unless contracts were produced that explicitly provided for the restricting or monopolizing of trade in sugar. But as Harlan said, contracts of that nature in all probability did not exist. The agreements entered into provided for the consolidation of refining facilities. To have entered into additional contracts to sell, over state lines, the sugar they produced, would have been both superfluous and illegal.[30] So long as federal judges treated buying and selling of sugar by the trust as merely "incidental" and "subsequent" to refining, it is difficult to see how the sugar trust case could have been won even by a trust-busting attorney general.

The day after the court's decision in the Knight case, Olney disclosed to the press that he had not been at all surprised at the outcome. In fact, he had expected just such a result from his study of the law and the facts of the case. Antitrust prosecutions by the Justice Department would be in no way affected because the department had launched no antitrust actions.[31] These candid remarks did not reveal the care Olney had taken to squelch the attempts of his more eager subordinates to get prosecutions under way.

Letters—whether from ordinary citizens, businessmen complaining of injury at the hands of some trust, or United States attorneys—giving information about various trusts and suggesting either investigations or prosecutions, were usually filed. Olney disposed of the balance in several ways. If a private citizen asked for federal assistance in prosecuting a combine, Olney would suggest that the applicant either give the information to the local United States attorney or himself initiate a private law suit.[32] To one subordinate Olney made clear his policy with respect to the role of the government in such prosecutions. "This government is not paternal in its character; . . . its action is to be limited to the fewest cases and the fewest subjects possible; and . . . private parties with ample remedies for the redress of their alleged wrongs in their own hands are not to be encouraged to expect governmental interposition in their behalf."[33]

United States attorneys who asked for funds or assistants to gather evidence in antitrust investigations almost always were granted their requests.[34] When they presented their cases to the attorney general for prosecution, however, he hedged and delayed. If the combines had been formed prior to the passage of the Sherman Law, he would point out that prosecution was impossible because no law could constitutionally be retroactive. Once the Knight case was under way, he recommended that all other cases be postponed until a decisive ruling came from the Supreme Court. If a district attorney continued to press, Olney would become indignant and write the offender an informal legal brief in the form of a letter, riddling the charges. The tone of these missives did not suggest that the district attorneys attempt to patch up their cases.[35]

The most persistent and annoying subordinate was Robert B. Glenn, United States attorney for the western district of North Carolina. Determined to bring the American Tobacco Company to trial for violating the antitrust law, Glenn, in August 1894, sought and received permission to go to Trenton, New Jersey, in search of information regarding the composition and structure of the tobacco combine. In October he sent the attorney general a copy of his bill of indictment against the company. Olney, "surprised" that the bill called for criminal rather than for civil prosecution, asked why. Glenn replied that the results of criminal action would be more "satisfactory" and was confident that he could easily win conviction of the defendants in a jury trial. Glenn requested that the bill be returned to him as soon as possible since the next term of the court began on 10 December. Olney held the bill, advising meanwhile that nothing be done during the election campaign then in progress. Finally, on 12 December, he returned the bill to Glenn with the admonition that since the recently argued Knight case involved substantially the same facts, "it would seem to be wholly unwise not to wait until the Supreme Court is heard from."[36]

In March 1895, Glenn again wrote to his chief to find out, in the light of the Knight decision, whether to proceed with the case. In his opinion the facts in his case were "a great deal stronger" than those presented in the sugar trust suit. He made the mistake, however, of adding that "a terrible pressure" had been brought to bear on him by the public to prosecute the tobacco company. "If persons are to be criminally prosecuted because of the 'terrible pressure' brought upon the law officer of the government," Olney shot back, "the indictment should certainly contain an allegation to that effect—that the Court may be in a position to pass upon the real merits of the charge."[37]

A few days later Olney sent an eight-page letter to Glenn in which he ripped to shreds the bill of indictment against the American Tobacco Company. He commented sourly that "outside of the epithetical charge of conspiracy," the indictment presented a case not essentially different from the sugar trust case. Although it was incumbent upon the Justice Department to institute suits to uphold the law, it was equally the department's duty, Olney concluded, to avoid the "expense and discredit of fruitless litigation." Undaunted, Glenn replied that he was undertaking a "more thorough examination" of the facts as a result of the attorney general's "valuable suggestions." Confident that he could obtain the needed evidence in Trenton or New York City, he requested another leave from his post. It was granted.[38] Before Glenn could draw up a new bill, Olney had become secretary of state.

Another United States attorney, George J. Denis, working with a special counsel for the government, Joseph H. Call, succeeded in getting permission from Olney during the Pullman Strike crisis to bring an antitrust suit against the Southern Pacific Railroad Company. The attorneys implied in their communications to the attorney general that the Southern Pacific, though able to do so, had refused to move mail and interstate commerce during the strike. A series of telegrams on the subject concluded on 13 July 1894, when Denis and Call wired Olney; "The situation in our opinion demands enforcement of Act of July 2, 1890 against unlawful combines of railroad and transportation companies. . . . We have evidence in our possession that Southern Pacific Company entered into illegal combination with Pacific Mail and Steamship company and other railroads in violation of Act above mentioned. Are we authorized to bring such suit?" Olney, anxious to put down the strike and to restore the flow of mail and interstate commerce, replied that the law was to be enforced strictly against all violators, including railroad and transportation companies.[39] An indictment was secured and in time a copy reached the attorney general's desk. Olney was upset to find that the bill had absolutely nothing to do with the strike but instead sought a court order breaking up the Southern Pacific railway system on the grounds that through a series of allegedly illegal consolidations—completed in 1888, two years prior to enactment of the Sherman law—the company had absorbed its competition and established a rail monopoly from Portland, Oregon, to San Francisco, Los Angeles, and New Orleans.[40]

Communicating with the chief counsel of the Southern Pacific, Charles H. Tweed, Olney learned that the consolidations had been designed to improve and make more efficient the flow of commerce, not to impede it. Further, according to Tweed, the consolidated lines had not been parallel competitors but actually made up a single line from Portland to New Orleans.[41] Olney, charging Denis and Call with misrepresentation of the facts, promptly ordered them to dismiss the bill. When they presumed to defend their cause, Olney sent them a blistering letter scoring their conduct of the whole strike situation in Los Angeles, accusing them of catering to the popular hatred of the Southern Pacific in order to make personal political capital, and concluding that they had deliberately deceived him in order to get his permission to prosecute the railroad in an action that he otherwise would never have approved.[42] He invited an answer, but if he received one it was not preserved in his personal papers or in the records of the Justice Department.

In accord with his view of the law, Olney initiated no new antitrust suits against business combines, and of the four cases inherited from the Harrison administration, he pushed only the sugar trust case to completion before the Supreme Court. The case against the Workingmen's Amalgamated Council of New Orleans (the first in which the Sherman law was used against strikers) was won in a lower court but, as noted, Olney denounced that decision as a perversion of the intent of Congress. The suit against the Trans-Missouri Freight Association remained dormant until Olney left the Justice Department. Finally, he allowed the case against the National Cash Register Company (*United States* v. *Patterson*) to be nolle prossed in November 1894, because the company that brought the suit and held the evidence against the defendant had subsequently been absorbed into the combine. "Under the circumstances," Olney observed, "it seems to be impossible for the government to push the case to trial."[43]

In defense of Olney's antitrust policy it has been argued that the Justice Department had too little money and too few men to conduct an antitrust crusade. Moreover, "since no one will believe that all existing statutes are equally necessary, useful, or wise," Olney was right to "exercise discretion" and not to prosecute under a law he regarded as poor legislation. His belief, after all, was shared by the federal judges who tested the Sherman Act prior to 1893.[44] The first contention is largely irrelevant and did not influence Olney's policy. When he believed it necessary to act he never allowed the scanty resources of the Justice Department to hold him back, as his later suppression of the Coxeyite armies and his crushing of the Pullman Strike would illustrate. Similarly, the fact that there were more laws on the statute books than could be enforced does not explain why Olney shunted aside the Sherman Act. That law was not an obscure or unimportant measure that somehow had slipped through Congress unnoticed. It was enacted in response to a widespread demand for a federal antitrust law—a demand so insistent that both major parties in 1888 pledged themselves in their platforms to enact such a measure. In 1892 the Democratic party went farther, calling for "rigid enforcement" of the Sherman Act and demanding "such further legislation in restraint of [trust] abuses as experience may show to be necessary."[45]

The crux of the matter was that Olney did not approve of the law and he simply did not enforce it. That the federal courts prior to 1893 had upheld his view of the law and in the sugar trust case continued to do so was hardly surprising. He had used his legal talents in helping them reach those decisions in his whiskey trust brief and perhaps in his 1893 annual report as well. Had Olney wanted to enforce the act, he would never have allowed the sugar trust case to go before the courts so poorly prepared. Moreover, once the courts confirmed his views as to the weaknesses of the law, rather than shelving the Sherman Act, he might have proposed legislation to strengthen it. Instead he self-righteously used the sugar trust decision as an excuse for ignoring the trust problem.

After the election of 1896, Finley Peter Dunne, speaking through the medium of this fictional Irish barkeep, "Mr. Dooley," summed up the reaction of the foes of the trusts to Olney's antitrust policy. "On'y wan class is iligible f'r Attorney-gen'ral," Mr. Dooley advised President-elect McKinley. "To fill that job a man's got to be a first-class thrust lawyer. If he ain't th' Lord knows what'll happen. Be mistake he might prosecute a thrust someday, an' th' whole counthry'll be rooned. He must be a man competint f'r to avoid such pitfalls an' snares, so tis th' rule f'r to have him hang on to his job with th' thrust afther he gets to Washington. This keeps him in touch with th' business intherests."[46]

7

Defending the
Income Tax

"No case can be trusted to take care of itself," Olney told the graduating class of the Columbian University Law School in June 1894. "The worst may be saved and the best ruined by aptness or inaptness in handling."[1] Within the year, Olney was to illustrate his assertion when his management of *Pollock* v. *Farmers' Loan & Trust Company*—the income tax case—contributed to the government's defeat.

Southern and western Democrats had united with Populists in Congress to add the income tax provision to the Wilson Tariff of 1894. The measure levied a flat two per cent tax on all personal incomes above $4,000 and on all corporate profits or income above the amount of actual operating expenses.[2] The alleged purpose of the new tax was to make up the anticipated loss of revenues caused by a reduction in tariff schedules. An important consideration to many congressmen, however, was the belief that the levy would tend to equalize tax burdens among the various classes. The tariff, which was the federal government's chief source of revenue, fell most heavily on the poorer classes (ran the argument) while the proposed income tax would be paid by the wealthier classes. President Cleveland reluctantly allowed the Wilson bill, with its controversial income tax provision, to become law without his signature. His quarrel was not with the income tax, which he approved in principle, but with the disappointingly small cuts in tariff rates. Senate Democrats, he charged, had betrayed the party's pledge to reform the tariff by amending the bill so often that its provisions were barely distinguishable from those of the protectionist measure that it was supposed to "reform."[3]

While the income tax was under debate in Congress, Attorney General Olney observed to one of his private clients that there was "very little about the bill that is logical or symmetrical or justifiable from any point of view—or rather from my point of view. Let us hope that it will not pass."[4] He does not seem to have engaged in active opposition to the bill, however, perhaps because the final debates on the measure took place while he was preoccupied with the Pullman Strike crisis.

Propertied interests across the nation vehemently denounced the new tax as an assault upon all property rights. Failing in their efforts to have the bill killed in Congress or vetoed by the president, they finally turned to the federal courts to have it overturned. Leaders of the opposition hoped to test the law before any of the tax could be collected, or better still, before tax returns had to be filed. This presented a problem because an act of Congress, passed in 1867, forbade federal courts to issue injunctions against the collection of a tax. The most obvious means for testing the income tax was for a taxpayer to pay under protest and then sue for recovery of his money, or to refuse to pay and then contest any suit instituted by the government for collecting the tax.[5] Either method involved considerable delay.

In striking contrast with the sluggish movement of the sugar trust case through the federal courts, the test of the income tax was speeded to a final decision less than nine months after enactment of the law. Legal action began on 22 December 1894, in a federal court in the District of Columbia, when one John G. Moore sought an injunction to restrain the collector of internal revenue from collecting an allegedly unconstitutional tax. Since this action was more apt to test the law forbidding such injunctions than the constitutionality of the income tax, William D. Guthrie of the New York law firm of Seward, Guthrie, Morawetz & Steele, undertook to devise a case that would result in a decisive ruling on the income tax without raising the extraneous issue of the 1867 law.

Guthrie persuaded the boards of directors of the Farmers' Loan & Trust Company and the Continental Trust Company to adopt resolutions to the effect that although there was doubt as to the constitutionality of the income tax, they were going to set aside funds from their profits to pay the tax when it fell due. With some difficulty Guthrie then induced a stockholder from each company to pose as plaintiff and seek an injunction against his company to restrain it from committing a breach of trust by paying an unconstitutional tax without first contesting it. To make the test effective, Guthrie hired the eminent New York attorney James C. Carter to defend the income tax and block the attempt to enjoin the trust companies. In the resulting suits, *Pollock* v. *Farmers' Loan & Trust Company* and *Hyde* v. *Conti-*

nental Trust Company, the purpose was not to enjoin revenue collectors from collecting the income tax, but to restrain trustees from paying it.

The *Pollock* and *Hyde* suits were not started until mid-January 1895, and Guthrie feared that the weaker *Moore* case might reach the Supreme Court first. To prevent this he made arrangements with the solicitor general, Lawrence Maxwell, for appeal to be taken directly to the Supreme Court.[6] The solicitor general, in accord with a long-standing practice of the Justice Department, was responsible for conducting and arguing cases for the government before the Supreme Court. On 19 January, Maxwell met with Attorney General Olney and outlined the procedure by which the cases were being hastened to a hearing before the high tribunal. Olney apparently offered no objections to the plan.[7] Accordingly, on 28 January, Maxwell, acting for the government, secured from the Supreme Court an early date for a joint hearing of all three suits.

But these preliminary actions by Maxwell marked the end of his participation in the cases. On 29 January Olney sent the solicitor general a curt, insulting note. In it, Olney stated that he had directed Assistant Attorney General Edward B. Whitney to act as his personal representative before the court on 28 January, when the date for hearing the income tax cases was set. After that session, he said, Whitney reported that he had not participated in fixing the date of the hearing because Maxwell claimed to have been put in complete charge of all arrangements after consultations with both Olney and Secretary of the Treasury Carlisle. Olney denied that any such consultations had taken place. "Under the circumstances," he declared, "your interference in the suits was a gross impertinence and quite of a piece with your recent underhand attempt to alter that part of the *Congressional Directory* relating to this Department to suit your own notions of your own importance. Neither performance disturbs me personally," he continued, "but an apology from you to Mr. Whitney, a younger man of whom you took advantage, seems to me very much in order." Olney concluded his note with the information that he had directed Whitney to take immediate charge of the income tax cases on behalf of the government.[8]

Maxwell's reply to this unexpected attack was equally intemperate. Regarding the changes in the *Congressional Directory,* he stated that his "corrections" had "covered grammatical errors, the remodeling of awkward sentences, the restoration of the exact language of certain statutes referred to, the elision of some obsolete matter, and a concise and accurate statement of the duties of the Solicitor General. No

Attorney General," he added caustically, "unless he were a petty spirit, could have taken exception to those corrections." Were Olney "half a man," he would have "had the courage" to mention the matter at any one of several recent meetings. Turning to the income tax cases, Maxwell said that Olney's charge of interference was "an impudent suggestion to make to the Solicitor General," especially since Olney himself had yet to argue a case for the government before the Supreme Court. Furthermore, Olney had not objected to the advancement of the cases when they had discussed the subject on 19 January. "You degrade your office by subscribing your letter to me as Attorney General," Maxwell continued. "I have a better opinion of the office. You will therefore regard this letter as addressed to you personally."[9] That same day Maxwell resigned. Apparently he hoped that the president would intervene, but Cleveland, accepting the resignation with regret, declined to hear details of the incident because "without regard to such details the situation admits of no change."[10]

Rumors were rife in Washington as to why Olney forced the solicitor general to resign. Maxwell's friends asserted that Olney was jealous of his skill in winning cases, of his great social success, and of his "strikingly beautiful" wife. Others charged that the break came because the two men differed over the income tax, Olney holding it to be constitutional while Maxwell believed it unconstitutional. More important, however, was the clash of the two men's personalities. Both were strong, aggressive, and domineering. Maxwell refused to subordinate himself to the attorney general or to pay him deference. He assumed personal charge of all cases before the Supreme Court and disposed of them without asking Olney's opinion, much less his permission. Olney is reported to have remonstrated with Maxwell on the point with no success. Maxwell's "corrections" of the *Congressional Directory*, de-emphasizing the attorney general's supervisory role over the solicitor general and enhancing the solicitor general's role in conducting the government's business before the Supreme Court, seemed to Olney an attempt to make the attorney general appear little more than a cipher. His temper already smoldering, Olney exploded when Maxwell disdainfully brushed aside his personal representative, Whitney, and agreed to an early hearing for the income tax cases.[11]

"It is annoying," Olney wrote Miss Straw, " . . . to have a row with my first lieutenant. But he is well got rid of at any price." He had foreseen and dreaded the confrontation for some time, he added, but now was "glad the thing is over & will not have to be done again."[12] Sigourney Butler wrote that "occasionally a man turns up in official life who thinks he is 'bigger than old Grant.' I should judge that Mr. Maxwell had reached that state of mind. I congratulate you, therefore on the way in which you have disposed of him. Knowing you as I do, I am convinced that only the most intolerable conduct on his part would impel you to proceed as you have."[13] Since Butler had had no direct contact with the matter, his views could only have reflected what Olney told him.

The sharp criticism that Olney received for the government's loss of the sugar trust case might also have prompted the sudden move. At his meeting with Maxwell on 19 January he apparently raised no objection either to Maxwell's handling the income tax cases or to his plan for advancing them to an early hearing. However, two days later, the Supreme Court handed down the sugar trust decision, and the press, although Olney had neither managed nor argued the case, belabored the attorney general for the defeat.[14] Perhaps Olney took over from Maxwell because he was unwilling to risk further denunciation in the press should Maxwell lose the income tax cases. Quite apart from its cause, however, Maxwell's resignation resulted in the government's case being conducted by men who, if not enthusiastic about the income tax, at least believed it to be constitutional.

To all appearances the task of the defenders of the income tax seemed much easier than that of its opponents. Certainly the weight of precedent was on their side. An income tax had first been levied in the United States as an emergency measure during the Civil War. The tax continued, though modified by various revenue acts, until 1872. Thus, for about ten years a tax not unlike that levied in 1894 had been collected by the United States government. Moreover, the earlier income tax had been tested in the federal courts and had finally been declared constitutional in 1881 by a unanimous ruling of the Supreme Court.[15]

The defenders nonetheless faced difficulties, some of which were of their own making. Solicitor General Maxwell's arrangements with the opposition to speed the suits directly to the high court by 7 March deprived the defense of the advantage of rehearsing its arguments before a lower court.[16] Furthermore, the 30 January resignation of Maxwell, who had made elaborate preparation to argue the case, left the attorney general and his assistant, Whitney, little more than a month in which to ready their arguments—a month during which part of their time, of necessity, was spent at the regular business of the Justice Department.

Olney indeed found it necessary to hurry his work on the income tax cases in order to get on with the preparation of the case against Eugene V. Debs—a case that seemed to him to be of greater importance. "Much obliged for the last revise of the income tax thing," he wrote Miss Straw on 24 February. "I am not proud of it, but it will have to do. I have got to get up a Debs argument in the course of three or four weeks—which may not be any better though I should like to have it." He complained of the slow pace at which he worked and lamented that in Washington he found little time for work.[17] Several years later Whitney declared that probably no question as difficult and important as that of the income tax had ever been presented to the Supreme Court with as little time for preparation.[18]

Opponents of the measure, meanwhile, were able to amass a sizeable war chest and to employ some of the best legal talent of the nation in their effort to reverse the precedents and to overturn the income tax. Although the defense team of Whitney, Olney, and James C. Carter was impressive, it did not match the opposition: William D. Guthrie, Clarence A. Seward, former United States Senator George F. Edmunds, and Joseph H. Choate.[19]

The first hearing of the income tax cases began on 7 March and continued for almost a week. The first three men to speak—Guthrie and Seward against the tax, and Whitney in defense of it—delivered lengthy, fact-laden addresses sketching out the main lines of argument and laying down the primary evidence for both sides. Edmunds followed with a presentation notable mostly for its emotional appeals and high-flown oratory.[20] In the briefest and most closely reasoned argument of the first hearing, Attorney General Olney reduced the remarks of the four preceding speakers to their essential points and then sought to destroy those of the opposition while reinforcing those of his colleague, Whitney. The only real contentions of the opposition, he declared, were two: that the income tax of 1894 was a direct tax which, according to the constitution, had to be apportioned among the states on the basis of population, and, secondly, that the tax violated the constitutional provision that all duties, imposts, and excises, had to be "uniform throughout the United States." All other objections, Olney asserted, were raised by his opponents "pro forma, by way of precaution, because of the possibility of a point developing in some unexpected connection."

The attorney general turned first to the direct-tax issue. Seward in his speech to the court had given a historical exposition of the term in an effort to prove that the Founding Fathers would have regarded the income tax as a direct tax. Whitney in his reply had traced the history of taxes since 1794 and demonstrated that both Congress and the courts repeatedly had held the term "direct tax" to include only capitation and land taxes. Olney, too, gave much weight to past decisions. Scientifically, economically, and practically, he argued, the income tax might be classified as either a direct or an indirect tax. The important question, he maintained, was whether it was direct in the sense in which the term was used in the constitution. In that sense the income tax was not direct, he said, unless "the five concurring judicial expressions of opinion" by the Supreme Court in the period beginning with the 1796 case of *Hylton* v. *United States*, when three members of the Constitutional Convention were sitting on the Court, and ending with the unanimous decision in the *Springer* case of 1881 were erroneous. That the judges had erred throughout the past century, Olney observed, was open to the "gravest doubt." But even if it were certain that they had been wrong, "no idea of reversing them ought now to be seriously considered," Olney continued. To upset a constitutional exposition almost coeval with the Constitution itself would "set a hurtful precedent" and would "go far to prove that government by a written constitution is not a thing of stable principles, but of the fluctuating views and wishes of the particular period and the particular judges when and from whom its interpretation happens to be called for."

It was chiefly upon the second requirement, uniformity in taxation, Olney contended, that the plaintiffs placed their reliance. They rejected the well-established interpretation that construed the phrase "uniform throughout the United States" as requiring only geographic uniformity. Instead, Olney observed, the opponents of the income tax insisted that the expression was to be applied both geographically and as between taxpayers, and indeed such had been the construction put upon the phrase by both Guthrie and Edmunds in their presentations. Granting their position for the sake of argument, Olney said that he did not see how it would advance their cause. Ideally and theoretically a tax should fall equally upon all persons in the community; it should be ratable and proportional; and it should be so adjusted that every member of the community would contribute his just and equal share. Such "uniformity" would be possible, however, he maintained, only if all members of the community were alike in respect to property, in their ability to bear taxation, and in the benefits they received from taxation.

But taxation, Olney declared, was "an uncommonly practical affair," and had to be adapted to the practical conditions of human life which were "never the same for any two persons, and for any community, however small, were infinitely diversified." He went on to demonstrate how a tax of the same percentage levied, without exception, on the incomes of all persons would bear heavily on the man of small means while it would be almost unnoticed by a person of great wealth, and how a tax levied in accord with benefits received from such tax-supported services as schools or highways would again fall upon the group of citizens least able to pay since the benefits to them outweighed the benefits to men of wealth.

Olney stressed that the taxing power could not be used in accord with abstract theories. By necessity, legislative bodies had to classify the members of the community for tax purposes. Such classifications, of course, had to be reasonable and in line with public policies and principles. The rate of taxation had to be the same for every taxpayer in a particular classification, and the same classifications, together with the rates for them, had to apply equally in all parts of the nation. So long as these limitations were observed, he held, Congress, and Congress alone—however mistaken it might be in its notions about taxation—had the power to establish classifications for tax purposes and to determine rates for them.

Olney's argument included not only an analysis of the points of law but also a rebuttal of the broader issues on which Edmunds had built his argument:

> It would be a mistake . . . to infer that this great array of counsel, this elaborate argumentation, and these many and voluminous treatises miscalled by the name of briefs, indicate anything specially intricate or unique either in the facts before the court or in the rules of law which are applicable to them. An income tax is preeminently a tax upon the rich, and all the circumstances just adverted to prove the immense pecuniary stake which is now played for. It is so large that counsel fees and costs and printers' bills are mere bagatelles. It is so large and so stimulates the efforts of counsel that no legal or constitutional principle that stands in the way, however venerable or however long and universally acquiesced in, is suffered to pass unchallenged.[21]

Edmunds, throughout his remarks, had urged the Supreme Court to assert its rightful authority and its independence by outlawing the income tax. "It is the grand mission of this court of last resort, independent and supreme," he had said, "to bring the Congress back to a true sense of the limitations of its powers."[22] This and similar arguments of the opposition were characterized by the attorney general as nothing less in essence than a call upon the judicial branch of the government "to supplant the political in the exercise of the taxing power; to substitute its discretion for that of Congress in respect of the subjects of taxation, the plan of taxation, and all the distinctions and discriminations by which taxation is sought to be equitably adjusted to the resources and capacities of the different classes of society." He concluded his remarks with a plea to the court to observe scrupulously the bounds that separated its powers from those of the Congress.[23]

The effectiveness of Olney's argument was attested to by both friends and foes of the income tax. The attorney general was especially proud of a note that he received after the hearing from one of the opposing lawyers, Clarence A. Seward. "The argument," Seward wrote, "seemed to me to be the work of a master mind and the composition of a trained, accomplished and most able lawyer. Its clear and methodical arrangement—its most chaste and felicitous style—its rigid adherence to the actual case—its skillful turning of points of pressure—and its absolute avoidance of all extraneous reference—really greatly impressed me. It was an argument of the highest order. . . . It seems to me," he concluded, "to be due to you that I should say this in this confidential way—not as a compliment, but as your actual due."[24] The congratulatory notes of Olney's colleagues were no more extravagant than this praise from his opponent.

Had the first hearing been limited to the two issues that Olney identified as controlling, the nature of a direct tax and the uniformity requirement for duties, imposts, and excise taxes, his argument might have prevailed. Certainly the remarks of the illustrious James C. Carter, who followed him, added no new legal points for the defense, though Carter's repeated references to class struggle and his warning to the court of what might follow when the masses reacted to an invalidation of the income tax drew much attention in the press.[25] It was the argument of Joseph H. Choate, who spoke last, however, that proved to be decisive. Like Edmunds and Carter before him, Choate sought to arouse the prejudices and fears of the judges. He labeled the income tax as communistic, socialistic, and populistic. He portrayed the case before the court as the one last opportunity to hold the line against the destruction not only of all property rights but of civilization itself. But it was not these remarks, however much they may have influenced the court, nor his analysis of the constitutional questions that Olney had defined, that provided the basis for the ultimate decision.

The critical point established by Choate was that while incomes from other sources might possibly be taxed by the federal government, a tax upon income derived either from state or municipal bonds or from rents on real estate was unconstitutional. State and municipal bonds ought to be exempted from federal taxation, he held, for the same reason that federal bonds were exempted from state taxation, that is, because such taxation interfered with the exercise of sovereign power. That income from bonds and not the bonds themselves was to be taxed, Choate dismissed with a rhetorical question: "What possible difference in principle is there between a tax on the bond and a tax on its income?"

As for taxing income from rents, Choate noted that all parties were agreed that a tax upon land would be a direct tax and hence would have to be apportioned among the states according to their populations. Quoting Coke, Choate again answered a question with a question: "For what is land but the profits thereon?" In principle, a tax on rents, he argued, was not different from a tax on the land itself, and while both rents and land could be taxed, such taxes were direct taxes and had to be imposed by apportionment. This the law of 1894 did not do.[26]

Charles F. Southmayd, a retired attorney, was the actual author of that portion of Choate's address dealing with income from state and municipal bonds and from rents. According to Choate, Southmayd possessed a sixth sense, "the sense of property," which had been aroused by the "iniquity" of the income tax. To help undo the measure, he had volunteered the brief that proved so valuable.[27] Olney confessed to Carter a few days after the hearing that although the Southmayd brief had been sent to him, his "attention was not attracted to it especially"; in fact, he had not read it at all. "Until I heard Mr. Choate's reply," he said, "I was not aware what particular line of argument he was going to pursue."[28] Apparently both Southmayd's and Choate's briefs were received at the Justice Department by 1 March—giving the attorney general over a week in which to prepare to meet their argument.[29] But, as noted, Olney had completed the final draft of his address by 24 February and had turned to preparing the Debs case. Working under rushed deadlines clearly did not help the government's case.

On 8 April, Chief Justice Fuller, speaking for six of the eight justices who participated in the initial hearing, delivered an opinion accepting Choate's arguments that income from state and municipal bonds must be exempted from the law and that a tax on income from rents, being a direct tax on land, had to be apportioned. Of the many precedents overturned by the court in reaching its conclusions, the *Springer* case, through which the court in 1881 had upheld the constitutionality of the older income tax legislation, involved the greatest amount of legal squirming. The chief justice dismissed the fact that a unanimous opinion in that case had held that an income tax was not a direct tax. "The original record," he noted, "discloses that the income was not derived in any degree from real estate but was in part professional as attorney at law and the rest interest on United States bonds. It would seem probable that the court did not feel called upon to advert to the distinction between the latter and the former source of income, as the validity of the tax as to either would sustain the action." He concluded, therefore, that the opinion of the court in that case did not control the question of the taxability of income from land. The court stood four to four on the other questions before it: whether the voided portions of the law invalidated the entire act, whether the tax on income from personal property was, like rent, a direct tax, and whether any part of the tax not considered a direct tax was invalid for want of uniformity.[30]

The decision—"sort of a drawn game," as Olney characterized it—pleased neither side.[31] Olney told the press that the government would accept the decision as rendered and would not ask for a rehearing. He added that he was not surprised that income from state and municipal bonds had been exempted, but he was certain that the ruling on rents would someday be reversed by the court.[32]

Opponents of the tax at once sought to find some way to bring about the invalidation of the remaining portions of the income tax law. Guthrie initiated new cases in lower courts, and on 15 April applied for a rehearing of the *Pollock* and *Hyde* cases before the Supreme Court. Olney stipulated that if a rehearing were granted, all questions, not just those that were still undecided, should be reargued. The government, he said, had not been heard on the matter of rents because at the first hearing it had assumed that the rulings of the past century had already settled the issue. Furthermore, the attorney general declared, Chief Justice Fuller's opinion had introduced novel limitations on the federal taxing power on which the government ought to be heard.[33]

A rehearing accordingly was scheduled for 6 May, this time before a full bench. Justice Howell E. Jackson, who had been too ill to participate in the first hearing, agreed to come to Washington, despite his illness, for the reargument. Each side was allowed two speakers: Guthrie and Choate for the plaintiffs, Olney and Carter for the defense. On 30 April, after several days of negotiation, Carter was dropped from the defense when the trust companies that originally had hired him declined to pay further fees to him and the attorney general did not feel justified in expending money to employ him.[34] Consequently, Assistant Attorney General Whitney was again pressed into service, this time with only a week to prepare his arguments.

Carter warned Olney that the opposition would probably attempt to convince the court that by excepting two of the main sources of income, it had destroyed the general scheme of the income tax and should therefore void the law in toto. Such a move, Carter insisted, should be "resisted to the utmost."[35] Olney, however, had already determined to restore the tax on rents or to scrap the law altogether. "You will see," he wrote to Miss Straw, "that if the landlords are exempt I want myself and others exempted also." Reargument, he thought, would "bring everybody in or leave everybody out."[36] This was a bold decision, one that in retrospect had little chance of success. It lent support to the view of Matthew Josephson and others that Olney might have deliberately scuttled the case. Yet a conclusion of that sort stems more from a knowledge of Olney's long service as a spokesman for propertied interests than from his actual handling of the tax cases. There were much readier and more likely means of losing the case than the course that he followed.[37]

Nevertheless, by attempting to restore rents to taxable income Olney virtually assured the loss of the entire tax measure. Not only would he have to win Justice Jackson to his side for victory, but he would also have to persuade two of the justices who had initially excluded rents from the income tax to reverse themselves. The opposition, on the other hand, had only to keep in line the justices who had already exempted rents and to convince one additional justice that without rents the whole income tax scheme was unconstitutional. Olney had no illusions about an easy victory.[38]

The arguments of Guthrie and Whitney at the rehearing went deeply into legal and historical precedent and again dealt extensively with the direct-tax and uniformity issues.[39] Olney, using less than one of the two hours allotted him, made a forceful attack on the idea that income from rents was different from income from other sources. He also argued strongly against the notion that rents and the real estate producing them were one and the same. As he afterwards wrote Carter, his remarks were really a criticism of the chief justice's opinion.[40]

Even people hostile to Olney admitted that his defense of the income tax at the rehearing was impressive. The correspondent for the *New York World*, Arthur Brisbane, to whom the whole rehearing seemed like "a sort of bench and bar composed of wolves discussing the advisability of killing and eating a nice little lamb," reluctantly admitted Olney's skill.[41] "Mr. Olney's argument," he wrote, "was so able, so ingenious, and so terse that it would really be interesting to know whether he actually believes in the principle of an income tax." Olney reminded Brisbane of "a good natured but cynical father telling his children about Santa Claus, and trying to keep his face straight."[42]

Nevertheless, it was Choate who again swayed the court. Speaking as though the positive rulings of the first hearing were irrevocable, he told the court that "this mangled and mutilated corpse has too long remained unburied. In its present condition it shocks the sensibilities of the entire people of the United States." Congress had enacted the income tax in order to tax capital, he asserted, but now it fell only upon labor. It had been aimed at great wealth, particularly in the form of real estate, a form of property that was now excluded; but inasmuch as it taxed the incomes of corporations, it struck "at the main source of income of thousands of widows and orphans whose incomes, individually small, are derived from corporation investments." Having convinced the court at the first hearing to exempt rents from the income tax, Choate now argued that such an exemption invalidated the whole law. "The biggest fish have got out through the rent that Your Honors have made in the meshes of the law," he punned. "Will you allow the little fish to be alone made the victims?" The constitutionality of the whole income tax measure, he contended, was a question now controlled by the customary rule of legal interpretation that when part of a law upon which other parts or the whole law depend is invalidated, the dependent parts are likewise void. Congress itself, he declared, would never have passed what now remained of the income tax as an independent measure.[43]

In its decision the Supreme Court, repudiating Olney's argument, adhered to its earlier opinion that a tax on income from real estate was the same as a tax on real estate itself, hence was a direct tax, and had to be apportioned among the states according to population. But the court went further and declared that taxes on personal property or on income from personal property were also direct taxes. Having thus excluded from the operation of the income tax law two of the main sources of income, the court held that the whole scheme of taxation was invalidated and the law void.[44]

Observers generally expected that the decision of the court would be determined by Justice Jackson. However, when the opinion of the court was made public, although Jackson voted to sustain the law, it still was declared unconstitutional by a five-to-four decision.

Immediately the cry went up for the name of the justice who had "switched sides." At the time the press placed the blame on Justice George Shiras, Jr., but even now the available evidence is too inconclusive to provide a definite answer.[45] Certainly as interesting to know would be which justice was persuaded to reverse himself on the question of including rents as a part of taxable income.

Olney was disappointed at the outcome. "Of course, the furor litis is on me & I wish I had beaten," he wrote Miss Straw. "[I]f I have or can form an unprejudiced opinion, it is that the decision is a great blow to the power of the Federal government & if the Union is worth preserving, a national misfortune. If the Court should follow up the work by deciding against me in the Debs business," he went on, "I should regret I ever came to Washington. . . . I take comfort in thinking I have saved the $200 or $300 of my own personal tax." Two days later he commented bitterly, "Bear in mind that one of the majority in the income tax cases is a man in his dotage—not fit to sit in any case."[46]

The conservative press hailed the decision as judicial statesmanship, while those newspapers and journals that were unhappy with the decision directed their criticism toward the court rather than against Olney or his tactics in managing the case. Olney himself maintained through the years that the income tax was constitutional.[47] Shortly before his death he saw the decision he had called "a national misfortune" overturned by the adoption of the Sixteenth Amendment.

8

Coxeyites and Strikers

The first half of Cleveland's depression-haunted second term was filled with labor unrest. The collapse of business in the spring of 1893 soon produced serious problems for the nation's workingmen. Those fortunate enough to have jobs faced repeated layoffs and wage cuts; antiunion employers, quick to take advantage of the bad times to rid themselves of unwanted labor organizations, staged lockouts and in other ways harassed unions; the number and severity of strikes increased; and unemployment reached perhaps twenty per cent of the total labor force.[1] In the spring of 1894 bands of unemployed men formed impromptu armies and marched on Washington, demanding relief legislation from Congress.

Frequently when strikes or other labor disorders blocked passage of the mail, stopped the flow of interstate commerce, led to the seizure or destruction of property under the protection of a federal court, or resulted in tumult or riot in a territory, the United States government was called upon to act. Having no overall policy for coping with such disorders, Cleveland left these matters to the Justice Department. There the attorney general, who also had no formula, improvised policy as incidents occurred. His decisions as to whether to intervene were as often reached after consultation with businessmen and corporation lawyers as with the president.

Wittingly, or unwittingly—for sometimes postmasters, United States attorneys and marshals, and other low-ranking federal officials made commitments that were not authorized in advance by the attorney general or the president—Olney allowed the power of the federal government to be used to break strikes and weaken labor unions as well as to protect property and maintain law and order. In handling the Coxeyite armies and the Great Northern Strike early in 1894, Olney and his subordinates forged the legal weapons that subsequently would be used to break the Pullman Strike.

No sooner had Olney taken office than he authorized federal officials to intervene in a labor dispute and break up a strike already in progress. The Bullion Beck & Champion Mining Company at Eureka, Utah Territory, was unable—or unwilling—to continue paying its employees three dollars a day. The employees, who were organized, refused to accept a wage cut, so on 15 January 1893 the company closed down operations. A short while later it reopened the mines and agreed to hire any laborers who would work for two-and-a-half dollars a day. The union, again refusing to accept lower pay, undertook to prevent the company from hiring nonunion labor. It was not long before mobs of union members were intimidating both "scab" laborers and company officials. The company demanded protection for its property and for the men who wished to work in the mines at the new wage scale.

On 15 March, Irving A. Benton, United States marshal for Utah, wired the Justice Department that unless "prompt action" were taken there was danger that the mounting tension at Eureka would lead to the destruction of property and to loss of life. He asked permission to hire up to one hundred deputy marshals to preserve the peace. If such permission were not forthcoming, Benton warned, the governor of the territory would be forced to call upon the president for federal troops.[2]

Olney regarded it as the duty of local officials to maintain law and order and asked by what authority federal intervention could be justified. The marshal pointed out that local officials, though sympathetic to the cause of law and order, were unwilling to act against so large a number of their constituents. Also, he cited an act of Congress that made it the duty of United States marshals to suppress riots and insurrections in the territories. Apparently without further investigation or consultation with the president, Olney wired the requested authorization.[3]

Marshal Benton read Olney's telegram to the Eureka mob, and declared that he would prevent all unlawful trespass on the company's property. Further, he announced that he and his deputies would protect the right of anyone to work in the mines who desired to do so. The results, Benton wrote Olney, were gratifying. "The moral effect of your telegram was excellent." It was "worth many deputies."[4] The disturbances, however, continued for some time and violence flared up on occasion. Peace was not restored in Eureka, in fact, until a federal grand jury indicted for riot and conspiracy as many of the labor leaders as did not flee the territory. A small force of federal deputy marshals, never exceeding twenty-two in number, guarded the mine property until 6 May.[5]

Meanwhile, in April, John Duggan, secretary of the miners' union, inquired of Olney whether federal marshals could legally act as employment agents for the company whose property they protected, and whether marshals could arrest men without warrants for violating city ordinances or carry arms beyond the limits of the property being protected. The Justice Department in reply sent a printed circular stating that the attorney general was empowered to render legal opinions only to the president and to members of the cabinet. When, in December 1893, the union asked for copies of Benton's report of the strike to the Justice Department and for a statement of the costs of hiring deputy marshals during the strike, the request was simply filed.[6]

In the autumn of 1893 Olney threw the support of the Justice Department behind the United States postmasters, marshal, and attorney in the Minneapolis-St. Paul area, when those officials openly assisted a private company in crushing a labor union. The Twin-City Rapid Transit Company, owned by Thomas Lowry, was battling with its employees over the question of union recognition. The company had attempted the previous June to compel its employees to pay for damages to streetcars resulting from runaway teams, collisions, or accidents. The employees rebelled, went on strike, and—supported by the townspeople—forced the company to back down. Humiliated, the company determined to smash the union.

On 19 October, the union accused the company of slowly replacing union employees with nonunion men. It also complained about the company official who collected fares from the car drivers. The drivers periodically turned in accumulated fares to the collector but were given no receipts. When there were losses, shortages, or counterfeit coins—and there often were—the collector deducted the amounts from the drivers' wages. The drivers regarded the collector as a scoundrel. Demanding recognition and a written contract, the union served notice that union members, who constituted all but thirteen of the company's employees, would no longer work with nonunion men or turn fares over to the distrusted collector.

President Lowry, declaring that he would not allow the union to dictate who could or could not work for his company, denied any discrimination against union members. With winter coming on and with armies of unemployed men waiting to take their well-paying positions, he warned, the union men were not wise to present such unreasonable demands.

Anticipating a strike on or about 29 October, Lowry and his associates laid careful plans to snuff out the union before its walkout could get under way. To accomplish this Lowry needed an adequate supply of men to operate the streetcars, the cooperation of postal officials, and protection by both the local police and the Department of Justice. The closing of the World's Columbian Exposition had left a throng of unemployed men in Chicago, and the transit company sent agents there to recruit strikebreakers. Meanwhile, Lowry convinced Minneapolis post office officials to change the schedule of mail deliveries over the transit company's lines. Ordinarily mail was carried at regular intervals from 9:00 A.M. to 4:30 P.M. on the interurban cars between Minneapolis and St. Paul. Beginning at 8:00 P.M., 25 October, all interurban cars, with the inscription "U.S. Mail" freshly painted in large black letters on their sides, began carrying boxes of mail.[7] That same night the federal marshal and the United States attorney met and decided "to take heroic measures, if necessary, to insure the safe and uninterrupted passage of the mail."[8] The next morning some 145 "agitators" were discharged by the transit company and thirty strikebreakers from Chicago, "a splendid class of intelligent men in hard luck," took their places. The company reduced its service to a minimum, except for the mail-bearing interurban line.[9]

Olney was brought into the affair that same day. Senator William D. Washburn of Minnesota showed the attorney general a telegram from Minneapolis, requesting the senator to "see the Attorney General and have him wire instructions to Marshal Donahower, St. Paul, to protect interests referred to. Do this today. Important. Answer."[10] Olney promptly wired Donahower that he was "reliably informed" that federal statutes against conspiracy and obstruction of the mails were being violated by "strikers" in Donahower's district. If true, the marshal was to uphold the law by hiring "a force of Deputies sufficient to arrest all violators."[11]

The transit workers were caught completely off-guard by the company's coup. Their leaders were dismissed without warning; nonunion men, protected by the local police, had been imported to take their jobs; all interurban cars bore the significant label, "U.S. Mail"; and local newspapers published Marshal Donahower's authorization from the attorney general to employ sufficient deputies to protect the mail. By the end of October the union had ceased to exist.[12]

By the spring of 1894, Jacob S. Coxey, a manufacturer from Massillon, Ohio, had worked out a scheme for solving the nation's unemployment problem. Local governments, he suggested, should undertake extensive public works programs financed by the issuance of twenty-five-year, noninterest-bearing bonds. Communities would exchange these bonds at the United States treasury for legal tender notes, which, in turn, would be used to hire the jobless for such socially useful projects as improving highways and building schools. When Congress failed to act on his recommendations, Coxey and some associates organized the "Commonweal of Christ" and laid plans for a massive "petition-in-boots." A band of unemployed men would leave Massillon on Easter Sunday; augmented by recruits from all sections of the country, a hundred thousand would parade up Pennsylvania Avenue on May Day to demand action from Congress. Thanks in part to bad weather, a scant one hundred men marched out of Massillon on the appointed day. However, thousands more, particularly in the Far West where jobs were scarcest, swarmed into "industrial armies" and began to drift eastward.[13]

To outward appearances President Cleveland and Attorney General Olney were unconcerned about the "crank army" from Ohio. Actually there was considerable apprehension in the administration. Secretary of State Gresham believed that the lawless bands held anarchical doctrines and portended revolution. According to Olney, all but a few of the politicians in Washington, "out of ignorance," saw little more to Coxeyism "than an eccentric and ephemeral demonstration. . . ." He professed to see in the movement the first symptoms of the impending industrial revolution that he sometimes spoke of in public addresses.[14]

En route to Washington, Coxey and his little troop were kept under careful surveillance. Secret-service men, in fact, marched with the army all the way. Meanwhile, in the capital itself, city authorities braced to meet the invasion, taking elaborate precautions to prevent "house-breaking, robbery, and pilfering of all sorts." Behind the scenes, Cleveland and Olney worked with District officials, prepared, if need be, to call out the army to support the local police in maintaining law and order.[15] The affair was put down with remarkable ease. Only about five hundred men actually marched on the Capitol on May Day, and when Coxey was arrested for trying to speak from the steps of the Capitol, his "army" stood by, awe-struck. "Edged" by the police out of the District into nearby Maryland and Virginia, the commonweal band soon "melted away and disappeared."[16]

Actually the federal government had won the battle against Coxeyism a week earlier on the railroads of the trans-Mississippi west. In that vast, sparsely settled region, thousands of men had been employed in the building of the transcontinental railroads. The panic suddenly halted all such construction. The workmen, lacking jobs, believed themselves entitled to free—or at least to inexpensive—transportation to the east. When the companies refused to accommodate them, some groups seized trains and ran them pell-mell over the mountains and plains toward the Mississippi River.[17]

State and territorial governors in the West in most instances lacked the military force needed to prevent trains from being stolen or to capture them when seized. Some openly sympathized with the commonwealers. It therefore was fortunate from the point of view of the companies and the attorney general that most of the great transcontinental lines were in federal receivership. This meant that although most railroads were being run by their usual managers, technically those managers were officers of the courts, operating the lines under the direction of a federal judge. To interfere with the operation of such a railroad was contempt of court. When the industrial armies formed and threatened these railroads, federal judges, at the request of attorneys for the lines, issued injunctions forbidding unauthorized persons, on pain of punishment for contempt, to seize, use, or in any other way interfere with a receiver's operation of a railroad. When the armies defied these orders, grounds for federal intervention existed.[18]

The policy that evolved for quelling the train-stealing Coxeyites of the West was the work of many persons—primarily railroad lawyers and federal judges, attorneys, and marshals on the scene. Olney, who directed the battle from Washington, was not himself especially creative in meeting the threat. For the most part he simply put himself and his department at the disposal of the railroads, receiving recommendations from them, working out any legal difficulties, and then presenting the case for intervention to the president.

Olney was in Boston on 21 April when the receivers of the Union Pacific notified the Justice Department that "Kelly's Army" had tied up rail traffic in the Omaha-Council Bluffs area. The receivers urged the government to put "a sufficient military force" at the disposal of the federal marshal to protect their property and "the large interests of the United States that are therein involved."[19] That same day, George Hoadly, the government's special counsel for Union Pacific affairs, suggested to Olney that a "military demonstration" in the Omaha area would show the mob that the United States intended to protect its property, and might well avert loss of life and destruction of property.[20]

Solicitor General Maxwell, who was acting attorney general in

Olney's absence, referred the matter to the secretary of war. Lamont, in turn, conferred with Cleveland and reported back that the president did not believe himself empowered to use federal troops until after a federal judge issued "legal process" and reported that his order was being "obstructed by force." Maxwell informed Hoadly of the strict conditions under which the president would send troops and asked him to pass that information on the Union Pacific receivers.[21]

When Olney returned on 23 April, he found not only Kelly's army harassing the Union Pacific at Omaha, but "Hogan's Army" blocking traffic in the yards of the Northern Pacific at Butte, Montana. Supported by a mob of townspeople, Hogan was defying the United States marshal, who wired Olney for instructions. Should he swear in a large force of deputies or call on the state militia or the United States army for assistance? Olney authorized him to assemble as many deputies as needed to execute any orders given him by the federal courts.[22]

On 24 April Olney learned that Hogan's army, threatened with an order of arrest, had seized a train and was running for St. Paul, Minnesota, at forty miles an hour, "with great danger to life and property."[23] The federal judge in Montana requested that troops be sent to stop the train because the marshal and his men could not. Knowing Cleveland's strict rule regarding the use of the army, Olney wired the judge that troops could be asked for only if the president were notified that the execution of a court order was being obstructed by a force that could not be "overcome in the ordinary manner." The judge responded accordingly: "Hogan and others resist an order to arrest them . . . by force which cannot be overcome in the ordinary manner."[24] Other telegrams from the marshal and from James McNaught of New York (counsel for the receivers of the Northern Pacific) added urgency. Both asked that the army be used to capture the stolen train and McNaught pointed out that a landslide temporarily blocked the train at Bozeman, Montana, making prompt action imperative.[25]

Thus armed, Olney went to the White House to persuade the president to order out the army. It was the "sole alternative left to the government," he argued: a court order had been issued and defied, the United States marshal lacked the power to recapture the stolen train, and the federal judge, marshal, and attorney for Montana all certified that troops were needed to execute the court's order.[26] Cleveland sent for the commanding general of the army, John M. Schofield. The general, earlier in the day, had expressed doubt that the army was actually needed to capture the train. The governor of Minnesota had plenty of militiamen at his disposal and "surely" it could not be difficult for the railroad company to halt the train "at any point" and thus to "detain the culprits" until state forces could arrest them. Schofield doubted that a governor could justifiably call upon the president for assistance until the state forces were tried and found inadequate.[27]

After a full discussion at the White House, Olney prevailed and troops were dispatched to Bozeman to capture the blocked train. Any misgivings that Schofield or the president might have had at sending federal troops into a state without first being asked were quieted the next day when the governor of Montana wired for help to recapture the stolen train, it being "impossible," he said, "for the militia to overtake" the commonwealers.[28] The band of Hoganites had meanwhile cleared the debris that blocked their train and resumed their flight. Only when they stopped to camp overnight on 25 April did the army catch up with them. The federal marshal took 331 into custody; 250 others escaped in the darkness.[29]

Attorneys for the railroad and the United States attorney for Montana urged the marshal to take the captured Coxeyites to Helena for trial. Because there was "a great deal of excitement in all the towns along the line of the Northern Pacific," the marshal feared that this could be done only if federal troops guarded the prisoners along the way and at Helena. McNaught wrote Olney that it was necessary and right to use the army to keep the "mob" under arrest until the orders of the court were executed and the prisoners could be proceeded against for both contempt of court and train-stealing. Following McNaught's advice, Olney ordered the marshal to take all prisoners, without exception, to Helena for trial and assured him that as many federal troops as were needed would be supplied.[30]

Meanwhile, another crisis was building up in the Pacific Northwest. Large armies of the unemployed were massing in Portland, Seattle, Tacoma, and Spokane. Perhaps 1200 men from Seattle and Tacoma had gathered at Meekers Junction, Washington, along the line of the Northern Pacific. Five hundred or so from Portland had marched along the Union Pacific as far as Troutdale, Oregon. Federal and railroad officials anticipated that both groups would soon demand or seize trains. To meet the threat in his district, the federal judge for Washington issued an order to the United States marshal to protect the property of the Northern Pacific. Olney confirmed the order and authorized the marshal to swear in as many deputies as he needed. Within two days the marshal stood guard with 200 men.[31]

At Troutdale, things got out of hand. There the United States marshal for Oregon seems to have provoked an incident by running an empty freight train to the campsite of the industrial army. Although copies of the orders of the federal court forbidding interference with the operation of the Union Pacific were plastered on the boxcars, the men clambered aboard. The marshal, unhitching the engine and abandoning the train, then telegraphed the Justice Department that a train had been seized and that he lacked the means to recapture it. He failed to mention either his role in the affair or the fact that the train was not moving.

The arrival next day of the private train of the Union Pacific's general manager provided the stranded men with locomotion. Blocking his train, they simply switched the engine to the freight and departed for the East. The marshal's earlier assertion that he could not capture the train was now true; neither he nor his two deputies were armed, the citizens of Troutdale, who for the most part sympathized with the commonwealers, refused to aid him, and when the local sheriff— at the marshal's request—called upon the governor for assistance, it was denied. The marshal and federal judge for Oregon wired Olney, asking that the army again be called out to intercept the stolen train.[32]

On 28 April, Olney met once more with Cleveland, Lamont, and Schofield to decide whether to send troops into Oregon. Unlike Montana, where the request of federal officials for soldiers was eventually supported by the governor, in Oregon the governor refused either to supply militia or to call for federal intervention. Olney persuaded the president that troops were needed to uphold a federal court order and that the views of state officials were irrelevant. The army was ordered into action. The next day the train from Troutdale was captured and the prisoners taken to Portland for trial.[33]

Arriving with news of the train capture in Oregon was a request for federal troops at Meekers Junction to forestall the theft of a train there. Unknown to Olney, three regiments of the Washington militia were already on hand. Railroad officials, however, persuaded the marshal that federal troops were needed as well. In response the administration dispatched army units to both Washington and Idaho, not to recapture stolen trains, but to guard against train seizures along the route of the Northern Pacific.[34]

Time and again over the next several weeks the army was employed to protect railroads from seizures or threatened seizures.[35] The formula used was the one initially prescribed by the president. In practice, however, requests for aid were rarely wholly spontaneous. Anticipating the calls, Olney made certain that when they arrived they were in proper form. Olney then took the telegrams, worded as the president wanted them, to the White House where results were almost automatic.

Although Olney was predisposed to yield to the advice and requests of federal officials on the scene or to railroad lawyers who represented companies under attack, he did not indiscriminately follow the advice of either. Knowing the president's strict views on the question, he out-of-hand rejected calls for federal troops not based on arguments acceptable to the president. Requests arguing that lawbreakers respected soldiers more than sheriffs or militiamen, or that the army was cheaper than special deputy marshals, or that Coxeyites scattered when troopers arrived, though persuasive, were not forwarded to the president.[36] Olney was careful that substance as well as form be scrupulously observed. He told one judge who asked for soldiers that since the marshal had not sought authorization for deputies or a posse, it could not be said that he had exhausted his ordinary resources for enforcing the law. Similarly, when troops were sent, Olney instructed the judge of the district to watch carefully that soldiers were used "only in case of exigency making such employment necessary and legally justifiable."[37]

Once Coxeyites were arrested, a whole series of new problems arose. The small towns of the West did not have jails large enough to accommodate so many men at one time. Citizens in some communities were openly on the side of the prisoners and threatened to free them or to prevent them from being brought to trial. The question arose whether all the captured Coxeyites should be tried and punished or only their leaders as an example to the others. The charges on which to try commonwealers also proved difficult since there were no federal laws against train-stealing. Finally, when jail sentences were meted out, confinement of the men became a problem.

The shortage of jail facilities was met in a variety of ways. The Hoganites, for example, were kept at a race track hired on a day-to-day basis and were guarded by both deputy marshals and soldiers. "Sanders's Army" from Colorado was taken to Fort Leavenworth, Kansas, where it was guarded on the military reservation by the marshal and his men. A second commonweal army from Colorado was confined in abandoned military barracks at Fort Sidney, Nebraska. At Boise, Idaho, the marshal housed his prisoners in a railroad roundhouse. In those communities where the townspeople were hostile, troops were sent in to assure orderly trials and to prevent mobs from freeing the Coxeyites.[38] Although Secretary Lamont was unenthusiastic about using military reservations as jails and soldiers as jailers, Olney persuaded him that the only alternative was to turn the Coxeyites free, unpunished.[39]

With regard to punishing the commonwealers, Olney leaned toward harsh punishment only for the leaders. "Does Court think it necessary to punish all the prisoners?" he wired one federal attorney. "Will it not do to make example of leaders and discharge the rest on their recognizances?"[40] However, when railroad companies favored sterner treatment, Olney deferred to their judgment. Officials of the Union Pacific, for instance, asked Olney to wire the federal judge in Idaho, stressing the "importance of holding entire army which committed outrage at Montpelier and hearing cases of all of them and imposing adequate punishment to make example such as will have effect of deterring others from like action."[41] Paraphrasing the company's request, Olney wired that it was "important that entire commonweal army arrested for lawlessness at Montpelier should be tried and adequately punished. Unwise to discharge any of them."[42]

Once the Coxeyites were brought to trial the question of the crime with which to charge them had to be answered. Judge James A. Beatty of Idaho, an early warrior in the battle against the Coxeyites, saw "no clear way" of punishing commonwealers. The Supreme Court had ruled that a person who violated a court order while committing a crime could not be punished for contempt of court unless it could be proved that he knew of the order. "The purposes of these parties in capturing trains," Beatty said, "is not to interfere with the Court or Receivers, and it would be difficult to show that they knew of the Receivers' or Courts' possession of the property."[43] The judge had a point; Olney himself, despite his intimate connection with the railroad community, had had to inquire whether the Northern Pacific in Idaho was in the hands of receivers, and, if so, who they were.[44] The attorney general apparently had no suggestions on how to proceed against the offenders. Other judges, less assailed by doubt, charged the arrested commonwealers with contempt or with obstructing and retarding the United States mail.[45] In sentencing Coxeyites, some judges sought to disperse the armies and deprive them of leadership. The leaders were given long jail terms or held for further court action, while the rank and file were given thirty- to sixty-day sentences and released a few at a time on condition that they discontinue train-stealing.[46] Both railroad and government officials hoped that this would result in a withering-away of the commonweal armies.

Despite his problem over means to punish Coxeyites, Judge Beatty proved resourceful in checking their march on the capital. "I feel that this wild crusade *must be stopped* at once before more dangerous complications arise . . . , " he wrote Olney. He believed that the policy of the government should be to send them westward towards their homes as far as lawfully possible.[47] The administration in Washington apparently had been discussing this very issue. When an industrial army stole a train or in some other way violated the law, the government had little difficulty in halting its advance on Washington, at least temporarily. But what about those armies that marched along peacefully and committed no crimes? And what could be done to prevent those arrested and convicted of crimes from resuming their eastward journey as soon as they had served their sentences?

General Schofield thought there was little that could or should be done so long as no crimes were committed. "Commonwealers have the same rights as other citizens to go West or come East at their pleasure," he wrote in a memorandum to Secretary Lamont. Most were "actuated by the laudable desire to get out of a country where they are no longer able to obtain subsistence." In his opinion there was no authority by which the War Department could bar Coxeyites from marching along roads that ran through military or Indian reservations, since these were public highways. To bar them on some technicality, as apparently had been suggested, would be to abuse rather than to enforce the laws, he asserted.[48]

That Olney held somewhat different views is evident from the aid he gave Judge Beatty in blocking the passage of Coxeyites eastward and in pushing back those taken into custody. Beatty proposed that all Coxeyites be tried in the state where they began their march. He was certain that this could be done even though "explicit proof" of their having committed an offense in that state could not be produced. The obvious advantage was that it would turn the Coxeyites back from their march on Washington.[49] The "course proposed by you seems eminently judicious," Olney wired the judge. "Marshal will be sustained in necessary expenses." The attorney general promptly instructed federal attorneys and marshals to assist in transferring men from one state to another.[50]

On 5 June Beatty wired Olney that he had sentenced 185 commonwealers to sixty days' imprisonment in a camp to be built at the western border of Idaho at the point where the Union Pacific Railroad crossed the Snake River from Oregon. The "board shed" in Boise where the prisoners lived and had been tried, was to be torn down and rebuilt at the new site. Costs would be reduced because the prisoners would do their own cooking. The location, moreover, was more healthful than at Boise. Beatty's real reason for confining the men in such an out-of-the-way place, however, was that it put them as far west as his jurisdiction allowed.

The location of the prison camp had yet a deeper purpose, however. The sentence could be carried out only if federal troops moved the prisoners to the camp and guarded them there. Since the site stood opposite the gateway from Oregon into Idaho, the troopers would both guard the prisoners and block the advance of other Coxeyites from the Pacific Northwest. "I must be sustained in what I have done," Beatty insisted, "or all will prove a failure, and it will be useless in me to further attempt to stem the tide."[51] Olney wrote to Lamont about the matter and conferred with Cleveland. Although troops could not actually be used to move or guard the prisoners, they decided, a detachment of soldiers would be stationed very near the prison camp and it would move to its new post on the same train that carried the Coxeyites into confinement.[52]

Although the movement ended by July, another year passed before all accounts for marshals' fees, wages for deputy marshals, and general expenses were settled. As early as 25 June 1894, Olney asked that the appropriation of the Justice Department be raised from $50,000 to $125,000 to cover these extraordinary expenditures.[53] Several marshals saw nothing wrong in allowing the railroads to pay for the protection given their property. In fact, some railroad officials guaranteed the fees and expenses of marshals in order to get prompt action. Federal judges, in turn, allowed such bills to be presented to, and to be paid by, the receivers of the railroads.[54] Olney, however, was indignant that the railroads should pay for the protection they were entitled to. "The United States, and the United States alone, owes you for any services lawfully rendered and any expenses lawfully incurred by you as United States Marshal for the protection of property in the hands of . . . Receivers . . . ," he wrote one marshal.[55] Marshals who accepted money from the railroads were instructed to submit bills to the Justice Department and then to reimburse the railroads in full. The Union Pacific, however, went a little far, presenting a bill for the fares of marshals who rode on its trains while protecting them against Coxeyites. Olney also rejected the bill of an Omaha lawyer who asked to be paid for defending 219 commonwealers in court.[56]

In the midst of the battle to halt the advance of the western industrial armies, a railroad strike in the region further complicated matters. Between August 1893 and March 1894, the Great Northern Railroad Company, headed by James J. Hill, imposed three wage reductions on its employees. Three times the established railroad brotherhoods accepted the cuts rather than strike. Eugene V. Debs and the newly founded American Railway Union—an organization committed to enlisting all railway workers in one big union—rejected the third cut. The decision was risky because only a small minority of the Great Northern's employees belonged to the ARU. Debs properly assessed the sentiments of the workmen, however, for despite the pleas of brotherhood leaders, the men threw down their tools and joined the strike. The tie-up was complete. Not a carload of freight passed over the Great Northern west of St. Paul for the duration of the strike. The union also carefully avoided violence, knowing that it would play into the hands of Hill.[57]

Hill, unable to secure men to break the strike, even with the assistance of the railway brotherhoods, turned to the federal government. On 19 April, the sixth day of the strike, he wired Attorney General Olney that a strike, "conducted by men not in Company's employ," was preventing the movement of trains. Probably meaning only to alert the attorney general to the situation, Hill made no requests, but informed Olney that the embargo was being "carefully met on strictly legal grounds."[58]

Two days later, coinciding exactly with the onset of Coxeyite train-stealing episodes while Olney was in Boston, a lesser official of the Post Office Department initiated a move to assist Hill and the Great Northern. James E. White, general superintendent of the Railway Mail Service and a long-time enemy of railway strikes, went to the Justice Department to secure a legal definition of a mail train. Whether he acted on his own or at the request of the Great Northern is not known.

What constituted a mail train and who should determine the exact make-up of a mail train had never been spelled out by statute, contract, or court ruling. The companies held that a mail train should consist of every car of any train (as made up by the companies) that included a car carrying United States mail. Under such a definition, of course, broad federal protection would cover all passenger service of a line during a strike so long as a mail car was affixed to each passenger train. Strikers, on the other hand, anxious to keep the government out of their disputes with the companies, objected to allowing the railroads to determine the make-up of mail trains. During most of the major railway tie-ups of the era, strikers announced their willingness to allow special mail trains, consisting of locomotives, tenders, and mail cars, to pass through their blockades. In this manner vital mail services could continue without interruption. At the same time the mails would not serve as a cover for continuing the regular passenger business of the railroad companies. Had the government accepted the workers' offer, the issue of the mails would not have become grounds for federal intervention in major rail strikes.[59]

In Olney's absence, White's conference on 21 April was with Acting Attorney General Maxwell. He found Maxwell wholly sympathetic to his (and the railroads') point of view. Like Olney, Maxwell maintained close ties to the railroad community while in office: before, during, and after his term as solicitor general, Maxwell was general counsel and a director of the Cincinnati, Hamilton & Dayton Railroad, and a director of the Cincinnati, New Orleans & Texas Pacific line. White was "astonished" when, after a brief discussion of the issues, Maxwell asked him to wait while he drafted an official opinion. White, who had "never waited for anything so cheerfully," characterized the opinion as "all wool and much more than a yard wide"—wide enough to win not only the Great Northern Strike, but the Pullman Strike as well.[60]

In the opinion, Maxwell stated that on the basis of statute law and previous court rulings, it was a federal offense to obstruct or retard the passage of any train carrying mail. Those who interfered with such trains could not excuse themselves by declaring that mail cars could pass on alone; the mail must proceed "in the usual and ordinary way." A striker who halted a mail train came within the scope of the law prohibiting conspiracies against the United States government and might well be charged and tried for that crime and if found guilty be subjected to the heavy penalties it bore.[61]

White's view that the opinion played a major part in ending the Great Northern Strike was erroneous. Because the railroad carried mail on but one passenger train each way each day over its lines, the ARU could safely allow passenger-mail trains to pass without ending their blockade of the more important freight business of the company. Passenger service brought so little income to the Great Northern that the company's small victory regarding mail trains had no effect on the outcome of the strike.[62]

After Olney returned from Boston on 23 April, he gave no hint as to his view of the opinion written by Maxwell. It probably coincided with his own views, since he neither rescinded nor modified it in any way. At the same time, Olney remained cool to all proposals that the government protect the Great Northern from strikers. Perhaps he resented Maxwell's presumption in acting on so important a matter without consultation, and so refused to endorse the policy. Olney also might have shared Charles E. Perkins's hostility for Hill, whose Great Northern competed with the Burlington for the traffic between the

Pacific Northwest and Chicago. It is even possible that Olney still held a narrow view as to the government's role in such affairs, limiting it to protecting the mails but assuming no responsibility for interstate commerce. If the latter were true, the Pullman Strike in the very near future would broaden Olney's outlook on this score considerably.

On 28 April, at the time that Cleveland and Olney were dispatching troops to Oregon and Washington to fight commonwealers, Hill wired the president that "the authority of law and its officers" was being "openly defied and ridiculed." He noted that federal marshals had called for troops to assist them. "I hope this may be done," he concluded.[63] Hill's message did not make clear whether he thought troops were needed to fight Coxeyites (who were in the area) or strikers. He probably made no fine distinctions between them, since both were blocking his railroad.

Writing to Secretary Lamont, Olney took the position that the government should stay completely clear of the controversy and not allow federal troops to be used either as strike-breakers or as mere constables "to help chase down and arrest" strikers accused of committing crimes. He pointed out that the troubles on the Great Northern were caused by a labor dispute between the company and its employees "in which the employees may possibly be right." Since newspaper reports indicated that settlement of the strike was near, he warned that "any unnecessary interposition of the military would, of course, aggravate matters."[64] His stand was vindicated the next day, when both parties accepted the findings of a board of arbitration and ended the strike.

A few weeks later, on the eve of the Pullman Strike, Olney again opposed sending federal troops into a labor dispute—at least until such time as state forces proved unable to cope with the situation. On 15 June the marshal for Southern Illinois telegraphed that armed strikers from nearby coal mines had invaded railroad property, and had broken into and looted freight cars. Since the companies were in the hands of federal court receivers, the judge ordered the marshal to protect them. The marshal and his men were unable to carry out the order and could not raise a posse because local sentiment strongly favored the strikers. Both he and the federal judge requested troops.[65] Olney recommended that the receivers seek assistance from local officials. If that proved inadequate, he suggested next calling upon the governor of Illinois, who was prepared to protect property against lawless violence with military force if needed.[66]

Prior to the Pullman Strike, Olney was also unwilling to invoke the Sherman Antitrust Act in labor disputes. When a number of businessmen in New York State sought an injunction under the act against a lumber-shovers' strike which blocked interstate commerce, Olney refused. Although the language of the act could be construed to embrace labor unions, he said, it was uncertain whether the courts would agree since it was "a matter of public notoriety that the provisions of the statute in question were aimed at public mischief of a wholly different character." As to the specific case in point, such a proceeding on the part of the government would put the "whole power of the federal government on one side of a civil controversy, of doubtful merits, between the employers of labor on one hand and the employed on the other." This, he declared, "wears an appearance of unfairness on various grounds," especially in that the costs of one party would be borne by the government. Olney suggested that the lumber importers were not without remedy. They could bring action against the union under state conspiracy laws and, of course, were free to initiate private action under the Sherman Act. The correct public policy, he stated, was for the government to limit its action to the fewest cases possible.[67]

By late June 1894, Olney had not revealed himself as either the friend or foe of organized labor nor had he followed a consistent policy regarding the role of the federal government in labor disputes. He had refused to invoke the Sherman Act against the striking lumbershovers because he thought it wrong to throw the weight of the federal government to one side in a labor dispute. He had argued against federal military intervention in the Great Northern Strike on the grounds that it would only aggravate a dispute in which the workers were possibly right. And, he declined to send federal troops against striking coal miners in Illinois in June 1894, because Governor John Peter Altgeld had sufficient power ready for use against strikers if force proved necessary. Even in using troops against the followers of Coxey, he carefully restricted their activities to the enforcement of federal court orders. How much these acts reflected Olney's own views and how much those of the more cautious Cleveland is not clear. There can be little doubt that Olney was restrained by his knowledge that the president believed the handling of labor troubles should be left to state officials wherever possible and that he preferred civil rather than military intervention when the federal government was obliged to act.

On the other hand, Olney's role in working out the precise wording of the requests from federal judges for military aid against Coxeyites strongly indicated that he was determined that the president send out the army. It can be argued that the unusual circumstances of the industrial-army movement caused Olney to act forcefully. The Coxeyites, after all, were lawless bands, not striking workmen. They stole trains in a region where state officials could not or would not act against them. In Olney's view, property rights, if not ordered society itself, were at stake and he followed the advice and recommendations of his fellow railroad attorneys in order to end this manifestation of lawlessness. When the railroad lawyers asked for troops, Olney ascertained the conditions under which the president would authorize them and saw to it that properly worded requests for intervention came from the officials on the scene. In minor labor disputes not brought to the president's attention—such as the Eureka Mine Strike and the St. Paul Streetcar Strike—Olney on his own authority threw the power of the federal government wholly to the side of management without a second thought.

The Coxeyite affair and the Great Northern Strike were important to Olney's later policies in that they supplied him with the levers to use against the Pullman strikers. The federal court orders against train-stealing which, when violated, induced Cleveland to send troops, would serve as a model for the blanket injunction against Debs, and the definition of "mail train" handed down by Maxwell during the Great Northern Strike proved to be the first weapon Olney would use in his attempt to break the boycott of Pullman cars.

In mid-June 1894, Olney told a commencement audience at Brown that the unrest of labor in America was part of a world-wide movement of working men "against the whole organized order of things." The stimulus was "neither the actual evils endured nor possible advantages coveted," he declared. "The former are not intolerable nor are the latter indispensable to happiness. The real stimulus is a sense of wrong—a conviction that they do not have fair play—that society by its very constitution necessarily works injustice and inequality. . . . "[68] If Olney were right in his diagnosis of the cause of labor discontent, his own conduct during labor disputes frequently bore out the suspicions of the working classes. Within a week's time he would depart even farther from the principles of "fair play" for labor.

9

The Pullman Strike

Labor disorders spawned by the panic of 1893 reached a climax during June and July 1894, when a minor strike at George M. Pullman's Palace Car Company exploded into a general strike against all railroads operating in and around Chicago and on westward to the Pacific. The employer-landlord had refused to negotiate a dispute with his men over wages and rents on company-owned housing. When the American Railway Union, to which many of the employees belonged, proposed arbitration, Pullman declared that there was nothing to arbitrate. Having little other recourse than abandoning their brethren at Pullman, the ARU convention, then meeting in Chicago, voted to boycott all Pullman cars on all railroads in the country after twelve noon, 26 June, unless the sleeping-car magnate came to terms.[1]

Citing contracts with the Pullman Company and an unwillingness to inconvenience their customers, the railroad companies insisted on running sleeping cars as usual. Also anxious to discredit Debs and the ARU—both of which they regarded as dangerous—the companies declared that they would allow no self-proclaimed labor leader to dictate to them the make-up of their trains. The twenty-four lines in the Chicago area were in a strong position to meet the challenge of the ARU, having worked closely together since 1892 in an organization known as the Chicago General Managers Association.

As soon as the ARU announced the boycott, the GMA moved to counter it. Meeting daily to formulate common policy, the organization's first acts were selecting a chairman to act as spokesman and instructing a standing committee to begin hiring replacements for men who went on strike or were discharged. They also agreed to share the burden of fighting the common enemy and set up a committee of lawyers to advise them on legal steps to initiate against the boycott. The GMA's original solution for the boycott was simple: any employee who refused to do his whole duty—including handling Pullman cars—was to be discharged.[2]

Attorney General Olney, watching the unfolding of events from Washington, also concluded that the boycott must be broken, by federal intervention if necessary. Why he felt so strongly is not clear, but at no point did he regard the Pullman boycott or the subsequent strike as comparable in any way to the Great Northern Strike that had occurred only a few weeks before. Perhaps the Pullman boycott offended him because it directly involved two of his major clients, the Burlington and Santa Fe railroads, and the interests of several of his close business associates—John Murray Forbes, Charles E. Perkins, Benjamin P. Cheney, and George M. Pullman.[3] Perhaps like other railroaders, he saw in the growing power of Debs and the ARU a threat to railroad property in general. More than likely, however, Olney looked at the matter from a strictly legal point of view. Whatever grievances Debs and the ARU had against the railroad companies (and they later claimed many), they instituted the boycott, not to win concessions for themselves, but to force their employers to pressure Pullman into yielding to his men. Many Americans, including a number of federal judges, questioned whether any sort of railroad strike was legal; by almost unanimous agreement in the legal community, sympathy strikes or boycotts were illegal.[4]

Whatever his personal motivation, Olney acted quickly. Three days before the boycott began, he sent to the Post Office Department for a map showing all railroad mail routes in the nation.[5] His initial plan for thwarting the boycott was to extend federal protection to all mail trains. As defined by Solicitor General Maxwell's opinion in the Great Northern Strike, every car of every train carrying mail, as made up by the companies, was part of a mail train and entitled to federal protection. To break the boycott the railroad companies had only to attach a mail car to every passenger train containing Pullman cars. When workmen halted these trains or cut cars from them, they automatically violated the law.

As soon as post office officials notified Olney that mail trains were being interrupted, he ordered United States attorneys in troubled areas to "see that the passage of regular trains carrying United States mails in the usual and ordinary way, as contemplated by the act of Congress and directed by the Postmaster-General, is not obstructed." He authorized the attorneys to "procure warrants or any other available process" from the federal courts against those obstructing the mails and he directed federal marshals to execute the court orders "by such number of deputies or such posse as may be necessary."[6]

Railroad and local postal officials quickly fell in with the plan. Several companies switched mail cars from their usual position immediately behind coal tenders to the very ends of trains so that if boycotters cut off sleeping cars they would have to cut off mail cars as well. Others, to win public support, halted mail trains on the pretext that disorder prevailed in Chicago.[7] The GMA resolved to turn over to the United States attorney the names of employees who interfered in any way with trains carrying mail pouches. In Chicago, postal authorities announced that beginning 1 July, most suburban passenger trains would be designated as mail trains and thereafter be fully protected by federal law.[8]

It is impossible to know how effective Olney's plan would have been had the boycott not developed into a general railway strike. Debs and the ARU, hoping to avoid trouble with the federal government, offered to allow any mail train to pass so long as Pullman cars were not attached. When the companies refused to cut off sleeping cars, however, the ARU in fact interfered with few mail-carrying trains. Postal authorities in Chicago reported no important delays in the movement of mail prior to the arrival of troops in the city on 4 July, except where abandoned freight trains blocked all traffic.[9]

Olney's plan for thwarting the boycott was itself short-circuited by the GMA's policy of discharging men for refusing to handle Pullman cars. Whenever an ARU member was fired, the union struck that company. One by one the Chicago lines were tied up until by 30 June most railroads between the Ohio-Pennsylvania boundary and the Pacific Ocean were struck. Traffic in that vast area, whether mail, passenger, or freight, was snarled.

If not quickly broken, the tie-up threatened to create a national emergency. Chicago suffered shortages of fresh fruits, vegetables, and ice, with prices sky-rocketing. Because it was the nation's livestock and grain processing center, and because strikers allowed milk trains to pass, the city suffered no acute shortages of meat, bread, or milk. Had the strike persisted, however, meat and grain supplies in time would have been exhausted. Eastern cities, relying on the Midwest for supplies, soon developed shortages of meat and other foodstuffs, and prices advanced. Isolated western mining communities, wholly dependent on the railroads for food, went hungry. The embargo of coal trains produced layoffs and shutdowns in factories around the country. Newspapers began to cry for federal action to halt the strike. Partly to bolster their arguments and partly to make the news more dramatic, reporters talked of impending crises, starvation, and intense suffering. Even allowing for exaggeration, however, there can be little doubt but that had the strike gone on for days or weeks, it would have menaced the health, safety, and well-being of much of the nation.[10]

Concerned at the success of the strike, the GMA's legal committee advised bringing the federal government fully into the battle. The lawyers believed that the boycott-strike violated both state and federal law, but recommended turning to the United States government because "the action which can be had under federal law will be more speedy and efficacious." The move was not difficult. As noted, postal officials obligingly altered mail schedules so as to bring more passenger trains under federal protection, and both the United States attorney, Thomas M. Milchrist, and the United States marshal, John. W. Arnold, offered to work closely with the GMA and its legal committee. Milchrist asked the companies to give him the names of workmen who obstructed mail trains, and offered his full cooperation. Arnold, hard-pressed for satisfactory deputies, turned to the GMA, which promptly supplied him with large numbers of loyal railroad employees willing to wear federal badges and do battle with the strikers.[11]

No federal official needed less wooing than Olney. His patience with Debs and the ARU had worn thin. Not only had the strike thwarted his efforts to end the matter quickly, it also threatened his plans to summer at Falmouth—something he had done regularly for twenty years. "The new war in which I am engaged has broken up all my plans for leaving Washington at present," he complained to Miss Straw. The annual summer exodus from the capital and its notorious hot, humid weather was well under way. Between 17 June and 3 July (the day on which it was decided to send the army to Chicago), daily highs in Washington ranged from 89 to 98 degrees except for three days.[12] Olney, his temper thoroughly aroused, would be satisfied with nothing less than a complete humbling of the strikers.

Although the illegal secondary boycott had become a bona fide strike, Olney continued to regard it as wholly outside the law. He refused to treat the strike as a labor dispute and made no effort whatever to effect a peaceful settlement. He was determined to crush it. On the day that the GMA decided to seek federal assistance, Olney asked a prominent Chicago railroad lawyer, Edwin Walker, to act as special counsel for the government at Chicago, and put him in full charge of the legal battle against the strikers. Walker, in his twenty-fifth year as solicitor in Illinois for the Chicago, Milwaukee & St. Paul Railroad, was the law partner of a member of the GMA's legal committee.[13]

The choice of so obvious a partisan of the railroads as counsel for the government gave rise to speculation. One newspaper suggested that Olney and Walker, both lawyers for major Chicago railroads, were personally acquainted. Another reported that the GMA, lacking confidence in the United States attorney, had proposed a special counsel and suggested Walker for the position. Olney allegedly complied with their request within two hours. It is doubtful that Olney knew the Chicago lawyer personally prior to appointing him. On the day of the appointment, Olney went to Secretary Gresham (a Chicagoan) and asked him his opinion of Walker.[14] It seems unlikely that the attorney general, who rarely sought out the advice of his cabinet colleagues on any matter, would have done this had he known Walker personally. Although the GMA's minutes reveal no recommendation of a special counsel, it would appear that someone, probably from Chicago, suggested Walker's name to Olney. Since Milchrist knew nothing of the appointment until Olney asked him to contact Walker, the most likely source of the recommendation was the railroad community.

On the other hand, less than a week after the appointment, Gresham received a letter reporting that railroad managers and attorneys in Chicago complained "bitterly" that Walker was a "disappointment and a failure," and thought it "a great mistake" that any railroad attorney should be appointed to "such a position." Walker was "vacillating and entirely lacking in resources or plans," and did not act "in harmony" with the railroad attorneys or with Milchrist.[15] Whether the railroad community had come to regret Olney's (or someone else's) choice, or repented its own, is not clear.

With the appointment of Walker, Olney was ready to begin a new phase in the campaign against the strikers. His objective, he wrote the special counsel, was "vigorously" to assert "the rights of the United States" in Chicago, thereby making the strike "a failure everywhere else" and preventing its "spread over the entire country." To accomplish this he would use the weapons recently forged in the struggle with the Coxeyites—federal court injunctions backed by the army. As in the case of the earlier troubles, Olney believed that President Cleveland "might have used the United States troops to prevent interference with the mails and with interstate commerce on his own initiative—without waiting for action by the courts or without justifying the proceeding as taken to enforce judicial decrees." Olney feared, however, that Cleveland "could be induced to move" only in support of court orders. The Justice Department accordingly "took measures to put itself in the position which had induced the President to authorize the use of troops against the Coxey movement," that is, it filed bills for injunctions. Olney did not expect the injunctions to be obeyed, however, nor did he think that the federal marshal would be strong enough to enforce them. He had, "of course," authorized the marshal to swear in a force of deputies, but believed that "the true way of dealing with the matter" was "by a force which is overwhelming and prevents any attempt at resistance."[16]

By 30 June, both government and railroad attorneys were drafting bills for injunctions. They had not yet reached complete accord, however, on the best legal grounds for justifying them. The legal committee of the GMA urged application under the Sherman Antitrust Act, largely because the strike had paralyzed interstate commerce and that law specifically outlawed conspiracies that restrained such commerce. On the other hand, United States Attorney Milchrist reported to Olney that he was examining the Interstate Commerce Act in the hope of somehow applying its provisions.[17]

Olney himself continued to think only in terms of protecting mail trains. Prior to 1 July, he mentioned neither the protection of interstate commerce nor applying the Sherman Act. His initial instructions to various United States attorneys had been to secure injunctions to protect the mails. In asking Walker to serve as special counsel he had wired: "Want you to act for Government in proceedings to prevent obstruction of United States mail." In a telegram to Milchrist on 30 June, Olney suggested ten federal court cases that might serve as precedents for an injunction. Five dealt with obstruction of the mail (but not with injunctions), one forbade a railroad boycott, and one enjoined a railroad strike on general grounds without reference to specific statute law. In one case reference was made to the Sherman Act, but in an aside not vital to the decision. In another the court granted an injunction against strikers but declared specifically that the Sherman Act might not be used to justify such an order. In his list, Olney carefully avoided mention of the case of the New Orleans dockworkers (or the circuit-court decision upholding it), where workmen were enjoined from striking specifically on the grounds of the Sherman Act. It was not that these two cases were unknown to Olney: he had cited them in his 1893 annual report as illustrating how the courts had perverted the intent of Congress.[18]

As it became increasingly evident that protecting mail trains would not unblock the railroads, Olney yielded. There seemed to be no other federal law to justify intervention and both railroad lawyers and United States attorneys urged use of the Sherman Act. Olney surrendered, but his conversion was reluctant, lasting only long enough to meet the immediate crisis. On 29 June he reportedly told one lawyer that "the only thing which the Anti-Trust law seemed to cover was just such combinations of disaffected laborers as the American Railway Union."[19] When, that same day, the United States attorney in San Francisco asked permission to file a bill for an injunction against strikers under the Sherman Act, Olney replied, "Act upon *your view* of the law, which is certainly sustained by adjudications so far as they have gone." Finally, on 1 July, he gave way completely. He authorized Milchrist to file a bill based in part on the Sherman Act and wired Walker that the "advantages of bill in equity restraining unlawful combinations against operation federal laws, whether under interstate-commerce law, act of July 2, 1890 [the Sherman Act], or on general grounds, are obvious and will doubtless be availed of by you, if practicable."[20]

Within hours injunctions began to issue out of federal courts across the land. The most important was the "blanket injunction" handed down in Chicago. There Milchrist and Walker, assisted by several railroad lawyers and by Peter S. Grosscup and William A. Woods—the federal judges sitting in the case—perfected the bill. Then passing on their own handiwork, Grosscup and Woods next day handed down a "very comprehensive" order addressed to Debs, several other ARU leaders, "all persons combining and conspiring with them, and all persons whosoever." The injunction prohibited any interference with engines, cars, track, equipment, buildings, or other property belonging to the railroads. It forbade the uncoupling of cars, engines, or parts of trains. All attempts by whatever means to persuade or prevent railroad employees from carrying out their duties, or other men from entering the employ of the railroads, were forbidden. "Any act whatever" that furthered "any conspiracy or combination to restrain" the operation of railroads carrying mail or interstate commerce was proscribed.[21]

At the time Olney authorized filing the bills for injunctions, he told the press that the problem had now passed out of his hands. "The filing of the injunction practically concluded my work, and it is for other branches to execute such action as the courts take." As a matter of fact, far from retiring, Olney moved to bring force to bear on the strikers as promptly as possible. Since he did not expect the court orders to be obeyed, he did not wait to see what might happen. He wired Milchrist to report to him "at once" if the strikers resisted the injunction by force that the marshal could not overcome. Conscious of the Coxey precedents, he added that the federal judge should join in the report. To Walker he telegraphed that "immediate, vigorous measures at center of disturbance immensely important."[22]

Having carefully laid the foundation for armed intervention, Olney went to the White House to prepare the president. He took with him "a bunch of telegrams" from Colorado and the Southwest reporting that bands of strikers in that region were obstructing trains in receivership. Cleveland had not regarded the strike as serious. Believing newspaper accounts to be "overdrawn for sensational purposes," he had not even planned to discuss the matter with the cabinet until its next regular session on 3 July. After listening to Olney's "official account," however, he at once authorized the use of troops to protect the property of railroads in receivership and alerted the soldiers at Fort Sheridan, just north of Chicago, for possible movement into the city. Although Olney probably discussed the contemplated injunctions with him, it is not evident that the president fully grasped their significance. His declaration that the government "must protect its own property, see that its business is transacted, and be ready to give prompt assistance wherever it could legally do so," did not indicate that he understood Olney's plan to use troops to break up obstruction of interstate commerce.[23]

Even as Olney talked with Cleveland, Marshal Arnold reported from Chicago that he was in trouble. "The situation here to-night is desperate. I have sworn in over 400 deputies, and many more will be needed to protect the mail trains." Expecting "great trouble" the next day, he asked permission to purchase a hundred riot guns "to quell the strike." Olney promptly sought out Walker's view of the situation and learned that the injunction would be served the next afternoon. Both Walker and Judge Grosscup expected that the army would have to be called out to enforce the court order.[24]

The next day at Blue Island, Illinois, strikers responded to Arnold's reading of the injunction by hooting, paying it no attention, or threatening not to allow Pullman cars to pass. Believing his forces inadequate, Arnold asked that infantrymen be sent "at once" from Fort Sheridan. Olney again contacted Milchrist. "Trust use of United States troops will not be necessary," he said, but assured the Chicagoan that if needed they would "be used promptly and decisively" as soon as the "justifying facts" were "certified" to him. Olney again carefully spelled out the formula used against the Coxeyites: the United States attorney, marshal, and judge (and in this instance the special counsel, Walker) were to join in the report.[25]

Olney was taken aback to learn that Walker wished to give the strikers a chance to obey the injunction before summoning the army. "Understand you think time for use of United States troops has not yet arrived," he wired. "If the time does come they will be used promptly and decisively," and once more he specified the form to be used in requesting troops. The wire to Walker, however, did not include the hope that the army would not be needed. As matters turned out, Walker had already changed his mind and was helping the federal marshal draft a formal request for troops when Olney's telegram arrived. Arnold dispatched the request—appropriately signed by Grosscup, Walker, and Milchrist—on the afternoon of 3 July.[26]

The telegram from Chicago was misleading. There had been no troubles in Chicago proper and none occurred there until 5 July, after the arrival of the army. The disorders that Arnold reported were those that had taken place at Blue Island several miles south of the city. Even there no new violence had occurred; the telegram simply rehashed the strikers' reaction to the reading of the injunction on 2 July. Although the situation had since cooled down, the marshal declared that he was unable to disperse the mob, to clear the tracks, or to arrest the chief troublemakers. In his opinion, only federal troops—he made no reference whatever to using local police or state militia—could "procure the passage of the mail trains or enforce the orders of the court." Arnold supplied a further note of urgency by adding—quite inaccurately—that "people engaged in the trades" were quitting work and joining the mob.[27]

Olney, meanwhile, had spent most of the day at the White House, arguing the case for dispatching troops to Chicago. During the forenoon the cabinet discussed the issue. Secretaries Gresham, Morton, and Smith opposed using troops and Secretary Lamont was distinctly cool to the idea. Gresham, formerly a federal judge, disapproved of courts using equity proceedings, backed by the army, in lieu of statute law and suspected that the Chicago bill might be "fatally bad" because it sought to enjoin the commission of a crime. Lamont, a practical politician, feared that the move might antagonize or discredit leading Democratic political leaders such as Mayor John P. Hopkins of Chicago and Governor Altgeld of Illinois, whose active support had helped reelect Cleveland in 1892.[28]

After the meeting, Cleveland continued the discussion with Gresham, Olney, Lamont, and Generals Schofield and Nelson A. Miles. Miles disagreed with those who thought that marching "two hundred regular soldiers" down Michigan Avenue in Chicago would end the disturbances. "[T]he trouble," he warned, "was very much more deeply rooted, more threatening and far reaching than anything that had occurred before," and might well "paralyze if not overthrow the civil government."[29] All debating ended when Arnold's request for troops, countersigned by Grosscup, Walker, and Milchrist, arrived from Chicago.

Despite his views as to the seriousness of affairs, General Miles, who commanded the military department that included Chicago, seemed reluctant to act forcefully. When on 2 July, troops were alerted for possible movement into Chicago, Miles was in the East. It had taken a number of telegrams to locate him and to summon him to the White House meeting. Once troops were ordered out, Miles "enlarged at considerable length upon the difficulties of dealing with the mob [and] of knowing when to fire and when not to fire upon a riotous mass of citizens. . . . " Finally, he asked the president point-blank whether he was to order his men to fire on rioters. Cleveland replied angrily that Miles would have to "be the judge on questions of that kind" since he would be on the scene and in full command. Miles then asked if the president wanted him to go to Chicago in person. "Considerably astonished," Cleveland replied that he "should think that the General would want to go there."[30] By dawn on 4 July the army was in Chicago; the following day General Miles arrived and took command.

Again it is not clear that the president or the military fully understood that troops were moving to Chicago primarily to break the blockage of interstate commerce. The order to the garrison at Fort Sheridan declared that "it having become impracticable, in the judgment of the President, to enforce by ordinary course of judicial proceedings the laws of the United States," troops were "to execute the orders and processes of the United States Court, to prevent the obstruction of the United States mails and generally to enforce the faithful execution of the laws of the United States." Though general, the order did not mention interstate commerce specifically as it did the mails. Similarly, Cleveland's declaration at the time that "if it takes the entire army and navy of the United States to deliver a postal card in Chicago, that card will be delivered," seemed to indicate that he was primarily concerned about the mails, not with interstate commerce.[31] Apparently Olney was still running well ahead of his chief.

As the army took up positions in Chicago on 4 July, Olney announced to the press: "We have been brought to the ragged edge of anarchy, and it is time to see whether the law is sufficiently strong to prevent this condition of affairs. If not, the sooner we know it the better that it may be changed."[32] It is doubtful that Olney seriously believed that the nation was teetering on the edge of anarchy. It is even unlikely that the Pullman Strike interrupted his usual routine for more than a few days. "Every afternoon I have been playing tennis with funny, gruff old Olney," Theodore Roosevelt wrote to his sister on 12 August.[33]

In choosing the word "anarchy," Olney had deliberately reached for a loaded term. Anarchism was much in the air. Only a few days before, headlines had reported the assassination of the president of France by an anarchist. To many Americans the city of Chicago and anarchism had been inseparably linked since the infamous Haymarket incident of 1886. General Miles, in one of his lurid reports from Chicago, warned of anarchists who were plotting "destruction, plunder and terror." Of the city's one-and-a-half million inhabitants, he pointed out, over half a million were "foreigners." Chicago was "ripe for rebellion"; it "probably contains more anarchists and socialists than any city on earth," and had "more men engaged in cruel occupations and living in scenes of blood and slaughter than any other."[34] "Anarchy" was also the right tocsin to sound in as much as Governor Altgeld, whose authority was being by-passed, was believed by many to be sympathetic to anarchism. Within the past year he had pardoned the last of the anarchists convicted of complicity in the Haymarket affair.

Altgeld immediately protested the presence of federal forces. In a lengthy message to Cleveland he argued that the Illinois militia was adequate, well trained, and fully prepared, and that he stood ready to order it into action whenever properly called upon to do so. He had repeatedly sent troops to the Illinois coal fields during June, he pointed out, and had already twice supplied militiamen to aid the United States marshal for Southern Illinois during the present difficulties. If the federal marshal for Northern Illinois or local officials in the Chicago area were to request assistance he would respond promptly. The president was "being imposed upon," he suggested. The problem of stalled trains stemmed less from obstruction by strikers than from the inability of the railroad companies to find men to run the trains. The dispatch of federal troops to end such obstruction before requested by the state was not only a breach of courtesy to him, it was an assault upon the fundamental principle of local self-government. He requested that the president withdraw the army from Illinois at once.[35]

Cleveland's brief reply—allegedly drafted by Olney—stated simply that the army had been sent at the request of postal officials who declared that the mail was obstructed, and of judicial officials who reported that court processes could not be executed and that conspiracies existed against interstate commerce.[36] The troops at Chicago were there to protect obvious federal functions, not to interfere "with the plain duty of the local authorities to preserve the peace of the city."

In rebuttal, Altgeld charged that the federal executive was asserting a new authority—the right to intervene in any locality, at any time, at the request of its own officials, under the pretext of executing some federal law. The statute under which the president sent troops to Chicago, Altgeld asserted, presumed that state forces would be used first. For the president to assume the power now claimed would destroy the concept of local self-government embodied in the Constitution and give him power no less absolute than that of the czar of Russia. Cleveland's second reply was more tense than the first: "While I am still persuaded that I have neither transcended my authority nor duty in the emergency that confronts us, it seems to me that in this hour of danger and public distress, discussion may well give way to active efforts on the part of all in authority to restore obedience to law and to protect life and property."

Olney, in a statement to the press, declared that it was "hardly worthwhile to discuss at length the false premise and the illogical non-sequiturs of the Altgeld manifesto." As a campaign document it would draw little support, he predicted. "The soil of Illinois is the soil of the United States, and for all United States purposes, the United States is there with its courts, its marshals, and its troops, not by license or comity, but as of right. The paramount duty of the President of the United States is to see that the laws of the United States are faithfully executed, and in the discharge of that duty he is not hampered or crippled by the necessity of consulting Chief of Police, Mayor, or even Governor." Denying that any violation of states' rights was involved, he concluded with a forceful assertion of federal authority. "The notion that any territory of any State is too sacred to permit the exercise thereon, by the United States government, of any of its legitimate functions never had any legal existence, and, as a rule of conduct became practically extinct with the close of the Civil War."[37]

Two distinct concepts of the proper relationship between the federal and state governments were at contest. Governor Altgeld supported the notion that the enforcement of all law—local, state, and federal—was primarily the responsibility of local law officers. If they found that they could not discharge their duties without support, they could turn to the governor of their state for military assistance. If state forces proved inadequate, the governor, in turn, could call upon the president of the United States for federal troops. Even federal court orders that United States marshals could not enforce on their own were to be executed with the assistance of local and state forces, and by federal forces only if the others proved inadequate. Such had been the practice in the past. President Rutherford B. Hayes, for example, at the beginning of the 1877 railway strikes, sent no troops into strike areas without the formal request of the governor of the state involved.

Cleveland, under Olney's tutelage, however, operated on the assumption that maintenance of law and order was a state and local function, but that protection of federal functions and enforcement of federal law was properly the duty of the federal government without reference to local or state authorities. Although Cleveland carried this doctrine farther than any of his predecessors, and was less sensitive to the feelings of state officials, there were precedents dating from the 1877 strikes for sending federal troops to enforce the orders of federal courts. As recently as the Coxey affair, however, it had been the custom—if not the invariable practice—for courts to apply first to local and state officials for assistance before calling on the federal executive for troops.[38]

The presence of the army at Chicago, far from quelling the disorders, may have been a factor in precipitating the rioting that began on the evening of 4 July. In part the difficulties stemmed from the equivocal attitude of General Miles. On the one hand he saw the strike as a dangerous rebellion against the federal government; on the other he was sympathetic to the unemployed and hungry men whose squalid and impoverished lives led them to rebel.[39] When first he assumed command, he found his force of 5,000 men broken up into squads of from ten to twenty who accompanied federal marshals on missions to clear the railroad lines of rioting and obstruction. The soldiers were under strict orders not to fire or use force unless they themselves were fired upon or assaulted. Under the circumstances, mobs hooted at them, insulted them, and pelted them as they went about their duties. Even so, General Miles' report on 5 July was optimistic: "Owing to the excellent discipline and great forbearance of officers and men serious hostilities were avoided yesterday. Several small fights and affrays occurred. Matters look more favorable to-day, although interference exists on five roads."[40]

Miles's cheery optimism was unwarranted, as his subsequent reports on 5 and 6 July showed. The vandalism and other disturbances that began on the evening of 4 July escalated. On the fifth, freight cars were overturned and burned and a great fire damaged buildings at the World's Columbian Exposition at Jackson Park. "The riot will soon embrace all the criminals of the city and vicinity," Miles warned. "Unless very positive measures are taken, the riot will be beyond the control of any small force." A later telegram that day told of the mobs' open defiance of the federal court injunction. On 6 July,

Miles reported to the secretary of war that only six of Chicago's twenty-three railroads were unobstructed. Thirteen roads abandoned all service in and out of the city and another ten lines limited themselves to passenger trains.[41] Rioting reached its climax that day when some $340,000 worth of railroad property—for the most part empty freight cars—was destroyed. Governor Altgeld ordered the militia into Chicago on the sixth, and the next day a pitched battle between a mob and a detachment of militia resulted in the greatest bloodshed of the strike; five militiamen were seriously wounded, four rioters were killed, and twenty of the mob were injured.[42]

Officials in Washington were less than pleased with Miles's performance. Upon reading one of the general's frequent press interviews, Olney, in a "petulant outburst," was alleged to have fumed that "if Miles would do less talking to newspapers and more shooting at strikers he'd come nearer fulfilling his mission on earth and earning his pay."[43] But the "brave peacock" (as Theodore Roosevelt later dubbed him) hesitated to order his men to open fire.[44] Late on 5 July he warned the War Department that if the growing mobs were not checked, "more serious trouble may be expected. . . . Shall I give the order for troops to fire on mob obstructing trains?" he asked.[45] None of his superiors, Schofield, Lamont, or Cleveland—had much stomach for issuing such an order. Schofield, in reply, ordered Miles to concentrate rather than scatter his troops so as better to protect federal property and to execute the orders sent him.[46]

Olney, to the contrary, was reported to be pressing for the order to fire to be given. On 9 July, Schofield declared in a general order that any mob forcibly resisting or obstructing the laws of the United States, or attempting to destroy property belonging to or under the protection of the federal government, was "a public enemy." Whether troops were to use "the fire of musketry and artillery," or "the bayonet and saber" in quelling such mobs was a tactical question to be determined on the spot by the immediate commander. Ordinarily the order to fire would not be given until warning was issued so that innocent parties might withdraw. Bayonets were to be used instead of bullets whenever practicable. No trooper was to fire unless his immediate superior gave the express order. However, once it was deemed necessary to open fire, commanders were not to concern themselves over the extent of losses "inflicted on the public enemy."[47]

It required ten days for the combined state and federal forces in Chicago to restore order and to get the railroads moving freely once more. Debs and the ARU found themselves standing alone against the government when other labor groups, sensing defeat for the strikers, refused to join in the struggle. Debs and his lieutenants eventually were taken into custody and the great strike gradually ground to a halt in the nation's main rail center.

Although Chicago was the principal battleground, the strike extended over the western two-thirds of the nation. Olney coordinated the overall struggle, authorizing or ordering requests for injunctions to halt obstruction of the mails or interstate commerce, approving the swearing-in of large numbers of deputy marshals, and presenting the case for using federal forces to protect trains from hostile mobs. The nationwide conflict, after two hectic weeks, sputtered out and an uneasy peace was reimposed on the nation's rail network.[48]

From the announcement of the boycott in late June to the collapse of the strike in mid-July, Olney's primary objective was to crush the strike. On 11 July, for example, he wired Walker asking whether additional indictments against Debs, however justified, might not make of him a martyr and drag out the disorders. "Securing earliest end of business paralysis is [the] first object," he reminded the special counsel, and suggested delaying additional indictments for the time being. "Full justice" could be meted out to the "conspirators" later and would "be the surer for being . . . deliberate and without temper . . . "[49]

Olney, however, allowed Walker to dictate tactics and the pace of action against Debs during the course of the struggle. From the first the special counsel concentrated as much on winning a major legal victory against strikes in general as on halting the strike at hand. Unlike Olney, who put his trust in injunctions backed by the military, Walker favored moving against the strike leaders with both equity and criminal proceedings. Although he admitted that any fines imposed after criminal convictions would be negligible, he believed that a federal grand jury investigating and returning indictments would have "a greater restraining effect" upon Debs and his men than the proposed injunction. Olney hailed Walker's suggestion of a grand jury investigation as "eminently wise."[50]

On 3 July, when Olney was working to persuade President Cleveland to send troops to Chicago, Walker was reaching "a thorough understanding" with Judge Grosscup. "[W]hile we may not proceed as rapidly as some of the impatient ones may desire, we shall be very careful to take no step in advance without sufficient evidence to support our position. . . . " As the rioting, burning, and bloodshed of 5–8 July took place in Chicago, and Olney and others chafed that Debs was not behind bars, Walker was busy gathering evidence and perfecting his criminal case. He reported to Olney that the grand jury would not meet until 10 July, and thus little change in the situation could be expected for nearly a week. When the grand jury met, however, he hoped to lay before it all telegraphic orders that Debs had sent out to his followers across the country. This evidence would result in several indictments against Debs and his lieutenants for conspiring to obstruct the mails and interstate commerce. If the strike leaders were convicted and punished on those grounds, Walker predicted, "a general strike upon any railroad will not again occur for a series of years."[51]

Olney, impatient as ever, wired on 8 July that it was "frequently asked" in Washington why Debs had not been jailed for contempt of court. Was it because his arrest would be "inopportune, inflammatory, possibly dangerous, until the situation was more in hand"? Walker replied that after consultation with General Miles and others he had concluded that Debs should not be arrested until indicted. Not only could he easily obtain bail and be released, but his arrest might lead to a sympathy strike by other labor groups.[52] As the level of violence rose, President Cleveland issued a proclamation warning people not to assist Debs or the strike in any way and to stay out of riot areas. Walker hoped that martial law would be declared if the troubles continued, and for that reason, he said, still had not arrested Debs. Meanwhile he was taking steps to lay before the grand jury not only all of Debs's telegraphic messages, but the "records and papers in the office of Debs'[s] association" as well. At all times he was "looking to final results instead of temporary advantage."[53]

On 10 July the grand jury began to issue indictments and Debs was taken briefly into custody. That evening federal authorities raided the offices of the ARU and seized all papers on the premises. Debs protested that his personal papers were among those taken and the court promptly ordered their return. Olney fired a telegram (which he at once made public) to Walker. The seizure, "if not according to law," was to be "publicly disavowed" and the papers returned immediately. "The Government, in enforcing the law," he said, "can not afford to be itself lawless." Even measures that were strictly legal, if "unusual" or "dangerously near invasion of personal rights" were not to be resorted to. "The Government is too strong and its cause too righteous to warrant anything of that nature."[54]

Walker was indignant. Debs's personal papers, taken by mistake, had been returned "unopened and without objection." This was not the time, he complained, "to make apologies to any officer of the American Railway Union," and he protested at being "publicly censured" by the release of the attorney general's telegram to the press. Olney at once smoothed the ruffled feathers of his special counsel, making it clear that he was more concerned with public relations than with abstract justice for Debs. He had not blamed Walker for the seizure, he said, but had acted only to disavow a case of "excessive zeal" that the "Government could not afford to defend." He had released the wire to the press because reporters at Chicago had somehow obtained a garbled account of it and he thought matters could best be set aright by publication of the original wire.[55]

Completely reconciled, Walker reported to Olney on 14 July that the strike had "practically ended." The summoning of the grand jury, the charge of the judge to that body, the indictment and arrest of Debs, and the continuing sessions of the grand jury had all "exercised a most wholesome influence" over labor leaders in Chicago, he believed, and had forestalled a general strike. Walker then outlined his strategy for punishing Debs and the other leaders. He intended to have the men brought before the federal court for contempt in that they had repeatedly violated the terms of the injunction. Meanwhile, he planned to seek from the grand jury one or two carefully prepared indictments against the same men for criminal conspiracy to block mail and interstate commerce. This course, "pursued with dignity and firmness," would make the Chicago strike "the last railway strike . . . in this country for many years." Again Olney was satisfied. "Your plan of procedure seems eminently judicious and is entirely approved."[56]

Debs surrendered to the police on 17 July and refused bail. Walker believed he preferred the calm and quiet of a cell to the hectic scenes under way at the headquarters of the dying strike. Within a week a contempt hearing began before Judge Woods. However, because of previous engagements, Woods could not remain in Chicago long enough to complete the case. Walker strongly opposed turning the matter over to a master-of-chancery for proof. Such proceedings would compel all parties to remain in Chicago for the rest of the summer and would have forced the government to produce most of the evidence that it planned to use later in the criminal case. Rather than do that, Walker said, he would have asked for a dismissal of the contempt charges. In a private conversation with Woods, Walker persuaded the judge not to appoint a master but to take testimony in open court in September.

Postponement offered several advantages beyond protecting the government's criminal case from premature exposure. For one, Walker did not feel well enough to continue for more than a few days. "The heat was really stifling," he complained, "and the crowd of strikers present at the hearing made the air of the room intolerable." More important, with the strike broken and its leaders warned that further trouble would aggravate the charges against them, there was little danger of renewed striking. The ARU was "badly demoralized" and local units were withdrawing from it daily. By September, Walker predicted, "there will be little left of this organization."[57]

Olney, who had been disturbed at the prospects of delay, was reassured. The "advantages resulting from delay as set forth in your letter, especially as regards ultimate results, are very great," he declared. "After all, the important thing is to vindicate the law and justify the preventive action taken under it."[58] From this point forward, however, Olney would increasingly take charge of vindicating and justifying the government's actions before the courts. Walker's role waned accordingly.

The crisis of arms was over and the government had won. "You are receiving much praise from every quarter for the firm and prompt action you have taken," Olney's brother Peter wrote from New York. In a later letter Peter noted that in politics too often "one fellow shakes the tree while the other fellow picks up and gets away with the persimmon." There were "many indications" that the public understood "the great public service the Atty Genl. has rendered in this crisis" and was "disposed to give credit to whom it is due. . . . I don't think little L. [Secretary of War Lamont] figures much in the public estimation in the present crisis. The public interest centers on the Pres. and his Atty. Genl."[59]

10

Changing Views
and Vindication

With the great strike over and the contempt case against Debs post-poned, Olney at last had time to reflect on his recent experiences. He immediately began tidying up his relationships with former clients—relationships that because of the strike had involved him in a flagrant conflict of interests. A few newspapers had questioned the propriety of an official so closely tied to the railroads being in charge of the government's strike policy. The *New York World*, which had hounded him from the day of his appointment for not enforcing the Sherman Antitrust Act, scattered sarcastic squibs across its editorial page. One had the attorney general saying, "Who says I don't enforce the laws? Watch me get at those workingmen!" "Those who are inclined to judge Mr. Olney severely because he prosecutes law-break-ing strikers and writes briefs in favor of law-breaking trusts," the item continued, "must remember that after all Mr. Olney never gets any fees from workingmen." Another noted that "an esteemed con-temporary refers to Mr. Olney as having 'left the service of the corpo-rations to become Attorney-General.' He has never left the service of the corporations. He simply took a public position in which his service to them would be more valuable. Does his interference in the Western railroad strikes look as if he had ceased to serve the corpora-tions? They could afford to pension him for life for this one service if he never rendered another." Alfred Henry Lewis, in the *Chicago Times*, accurately described Olney's connections with the strike-bound Santa Fe and Burlington railroads and accused him of using his position to defeat the strike and to destroy labor unions among railroad employees.[1]

Meanwhile, Congress received a sprinkle of petitions, mostly from labor organizations, denouncing Olney and calling for his impeachment.[2] When a resolution was introduced in the House of Representatives to commend the administration's handling of the Chicago strike, Congressman Lafayette Pence, a Populist from Colorado, strenuously objected. "[T]he American people," he said, "will never believe that the Attorney General who orders the indictments, who orders the injunctions, who orders the military, should be either the attorney for one of those corporations, a stockholder in any one of them, or a member of the board of directors of any one of them."[3] The resolution passed easily, however, without further inquiry into Olney's private affairs. An attempt by Populist senators to have all official correspondence related to the strike made public (presumably to detect any ties between Olney and the GMA) was squelched when the attorney general protested privately to Senate leaders that the move would prematurely expose the government's case against Debs.[4] Congress, most of the press, and the public, if they noticed the charges at all, apparently dismissed them as mere labor propaganda, or regarded them as irrelevant to the more important issues of the strike.

Olney made no attempt to answer his critics or to explain his position; most of the accusations, after all, were true. Instead he quietly lessened his connections with the railroads. Sometime after drawing his last quarterly salary payment of $2500 from the Burlington on 3 August 1894, Olney asked that the payments be stopped so long as he remained in the cabinet. He continued, however, to serve as counsel and as a director of the Burlington without pay.[5] About the same time he reduced his connection with the Santa Fe by finding another lawyer to "assist Mr. Cheney in the management of his Atchison interests." After August, Olney apparently did only enough work for his clients to maintain ties against the day when he would return to private practice.[6]

Cutting direct financial ties, of course, did not answer the complaint that during the strike he had acted for the companies and against the workers. That charge apparently stung Olney deeply. Throughout the strike and for many years after, he repeatedly asserted that the government had been completely even-handed and that it sought only to enforce the law, not harm the rights of workingmen. No doubt in his own mind he did not see himself as hostile to labor. In fact, prior to entering public life he had never given workers, unions, or the rights of labor any serious thought. Growing up as a boy in Oxford he had learned little about labor problems. As an adult his contacts with working people—aside from servants—were few. His specialities—trust estates and railroad and corporation law—rarely involved laborers. Olney was aware of hardships faced by the lower classes, to be sure, but his sympathies at best were detached and passive. "A terrible night for the *poor* people!" he would exclaim to his family on cold winter evenings.[7]

The ferment touched off by the great strike set Olney for the first time to thinking deeply about the labor question. He soon began to modify his views. At the close of the Pullman Strike, Olney drafted some notes for use in his annual report. Although not used, they pointed out three lessons that he then believed the strike had taught. (1) Hereafter any strike involving interstate commerce "must count upon the United States [government] as an important factor." Strikers acting "within legal limits" need not fear intervention, but when intimidation, violence, or terrorization of nonstrikers occurred, action by the federal government could be expected. (2) Sympathy strikes, which had "never rested upon any rational basis," ought now to be "wholly discredited even in the eyes of . . . labor organizations." (3) Some sort of arbitration tribunal was needed for settling railway labor disputes. Olney condemned the ARU for rejecting compulsory arbitration at its Chicago convention, but conveniently overlooked both Pullman's refusal to arbitrate and the administration's failure to press for voluntary arbitration under the arbitration act of 1888.[8] Only after the defeat of the ARU had the president named a commission (as the act provided) to investigate the strike and its causes.

The next indication of Olney's new thinking grew out of a conversation with Supreme Court Justice John Marshall Harlan regarding the legality of an injunction that prohibited a strike. In December 1893, Judge James G. Jenkins of Milwaukee, at the request of the receivers of the Northern Pacific Railroad, had issued a comprehensive injunction expressly forbidding employees of that line from striking to protest a wage cut. In modifying and justifying the original injunction, Jenkins, in April 1894, defined strikes as illegal because they invariably involved violence, intimidation, destruction of property, and resort to force. Talk of a peaceable strike, he said, was "idle" and "impeachment of intelligence" because "none such ever occurred."[9] Railway workers appealed the order to Harlan, then on circuit duty, and he in turn discussed the matter with the attorney general. After the conversation, Olney set forth his views in a letter to the justice.

Olney raised no objection to restraining workers from combining and conspiring to quit work together so as to cripple operation of the railroad. However, he rejected Jenkins's assertion that all strikes of necessity were violent and hence lawless. The injunction might better have rested on grounds that a strike would have constituted gross contempt of court, Olney suggested. Since both the receivers and the employees technically were officers of the court, what "more flagrant contempt" could there be than for the men, by a "sudden, premeditated and unanimous abandonment of their positions . . . to necessitate the shutting up of the railroad because no reasonable opportunity had been given to supply their places."

An even stronger justification, he said, was that a strike could create a "great public nuisance." Nothing at law had "longer" or "more clearly and absolutely" been settled than that a court of equity could issue an injunction to prevent the obstruction of a public highway. A railroad, of course, was nothing more than a "specially contrived and improved species of public highway." Obstructions of ordinary highways commonly took the form of physical blockage. A railroad, however, because it required the services of "a corps of trained employees," could be obstructed either by physical blockage or by the withdrawal of service by the "expert officials and agents" who operated it. To enjoin such a strike, therefore, was not essentially different from enjoining an abutter of a public highway from erecting a fence across the road that would block the right of way.

Railroad employees might have a right to strike in spite of the nuisance created, Olney admitted, but that right had to be established and proved, not simply assumed. The employees of the Northern Pacific, for example, had no agreement with the company that they could quit work on any stipulated term of notice. Therefore, whether they could strike was governed by the "nature of their employment and all the conditions and circumstances attending it." A single employee, because his quitting probably would not affect the operation of the railroad, could quit at will so long as he did "not subject the employer's property to peculiar risks or injuries" or "endanger human life." Whether several employees could quit in unison depended on the amount of harm their quitting would do to operation of the line. If all employees wished to halt work together, it seemed to Olney that they would be obliged "to give such notice of their purpose" as would be "reasonably sufficient to enable those in charge of the railroad to procure another body of employees and thus prevent a public nuisance."[10]

Harlan's subsequent modification of Jenkins's injunction disappointed Olney because it avoided the issues he had raised. Since the ruling was "theoretical rather than practical," he hoped—but did not expect—that it would be appealed to the Supreme Court.[11] The decision no doubt gave Olney pause as to the ultimate fate of the blanket injunction issued at Chicago should it be reviewed by the High Court. Among other things, Harlan had warned federal judges that injunctions were to be used with great restraint. "There is no power the exercise of which is more delicate, which requires greater caution, deliberation, and sound discretion, or is more dangerous in a doubtful case, that the issuing of an injunction."[12]

Olney continued to explore the idea that railroad strikes could be enjoined because they created public nuisances. The chief attraction of the argument seems to have been that it could serve as a substitute for the Sherman Antitrust Act in justifying injunctions. Only reluctantly had Olney allowed federal attorneys to seek court orders under the Sherman Act during the strike and he preferred to rest the government's case on other foundations. In September he urged the proposition on Walker. The Chicago attorney had reported that he expected the court to uphold the blanket injunction against Debs, but feared that it might reject Section 4 of the Sherman Act—one of the justifications for the injunction—as unconstitutional. Olney doubted that the section in question was invalid and regarded Walker's other arguments as unanswerable. He suggested, however, "a still broader ground" on which to justify the bill, "even if no such act as that of 1890 were in existence," namely, the "indisputable jurisdiction of a court of equity in the case of a public nuisance." Olney spelled out, step by step, with appropriate citations, the argument he earlier had sketched out for Justice Harlan.[13]

After the hearing in Chicago, Walker reported that he had "anticipated the precise points suggested. . . . " The balance of his letter, however, revealed far less interest in the public-nuisance argument or any other grounds, than in winning approval of the right of the federal courts to enjoin threats to interstate commerce. Affirmation of that point, he believed, would forestall future general strikes on the railroads.[14] Once the case was argued and under advisement, Walker and Olney waited for two-and-a-half months while Judge Woods pondered his decision.

Meanwhile, Olney's views on the rights of workingmen continued to evolve. In late September, Edward A. Moseley, secretary of the Interstate Commerce Commission and a fellow-citizen of Massachusetts, called the attorney general's attention to the situation of a group of employees of the Philadelphia & Reading Railroad. The receivers of that line, invoking an old company rule, had ordered all employees to give up union membership or be fired. The men, who had belonged to the Brotherhood of Railway Trainmen for many years and paid regular dues and assessments, stood to lose accumulated disability and

death benefits if they dropped their membership. They were considering an appeal to federal Judge George M. Dallas, who had appointed
the receivers. Moseley asked Olney's opinion and when Olney replied
that the complaint seemed reasonable, Moseley asked if the attorney
general would discuss the matter with Stephen E. Wilkinson, grand
master of the BRT. He thought Olney should grant the interview,
if for no other reason, because Wilkinson and the BRT had helped
the government indirectly during the Pullman Strike by refusing to
support the ARU.[15]

Olney agreed, and learned from Wilkinson that he had shaved off
his whiskers as a partial disguise and taken up arms against the strikers.
When the disorders ended, the BRT suspended or expelled "as many
as twenty thousand" members for having disobeyed orders and participated in the strike. "Wilkinson's account interested me both during
the interview and afterwards," Olney wrote, "and made me keep in
mind the case of his employees [*sic*]."[16]

Apparently gratified that the BRT had supported the government,
Olney repaid its loyalty by sending Moseley "a hastily dictated draft
of a petition" outlining the main points to be included in an appeal.
A few days later he recommended Philadelphia lawyers who might
present the BRT's case to Judge Dallas.[17] The more he thought about
the issue, however, the more concerned he became about a growing
opinion, even among federal judges, that labor unions, because they
might promote successful strikes, were "in their essence illegal." This
seemed "so entirely unfounded" and "so mischievous in its tendency
and operation," that he decided to intervene in the Reading case.[18]
"It seemed to me," Olney later wrote, "that there was a great public
question involved which could be best presented to the court by some
lawyer who was not retained for either of the litigants and who would
act and would be deemed by the public to act purely from public
considerations."[19] On 6 October Olney asked permission of Judge
Dallas to "submit for consideration . . . a few suggestions" that
seemed to him to be "pertinent from a public point of view . . . "
He twice changed his mind about intervening, but finally, on 6 November, submitted an informal brief as amicus curiae.[20]

Olney declared that the order requiring men (against whom the
receiver had no complaint) to quit a union (with which the railroad
had never had difficulties) was unjust because it would deprive them
of union benefits already paid for. The only excuse—that the union
might provoke strikes—was invalid. Not only did the BRT's strike-
calling procedure tend to discourage strikes, but the workmen knew
full well that any strike against the receivers would be "summarily

controlled and punished through the process of contempt." While union membership in and of itself might be sufficient grounds for a private employer to discharge employees, a court of equity ought not allow its receivers to act in so unjust a manner.

Passing to broader issues, Olney declared that strikes were "not necessarily unlawful." Only when to the necessary and legal elements of a strike—"1) the quitting of work 2) by concert between two or more 3) simultaneously"—were added such ingredients as "malicious intent, followed by actual injury, intimidation, violence, the creation of a public nuisance, or a breach of the peace of any sort," did a strike become illegal. This being true, unions ought not to be proscribed solely because they sometimes conducted strikes. "Men deeming themselves aggrieved," Olney pointed out, whether or not formally organized into a union, frequently and easily united "for the single purpose of a strike."

More central was whether labor had the right to organize for settling its differences with capital "whose right to organize is apparently not denied." Again, how an ordinary employer answered the question was of little consequence, but the stand of a court of equity involved "the whole confidence of judicial impartiality and capacity." The "best service" was not to be expected from employees smarting under "a sense of injustice" and in "a chronic state of discontent." Such feelings were inevitable, however, when workmen saw capital not restricted from organizing, as they were, and when treatment "so apparently unfair" was administered through the courts, the law itself seeming "to have got wrong and in some unaccountable manner to have taken sides against them."

Allowing workmen to organize freely, Olney argued, avoided the "necessarily invidious, if not illegal, position that a man shall go without work unless he gives up a legal right"—freedom to associate with others—which he may value. A favorable ruling would be conciliatory to the workmen, would indicate that no injustice was contemplated against them, and would stand as "practical proof" that the courts fully understood and appreciated "the greatest social problem of the day." Olney went on to proclaim what for the time was an advanced stand on the labor question:

> Whatever else may remain for the future to determine, it must now be regarded as substantially settled that the mass of wage-earners can no longer be dealt with by capital as so many isolated units. The time has passed when the individual workman is called upon to pit his feeble single strength against the might of organ-

ized capital. Organized labor now confronts organized capital . . . and the burning question of modern times is how shall the ever-recurring controversies between them be adjusted and terminated. If the combatants are left to fight out their battles between themselves by the ordinary agencies, nothing is more certain than that each will inflict incalculable injury upon the other; while, whichever may triumph, will have won a victory only less disastrous and less regrettable than defeat.

As a practical solution, Olney proposed that the court itself act as arbiter between its receivers and employees, setting an enlightened example for others to follow. "No better mode" for resolving such disputes had yet been devised and the court was in an ideal position to act as arbiter: both sides would have confidence in it and, empowered to deal summarily with contempt, it could enforce its award.

Olney's brief caused no little stir in court. Neither Judge Dallas nor Samuel Dickson, attorney for the receivers, knew how to deal with it. Dallas declared that he had only glanced at it and so in no way had been influenced by it. Dickson, who did not "care a button" about the letter, questioned whether it was from Richard Olney, private citizen, or Richard Olney, attorney general. It must be the latter, he concluded, because if Olney had remained "in the comparative obscurity in the city of Boston" where he was at the time of his appointment, it "would never have occurred to him" to address the court in a matter in which he was neither litigant nor counsel. Dickson was confident that Judge Dallas would not be swayed by the influence of high office. Concluding that Olney was ill-informed as to the proper role of amicus curiae, Dallas accepted the document for consideration only when the petitioners' attorney adopted it as a supplementary brief.[21] So ended Olney's hope that the letter would be accepted as an impartial statement on a matter of public concern.

Outside the Philadelphia courtroom Olney's brief attracted little attention except among partisans. Debs denounced it as hypocrisy, while Alford E. Brown, vice-master of the BRT, wired Olney that "thousands" of union men and other working people saw "nothing but honest motives" behind the brief. "We do not see that the Reading letter was necessary to justify any action in connection with the Pullman strike, nor do we think the Reading letter a piece of politics," he declared. Joseph Nimmo, Jr., a government statistician who frequently corresponded with President Perkins of the Burlington, observed that Olney seemed to have made "a rather undignified flop."

His recent course illustrated an old saying about the influence of political power in Washington: "It is like the rose tree of Trebizond, its honey drives men mad."[22]

If political ambition lay behind Olney's new stance, he revealed little aptitude for exploiting it. He did not leak the contents of his letter to the press, for example, nor did he otherwise call attention to it. By mailing it to Judge Dallas on election day, he assured that it would be overshadowed as news by election results. The platform he used—a legal brief in a relatively obscure law case—gave him minimal attention as compared with the audience that an article or essay in a leading magazine, or a statement to the press setting forth his new views would have drawn.

Judge Dallas ultimately upheld the receivers with respect to the complainants. As for Olney's broader arguments, the judge contemptuously disposed of them without so much as alluding to the attorney general by name or title. It had been proposed, he said, that the matter be considered "abstractly" and "without regard to the merits of the particular case." Coming as it did from a party without standing in the case, the proposal ordinarily would have been ignored. To require the receivers to answer charges volunteered by any "mere meddler" or "litigious busybody" would be unreasonable and "mischievous" and would unnecessarily burden them in the performance of their duty.

Dallas made an exception for this particular unwarranted interference, but then refused to consider the questions raised. The character of the BRT was completely irrelevant, he said. The pleas that the court should "discuss and rule upon the good or evil influence and tendencies" of unions because they involved " 'vexed and new questions' " and were " 'the greatest social problem of the day' " and " 'the burning question of modern times,' " were the very reasons why the courts should avoid ruling. "The solutions of social problems, and of vexed, new, and burning questions" had "not been confided to the judiciary," but were functions properly assigned to the legislative branch of government. The question before the court was not "whether the Brotherhood of Railway Trainmen is or is not inimical to the general welfare, but whether these receivers should be ordered to retain its members in their service, despite the company's pre-existing rule to the contrary and against their own unanimous judgment." Nothing in the evidence before him suggested that he should override the receivers.[23] Olney took the rebuff calmly: "the judge has contrived to beat the plaintiffs on another point," he wrote Miss Straw, "and to dodge any decision on the points made by me."[24]

By the time that Judge Dallas handed down his ruling, Olney's attention had shifted to the findings of the Pullman Strike Commission. Made public in mid-November, the report showered blame generously. It criticized the ARU for admitting Pullman's sleeping-car employees (who did not work for railroads) into the union and for undertaking the boycott-strike at a time when extensive unemployment made the move obviously futile. It accused Pullman of precipitating the troubles by refusing to arbitrate or to deal with the union to which many of his employees belonged. The railroad companies, the report charged, were presumptuous in refusing to recognize the right of their employees to band together in the ARU, given the nature of their own organization, the GMA. "Some of our courts," the document noted scornfully, "are still poring over the law reports of antiquity in order to construe conspiracy out of labor unions."

Of greatest concern to Olney was the charge that the Justice Department had allowed railroad companies to supply loyal employees to serve as deputy United States marshals. Not only had the companies selected the men, they had fed, housed, armed, supervised, and paid them. In return, the men made arrests and exercised "unrestricted United States authority" while operating the trains of their employers. "This is placing officers of the Government under control of a combination of railroads," the commission declared. "It is a bad precedent, that might well lead to serious consequences."[25]

Outraged, Olney was about to accuse the commission of misrepresenting facts when he was shown sworn testimony of railroad officials completely confirming the charge. Considerably taken aback because he had forbidden marshals to allow the railroads to pay wages to deputies hired to protect trains, he immediately launched an investigation.[26] The replies his inquiries brought from Walker, Milchrist, Arnold, and George B. Harris, vice-president of the Burlington, bolstered the commission's findings. Arnold, Olney learned, had at first recruited "idlers" and other undesirables, including (to the dismay of the railroad officials) even strikers. When the GMA offered to supply loyal railway employees at no cost to his office, Arnold willingly swore in 2,887 to supplement 1,589 men procured elsewhere.[27]

Most respondents were indignant that anyone questioned the propriety of using these men as marshals during the strike. "It would appear obvious," Harris replied, that on such occasions it was "important to get men whose natural sympathies and tendencies are in favor of the protection of life and the preservation of property, rather than those who favor anarchy and chaos." Milchrist, though admitting that "technically it was a mistake to commission these men," believed that the "turbulence, violence and lawlessness" of the strike justified the action. That the deputies killed no one during the disorders seemed proof that their use had not been wholly unwise.[28]

"What has been done cannot be undone, of course," Olney wrote Walker. Still, he was upset that his orders had been disobeyed. It seemed that in "these ever recurring and ever intensifying collisions between labor and capital," that "the Government should not only be impartial in fact but impartial in appearance also. To unnecessarily afford any pretext . . . for the charge that the Government is nothing but the paid agent and instrument of capital in a vital mistake." But how was the charge to be avoided, or its truth from being accepted, if the government came forth to protect property "not in the due discharge of its legitimate public functions but only when capital opens its purse and agrees to pay the bills?" Money taken under such circumstances must appear to those against whom the government acted "to be nothing more or less than a bribe."[29] Incredibly enough, Olney saw no impropriety in railroads selecting, arming, and directing the deputies. He was disturbed only in that they paid them, and to undo that evil, he ordered repayment to the companies of every cent paid to their employees who served as deputies.[30]

Among other things, the Strike Commission Report recommended substituting arbitration for strikes in resolving railway labor disputes. Despite strong opposition to the idea, Commissioners Carroll D. Wright and John D. Kernan prepared a draft bill to replace the weak arbitration act of 1888 and submitted it to the House Labor Committee. Because Olney had championed arbitration in his Reading brief, Moseley and Wright sought to enlist him behind the measure and Lawrence E. McGann, chairman of the House Labor Committee, asked him to evaluate Wright's bill.[31]

After consultation with the president, Olney prepared a critique and drafted a bill of his own incorporating the changes he proposed. Wright and Kernan had proposed a permanent commission both to investigate railroad labor conditions and to arbitrate disputes. Arbitration was to be voluntary, but once agreed to, the award was to be binding and enforced by the federal courts. The bill also outlawed yellow-dog contracts, blacklisting, and the discharge of employees for belonging to labor unions. Olney objected to a permanent, full-time, "expensive, cumbrous and costly board." Like the Interstate Commerce Commission, the longer it existed the more entrenched and expensive it would become. Further, it would "inevitably" serve as "a standing invitation to arbitrate or to find something to arbitrate." So far as possible, capital and labor should be encouraged to resolve their differences "without governmental interposition." A permanent commission, moreover, would destroy "the most attractive feature of arbitration," namely, the right of each side to choose at least one member of the panel. Wright had attempted to get around this by providing that at least one member of the commission was to have had experience as a railway manager and another as a railway labor leader. These representatives, Olney believed, would "soon cease to be in touch" with the class they came from, and "without consciously deserting the interests and principles" of that class, would "sooner or later be found to have transferred allegiance to the commission itself."

Following Cleveland's suggestion, Olney left the investigation of railroad corporations and unions to the ICC and to the United States commissioner of labor, and proposed ad hoc commissions for arbitration. Cleveland had also objected to Wright's proposal that any single railway employee be enabled to set the machinery of investigation and arbitration in motion. Olney's bill provided that in addition to railroad companies, only organized laborers or whole classes of workers could be parties to arbitration. He also preserved Wright's provisions against blacklisting, yellow-dog contracts, and firing men for joining unions.

By this time, Olney had come to believe in compulsory arbitration of railway labor disputes. He knew, however, that neither the companies nor the brotherhoods would accept so radical a proposal. Determined, nonetheless, that when the parties accepted arbitration, the award must be final, his bill called for the enforcement of awards by the courts. Unlike Wright's bill, Olney's would allow appeals from awards only on matters of law apparent on the record. Judges were not equipped, in his opinion, to rule on questions of wages, hours, or working conditions that were, after all, matters of "business expediency and policy" rather than of right. Once an award was handed down, decided issues could not be reopened for at least two years.

Given Olney's handling of the Pullman Strike, the most interesting feature of his bill was its provision for dealing with railway strikes or strike threats. When one or both parties refused to submit to arbitration, or if one or both refused to abide by an award, the attorney general was empowered to seek relief in a court of equity. Not only would the court be asked to enjoin strikes, it would also be asked to appoint receivers to operate the railroad until such time as the dispute was resolved. This, Olney predicted, would be equally distasteful to companies and employees because it would strip the one of control over its property and the other of the power to withhold services.[32]

These provisions more than any other stood as an index of Olney's growth on the labor question. Not only did they provide for halting strikes that endangered the public welfare, they did so without prejudice to either side. Under these provisions, labor disputes would be dealt with as labor disputes, not as rebellions, and effecting peaceful settlements, not smashing strikes, was to be the chief objective of the government. This was as close as Olney ever came to repudiating his management of the Pullman Strike.

The House Labor Committee accepted Olney's draft and the railway brotherhoods endorsed it, though not enthusiastically. After passing the House near the close of the session, the bill bogged down in the Senate.[33] "It is very surprising that [Olney] should favor legislation of this kind," Charles E. Perkins observed, "and fortunate that it cannot go through at this session. At the next session we may have to do something to oppose it." To Forbes he wrote, "I do not understand what has come over Olney."[34] Congressional interest in the bill revived periodically, and in 1898, after Olney left office, his bill, without the provision for placing railroad companies in receivership during disputes, was enacted as the Erdman Act.[35]

By early 1895 Olney had come to see organized labor as a natural consequence of the growing concentration of capital. Since he regarded it essential for capital to be free to combine without restraint, both logic and justice argued that the same right be extended to labor. Olney called for recognition of labor's right to organize, not because unionization as such was necessarily good, but because he saw it as inevitable. Moreover, unions were potentially a conservative force. Given recognition, over the years unions and their leaders would become more experienced and responsible. As this happened they would become useful buffers between management and the extreme demands of impromptu groups of disaffected workmen.

Olney's defense of the right of workers to strike was most conservative. His definition of the term made it synonymous with "quit." Furthermore, a strike was legal only so long as it did not involve malicious intent, injury, intimidation, violence, breach of peace, creation of a public nuisance, or interference with the right of others to take the places of those who struck. Railway employees could strike only if they gave their employers sufficient time to secure replacements so as to maintain normal operations.

On the other hand, with regard to arbitration, Olney was in advance of most of his contemporaries in the business world. He realized that although unionization would tend to reduce the number of railroad strikes, it would make the strikes that did occur between giant corporations and giant unions infinitely more serious. Since paralysis of the railway network was intolerable from a public point of view, strikes could not be allowed. Since suppression offered no just solution, compulsory arbitration seemed the best alternative. Until mandatory arbitration was adopted, Olney supported voluntary arbitration, backed by receiverships for the companies and injunctions against strikes. In the years that followed, Olney returned to the service of the railroads and other corporate interests. However, he never retreated from the positions respecting labor that he formulated in the closing months of his term as attorney general. Eventually he would assign to organized labor an even more significant role in the economic, social, and political life of the nation.

This transformation in Olney's thinking took place prior to his appearance before the Supreme Court in March 1895 to argue the *Debs* case. Judge Woods, of the circuit court in Chicago, had weighed the matter from late September until mid-December because he realized that both the Justice Department and "those representing the business interests of the entire country" regarded the decision "as most important." Walker inferred from a conversation with the judge that his opinion would be "very carefully prepared," as he evidently regarded it "as his opportunity."[36] In the end, Woods found Debs guilty of contempt and sentenced him to six months in jail.

The forty-page decision fully vindicated the original blanket injunction. After a rambling discussion of various grounds for enjoining strike activities—including Olney's public-nuisance doctrine—Woods concluded that the Sherman Act of itself provided all the justification needed.[37] If Woods thought the decision might put him in line for promotion, he was mistaken. Olney regarded the circuit-court proceedings as but a necessary preliminary to a hearing before the Supreme Court and fretted at the time wasted. Woods's tardiness prevented Olney from mentioning the case in his annual report (as he had hoped to do) and threatened to hold up a final ruling, because the Supreme Court adjourned in May. Moreover, as Olney wrote to President Cleveland many years later, Woods had "decided rightly enough but upon the wrong ground—namely the Sherman Anti-Trust Act."[38]

During December and January, Olney cooperated with Debs's lawyers to appeal directly to the Supreme Court, but only if "questions of law, clearly presented, and not accompanied by cumbersome record" were contested.[39] Argument was ordered for late March. In the interim, Olney worked on the income tax cases while Walker pursued the criminal prosecution of Debs in Chicago. From "a public point of view," Olney advised, "no man should be allowed to play the part Debs did last summer and go unwhipped of Justice." As he saw it, no punishment the labor leader received, even if he were "convicted and sentenced on all pending indictments," would be "commensurate with his offense." Olney was far more concerned, however, that the injunction be upheld in the contempt case than that Debs be convicted and imprisoned under the criminal charge.[40]

Proceedings in Chicago aborted. Clarence Darrow, one of Debs's lawyers, denied that his client had conspired to obstruct the mails or interstate commerce, and countered that the workers were themselves the victims of a conspiracy of Chicago railroads to reduce wages and pursue a common antilabor policy. To substantiate his charge, Darrow called for the secret minutes of the GMA—much to the discomfort of the railroad attorneys. On 8 February a juror fell ill. Although the defense stipulated that the trial might continue with a new juror, the judge halted the proceedings. Debs and his supporters claimed that the dismissed jurymen all shook hands with Debs and told him that in their opinions he was winning. Walker vehemently denied the story and repeatedly urged Olney to seek a new trial.[41] Matters drifted until late April, when John C. Black, United States attorney for Northern Illinois, after a conference with the attorney general, announced that the government would halt criminal proceedings until the Supreme Court had ruled in the contempt case.[42]

Olney was careful from September 1894 to late May 1895 not to prejudice the contempt proceedings. He repeatedly urged United States attorneys to seek continuances of cases against Debs and other strikers rather than to press for trials. The threats hanging over the defendants' heads would guarantee their good behavior while suspensions avoided the appearance that the government was persecuting the laborers.[43]

The most troublesome and persistent labor problem during the interim involved New Orleans dockworkers who periodically went on strike and obstructed international trade in the port city. In November 1894, Olney authorized the United States attorney in Louisiana to secure an injunction such as had been used at Chicago—but only if absolutely necessary. State officials, he pointed out, were responsible for quelling disorders. "Any interference or proceedings involving resort to military force of the United States," he warned, were to be "deprecated and if possible avoided." The injunction was not sought that fall, but the next spring dockworkers again went on strike. A spokesman for shippers who called on the attorney general found him completely unwilling to act as he had at Chicago. The Justice Department did not wish to proceed again under the antitrust law until the *Debs* decision was rendered.[44]

Olney argued brilliantly when the contempt case came before the Supreme Court on 25 and 26 March 1895. Gone was all evidence of his new thinking on the rights of labor. Vanished, too, were any doubts he may have harbored over the government's course at Chicago. It was not that Olney had abandoned his new views; under fire the old Olney simply reappeared. As he confidently addressed the Court, his one objective was vindication, not only of the injunction and his policy, but of himself.

The "single question" before the Court, Olney argued, was whether the lower court had the power to issue the injunction in question. The defense's claim that the government had no right to injunctive relief because it had no property threatened with irreparable damage was false, he said. The government owned mail bags and had "possessory rights" over mail in transit. This was unimportant, however, because the lower court had granted the injunction, not to protect property, but to prevent restraint of interstate commerce under the Sherman Act. Opposing lawyers to the contrary notwithstanding, Olney argued, nothing he had heard or read cast "the slightest doubt" on the findings of the court below. Clearly the Act of 1890 applied to restraint of interstate commerce such as was complained of, and Section 4 authorized injunctions such as had been issued.

Olney then skillfully shifted the whole basis of the government's contention. The original request for an injunction had rested largely on the Sherman Act. When granted, the injunction had been justified by the same law. Judge Woods, in December, had upheld the injunction solely on the authority of the antitrust act. Both Olney's colleagues (whose arguments preceeded his) and Debs's lawyers had discussed at length the applicability of the Sherman Law. Now Olney completely abandoned that act. The government's case, he said, should not "be thought to turn upon the Government's technical relation to the mails and the mail bags," or "appear to depend upon the novel provisions of an experimental piece of legislation like the act of 1890." Rather, it based its actions on the constitutional power of Congress to regulate interstate commerce.

The courts, he pointed out, had ruled that once Congress acted to regulate interstate railroads, no other agency—governmental or individual—could interfere. By law, Congress had declared all railroads to be interstate carriers for governmental and private purposes and by the Interstate Commerce Act had "inaugurated measures more radical and comprehensive than anything ever before attempted" under the commerce clause. In effect that law "practically put" the railroads under the "charge of a commission, which is to see to it that their duties as interstate carriers as prescribed by Congress are faithfully discharged."[45]

At the time of the Pullman Strike, all interstate railroad transportation was within the exclusive keeping of the federal government. Any interference with it from any quarter—whether state governments or groups of strikers—was illegal. In July 1894, there was interference on a massive scale. It "was not sentimental, nor brought about by persuasion or cajolery, nor even by threats only. It was accompanied with the burning of cars, with the derailment of trains, with the destruction of signal towers and other appliances for the safe operation of trains, with assaults upon passengers and employees by which many were killed and many more wounded, with howling and excited mobs in full occupation of entire districts and terrorizing entire communities." That interference, "with all its consequences and incidents," was "to the fullest extent" the responsibility of the petitioners—

> unless it be true that men can wantonly touch the match to powder and yet be blameless because not rightly realizing the ensuing devastation; unless it be true that men can make vehement appeals for something to be done and yet plead not guilty when their tools and dupes resort to the only means by which that something can be done; unless it be true that those who seek to execute a plot by the only means possible, in the open, and taking the legal consequences upon their heads, are to be branded as criminals, while those who sit in an office and hatch the plot and urge on its consummation are to go unwhipped of justice because of loud-mouthed professions of virtue in general and respect for law and order in particular.

Given the "most extensive," "most ruinous," and "most irreparable character" of the interference, and the fact that Chicago, cut off from the rest of the nation, was reduced to slow starvation and famine, what was to be done? State and local forces were responsible for preventing crimes and rioting, of course, but the duty of "relieving interstate railroad transportation" fell to the United States government. In performing that duty, the federal executive could have arrested and prosecuted those who conspired against and obstructed the mails. Such a remedy, however, would have been of little value against mobs of thousands—especially when the government's objective was not so much to punish interference with interstate commerce as to end it. The "exact remedy" was the one that was used: application for injunctions against obstruction of the mail and interstate commerce. The defense's contention that the government, lacking proprietary interest, had no right to seek the injunction was unsound, Olney declared. "A trustee's right and duty to protect by suit the subject matter of the trust" was in no way affected because the trustee did not have a private interest in that subject matter. And, after all, with regard to interstate railroad transportation, what was the United States government "but a trustee for all parties and interests concerned?" Railroads were "national highways" over which the United States had a "jurisdiction and control" that was the "equivalent of ownership."

Olney noted that the court had been "harangued upon the absurdity and folly of quelling mobs by injunction." To invoke the powers of equity against "political revolution or armed insurrection" ordinarily would be unwise because futile. But the Chicago injunction had not been "ridiculous or ineffective," and he quoted Debs's own testimony before the federal Strike Commission to the effect that the injunction and his subsequent arrest for contempt had broken the strike. It was the success of the injunction, indeed, that lay behind the bitterness with which it was condemned, he contended.[46]

For two months, Olney, Debs, and the nation awaited the decision. On 27 May, by unanimous vote, the Supreme Court upheld the government's contentions, declaring that "the entire strength of the nation may be used to enforce in any part of the land the full and free exercise of all national powers and the security of all rights entrusted by the Constitution to its care." The Court held that the government in an emergency might not only use the army and the militia, but also could turn to the courts for injunctions. Declining to discuss the applicability of the Sherman Act, the Court rested its judgment on "broader grounds": the constitutional power of the United States to protect the mails and interstate commerce.[47]

Olney was pleased and did not greatly exaggerate when he wrote to Miss Straw, "Nothing new—except that Supreme Court to-day decided Debs case in my favor on all points—in fact took my argument & turned it into an opinion." The victory somewhat eased his disappointment at losing the income tax case. Taking the two together, he said, "I think a fair average."[48] Edwin Walker, writing to Olney less than a week before, had once again urged the attorney general to revive the criminal case against Debs. "Of course," he admitted, "we have to take our chances with the jury, but certainly a mistrial will be better than a dismissal of the case."[49] Olney must have wondered how even a victory—much less a mistrial or defeat—could possibly improve upon the situation. As matters stood, he had won a unanimous and complete vindication from the Supreme Court on exactly the terms he wanted. The criminal trial was never resumed and after Olney left the Justice Department his successor quietly quashed the indictment.

Suppressing the Pullman Strike and winning the *Debs* case were great personal victories for Olney that brought him the praise of businessmen, lawyers, and politicians alike. He had achieved fame and reputation undreamed of two years before when he entered public life. By the end of May 1895, however, the Justice Department had little more to offer in the way of excitement or challenge. The significant work was done: the sugar trust ruling had stilled—at least temporarily—the demand for a crusade against business combinations; the controversial income tax had been tested and found unconstitutional; the *Debs* decision had capped the victory at Chicago and given the government new weapons for controlling railway strikes; Olney's plan for financing the debts of the Union Pacific and his bill for arbitrating railway labor disputes were both in the hands of Congress. Only routine matters remained. Without new battles to fight, Olney would soon have tired of time-serving in Washington and might well have returned to Boston. This did not happen, however. The day after the Supreme Court's decision in the *Debs* case, Secretary of State Gresham, who had been ill for several weeks, suddenly died, leaving vacant the first place in Cleveland's cabinet.

11

The Shaping of
Foreign Policy

Gresham's unexpected death suddenly changed Olney's prospects. Sigourney Butler thought that his cousin "unquestionably" should be appointed to fill the vacancy and offered to propose his name to the president unless Olney thought it "a bit delicate." "Wire me if you want me to write," he said. "Just say 'Write' or 'Don't Write' . . . " Characteristically, Olney made no move to secure the appointment. "[W]hile I have my own views as to what would be simple justice under all the circumstances," he wrote Miss Straw, "I do not expect to change my present position." Staying on as attorney general had an advantage, he observed: "it will leave me free to get out of here when I choose."[1]

While newspapers speculated on Gresham's successor, unsolicited recommendations piled up at the White House. The president, deeply affected at the loss of his trusted adviser and friend, held his counsel and refused even to look at the suggestions. Finally, on 3 June, two days after Gresham's funeral, Cleveland closeted himself with Secretaries Lamont and Carlisle to discuss the "Cabinet situation." He assumed that Carlisle would prefer to remain on at the Treasury Department. The secretary, willing to "undertake any duty," preferred his existing position because, after two trying years, the "situation was clearing up. . . . " Pleased that Carlisle saw matters as he did, the president said that he thought it best to move Olney to the State Department. Both secretaries "cordially assented." No other names were discussed, the nomination was made, and after Senate approval, Olney was sworn in on 10 June.[2]

Cleveland's choice met with general approval. The press discussed the attorney general's "courage" as demonstrated in putting down the Chicago Strike and his "fairness" as displayed in the Reading brief.

Democratic leaders were pleased that a loyal party man would succeed the Mugwump Republican, Gresham. Because Olney was regarded as above partisanship, even Republicans praised the appointment. In their opinion Olney was the "one success" to emerge from the second Cleveland administration.[3]

Years later, Cleveland wrote that Olney was "exceptionally strong and able" and "in every way especially qualified" to fill Gresham's place.[4] There is no doubt but that Olney was skillful and tough-minded and that the president admired the forceful and determined manner in which the New Englander tackled problems. To be sure, the attorney general's aggressive policy during the Pullman Strike had given Cleveland a few sleepless nights, but his decisive moves, his relentless determination to win, and his legal adroitness had brought the administration safely through to victory both on the railroads and in the courts. The president was also impressed by Olney's Cleveland-like stubbornness, his competence at law, and his apparent disdain of newspaper publicity and public acclaim.

Many of the characteristics Olney displayed while attorney general augured favorably for his new assignment. His capacity for hard work, his orderly work habits, and his penchant for cutting though nonessentials indicated that the State Department would be run efficiently. That he was quick to grasp new situations, to learn, to adapt, to grow, suggested that he would bring intelligence to his work. At the same time, the very traits that Cleveland looked on as strengths, others might have regarded as handicaps if not weaknesses. The most serious of these, perhaps, was Olney's quick temper, that led him to strike out impulsively—even rashly—at those who opposed him. Also, in defining his position on controversial issues, he was given to blunt, tactless language that left little room for compromise. Olney was ruthless in crushing opposition, as the American Railway Union had learned, and it was only after he had obtained unconditional surrender that he would survey the damage and try to find ways to prevent such confrontations in the future. When dealing with "inferiors"—his wife and daughters, his employees and subordinates, and Coxeyites and strikers—such methods often produced the results that he desired. How they would work when employed against sovereign nations remained to be seen.

Although Cleveland was right in choosing Olney because he trusted his character and judgment, the president was talking nonsense when he referred to Olney as being "in every way especially qualified" for his new post. Olney lacked many attainments that might be expected of one who was to conduct the foreign relations of a major power. His education, training, and experience lay wholly outside the realm of international politics. His law practice rarely involved matters beyond the jurisdiction of the United States. He had not traveled outside the country except for a brief vacation in the British Isles in the 1870s and two short business trips—one to London and Paris, the other to Cuba. Until Olney came to Washington in 1893, even his social life had been largely confined to a narrow circle of Bostonians. The little he knew of foreign affairs he had picked up at Cleveland's cabinet table.[5]

In naming so inexperienced a man to office, Cleveland broke no tradition. Most of the post-Civil War presidents chose their secretaries of state, not because of broad training and experience in diplomacy, but in spite of the lack of such a background.[6] As late as the 1890s, foreign affairs were only beginning to emerge as a major concern of the federal government. The executive still largely improvised foreign policy, reacting—or overreacting—to foreign stimuli rather than consciously pursuing broad national objectives. More often than not, domestic politics determined foreign policy and copy-book maxims rather than careful analysis guided decisions. Under these circumstances it could be argued that a secretary of state needed astuteness, nerve, and luck more than formal training or experience in international diplomacy; if so, Olney in many ways was a happy choice.

In the execution of foreign policy, Cleveland ordinarily left matters in the hands of his secretary of state. Only when a problem became obviously serious or threatened to produce a domestic political crisis was he apt to intervene. Once convinced that something must be done, he discussed the situation with the men around him. Secretary Gresham complained that he had never seen the president read a book, but on the basis of "fragmentary information" picked up in conversation, "was likely, when the time came to take a position, to take it suddenly and then to adhere to it." John Bassett Moore, who also observed Cleveland's style first hand, agreed and added that the president's "remarkable good fortune had tended to confirm him in that disposition, and to give him undue confidence in his opinions."

Persuading the president to change direction was most difficult. Gresham found it "quite useless to attempt to advise him directly" on such occasions because "he never forgot anything and would remember what he had said formerly." For that reason the secretary recommended watching until the president "seemed to be inclining to views similar to your own, and then to endorse and support them, not as your own, but as his."[7] Olney's tactics in handling Cleveland, though never so explicitly spelled out, seem to have been about the same. The New Englander had certain advantages over Gresham in dealing with the president, however. He was shrewder, shared more of the president's views, and, above all, was decisive and certain where Gresham was frequently hesitant and wavering.

The contrasting styles and work methods of Olney and Gresham became evident as soon as the new secretary took over. Gresham had been friendly, easy-going, and informal. He enjoyed holding court in his shirt sleeves, receiving in his office at almost any hour congressmen, news reporters, and general visitors. Because he was careless in budgeting his work day, he consumed much time and energy in conversation. Consequently, Gresham often found it necessary to work late at his desk and complained of feeling harried and rushed—especially during his last weeks. His practice of taking newsmen into his confidence, both to learn from them and to assist them in understanding events correctly, frequently backfired. Some gentlemen of the press viciously attacked the administration's policies, using information gleaned from the secretary as ammunition.[8]

Olney, on the other hand, was brusquely courteous, businesslike, and reserved. His dress was always "beyond criticism," his surroundings neat, quiet, and in good taste. He followed a rigid daily schedule, rising early, breakfasting, and arriving at the department just as the clock struck eight—an hour ahead of most of his staff. There he and his private secretary, Walter Blandford, cleared his desk for action by nine. After checking his personal mail, Olney took up official matters for the balance of the morning. Disliking confusion of any sort, he worked alone, summoning his assistant secretaries or bureau chiefs only if the information at hand was not satisfactory. Wholly routine matters he left to his subordinates, but he closely scanned their work each day. Any state paper of consequence he drafted himself. After carefully studying the question at hand and making notes, he would summon Blandford and begin dictating. Because of his clarity of expression and precision of language, his dictation rarely needed revision or correction.

Anyone wishing to see Olney had to go through Blandford, whose duty it was to shield the secretary from those who might waste his time. Only cabinet members were allowed unrestricted entree to his office. General visitors and unscheduled callers he refused to see. Even congressmen and senators were guided to assistant secretaries or other officials. Newsmen were frozen out completely unless Olney wished to use them to publicize some matter. Thursdays he set aside to receive representatives from foreign governments, and unless urgent matters arose, Olney saw them at no other time.

Except for cabinet days (Tuesdays and Fridays when he was at the White House from ten until one or two), Olney left his desk at twelve-forty-five and walked home for lunch. Back by two, he devoted about half an hour to signing documents prepared by his staff. So that he might concentrate on these, he saw no one until finished. He then assembled the assistant secretaries and bureau chiefs for conferences on current problems facing the department. Unless a particularly pressing subject required him to take papers home at night, Olney left his desk and his work at four o'clock sharp. Except in the worst winter weather, he walked from his office in the State Department building to Capitol Hill, and from there along Massachusetts and Rhode Island Avenues to his home. This four- to five-mile walk was at top speed. Although he rarely started out alone, his companions usually dropped along the way, most finding it pointless to attempt conversation at the speed they were obliged to trot. In summer, lawn tennis, at Olney's usual furious pace, displaced the brisk walks.[9]

Evenings were reserved for relaxation—sometimes quietly at home, but more often at dinner parties or receptions. Entertaining and attending social functions were inescapable duties of his post, but Olney did more than his position required because he had the means and because he enjoyed the capital city's social life. "Olney lives in a fine house and entertains well," Postmaster General Wilson recorded in his diary. Gresham, by contrast, had lived in an apartment in the Arlington Hotel and had lacked both the wealth and the facilities for extensive party-giving. Contrary to prevailing custom, Olney's entertainments were bipartisan. Hating to be bored, the secretary himself carefully guided conversation. In mixed company he preferred the conversation of witty women to that of men and, given the choice, chatted with bright Republicans rather than unimaginative Democrats, however influential.[10] In return, Olney was entertained by prominent Republicans, including Senators Henry Cabot Lodge, Don Cameron, and others of the Henry Adams set. How the president reacted to his secretary of state's mixing socially with the enemy—and especially with the Adams clique, which he detested—can only be guessed, since nothing was ever said.[11]

Cleveland, assisted first by Gresham and then by Olney, presided over foreign policy in a difficult era. European imperialism was rampant. The great powers were reaching out—in the Transvaal, along the Upper Nile, in East Africa, East Asia, and the Eastern Mediterranean, and (at least so the Cleveland administration came to believe) in Latin

America. To frontier-conscious Americans, the underdeveloped areas of Africa, Asia, and South America offered the last opportunities on earth for exploration, conquest, settlement, and exploitation. Whenever part of this expanse fell to one of the imperial powers, it appeared to be forever closed to all other nations. Since the great powers, with the exception of France, were monarchies, the political threat that imperialism posed to the future growth of republican ideals and institutions seemed obvious to a generation steeped in the notion that only the fittest survived.

Imperialism's economic implications were also evident. When an area became a colony or came under the influence of one of the European nations, its trade and commerce passed into the hands of that power—by favor and special concession if not by law. Preemption of world markets by the powers of Europe caused great concern among a small but influential and growing segment of American opinion-shapers. This handful of intellectuals, businessmen, and politicians believed that the rapid industrial and technological development of the United States during the post-Civil War years had reached a crisis stage. America's economic establishment could now produce more goods than the domestic market could consume. The only apparent alternative to economic stagnation, long periods of depression, and possibly social upheaval, would be for the United States to dispose of those growing surpluses abroad. Underdeveloped areas seemed to offer particularly attractive markets because they would serve both as suppliers of inexpensive raw materials and as consumers of relatively more expensive manufactured goods.[12]

Accordingly, the march of European powers into the less developed areas of the world aroused among Americans a mixture of uneasiness, envy, and hostility. Increasingly the cry went up for the United States to construct more warships, expand its overseas trade, increase the work of its missionaries among the heathen, obtain coaling stations and naval bases, build a canal across Central America, and even acquire colonies. Noisy critics cursed Cleveland for a lack of backbone, charging that he too lightly accepted slights to America's honor, that he failed to take advantage of opportunities for national aggrandizement, and that he too supinely backed down, particularly to the British.

Cleveland and his second-term secretaries of state held to old-fashioned and unsophisticated views of America's role in world affairs. Their policy was bounded on the one side by Washington's admonition to avoid entanglement in the affairs of Europe and on the other by Monroe's corollary, that non-American states must not interfere in the affairs of the New World. They regarded foreign adventures and the acquisition of colonies as undesirable, inconsistent with American character, and contrary to the teachings of the Declaration of Independence and the Constitution. Since the United States had no "grand design" or "larger policy" to pursue, no alliances to maintain, and no empire to build, the functions of foreign policy were simple, few, and essentially unchanged from the past. The State Department's purpose was to maintain peace with other nations, to protect the lives, rights, and property of American citizens overseas, and to promote trade and commerce so long as the government itself remained free of entangling responsibilities or commitments. In the early 1890s most Americans probably subscribed to this limited concept of foreign policy.

Nevertheless, throughout Cleveland's second term, a jingoist faction in Congress, aided by an influential segment of the press, repeatedly tried to magnify small incidents into major foreign policy crises. The motivation of many of these men was not hard to discern. Cleveland, by successfully thwarting the annexation of Hawaii at the very beginning of his term, deeply embittered both the Republicans who sponsored the treaty and members of his own party who favored expansion. His Hawaiian "victory" doomed all hope of bipartisan support in foreign policy matters, replacing it with partisan bickering. Once the Republican-dominated Fifty-fourth Congress assembled in December 1895, tensions increased. Those who desired to launch the nation on a course of imperial ventures united with those who sought only to make political capital by embarrassing the administration and creating issues for the upcoming presidential campaign. As Postmaster General Wilson observed at the close of Cleveland's term, "These jingo senators have for most of the administration vapored first against this and then against that nation, knowing that while they were indulging their bravado, the strong and cool-headed man at the White House would protect the country from foreign quarrels."

Less easily explained was the apparent willingness of the public to be swept along on these emotional and often insubstantial binges. Especially strong responses seemed to mark every charge that an imperial power was encroaching on the Western Hemisphere in violation of the Monroe Doctrine. Wilson, even after making allowance for "political maneuvering" and the "ridiculousness" of Congress's attempts to conduct foreign affairs in a "town meeting" atmosphere, still found "the jingoism in the air . . . a curious craze and unaccountable. . . . " Perhaps, he concluded, it was "on account of the unrest of our people" and their "willingness to turn from domestic to foreign affairs . . . "[13] The postmaster general may have been right. After two years of fretting and struggling with the Panic, with monetary problems, with Coxeyites and strikers, the public may have craved other diversions. Specific foreign threats provided more obvious and satisfying targets for venting spleen than the vague forces that lay behind the nation's economic problems. Moreover, for some, the chief threat from abroad—Great Britain—was also the architect of America's domestic monetary and financial woes and so doubly worthy of hatred.

In all this, Cleveland, who worried much about the increase of "war fever" among his countrymen, pursued his essentially uncomplicated policy of avoiding both wars and such new responsibilities as colonies. He was "very vigorous in his opposition to our meddling with affairs at a distance," Gresham noted, and wanted the United States to get out of such areas as Samoa and Hawaii. He declared that if the American people "did not stay at home and attend to their own business, they would go to hell as fast as possible."[14] Whenever foreign problems arose that might justifiably give the public cause for concern, Cleveland and his secretaries of state moved quickly to settle them. The administration also tried to quiet or forestall foreign issues, genuine or false, that demagogues might use to inflame the public.

During summer recesses of Congress in both 1895 and 1896, Secretary Olney worked diligently to put irritating questions to rest before the legislative branch reassembled. When Congress was in session the administration found it necessary to outmaneuver the jingoes—sometimes by appearing to be more aggressive than their critics, sometimes by buying time, and on a few occasions by confronting their critics directly and challenging the right of Congress to meddle in foreign-policy matters. Throughout Cleveland's second term, domestic politics often lay at the root of foreign policy.

But perhaps political considerations were only a facade behind which the "real"—or economic—forces that actually shaped Cleveland's foreign policy were at work. "The key" to understanding America's behavior on the world scene after 1893, a number of prominent scholars insist, was the crisis caused by the Panic of 1893. At heart, this position attributes to Cleveland, Gresham, and Olney a much more sophisticated understanding of economics than hitherto has been suspected. All three statesmen, it is argued, saw overproduction as the cause of the panic and of the widespread unemployment that accompanied it. Depressed wages and joblessness, in turn, produced labor unrest, as in 1893 and 1894, which if not checked could lead to revolution. The solution, Cleveland, Gresham, and Olney are said to have believed, was expanded American exports to relieve the surpluses and create jobs. Acting in accord with this understanding of the problem, the administration allegedly pursued a consciously aggressive foreign policy designed to capture foreign markets for American goods, particularly in Latin America and China. The administration's handling of the Brazilian Naval Revolt (1893–94), the Corinto affair in Nicaragua (April 1895), and the onset of the Cuban Revolution (1895–97) are all interpreted as reflecting this purpose. Most important, Olney's and Cleveland's deliverances during the Venezuelan boundary dispute with Great Britain are seen as studied attempts to establish American commercial and political hegemony over the Western Hemisphere. In Asia, when the activity of other governments resulted in the loss of markets to Americans, the Cleveland administration, it has been stated, abandoned its passive policy and moved directly to assure equal access to the trade of China for American merchants.[15]

Though plausible, these conclusions rest on several unproven assumptions and a considerable straining of evidence. One unprovable assumption is that Cleveland's, Gresham's, and Olney's scattered references to economic considerations, however slight, somehow were more important and more revealing of their true concerns than their more frequent and detailed references to other factors. A serious error is the implication that Cleveland, Gresham, and Olney shared essentially similar beliefs about overproduction, the cause of labor disorders, and the importance of foreign commerce to domestic prosperity. Between 1893 and 1900 the concept that American overproduction made expanded overseas commerce indispensable spread widely and certainly reached the ears of these three men. When, and the degree to which each was influenced by that concept, however, varied considerably. That it became the basis for the foreign-policy decisions of any of them seems unlikely and is at best conjectural.

Secretary Gresham, for example, saw overproduction as the cause of growing unemployment and social unrest, and feared revolution. It is also true that he thought American production might be disposed of overseas—but not by pursuing a vigorous foreign policy. In his discussions of the problem he invariably called for tariff reductions, especially on raw materials, so that lower production costs would enable American manufacturers to compete favorably with Europeans in the markets of the world.[16] In the end, however, he saw that expanded trade offered no lasting solution to overproduction, which was a problem for all advanced nations. He feared that "with at least a dozen strong nations with a large surplus competing for the single world market," hostilities rather than prosperity would be the outcome. War between the industrial powers for control of world markets, he declared, was not the answer to surplus production. "This world-wide problem was to be solved on principles of righteousness and justice," he believed. Put bluntly, Gresham had no specific answer. As for his apocalyptic views on revolution, they were chronic with the secretary. As federal judge in Indianapolis during the 1877 railway strikes (when too extensive suffrage rather than overproduction gave him concern), he had also seen revolution and organized a vigilante-type "committee of public safety" to protect lives and property.[17]

Cleveland, much less philosophical than Gresham, was not given to speculation about the long-range outcome of anything. If he feared social revolution, he never spoke of it. Far and away the most important cause of the panic, he believed, was the government's unsound money policy. Hence, the solution lay in monetary reform, not in bold foreign-policy moves. During his second term, to be sure, he spoke on occasion of the need to expand exports so as to use up surpluses and to create jobs for the unemployed, but like Gresham, he always linked increased trade to tariff reduction. The president had long maintained that tariff reform was the key to solving a number of America's ills. During his first term he had argued that a reduced tariff would lessen the tax burden on the working classes and get rid of the embarrassing surplus of money in the federal treasury. He also argued that a lower tariff would create jobs for American workingmen by stimulating exports.[18] His assertion that a lower tariff would eliminate treasury surpluses unfortunately lost much of its appeal by 1894 when surpluses were only a memory. Thus, when Cleveland promoted the expanded-trade-for-more-jobs argument to first place, he appears to have been shifting to a stronger debating position on his favorite reform rather than revealing a penetrating new insight into the nation's economic plight. Clearly Cleveland ranked expanded trade through reduced tariffs well behind monetary reform as a cure for depression. Once the panic began in April 1893, he promptly demoted tariff revision from first priority, putting currency legislation in its place. Had he seen expanded trade as the solution, he certainly would have given tariff reduction equal billing with—if not preference to—currency reform when he called Congress into special session to deal with the crisis.

Tying Olney into the economic argument, despite his strong business connections, is especially difficult. Although he was well aware of labor unrest and saw it as part of a world-wide industrial revolution, he attributed it not to overproduction, but to the belief of working people that they were being cheated and that their governments often worked to promote the interests of their exploiters. His associations with the Lodges, the Camerons, Henry Adams, Henry White, and

Theodore Roosevelt, especially *after* the Venezuela crisis, undoubtedly exposed him to the overproduction argument (among others) for American expansion. That he was won over prior to leaving office is not at all certain. "Of course I know—or think I know—that you were 'one of us' in sentiment all along . . . , " Mrs. Cameron wrote him afterwards on the eve of the Spanish-American War.[19] But Olney's conversion to the overproduction concept was cautious and became evident only after he left office. Never did he express the notion that the depression was caused by overproduction and at no time before or during his tenure as secretary of state did he suggest that the United States should seek overseas commercial expansion to solve its domestic problems. Only *after* he left office and, interestingly enough, only after prosperity had returned, did Olney begin to speak of the need for expansion of United States commerce.[20]

Although it may seem reasonable to assume that Olney held these views earlier, he characteristically was not given to theorizing or philosophizing in advance of direct experience. His statements favoring the recognition of labor unions and compulsory arbitration of labor disputes, for example, came on the heels of the Pullman Strike, but by no means represented his thinking before or during that affair. So, too, in the matter of America's role in the world at large. He had been totally uninvolved with such matters before becoming secretary of state and there is no evidence that he held fixed ideas about them when he assumed office. However, once he had served as secretary of state and later observed the Spanish-American War and the onset of American imperialism, he temporarily changed his views and became an advocate of a more active role for the United States in world affairs.

None of this is to argue that foreign trade played no part in shaping Cleveland's foreign policy. Although not the determining factor, it was important and could hardly have been otherwise. Even if the administration had chosen to ignore overseas commerce and investments, or to leave them unprotected, American businessmen, with easy access to Congress and the press, would have found willing ears and ready tongues eager to generate public support for their cause. Nor was such concern as the Cleveland administration showed for foreign trade something new brought about by the Panic of 1893. The concern was as old as the republic itself. Almost every president and secretary of state, in good and bad years alike, expressed interest in and concern for the expansion of America's trade.

Cleveland, Gresham, and Olney believed that in a truly free and competitive world market, American merchants would be able to hold their own. All they needed, as Olney (and many others) once put it, was "a fair field and no favor." The chief deterrents to overseas commercial expansion were the American protective tariff system and the preferential and exclusionist policies of the imperial powers. Consequently, the Cleveland administration worked for tariff revision at home and for unhampered access to markets abroad.[21]

Although the administration made no effort to win special concessions overseas for American businessmen, it did resist attempts by European powers to use political influence or military pressure to block Americans from the markets of Latin America or East Asia. Even this restrained policy was a form of expansionism, some scholars argue, because with equal access to markets Americans expected to win a substantial share of the trade in question. Apparently the only way the United States could have escaped the charge of expansionism would have been for neither American businessmen nor the government to have raised objections at being excluded from these markets by the political maneuvering of European powers. The issue of colonialism is handled similarly by the same scholars. To them, the refusal of the Cleveland administration either to annex Hawaii or to intervene in the Cuban Revolution was not due to anti-imperialism. Rather, it was imperialism in a new form. Cleveland and his advisors pursued a course of "anti-colonial imperialism" in a quest for "informal empire."[22] Since nonannexation of Hawaii and nonintervention in Cuba were as surely "expansionist" as annexation or intervention would have been, the Cleveland administration by definition simply could not have been anti-imperialistic. By the same token, such all-inclusive definitions become useless as tools in trying to understand or analyze the conduct of foreign policy by the Cleveland administration.

A more accurate though less novel appraisal of policy in the 1890s would be that American overseas economic interests were expanding rapidly and that the Cleveland administration welcomed that expansion and stood ready to protect it from undue harassment. To insist that the administration actively and calculatingly promoted expanded trade in order to solve a growing domestic economic crisis, and that it consciously tried to evict the European powers from the Western Hemisphere while holding open the doors of Asia in order to capture the markets of those areas for American exploitation, overstates the case and is inconsistent with the known beliefs and behavior of Cleveland and his principal advisers.

Prior to becoming secretary of state, Olney was involved in one major foreign policy question: what to do about Hawaii. In the dying days of the Harrison administration, American and European planters in Hawaii had revolted against the native queen, Liliuokalani. In the course of the bloodless coup, the American minister to the islands, John L. Stevens, ordered a detachment of marines from the American naval base at Pearl Harbor into Honolulu, allegedly to protect the lives and property of United States citizens. Taking this as proof of American support, the rebels occupied the government buildings, announced the deposition of the queen, and established a provisional regime that Stevens promptly recognized as the legitimate government of Hawaii. The queen, thinking that the marines were supporting the revolt, yielded up authority under protest and called upon the president of the United States to see justice done. Stevens ran up the American flag and proclaimed Hawaii a protectorate of the United States while representatives of the provisional government went to Washington to draw up a treaty of annexation. In due course the treaty was submitted to the Senate for ratification, but because of the imminent inauguration of Cleveland, was delayed.[23]

One of Cleveland's first acts as president was to withdraw the treaty and to send James H. Blount as his special commissioner to investigate fully "the conditions of affairs in the Hawaiian Islands, the causes of the revolution by which the Queen's Government was overthrown, the sentiment of the people toward existing authority," and anything else that might "enlighten the President" on affairs in the islands. Blount promptly ordered the lowering of the American flag at Honolulu and sent the marines who patroled the city back to their barracks. A few weeks later he forwarded his findings to Washington. But for the encouragement of Minister Stevens (an ardent advocate of annexation), he concluded, the planters would not have revolted when they did. The presence of the marines convinced the queen that resistance was useless, so, appealing to the president, she had stepped down. As for the native Hawaiians, they overwhelmingly opposed annexation.[24]

By mid-September, Secretary Gresham had digested the report and begun to formulate his policy. Like the president, Gresham tended to jump to conclusions on the basis of broad moral judgments rather than careful analysis. Since the United States, through the improper acts of Stevens, had deprived the queen of her throne, he reasoned, the obvious course dictated by honor was for the United States to restore the queen and to withdraw. Apparently he believed that the provisional government existed solely at the sufferance of the United States and would crumble if that support were withdrawn. His plan was to send a new minister to the islands to demand that the provisional government render authority back to the queen. If necessary, troops would again be marched into Honolulu. Gresham doubted that the planter element would resist with arms.[25]

According to Gresham's wife, the secretary's policy grew out of his inherent sense of chivalry and justice. "A woman in trouble, my husband would certainly side with her against the power, greed, and lust of man. . . . " She was pleased that some commentators likened her husband's course less to diplomacy than to the ruling of a judge in equity. "[H]e believed that there was such a thing as public morality, [and] that 'right and justice' should govern the conduct of nations the same as that of individuals. . . . "[26]

Gresham clearly acted from a sense of duty in a situation in which he believed the United States had perpetrated a wrong. He adamantly opposed any acquisition of territory outside the continental bounds of the United States and regarded the attempt to annex Hawaii as a corrupt fraud, based on the greed and selfishness of the planters and their allies and completely opposed by the native Hawaiians. Even if he favored expansion, he told one critic, he was "unalterably opposed to stealing territory, or of annexing a people against their consent, and the people of Hawaii do not favor annexation." Were the islands tendered "with the consent of the *inhabitants,* the question would be quite different from the one we are now dealing with."[27]

On 6 October, the Hawaiian question was broached at a cabinet meeting. The president apparently shared Gresham's views as to the demands of chivalry, right, and honor. Olney, who until then had not been involved, was troubled that the president and secretary of state were proposing to restore the queen with little or no concern for the practical difficulties or possible consequences that might follow. Accordingly he wrote a carefully reasoned letter to Gresham, urging caution. Olney accepted the legal and moral conclusions of Cleveland and Gresham, but pointed out that righting the obvious wrong done by Minister Stevens would not be simple.

If the queen, dethroned by a show of force, could be "reinstated by a like exhibition of force without actual resort to it," there could be little complaint. But the "Stevens Government" had been in authority "with our acquiescence for many months," it had full possession of Hawaii and its resources, had received the revenues and collected taxes, and had administered justice and enforced laws. In effect, the provisional government had generally exercised "all the functions of a legitimate Government." It was possible that the planter regime could be displaced "only by actual force and after more or less loss of life and destruction of property."

Olney raised three objections to the use of force to restore the queen. "[H]owever righteous the cause," the attempt would be an act of war "beyond the President's constitutional power." To return to the queen a land torn by war, with its property devastated and its population decimated and alienated, would be "but a poor substitute" for the peaceful kingdom wrested from her. Finally, there was the problem of public support for the provisional government both in the United States and Hawaii. That a large number of Americans supported the regime was evident. Should the same be true of Hawaiians, the administration might find itself sacrificing the interests of the Hawaiian people to those of the queen and her dynasty. We had "no right," Olney declared, "to redeem the original wrong by the commission of another still greater wrong, to wit, the imposition upon Hawaii of a Government not wanted by its people. . . . " He raised these points, not because he expected armed resistance to anything that the United States might do in Hawaii, but because "it is the unexpected that proverbially happens in politics," and he did not want the administration to act without taking into consideration "every contingency however remote."

What if the queen, he asked, when restored, attempted to punish those who had engaged in the revolution? After all, the provisional government, however illegitimate in origin, was the lawful government of Hawaii and had been so recognized by the United States and other nations. Since it governed "by the consent of all parties," its acts should be recognized as binding and its officials ought to be exempted from punishment or loss of rights and property in consequence of their official actions. The honor of the United States was as fully involved "in securing justice and fair play" for those men as in restoring the queen. "It must ever be remembered," he said, "that the Stevens Government is our Government; that it was set up by our Minister by the aid of our naval and military forces and was accorded the protection of our flag; and that whatever be the views of this Administration, its predecessor practically sanctioned everything Minister Stevens took upon himself to do."

Olney recommended that the United States make every diplomatic effort to restore the queen by "peaceful methods and without force." If that failed and force proved necessary, the matter should be referred to Congress which alone had power to declare war. The United States, as a condition of attempting the restoration, should require that the queen give it "full power and authority" to negotiate "such reasonable terms and conditions as the United States may approve and find to be practicable." Among those terms, Olney insisted, must be "full pardon and amnesty" for all those in the present government of Hawaii. With these conditions fully understood by all, Olney believed that the confidence of all parties would be won and the affair could be settled satisfactorily.[28]

"I do not mind saying to you," Olney wrote his daughter, "that the letter was timely and I think kept the Administration from making a serious mistake."[29] Olney influenced the president, not Secretary Gresham. On 18 October Gresham set forth his recommendations. The treaty of annexation should not be resubmitted to the Senate and the United States should restore the queen. "Our Government was the first to recognize the independence of the Islands and it should be the last to acquire sovereignty over them by force or fraud," he declared.[30] He did not say how the queen was to be restored, whether force should be used, or whether the United States should concern itself with the fate of officials of the provisional government. At a cabinet meeting that day, Olney, Carlisle, and "perhaps others" openly raised the points in Olney's letter. Whatever steps the United States took to restore the queen, the cabinet concluded, care was to be taken to protect the rights and interests of American citizens and others who had joined in the revolt "in reliance upon the United States as apparently represented by its Minister, Mr. Stevens."[31]

After the meeting, Gresham dictated instructions to Albert S. Willis, the new minister to Hawaii. The treaty of annexation would not be returned to the Senate and Willis was to convey to the queen the president's "sincere regret" at Minister Stevens's "reprehensible conduct," and to assure her that the United States would "undo the flagrant wrong" done her government. The balance of the instruction reflected Olney's influence. The president, Gresham declared, expected the queen, when reinstated, to grant full amnesty to those who had participated in the revolution. They were to be deprived of no rights or privileges enjoyed prior to the revolution, and all obligations undertaken by the provisional government were to be assumed by her government. When the queen agreed to those conditions, Willis was to advise the provisional government that the president was determined to restore the queen and that he expected that government promptly to relinquish authority to her. If either party refused, Willis was to report and await further instructions.[32]

Olney's letter and Gresham's instruction contained two notable features. Neither showed concern for the economic, commercial, or strategic importance of the islands to the United States, but both assumed that the United States had the right to determine the settlement. The document by which the queen had surrendered and appealed to the president to see justice done, the two men agreed, justified the contemplated intervention. When the provisional government accepted the queen's surrender on those terms, it too, in effect, had agreed to submit the matter to the president for final disposition.[33]

This legalism was undone by the attitudes of both parties in Hawaii. When Willis met with the queen and advised her of the conditions attached to her restoration, she replied that the rebels "should be beheaded and their property confiscated. . . . " Willis at once cabled Washington that the queen's views were "so extreme as to require further instructions."[34] Gresham replied that "amnesty and recognition of obligations of the provisional government" were "essential conditions of restoration." If the queen refused to agree in writing, she was to be told that the president would discontinue his efforts on her behalf.[35]

The queen's intransigence prevented Cleveland from reporting to Congress in his annual message that the Hawaiian question was on the way to settlement. Instead, he reported that he was attempting to "undo the wrong that had been done . . . and to restore as far as practicable" conditions to what they had been prior to "our forcible intervention." He promised to inform Congress as soon as definite results were reached.[36]

During the next two weeks, the administration's hopes for resolving matters collapsed completely—both in Hawaii and in Washington. On 9 December, Willis wrote from Honolulu, raising a number of knotty questions not adequately covered by his instructions. Should the queen, when restored, be advised not to tamper with the Constitution of 1887 which gave the planters considerable influence in the Hawaiian government? It had been her attempts to revoke that constitution and to supplant whites with native advisers that led to the revolution in 1893. A similar move by her in the future would provoke a like response, Willis feared. Having once expected the grateful queen to name leaders of the revolution, who before the troubles had been officials in the queen's government, to important posts in the restored government, Willis now asked to what posts, if any, these men should be appointed. The queen had called for their heads and even Willis questioned whether the post of justice on Hawaii's highest court should be given back to Dole or be declared vacant considering Dole's part in overturning the queen. These and like questions pointedly illustrated how right Olney had been when he suggested that restoring the *status quo ante* would not be easy.[37]

After further conferences with Willis, the queen capitulated and signed a document granting amnesty to the revolutionaries and assuming all lawful obligations of the provisonal government. Willis then approached the provisional government, only to be told that the president of the United States had no right to interfere in the domestic affairs of Hawaii. Only by request of the lawful government—that is, the planter regime—or by conquest, could Cleveland intercede. The planters thereupon prepared to defend themselves by arming their supporters and sandbagging public buildings.[38]

As yet unaware of developments in Hawaii, the administration in Washington wrestled with the full report of Willis's first interview with the queen, which had just arrived. Her vengeful attitude gave the president "much anxiety," and he decided to lay the whole matter before Congress. Cleveland asked Gresham to draft a special message and the secretary, in turn, asked John Bassett Moore to assist him. The Gresham-Moore draft in effect recommended that the administration press on rather than give up, and suggested that Cleveland report to Congress that he was "attempting to effect such an arrangement between the Queen and the leaders of the revolution as would afford security to all, without the exclusion of any party from the Government." Although he used a few passages from the draft in his message, Cleveland rejected the recommendation and asked Olney to try his hand at preparing the message. In the end, Cleveland relied heavily, though not exclusively, on Olney's draft.[39]

Olney believed that the United States would do well to wash its hands of the whole affair and leave the queen and provisional government to work out their own salvation. He proposed reporting the queen's unreasonableness and submitting the matter to Congress "for such action, *if any*, consonant with the obvious merits of the case, as its wisdom may advise and its more extended powers may render practicable."[40] Cleveland, unwilling to suggest that Congress do nothing, simply commended the matter "to the extended powers and wide discretion of the Congress," and offered to cooperate "in any legislative plan . . . consistent with American honor, integrity and morality" that it might devise.[41]

Turning the matter over to Congress was a blunder that resulted in much partisan strife in Congress and devisive bickering within the Democratic party. After a flurry of recriminating debate, the House passed a resolution endorsing the president's course, but proposing nothing more. The Senate explored the relative merits of imperialism and nonimperialism for months without reaching positive conclusions. Meanwhile, the Foreign Relations Committee of the Senate published extensive testimony, much of it friendly to annexation, and a set of conclusions over which the committee was badly split. The Hawaiian debates effectively destroyed for some time to come the ability of

Congress to view foreign-policy questions on their merit rather than as party issues.[42]

Meanwhile, in the islands, the provisional government gave way to a republic. Liliuokalani abdicated and the Cleveland administration made its peace with the new planter regime. In 1894 the Wilson Tariff restored prosperity to Hawaii by ending a special bounty previously paid to domestic sugar producers and admitting Hawaiian sugar to the mainland duty-free. When an attempted royalist revolt was suppressed in January 1895, Secretary Gresham found it necessary to intervene to protect the lives of American citizens involved on the losing side.[43] Aside from minor incidents, American relations with the Republic remained peaceful until the United States quietly annexed the islands during the war with Spain.

The Hawaiian episode confirmed Olney's belief that foreign policy could not be formulated solely on the basis of abstract justice, right, and honor. Practical considerations had to be reckoned with and every possible consequence, however remote, evaluated. The experience also taught Olney that however intractable a foreign question became, turning it over to Congress was no solution. Picking out Gresham's shortcomings was easy. As secretary of state, Olney would make mistakes of his own.

12

A Heady Summer

As Secretary of State, Olney fell heir to a number of unresolved problems that Gresham, for reasons of temperament or perhaps illness, had allowed to drift. With characteristic vigor, the new secretary set to work to clear up two matters in particular that had dragged on for decades and upon which Congress had recently passed resolutions demanding action: the disputed boundary between British Guiana and Venezuela, and the Mora claim against Spain. Concluding that both had long since reached the stage for settlement, Olney decided to inform the two powers of the exact position and precise demands of the United States, to insist upon prompt responses within fixed time limits, and to indicate that nothing less than conclusive settlements along lines he prescribed would be acceptable. During June he drafted a formal note to London, calling for submission of the boundary dispute to arbitration, and opened informal correspondence with the Spanish minister to Washington, demanding immediate payment of the Mora claim.

In July, Olney retreated to Falmouth for the summer, leaving an old State Department hand, Assistant Secretary Alvey A. Adee, in charge in Washington. One minor crisis after another plagued the department in Olney's absence: harassment of American citizens in Cuba, massacres of Armenians and attacks on missionary stations in Turkey, and antiforeign riots in China. Adee, who initiated action in the first incident, quickly learned that Olney never really trusted anyone to act in his stead. Reprimanded by the secretary, Adee thereafter was careful to consult with Olney in advance on everything. "Although Mr. Olney is not in the State Department building," one underling wrote, "nothing is permitted to be issued from it without his approval, and both the wires and postal car are kept busy conveying from Washington to East Falmouth a detailed statement of the conduct of foreign affairs."[1]

Of all the affairs that summer, the note to Britain overshadowed all else. By year's end it produced the most serious breach in Anglo-American relations since the Civil War. Studied in isolation, the Venezuela incident has given rise to elaborate explanations of Olney's purpose. In the context of other matters that he tackled with similar directness that first summer in office, Olney's motives appear somewhat less complicated.

The claim of Antonio Maximo Mora, for example, had run against Spain for a quarter-century. In 1870, during a revolt in Cuba, Spanish officials had court-martialed Mora in absentia, condemning the wealthy landowner to death and ordering confiscation of his estates. Mora, who meanwhile had fled to the United States, had become a naturalized citizen. Since Spain was barred by treaty from alienating the property of American citizens in Cuba, the State Department filed a claim. In 1873 the king of Spain pardoned the planter and ordered restoration of his lands. For one reason and another, the estates were never returned; some were sold, the rest laid waste. Under pressure from the United States, Spain in 1886 agreed to quiet the claim by a cash settlement of $1,500,000. Because Mora had contributed heavily to the rebel cause, however, sentiment in Spain remained adamant against payment. A long, unproductive exchange of courteous diplomatic notes followed. As State Department folios slowly filled, Spain stalled payment for a decade.[2]

The day after taking office, Olney instructed Hannis Taylor, the United States minister at Madrid, to press for immediate partial payment of the Mora claim and to arrange a schedule for future payments.[3] Relishing his assignment, Taylor, two days after receiving the instruction, reported that he had talked with the foreign minister and wished now to be armed "with the moral power to coerce" Spain. With a new rebellion raging in Cuba, he suggested, a mere hint that the United States might relax its vigil against gun-running to the island (not to mention possible recognition of the rebels) would provide the needed leverage to effect settlement.[4]

Notwithstanding Taylor's zeal, Olney took matters into his own hands. If Spain did not promptly pay the Mora claim—a "long-standing grievance and source of irritation"—Olney warned the Spanish minister, Enrique Dupuy de Lôme, the United States would be obliged to determine the course called for by "its honor and interest and the due protection of its citizens." Since the matter was beyond all discussion of possible merits, offsets, or conditions, only "speedy actual payment" would "satisfy the situation." Lightly masking the threat suggested by Taylor, Olney observed that payment would indicate Spain's reciprocation of the good faith shown by the United States in discharging its obligations with respect to the Cuban revolt. It would also prove that the rebellion had not crippled Spain's economy.[5]

Meanwhile, the Spanish council in Madrid authorized payment of the claim in full. Details, however, were to be worked out by the foreign ministry.[6] Negotiations snagged when de Lôme reversed himself on the issue of interest since 1886, when Spain first acknowledged the obligation. Having previously agreed to defer that question until the principal was paid, de Lôme now insisted that it be resolved first. Sensing that postponement might again prove fatal, Olney loosed his vitriolic pen. "A careful perusal" of the minister's latest "purport[ed]" reply to the demands of the United States only confirmed the suspicion that Spain was stalling, Olney said. He would "not stop to note various inaccuracies" that had "inadvertently, of course," crept into de Lôme's "recital of facts," because they were immaterial. The "elaborate argumentation" in which de Lôme indulged, "while interesting in itself," only served "to demonstrate the weakness of the contention" that required "the exercise of so much ingenuity in its support."

The truth of the matter being "too plain for discussion," Olney declined to "waste any more words upon it." He demanded explicit answers to two questions: Would Spain pay the $1,500,000 at once, setting aside the matter of interest for the time being, and would the money, when and if paid, be in American gold dollars or their equivalent? If he did not receive a reply within one week, Olney said, or if the reply did not conform to requirements that he laid down, nothing would remain but for him to report to the president that his "conciliatory efforts" to collect the indebtedness had failed and that it was for the president "to resort to such other means" for collecting the claim "as he may deem expedient."[7]

Eight days later, de Lôme and Olney signed a memorandum providing for payment in full, in gold, on or before 15 September. Payment was made on schedule, but de Lôme did not allow Olney's insulting communications to go unchallenged. In twenty-seven years of diplomatic service, he declared, he had never seen negotiations "conducted in less friendly terms," nor had he encountered letters like Olney's. From the first the secretary assumed "not the position of Counsel for the United States but of Judge, although only details were contested." Each of the notes, de Lôme complained, contained "a threat and an ultimatum totally unnecessary . . . . "[8] The rebuff paid off because it won Olney's respect. He and de Lôme became friends and worked closely together to suppress violations of American neutrality laws during the Cuban insurrection.

As Olney left office in March 1897, he drafted one of the few apologies of his career:

> Some things occurred in the earliest days of our intercourse for which I have always felt I owed you an apology. They arose partly no doubt from natural infirmity of disposition, partly from newness to a position for which I was unprepared, & into which I was thrust against my will & partly from complete misconception of the character of the person with whom I had to deal. I am under obligation to you for not permitting those incidents to embarrass our subsequent relations, which have, I believe, been as open & cordial as it is possible for the representatives of two governments to maintain.

Whether Olney sent the letter is not known.[9]

In late July, Assistant Secretary Adee apparently panicked over anticipated troubles in Havana. Telegrams from the brothers of two Cuban-born naturalized American citizens, jailed in Cuba for alleged revolutionary activities, warned that the prisoners were in great danger. The Havana Volunteers—a militant group loyal to Spain—were about to hold a massive parade and demand execution of the jailed men. Adee, remembering that similar groups in the previous Cuban revolt had forced drumhead trials and summary executions, believed that the 1895 volunteers were equally dangerous and doubted that Spanish authorities would resolutely resist their demands.

With both the president and Olney on vacation, Adee conferred with Secretary of the Navy Herbert. The two concluded that a warship should be sent to Havana to insure the safety of Americans there. Their chief misgiving was that a single warship might provoke rather than overawe the volunteers and lead to an incident. Adee wired Olney, outlining the bare facts and stating his and Herbert's belief that a warship should be sent.[10] Olney agreed. The *Atlanta* next day sailed into a festive harbor. The volunteers had called off their parade, and the city was celebrating the Queen Regent's birthday. Dressing his ship with appropriate flags, the *Atlanta's* commander exchanged the salutes and formal visits prescribed by protocol, and left.[11]

Olney was more than a little annoyed. He had not been impressed with the seriousness of the case and suggested that Adee had not given "sufficient weight" to the fact that the fears of relatives, "even if genuine," were probably exaggerated, nor to the "strong probability" that their alarm was "largely artificial." The rebels and their sympathizers, he observed, were "seizing with avidity upon every possible opportunity of prejudicing Spain in the eyes of the people of the United States." Similarly, Olney had not shared Herbert's fears that the *Atlanta's* appearance might antagonize the volunteers. Such hostile feelings as existed were not against the United States government, "whose earnest and friendly efforts to fulfill its neutral obligations" were appreciated, but were "mainly against Cubans whose treacherous combinations against their own government derive more or less immunity from their masquerading as naturalized citizens of the United States." He approved sending the ship only because Adee possibly had information that he did not and because Secretary Herbert seemed to agree. Olney was displeased that Adee had conferred with Herbert in the first place. Herbert could not have refused the request for advice without appearing discourteous, and once given, Olney had to "fall in" with it or seem to attach little value to a colleague's views. If, despite existing facilities for communication, the department could not be "satisfactorily run" while he was on vacation, Olney declared, he would return to Washington rather than impose on other cabinet members.[12]

Even as Olney polished the Venezuela note and pushed for settlement of the Mora claim, trouble arose in another quarter. Periodically the Turks unleashed their pent-up hostility against the Christian nations that hovered like vultures over their sick empire by assaulting isolated Western missionary stations and perpetrating massacres of Armenians within the Ottoman Empire. Each such incident brought demands in Europe and the United States for intervention to protect the missions and other Western interests, and to save the Armenians. Throughout the summer of 1895, such demands poured in upon Olney.[13] On 4 August, the ultimatum to de Lôme just mailed, Olney asked Adee if the claims against Turkey were in such shape that "a demand that must be attended to" could be made. If so, he was prepared to give "proper instructions" to the United States minister at Constantinople and was certain that the president would back him with as much force as might be needed. Deciding that the time was not yet ripe, Olney contented himself with maneuvering American warships in Turkish waters so as to afford such protection to Americans as was possible.[14]

Two instances of antiforeign rioting in China caused similar problems. The first, at the end of May 1895, occurred at Chengtu, in Szechuan Province, a thousand miles from the sea. No lives were taken, but considerable damage was done to mission properties and all foreigners—including twenty-five Americans—were driven from the area. In early August, a bloodier uprising at Kutien—about a hundred miles north of the seaport of Foochow—resulted in the deaths of ten British subjects and injury to an American woman.[15]

Learning of the Chengtu riot, Charles Denby, the United States minister to Peking, asked an American missionary to join a proposed British commission that was to investigate the incident. In a report to Washington, Denby attributed the outbursts to the connivance of high local officials who were never punished by the Chinese government for the outrages, and to the need of the Chinese for the employment created when their government was forced to rebuild the facilities. To end the disorders, Denby recommended that the Western powers announce their intention to use gunboats to batter down towns where rioting occurred. For places like Chengtu, well beyond the reach of gunboats, reprisal would be taken against localities nearer at hand.[16]

Adee forwarded the dispatch to Falmouth, noting that in international practice, threats to bombard were common when dealing with "savage tribes," but were not ordinarily issued to "an ostensibly organized and responsible government." A few days later the acting secretary notified Denby that his proposal had been rejected, but "without prejudice" to possible later instructions.[17] Olney, meanwhile, hastily undertook to educate himself on Chinese matters, sending to the department for Arthur H. Smith's *Chinese Characteristics* and Chester Holcombe's *The Real Chinaman*.[18]

Knowing—as Denby could not—that the Venezuelan note might well strain relations with Britain, Olney and Adee were not enthusiastic about the joint commission to Chengtu. They sanctioned it only because it appeared to be a fait accompli. As for Kutien, Adee instructed Denby to limit cooperation with Britain to what was absolutely necessary to protect American interests, and to name a wholly American commission to investigate the disorders.[19]

When American missionaries in China objected to the United States tagging along on a British commission to Chengtu, Denby withdrew and sent for permission to appoint an American commission. Confused by the switch, the department instructed him to stick with the original plan. A British decision not to investigate ended that plan.[20] Meanwhile, an independent French investigation confirmed Denby's suspicions that the viceroy of Szechuan, Liu Ping-chang, had been involved in the rioting. Denby at once demanded that Liu be degraded and barred from ever again holding public office, and that his offenses and punishments be published in the *Peking Gazette* as a warning to others. The Chinese government's refusal led Denby to call on Washington for support. Unwilling to press demands on the basis of the French findings, Adee instructed Denby to send a three-man American commission—with escort—overland from Tientsin, near Peking, to Chengtu, a journey of well over a thousand miles.[21]

Efforts of the Tsungli yamen (China's Foreign Office) to block the commissions to Chengtu and Kutien failed, despite arguments that no Americans had been killed, that five Chinese implicated at Kutien were already under arrest, that stringent orders had been sent to all viceroys to protect Christian missionaries, and that the Chinese government had sent no such commission to investigate recent killings of Chinese laborers in the United States. The State Department insisted that if China would not cooperate, the commission to Chengtu would proceed on its own. If suitable escort were not provided, Denby warned, he would recommend that United States marines accompany the mission. Unable to prevent either expedition, the Tsungli yamen stalled, quibbling over the rank of the commissioners going to Kutien, and in a final bid to lessen the impact of the proposed parade into the heart of the empire, suggested that the Chengtu commission go by river rather than by land. Olney stood firm. Although the overland route would be "more fatiguing" and unwelcome to China, it would provide a "demonstration . . . of the utmost importance to us."[22]

In a review of Chinese matters, Olney informed Denby that the department had gone along with the joint commission to Chengtu until the "alarming occurrences at Kutien" forced reconsideration. The large number of American missionary stations in Szechuan and neighboring provinces made "a more impressive demonstration" of American power "expedient." China's repeated efforts to thwart the investigation served only to convince Olney of the need for a display that would leave no doubt in the minds of Chinese officials or peasants "that the United States Government" was "an effective factor in securing due rights for Americans resident in China." Chengtu was "the crucial test," and the department would push the matter to "a successful conclusion" on the assumption that if the determination of the United States to protect the lives and property of its citizens were conspicuously manifested, there would probably be no occasion to repeat the performance.[23]

Under simultaneous pressure from the Americans, the British (who sent a fleet), and the French to punish all guilty parties at Chengtu, China capitulated. Denby cabled results: "Six criminals executed Chengtu; thirteen punished—banished, imprisonment, bambooing." Three days later he reported that Liu had been permanently deprived of all offices and that others would be punished soon. By its stand,

Denby boasted, the United States had set in motion events that assured a new era "in the treatment of foreigners in China." Although China met all demands of the United States at Chengtu, the commission set out. Following its return and report, the United States demanded and collected from China over $16,000 in damages.[24]

Meanwhile, at Kutien, convicted rioters appealed to the American commission for clemency. Neither Denby nor Olney approved. The law should be allowed to run its course, Denby believed, because clemency, "in the Chinese view," was weakness. "If under Chinese law a certain number of murderers ought to be decapitated, a certain number ought to be strangled, and still others to be banished for life, I incline to the opinion that it is better for England and the United States to stand by and see these penalties inflicted. It is severe, perhaps, but the crime was terrible." Only if Queen Victoria recommended clemency should Cleveland consider it.[25]

Olney's objections were different in character. The "real purpose" of the commission was to secure first-hand information to support a demand for the punishment of high officials who were guilty of "culpable neglect of duty." The United States would not measure justice "by the number of decapitations which may ensue," nor would it "rest satisfied with the infliction of punishment upon humble actors in the outrages." Adequate "chastisement and reparation for actual injuries" would be required, but the "chief and higher aim" was to prevent the recurrence of injuries by holding the Chinese government and its agents responsible for taking necessary "precautionary measures."[26]

After the Kutien riot, the commander of United States naval forces in Asiatic waters inquired if missionaries ought not be moved temporarily from the interior to the treaty ports for protection. Bowing to Denby's "better knowledge of affairs," Olney left the decision to him. The minister thought the proposal unwise. Because missionaries were scattered throughout China, it was impossible to know the forces at work in the remote local areas where they were stationed. To advise them to abandon their homes and work might result in "an exodus of hundreds of men, women and children under the most distressing circumstances." To advise them to stay could result in the loss of life and property. Since the missionaries knew best the conditions where they were, Denby favored leaving the decision to them.

His motives ran deeper. To suggest moving would be to "confess weakness," he warned. The Chinese would soon learn that they could induce an exodus at any time by simply rioting. The solution lay in the construction of railroads into the interior. Once "the first great railroad in China" was open, "the strange anomaly" of allowing missionaries to settle in the interior and to engage in such occupations as medicine, teaching, and manufacturing in industrial schools, while denying similar privileges to merchants and professional men, would disappear, he predicted.[27] Denby's chief concern was keeping open the China market. Olney's was not. He raised no objections to Denby's views, but protecting the lives and property of Americans living and traveling in foreign countries was his first duty.

Taken together, Olney's actions in the summer of 1895 indicated nothing more complex than a desire to get matters settled promptly, a general unwillingness to trust others to handle important problems, and a naive assumption that straight talk and a show of determination of themselves would turn the trick. Olney, all told, had had a heady summer. Harsh words and an ultimatum had ended diddling over the Mora claim. Shows of force in the Eastern Mediterranean and in China had slowed attacks on American interests in those areas. From his private secretary in Washington came word that news correspondents were speaking favorably of Olney's conduct of the department. Contrasting his "prompt action to the non-action of former administrations," the reporters were particularly impressed with Olney's handling of the Mora claim and his swift moves to protect American citizens abroad, especially in Cuba. Had Olney remained in the department a few years more, one man later commented, "he would have got the docket cleared for once."[28]

In his annual message in December, it was evident that the president was pleased with the summer's work. "The energetic steps" taken in China were "likely to result in future safety to our citizens there"; the presence of warships off the coast of Turkey would "afford opportunities" to gather information about conditions in that country and "enable us to take suitable steps for the protection of any interests of our countrymen within reach of our ships. . . . " The "longstanding demand of Antonio Maximo Mora against Spain" had "at last been settled." No doubt Cleveland had hoped to report that Britain had agreed to arbitration of the long-standing boundary dispute with Venezuela. Because the London government failed to reply within the time stipulated by Olney, the president could only report that Olney's note had been sent and that when the reply, which was "expected shortly," arrived, "further communication" would "probably be made to Congress."[29]

The Venezuelan controversy had begun to trouble the Cleveland administration seriously about three months before Olney became secretary of state. Three closely interwoven developments between August 1894 and March 1895 had brought the issue to the fore: (1) propagandizing by William L. Scruggs, one-time United States minister to Caracas, who had been employed by Venezuela to lobby on her behalf in Washington; (2) increasing efforts by Republican leaders, abetted by the jingoist press and a handful of "patriotic" Democrats, to make British "aggressions" in Latin America a major political issue; and (3) a growing suspicion within the administration itself about the motives behind recent British moves in the Western Hemisphere.

Scruggs had been particularly successful. He had written, published, and widely distributed a pamphlet entitled *British Aggressions in Venezuela, or The Monroe Doctrine on Trial,* the burden of which was that in defiance of the Monroe Doctrine, Britain was using the boundary dispute to cloak encroachments against Venezuela. Once England obtained possession of land at the mouth of the Orinoco River, Scruggs warned, she would control the commerce and ultimately the political life of the northern quarter of South America. The lobbyist for Venezuela also skillfully converted an innocuous announcement in the president's annual message—that he intended to renew efforts to bring about arbitration of the boundary dispute—into the resolution urging action that Congress had adopted in February without a dissenting vote.[30]

Agitation over British activities in the New World, much of it politically motivated, swelled in Congress during January and February. Then, in March, Senator Lodge blasted "Our Blundering Foreign Policy," in *Forum.* Cleveland, who longed for the session's end on 4 March, enjoyed no respite after Congress adjourned.[31] In the June *North American Review,* Lodge warned that if the administration failed to take steps to uphold the Monroe Doctrine, it would be "the duty and the privilege of the next Congress to see that this is done."[32] Meanwhile, Senators Lodge, John T. Morgan of Alabama, William M. Stewart of Nevada, and others, steadily fed statements to the press, calling upon the administration to defend American interests from the British. Even less welcome to the president was the prospect of the Republican-dominated Fifty-fourth Congress that would assemble in December. Cleveland and his advisers knew that in that final session before the 1896 presidential campaign, Republicans and anti-administration Democrats alike would leave no stone unturned in their quest for issues.[33] If further harassment were to be avoided, the administration would somehow have to defuse the British question before December.

Concern over England's behavior was not limited to the jingo press and enemies of the administration. Even to the president and members of his official family, it seemed that Britain was on the march all around the world—in South Africa, in the Sudan, in Siam, in China, in the Pacific, and perhaps even in the New World. Britain was known to be strengthening her bases in the Caribbean, and Secretary Gresham believed that she had given aid to the rebels who had tried to restore monarchy in Brazil in 1893–94.[34] A quarrel with Nicaragua in March 1895 led Britain to threaten to occupy the Pacific coast port of Corinto unless the Central American republic came to terms. Despite United States efforts to forestall a take-over, British forces seized Corinto on 27 April and held the town until 3 May, much to the outrage of the American press.[35] Because the deepening Anglo-Venezuelan dispute possibly fit into a larger pattern, Olney, still attorney general and busy with the income tax and *Debs* cases, took time "to beat the tomtom" in the matter. In April, dispatches from London disturbed the president. Not only did Britain refuse to initiate a restoration of relations with Venezuela, she introduced what seemed to Cleveland a bold new assertion. Only if Venezuela first surrendered a substantial portion of the territory in question (including land at the mouth of the Orinoco, Bayard pointed out) would Britain agree to submit the balance to arbitration.[36] This condition appeared to confirm Scruggs's charge that Britain had her eye on mastery of the Orinoco Valley.

Given the growing jingoism across the country and in Congress, Cleveland and Gresham concluded even before the April dispatches that the Venezuelan question was most dangerous. If not resolved, Venezuela might well be goaded into war with Britain. In that event, adherence to the Monroe Doctrine would force the United States to take up arms to prevent alienation of American territory by a European power.[37] The administration decided to bring matters to a head with Britain, short of war. That decision would not be executed as long as Gresham was secretary of state. Wavering indecisively, he asserted in March that Britain's position in Venezuela was "contradictory and palpably unjust."[38] Under the coaching of the pro-British American ambassador to London, Thomas F. Bayard, and Professor John Bassett Moore, a frequent adviser to the State Department, Gresham reversed himself by mid-April. Accusing the Venezuelan government of trying "to dump the controversy on us," he concluded that the Latin republic had "better settle, if she can," on terms offered by Britain.[39]

In the final weeks of Gresham's life, the administration was preparing new steps to bring the controversy to arbitration. The State Department urged Venezuela to restore relations with Britain, pledging in return to make "earnest endeavor" to induce Britain to submit the territorial question in its entirety to judgment by an impartial tribunal.[40] A new note to Britain was also contemplated. Because the secretary of state was ill, Cleveland asked Olney to begin a draft. Gresham, meanwhile, laid plans to examine—with Moore's assistance— the merits of the dispute and to inform Venezuela of the findings. Then a firm note, but one that would not contain an ultimatum such as Olney later used, would be sent to Britain.[41] Gresham's plans for resolving the problem died with him at the end of May.

As soon as Olney was named secretary of state, he undertook a thorough examination of the Venezuelan controversy. He had much to learn, knowing little about Venezuela or British Guiana and less about their boundary dispute. It is doubtful that he had ever given serious thought to the relationship of the United States to the Latin American republics or to the meaning, scope, or implications of the Monroe Doctrine. Olney's research was limited by time and, because he did not read Spanish, to English-language sources. More concerned with bringing the parties to the negotiating table than with determining the merits of their respective claims, he saw no need for data from foreign archives. Instead he read Scruggs's pamphlet (the lobbyist had sent a copy to everyone of importance in Washington), a compilation of correspondence on the question between Britain, Venezuela, and the United States, assembled at the request of Congress in 1888 when the controversy had flared briefly, and recent files of the State Department. He also seems to have gone through the messages of the presidents, searching out references to the Monroe Doctrine and to relations with the Latin American states. During his first two weeks in office he spent much time in conversation with Cleveland about the affair.[42]

The dispute stemmed from conflicting, ill-defined Spanish and Dutch claims dating from the age of exploration.[43] Venezuela and Britain, successors to the original claimants, first fell to quarrelling in 1841 when the British authorized Robert Schomburgk to survey a western frontier for British Guiana. Venezuela protested, insisting that her territory extended at least to the Essequibo River. Britain, in response, disavowed the Schomburgk line and fell back on vague claims to lands far west of that line. Although to reach accommodation during the 1840s both parties offered compromise lines, they could not agree and in 1850 gave mutual pledges not to encroach upon or settle the disputed zone.

Civil disorders preoccupied Venezuela until 1876 when the two governments exchanged protests over alleged violations of the 1850 agreement. Discovery of gold in the region in the early 1880s increased tensions. At that time Britain reasserted claim to the entire watershed of the Essequibo and all its tributaries, including the Cayuni and Yuruari rivers, and to a tract running westward along the Atlantic coast to Point Barima where the Amacuru River flowed into the mouth of the Orinoco. As settlers moved into the gold fields, Britain in 1886 declared the Schomburgk line to be the provisional western boundary of British Guiana and thereafter held that areas already settled and administered by British subjects could not be submitted to arbitration.

Beginning in 1876, Venezuela regularly sought to enlist the United States on her side in the dispute, arguing that Britain was violating the Monroe Doctrine. Every American secretary of state from Hamilton Fish to Walter Q. Gresham was importuned at least once by Venezuela to intervene. Only Fish, who received his note shortly before leaving office, did not reply.[44] The others all regarded the controversy as within the province of the United States, though they differed in their responses. William M. Evarts and James G. Blaine, for example, accepted Venezuela's charges without question and spoke forcefully of taking steps to defend the Latin republic from British expansion.[45] Secretaries Frederick T. Frelinghuysen and Thomas F. Bayard, on the other hand, while urging prompt settlement of the dispute, assumed an attitude of strict neutrality and disclaimed knowledge of the merits of the case in hopes that the United States would be invited to arbitrate the question.[46]

The United States first directly contacted Britain with respect to the controversy in 1884, proposing arbitration. During the first Cleveland administration, Secretary Bayard extended the good offices of the United States. As Anglo-Venezuelan relations worsened and finally broke, the United States repeatedly pleaded with England, as the stronger party, to negotiate or arbitrate, and each time was politely but firmly rebuffed.[47]

Olney's study strengthened the administration's suspicions that England was encroaching. Repeated westward shifts of her "minimum limit," granting protection to British subjects who settled in the disputed zone subsequent to the pledges of 1850, assertion of the Schomburgk line (with its toe-hold on the Orinoco) as the provisional boundary, and stubbornly refusing to arbitrate any area east of that line, all pointed to British guilt. By contrast, Venezuela's persistent claim of the Essequibo line, coupled with an eagerness to arbitrate, implied innocence. These conclusions reached, the problem remained: how to force Britain to accept prompt arbitration of the controversy?

Olney's reading of the decade or so of correspondence between

Washington and London convinced him that the soft words and tactful language of conventional diplomacy had produced few results. If anything, past notes, combined with the "constant stream of taffy" that Ambassador Bayard "played" over the British in the form of sentimental and laudatory speeches, undermined respect for the United States.[48] The need for a speedy solution, the relative disparity of strength between the antagonists, and perhaps a concern for Venezuela's competence and reliability, prompted Olney to suggest a marked shift in tactics.

Instead of another note beseeching the British to deal justly with Venezuela, Olney proposed calling the London government up short and demanding that it deal directly with the United States. This would reduce the time required by three-cornered diplomacy, redress the imbalance of power between the antagonists, and remove any uncertainty as to Venezuela's conduct, thereby making possible a reasonable settlement by responsible powers. On the latter point, it should be noted, Olney took up the matter without Venezuela's knowledge, consent, or participation.

Cleveland apparently agreed with Olney on these points.[49] The president, however, insisted that in taking its stand the administration must squarely vindicate the Monroe Doctrine. As already noted, Cleveland believed that if the affair dragged on and resulted in an Anglo-Venezuelan war, the United States would be obliged to intercede to uphold the doctrine. In that event, British honor would be at stake, retreat would be difficult if not impossible, and the United States would have to go to war. Since the doctrine ultimately would be resorted to, the president thought it best to advance it early in the negotiations while all parties had time to maneuver.[50]

Cleveland's concept of the scope and meaning of the Monroe Doctrine was muddy. He regarded it with considerable awe, having seen the magic it could work on public opinion whenever invoked by the jingoes. To merely utter the phrase seemed a sort of ultimate weapon to use against Europeans who interfered in American affairs. Although so potent an incantation had to be used sparingly, when fully justified it could be advanced as the clinching argument to end all argument in forcing the withdrawal of European aggressors.

Writing to Bayard at the height of the crisis, Cleveland explained that during his first term he had avoided the doctrine that he "knew to be troublesome" and about which he had little "clear conception or information." He knew, however, that Bayard and his predecessors regarded it as "important" and supposed that when they quoted it in reference to the Venezuelan dispute it was because they deemed

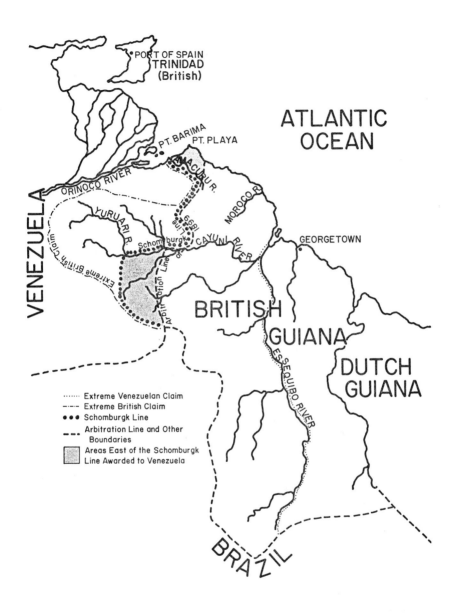

The *Venezuela-British Guiana Boundary Dispute*

it relevant. Since "all consequences" had to be "appreciated and awaited" before applying the doctrine, Cleveland had been "quite willing, if possible within the limits of inflexible duty, to escape its serious contemplation." Recent revival of the issue at a more serious level, however, had led him to examine the question more fully. It was "now entirely clear" that the doctrine was not obsolete, that it should be defended and maintained for "its value and importance *to our government and welfare*," and that that defense and maintenance meant applying the doctrine "when a state of facts arises requiring it."[51]

Secretary Olney did not wholly share these views. He had reservations about using the Monroe Doctrine to justify intervention. The doctrine had no standing in international law, he knew full well, however much the American people revered it. Moreover, he was disturbed by the penchant of jingoes for invoking it to block European powers from punishing Latin American states for various offenses (as in the recent case of Nicaragua), or to promote the expansion of United States interests in Central and South America.

On 17 June, the president went to Buzzard's Bay for the summer, leaving Olney in Washington to draft the note to Britain. The task would not be easy. The issues were highly complex and Olney had little time to master them. The administration's goals called for unusual diplomatic finesse, and Olney was a novice in the field. The president insisted on assertion of the Monroe Doctrine while Olney had reservations about its use. The result was a document in excess of twelve thousand words. Overly long and sometimes self-contradictory, it mixed sensible propositions with dubious history and contentious arguments.

Olney began with a brief account of the boundary dispute and the relationship of the United States to it. Summarizing his findings, Olney noted: (1) that the controversy involved title to an "indefinite but confessedly very large" territory, (2) that the disparity in strength between the antagonists precluded any but a peaceful settlement for Venezuela, (3) that during the half-century the controversy had run, Venezuela had repeatedly and unsuccessfully sought to reach a negotiated settlement, (4) that conventional means having failed, Venezuela for twenty-five years had pressed for arbitration, (5) that Britain consistently refused to arbitrate unless Venezuela first surrendered a large portion of the territory at dispute, and (6) that the United States, "by frequent interposition of its good offices," had made clear "to Great Britain and to the world" that the controversy involved its honor and interests and that it could not regard continuation of the dispute "with indifference." Olney also observed that neither party claimed a line "predicated upon strict legal right." Britain, beginning in 1844, had offered various compromise lines, each west of its predecessor. Even the present "minimum boundary," the Schomburgk line, lay east of the extreme British claim. Venezuela, on the other hand, alleged that the Essequibo line represented "a liberal concession to her antagonist."[52]

To justify American intervention, Olney undertook the difficult task of invoking the Monroe Doctrine without claiming it as part of international law. This he did by pointing out that international law recognized the right of a nation to intervene in any controversy among other nations if that controversy posed "a serious and direct menace to its own integrity, tranquility, or welfare." Since this broad right had often served as "a cloak for schemes of wanton spoliation and aggrandizement," the United States, beginning with Washington's Farewell Address, had deliberately confined its interests by proscribing all involvement in European affairs. A generation later in the Monroe Doctrine, the United States continued to confine its interests to the Western Hemisphere, but logically insisted in return that European powers not interfere in American affairs.[53]

Anxious to dispel the wilder pretensions of domestic jingoes, Olney defined most precisely the scope of the Monroe Doctrine. It did "not establish any general protectorate by the United States over other American states," it did "not relieve any American state from its obligations as fixed by international law," and it did not "prevent any European power directly interested from enforcing such obligations or from inflicting merited punishment for the breach of them." Neither did the doctrine "contemplate any interference [by the United States] in the internal affairs of any American state or in the relations between it and other American states," nor did it "justify any attempt" by the United States "to change the established form of government of any American state or to prevent the people of such state from altering that form according to their own will and pleasure." The rule laid down by Monroe had but a "single purpose and object . . . no European power or combination of European powers shall forcibly deprive an American state of the right and power of self-government and of shaping for itself its own political fortunes and destinies." As Olney later told his brother, never had the Monroe Doctrine been "so carefully defined and so narrowly restricted. . . . "[54]

Although strictly confining its application, Olney had no intention of denigrating the doctrine. It was, he declared (borrowing a phrase from Scruggs), an "accepted public law" of the United States.[55] His efforts to prove this point resulted in a tangle of strained historical interpretation and gratuitous assertion. Congress had never formally affirmed the doctrine, he admitted, but since the executive had openly declared and acted upon it for over seventy years without repudiation, it could be "conclusively presumed" to have legislative "sanction."[56] Practical results had further validated the rule. Among other things the doctrine had been "the controlling factor in the emancipation of South America." Its "most striking single achievement" had been to force the French from Mexico in 1867, it had served as the basis of the Clayton-Bulwer Treaty of 1850, and most recently had been "influential" in bringing about "relinquishment" by Britain of its "supposed protectorate" over the Mosquito Reservation in Nicaragua. The list not only revealed varied instances when the doctrine had been "affirmed and applied," Olney observed, it also demonstrated that the Venezuelan boundary dispute fell "far within" the doctrine's "scope and spirit."[57]

The Monroe Doctrine rested upon "facts and principles" that were both "intelligible and incontrovertible," Olney declared. "[D]istance and three thousand miles of intervening ocean" rendered "any permanent political union between an European and an American state unnatural and inexpedient."[58] Further, while European nations needed "enormous armies and navies" to defend themselves and their interests, the American states had no reason to impoverish themselves "by wars or preparations for war with whose causes or results they can have no direct concern." And, finally, except for France, Europe was monarchical in its form of government while America was "devoted to the exactly opposite principle—to the idea that every people has an inalienable right of self-government." Given these "irreconcilable" differences, it was obvious that "any European control" of an American state would be "both incongruous and injurious."

To prove that the "safety and welfare" of the United States depended upon maintaining the independence of "every American state as against an European power," Olney observed that the countries of North and South America, "by geographical proximity, by natural sympathy, by similarity of governmental constitutions," were "friends and allies, commercially and politically of the United States."[59] To allow any of them to be subjugated by a European power would "reverse that situation" and signify "the loss of all the advantages incident to their natural relations to us." Equally important, the people of the United States had "a vital interest in the cause of popular self-government." Having purchased it for themselves at great cost, they believed it to be for the "healing of all nations" and that "civilization must either advance or retrograde accordingly as its supremacy is extended or curtailed." Disclaiming any crusade to spread self-government, Olney observed that Americans were content to defend it "as their own security and welfare demand."

"Today the United States is practically sovereign on this continent," Olney declared, "and its fiat is law upon the subjects to which it confines its interposition." This was because "in addition to all other grounds," the nation's "infinite resources, combined with its isolated position render it master of the situation and practically invulnerable as against any or all other powers." All of the advantages deriving from this superior position, however, would be immediately imperiled were the United States to allow a European power to convert an American state into a colony. "What one power was permitted to do could not be denied to another," and South America would soon suffer the fate of Africa, then in the process of being partitioned among the powers. Accordingly, the United States would lose prestige, authority, and "weight in the councils of nations." Previously it had been spared the burdens and evils of maintaining large standing armies, but with its "only real rivals in peace as well as enemies in war" camped on its doorstep, the United States would be obliged to keep itself "armed to the teeth."

In anticipation of possible British objections, Olney argued that the dispute involved much more than a boundary line. Political control over a considerable territory was at stake and (again borrowing from Scruggs) if "command of the mouth of the Orinoco" was involved, the dispute was of "immense consequence" to the "whole river navigation of the interior of South America."[60] To the argument that British Guiana was itself an American state and hence exempt from the Monroe Doctrine, Olney agreed, but only if Guiana carried on the dispute without the support of the British empire. As for the proposition that the Monroe Doctrine did not apply because it recognized existing European colonies, Olney observed that colonies had been recognized with boundaries as of the date when the doctrine was issued. That Britain was not planting a new colony was of no consequence. If she was using the disputed line of an existing colony to appropriate Venezuelan territory, the doctrine applied.

Olney insisted that the United States did not assume British guilt. However, Venezuela had repeatedly charged encroachment and England denied that charge. Since the United States was "entitled to resent and resist any sequestration of Venezuelan soil," it was "necessarily entitled to know whether such sequestration has occurred or is now going on." Attempts to resolve the matter by negotiation had borne no fruit in half a century. To settle it by force of arms was "even more impossible" because war was a "relic of barbarism," and because so one-sided a contest would be a "distinct disparagement" of Britain's "character as a civilized state." The "one feasible mode" remaining was arbitration. Even Britain admitted the desirability of the principle, Olney declared, but nullified it in practice by insisting that Venezuela first surrender part of the land at dispute. Only Venezuela's relative feebleness deprived her of the right to an impartial judgment.

Olney denied that long occupation of parts of the disputed territory gave clear title and rejected Britain's claim that arbitration was therefore inapplicable. It simply raised an additional topic for arbitrators to consider, namely, "the validity of the asserted prescriptive title either in point of law or in point of fact." Olney declared that Britain's stand—that Venezuela could get none of the disputed land by force because she was too weak, nor by treaty because Britain would not agree, and perhaps a part by arbitration, but only if she first gave over a stipulated portion to Britain—was indefensible, and unworthy of the British "love of fair play." The United States could only regard it as "amounting, in substance, to an invasion and conquest of Venezuelan territory."[61]

The note concluded with a threat, an inducement to arbitrate, and a time limit for reply. The president's duty, Olney said, was "unmistakable and imperative." Britain's assertion of title and refusal to have it investigated constituted a "substantial appropriation" of Venezuelan territory. For the United States not to give warning that it regarded this "as injurious to the interests of the people of the United States" would be to ignore an established policy closely identified with the nation's honor and welfare. It was for Congress to determine the measures "necessary and proper" to vindicate that policy, he warned. He suggested, however, that it was "clearly for the Executive to leave nothing undone which may tend to render such determination [by Congress] unnecessary." In effect, Olney was hinting, Britain would find it easier to deal with the executive than with Congress.[62] The United States, he concluded, insisted on a definite decision as to whether Britain would submit the dispute in its entirety to impartial arbitration. If the president were to be disappointed in that hope—an event calculated to "greatly embarrass the future relations" of the two countries—it was his wish to be notified "at such early date" as would "enable him to lay the whole subject before Congress in his next annual message."

On 2 July, Olney left Washington for Falmouth. En route he delivered the note to the president at Buzzard's Bay. Without other explanation or comment, he told Cleveland that the document represented his judgment in the matter, but that the president might not agree. For the next few days Olney endured the greatest nervous suspense of his career. The note was his first assignment as secretary of state and he was anxious that it meet the president's approval. He feared the president might reject his deliberately jolting language as too strong, or perhaps object to his roundabout application of the Monroe Doctrine. So confident was Olney that he was right, however, that he was prepared to resign if Cleveland did not support him.[63] Five days later the president sent his anxiously awaited response. "It's the best thing of the kind I have ever read and it leads to a conclusion that one cannot escape if he tries—that is if there is anything of the Monroe Doctrine at all. You show there is a great deal of that and place it I think on better and more defensible ground than any of your predecessors—*or mine*." The president proposed meeting with Olney to consider "a little more softened verbiage here and there." Olney was most pleased at the "extraordinary" extent of Cleveland's praise.[64]

The later meeting produced slight changes, if any. At Cleveland's suggestion, Olney then took the document to Washington and read it to such cabinet members as were in town—Lamont, Carlisle, Herbert, and Harmon. No one raised objections, so the note was printed and dispatched to London on 20 July.[65] Olney then returned to the Cape to await the reply of the Foreign Office. If negative, he and Cleveland would have much work to do before Congress assembled. If positive, as both men expected, the president would be able to report in December that the Venezuela boundary dispute was on the way to settlement.[66]

Except for the immediately favorable responses of politicians and news editors, Olney's note of 20 July has drawn heavy criticism, especially from the scholarly community. At the time and since, critics attributed its haughty, bombastic tone and tactless language to Olney's bad temper, to his long career as the advocate of only one side of legal questions, and to his unfamiliarity with diplomatic practices. The note, they contend, naively championed Venezuela's absurd claim to the Essequibo frontier, ignored the rights of British settlers, and accused Britain of deliberately encroaching on Venezuelan territory. Further, Olney allegedly distorted the Monroe Doctrine from a wholly defensive statement into a manifesto justifying the extension of United States domination over the hemisphere. Replete with bad history, the note violated the first canon of diplomacy by serving an ultimatum on Britain. The critics contend that Olney then somehow misled Cleveland—an outspoken foe of expansionism and jingoism—into approving the document, thereby launching the nation on an adventure that would take it to the brink of war.[67]

Critics at the time felt that Cleveland had betrayed them. Olney's stance was all too reminiscent of the blustering jingoism of Blaine, whom the critics had vigorously opposed. Later commentators, no doubt influenced by two world wars in which Anglo-American cooperation seemed indispensable to the preservation of civilization, shuddered to think of the consequences that Olney's rash note might have had. At all stages, most scholarly critics have seen Britain's good will as infinitely more valuable to the United States than that of all the Latin American states. Quite understandably they also favored careful diplomacy, restrained language, and reliance upon reason and law in the dealings of one nation with another. Olney's note badly wrenched Anglo-American relations, appealed to the baser aspects of nationalism, and blustered much of power and force. These elements in the note of 20 July tended to blind critics to such merit as the document contained.

Bayard and Moore were among the first to fix full blame for the note on Olney and to accuse him of having manipulated the president. According to Moore, Olney was reputed to be "the worst tempered man in Boston."[68] Over the years other critics picked up the theme. Cleveland "strangely approved" the harsh note, having "fallen under the spell of Olney's belligerence."[69] The secretary's "mere irascibility" and "uncontrollable temper" were important factors in the wording of Cleveland's December message to Congress as well as the July note. The president's blunder was due, in important part, to his "unthinking acceptance of advice from Olney."[70] The implication of all this was that Olney, angry and intemperate, dashed off the offensive note filled with errors, distortions, and absurdities, and induced the president to approve it.

The "bad temper" explanation, however, ignores the long gestation period between December 1894 and May 1895 when Cleveland and Gresham worked on the policy that Olney formulated in July, and fails to take into account the two weeks or so in June when Olney and Cleveland together mulled over the problem. Even if suspected British aggressions angered Olney, it is difficult to believe that he could have maintained a white-hot, irrational hatred of England through the four weeks of intense work involved in preparing the note. Reading the blatantly self-serving notes of Venezuela (obviously designed to entangle the United States in the dispute) alone should have tempered Olney's anger at Britain. The interpretation also does not explain how Cleveland, after studying the note without pressure of any sort from Olney, was so easily and completely won over to so radical a position, or why, when the two men later went over the note they made no changes in it.[71] Surely by then, through the influence of Cleveland's supposedly cooler head, Olney's temper tantrum would have been brought under control. Clearly the note of 20 July was not the product of one man's fit of temper. Whatever its faults, the note was the outcome of months of consideration by Cleveland, Gresham, and Olney and of at least a month of intense study, thought, and careful weighing by Olney.

That the note contained historical inaccuracies and exaggerations is beyond question. But Olney was not a professional historian, and he had neither the time for nor the intention of writing a historically accurate account of the dispute. He was trying to state his case forcefully and to persuade Britain that arbitration must be accepted at once. Anyone familiar with state papers knows that "good" history is rarely found in the ex parte communications of one foreign office to another. When more than passable accuracy is achieved in such documents, it is the incidental by-product of other purposes, not a goal in itself. The history in Olney's note, bad as it was, set no record for inaccuracy in diplomatic correspondence.

A fair reading of the note disproves the charges that Olney asserted England's guilt (whatever he may have suspected), or that he intended to expand the scope of the Monroe Doctrine (whatever may have happened as a result of the note). Rather, Olney asked Britain to answer the charges brought by Venezuela with proofs instead of denials, and suggested that arbitration would both prove the facts and resolve the dispute. With respect to the Monroe Doctrine, Olney believed that he had "defined it and confined its application within narrower limits than had ever been fixed by previous administrations or public men."[72] Over the years he consistently held to this contention, privately and publicly denouncing Theodore Roosevelt's Corollary of 1904, for example, as a perversion of both the Monroe Doctrine and the Cleveland administration's policy in 1895.[73] Nor did Olney assert or believe that the doctrine was part of international law. As he afterwards explained, the doctrine was "a matter of policy and not of right" and was "without recognition in international law."[74]

Possibly Olney's insistence that the dispute must be arbitrated could have resulted in distortion of the original doctrine. If, for example, the independent states of the Americas challenged the boundaries of all existing European colonies in the New World and demanded arbitration, the doctrine's recognition of existing colonies might have been nullified. But Olney laid down no general rule; he spoke only to the specific problem of Venezuela's boundary which had been contested for over half a century, which despite numerous efforts to solve remained unsettled, and which so long as it remained unresolved worked to Venezuela's disadvantage.

In charging him with extreme naivete and lack of diplomatic skill, Olney's critics have seriously underestimated him. However ignorant he might have been of international diplomacy, he had had considerable experience as an arbiter of disputes in his private law practice. He made use of that experience when he insisted that all lands at dispute be included in the arbitration. It was not that he necessarily believed the Essequibo to be the proper boundary of British Guiana, or that British settlers in the disputed zone had no rights. His demand cut both ways. Arbitration was to include not only Venezuela's "unreasonable" claims, but Great Britain's as well. As for the rights of British settlers, Olney conceded that their prescriptive claims were subject to adjudication.[75]

The problem, as stated in the note, was that neither party's claim rested on clear title. Venezuela's claim derived from Spain's original discovery of the region, while Britain relied heavily on prescriptive rights—long occupation, settlement, and use of the land in question. Of the two, prescriptive rights historically had prevailed over titles based on the mere right of discovery. Britain's case, therefore, was stronger, especially in districts where its subjects actually occupied the land and where its officials had exercised jurisdiction for many years. It was, in fact, because Britain's claim rested on prescription that Olney was anxious to settle the matter as quickly as possible. Delay worked to Britain's advantage since any time gained made it possible for British subjects to extend their holdings into new areas and to perfect title to areas already settled.

From his experience, Olney knew that one of the principal objections to arbitration was the tendency of tribunals to split the difference between contending parties. For that reason as much as any, Britain consistently had declined to submit the whole area to arbitration lest some tribunal award Venezuela a "share" of land without regard to British nationals living there.[76] On the other hand, Britain's willingness to arbitrate only the area west of the Schomburgk line was no concession whatever. Lands settled by British subjects all lay east of that line and the remaining unoccupied territory, to be apportioned by the arbiters, was land to which Britain had tenuous claim. If Venezuela acceded to Britain's terms, she would not only give up all lands east of the Schomburgk line, but probably lose up to half of the land west of the line as well.

Olney's response was that of any good attorney in such a case: assert claim to the whole area west of the Essequibo without regard for British settlements. Because prescriptive rights carried greater weight, the tribunal could be expected to award to Britain much if not all lands settled by her nationals. At the same time, having made so substantial an award to Britain, the tribunal would probably award most unsettled lands, including all lands west of the Schomburgk line, to Venezuela. The difference would not be great, but under Olney's scheme Venezuela would not necessarily lose everything east of the Schomburgk line and would be far less apt to lose any land west of that line. All else aside, Olney's tactics were shrewd.

Few of Olney's critics suggested alternatives by which the long dispute might better have been resolved. Some believed that the issue in no way involved the Monroe Doctrine or American interests, and that without encouragement from the United States, Venezuela eventually would have negotiated a reasonable settlement with Great Britain.[77] This view not only defined the doctrine out of existence, it assumed Venezuelan cupidity and British innocence, and forgot that the dispute had gone on for decades before the United States intervened. In all probability demagoguery in Venezuela would have continued, as in the past, to block any "surrender" of the homeland. And, had the dispute run on, British settlers in all likelihood would have continued to pour into the disputed zone (especially into the gold fields) west of the Schomburgk line. By the time of the next confrontation, Britain's "minimum boundary line" might well have again moved westward.[78]

Olney's Venezuelan note was purposefully undiplomatic in tone. The gentle diplomatic hints previously employed by the State Department with reference to Venezuela, Olney suspected, had lulled the British into believing that they could defer settlement indefinitely. The note of 20 July, he later explained, was designed "effectually even if rudely" to dispel British complacency.[79] Its phrases were of a "bumptious order," he admitted, but the "excuse was that in English eyes the United States was then so completely a negligible quantity that it was believed only words the equivalent of blows would be really effective."[80] Possibly Olney could have achieved the same ends with a less aggressive note. In light of the failure of earlier diplomatically worded communications, however, Olney rightly could argue that the burden of proof lay with those making the assertion.

Olney's note deserved criticism, to be sure, but its chief faults were not those that have received the most attention. The principal problem was that Olney tried to accomplish too many goals within a single note. On the one hand he was trying to jar the British into settling the dispute while, on the other, hoping to coax them into accepting arbitration as the means. He was attempting to apply the Monroe Doctrine specifically to the Venezuelan dispute without asserting that it was applicable to other incidents that might arise between European and American powers. He was trying to quiet the affair as a domestic political issue before the December meeting of Congress by stirring it up as an international incident in July. It is doubtful that anyone could have framed a note that would have accomplished such diverse objectives. The result was not, as some have charged, a typical lawyer's brief (Olney's briefs at any rate were short, cogent, forceful, and tightly reasoned). The Venezuela note was wordy, more provocative than convincing, and gratuitously quarrelsome. Few read the long document in its entirety; fewer still remembered its contents in detail. What most easily caught the eye was bombast, taken seriously at face value. Quieter, more thoughtful passages were overlooked, forgotten, or dismissed as unimportant. Unfortunately, even diplomats at the Foreign Office, swept along by Olney's intemperate phrases, managed to miss the message that he was trying to convey.

13

Crisis and Detente

After 20 July, the pace of events in the Venezuelan dispute passed from Olney's control to that of Ambassador Bayard in London and to leisurely officials at the Foreign Office. Ever hesitant about conveying irritating messages to the British and even slower in relaying negative responses to Washington, Bayard held Olney's note for six days before delivering it. As an introduction, he reviewed the previous correspondence on the subject for Prime Minister Salisbury (who was also serving as foreign minister). Apparently Bayard hoped to cushion the impact of the note by implying that it was only the latest in a long series. Afterwards he urged Salisbury to maintain an "atmosphere of serene and elevated effort" by avoiding "all irritating issues," and to keep the matter out of the "arena of party strife."

Instructed to read the note in its entirety, Bayard reported—two days after the event—that he had "fully conveyed" the "grave instruction." The prime minister, he said, made "courteous expression of thanks," but expressed regret that Olney thought it necessary to present "so far-reaching and important a principle" and "such wide and profound policies" in relation to so comparatively small an issue. Before replying to the secretary's "able and profound" argument, he wished the law officers of his government to examine the note carefully. Their study would probably require considerable time and might possibly give rise to a "long and difficult discussion and much controversy," but a reply would be made.[1]

Salisbury's version of the meeting (sent immediately afterwards to the British Embassy in Washington) was somewhat less effusive. Bayard read Olney's note to him "in part," but the issues were "much too large and much too complicated" to be dealt with at the interview. Invoking doctrines of such scope, and containing "so much disputable matter," was not likely to bring the controversy to a speedy conclusion, he told Bayard. Although the dispute itself was not extensive, Olney's "elaborate and exhaustive statement" would require detailed investigation because the British government did not wish at some future date to find itself committed to principles it did not accept.[2]

Yet a third account of the interview appeared in the *London Daily Chronicle* of 22 October. "An official of high standing" revealed that "midway" in Bayard's reading of the note, Salisbury interrupted to say that he "need not proceed further." The British government "could not even entertain the arguments put forward and absolutely declined to recognize such an application of the Monroe doctrine." Using nearly identical words in a memorandum to a colleague, the prime minister complained that the tone of Olney's message made the situation more difficult.

Outraged, Bayard sent a copy of the *Chronicle*'s account to Olney and denounced its author as a sensation-seeker. The correspondent, who had called at the embassy, revealed that his informant had seen the memorandum, written in Salisbury's hand, addressed to Colonial Secretary Joseph Chamberlain. Vigorously denying the story, Bayard inadvertently attested to its partial accuracy when he complained that "giving such information was, of course, a gross and disreputable breach of trust," that probably would be punished.[3] From the three versions one fact stood out: Bayard had tried to soften the impact of both Olney's note and Salisbury's reaction. Thereafter Olney questioned how far he could trust Bayard in handling such assignments.

Short-handed because of vacations, and preoccupied with the supposed imminent collapse of the Ottoman Empire, Foreign Office officials nonetheless began to pore over Olney's words. Meanwhile, Chamberlain at the Colonial Office concentrated on practical matters. Conditions in the disputed territory in Guiana were "almost intolerable," he reported on 30 August. The time had come to make a determined effort to end the controversy. The recent arrest and alleged mistreatment by Venezuela of a British officer at Uruan (in the disputed zone), the need to protect the Schomburgk line as the colony's "minimum boundary," and the problem of Venezuelan encroachments west of that line, all called for action. Britain ought to demand "the fullest possible compensation" for the Uruan incident and should intimate to Venezuela that if redress were not secured within a reasonable time, "forcible means" would be adopted to obtain satisfaction. Future trespasses in the area should be dealt with by force rather than diplomacy. Finally, when it demanded compensation for the Uruan affair, Britain should insist that all disputed lands west of the Schomburgk line be submitted to arbitration. An unfavorable award was possible, Chamberlain admitted, but Venezuela's acceptance would "*pro tanto* be an admission of the British claim to the Schomburgk line."[4]

In a later communication, Chamberlain again pressed for a prompt settlement of the dispute. The Schomburgk line passed through "a very rich territory," the development of which he was trying to persuade London firms to finance. If the area proved to be as valuable as the gold officer of the colony believed, it might "turn out to be another Transvaal or West Australia."[5] In September, Chamberlain proposed remedies to the governor of British Guiana for the colony's chief economic problem—overdependence on sugar, the world price of which was depressed. The governor should encourage new crops suited to the colony's soil. "More particularly," he should "foster and develop" gold mining, which had "already made some advance." Potentially a source of considerable wealth and revenue, gold production required roads opening the back country and making gold fields more accessible. Venezuelan incursions must be halted, too, and capital from both Guianan and English sources was needed for development. Chamberlain inquired whether the colony's police force was adequate to protect the area, presumably against Venezuelan interlopers. By mid-October Maxim guns had been sent to Guiana and Salisbury had dispatched an ultimatum to Caracas, demanding damages in the Uruan incident. No mention, however, was made of arbitrating disputed lands.[6]

Competent witnesses have suggested that Salisbury might deliberately have stalled his reply so as to miss the deadline fixed by Olney.[7] Certainly he did not rush his answer. Seeing no need to discuss details, Salisbury limited himself to denying the applicability of the Monroe Doctrine to the dispute, rejecting any British obligation to the doctrine if it did apply, and refuting the right of the United States to insist upon arbitration of a quarrel that apparently was not its concern. Time had nearly run out when Salisbury submitted his proposed draft to the queen and cabinet for approval. The ministry was not satisfied and insisted upon a second note, setting forth Britain's side of the dispute.[8] Preparation of the second note, coupled with insistence that the replies be hand-delivered rather than cabled, precluded meeting the deadline.

Throughout the summer and autumn, Olney fretted. First he pestered Adee about whether Bayard had received and delivered the note. Then he watched for unofficial hints as to the British reply, wondering at remarks that Pauncefote made in Ottawa to newsmen's questions about Venezuela. He also scanned editorials that bore "the ear-marks of official suggestion" which Bayard clipped and sent from

London. In October, Olney reminded Bayard that the president wanted any "negative response" prior to the meeting of Congress, then eight weeks away. He urged the ambassador to use the cable "freely" to convey any information as to the "time and tenor" of the reply.[9]

With little more than two weeks remaining, Olney again cabled. "Without betraying uneasiness and preserving the dignified attitude hitherto maintained," Bayard was to determine if an immediate reply could be expected or whether the Eastern Question "precluded consideration of all else."[10] To the reply that Salisbury and his staff were "anxiously occupied" with Turkish matters, Olney suggested, "in the interests of good relations," that the Foreign Office assign an official reason for not responding as requested, and fix a date when a reply could be expected.[11]

Time and again Bayard raised hopes that an answer was imminent, only to dash them with reports of fresh delays. Finally, on 26 November, the Foreign Office gave him advance copy of the notes but insisted that he sign a pledge to treat them as confidential until Pauncefote could deliver them in person to Olney. As Bayard interpreted his promise, he could not even cable the substance of the messages. He doubted that the brief delay would do any harm.[12]

Commenting on the Venezuela dispute in his annual message, President Cleveland neither referred to the Monroe Doctrine by name, nor mentioned Britain's failure to respond within the time limit. If the administration—as later critics charged—hoped to use the issue to divert attention from domestic problems, Cleveland certainly muffed an opportunity.

Despite hints to the contrary, Olney and Cleveland apparently clung to the belief that the reply would be favorable. Salisbury's failure to respond before expiration of the deadline for a negative answer, and Bayard's decision not to cable the reply, probably nursed that hope. Certainly Cleveland sensed no crisis when he left on 5 December for a ten-day duck-hunting trip. Since the reply was coming by steamship and could not arrive for at least a week, he suggested that Olney pocket it until his return. "In the meantime," he added, "*if* its transmission [to Congress] should be accompanied by any particular message, you can if you have time be blocking it out."[13]

The lofty "ho-hum" tone of Salisbury's response ended all hope that the Venezuelan question would be ended speedily, and threatened to loose a fresh flood of jingoism. The first note suggested that the

Monroe Doctrine had "undergone a very notable development" at Olney's hand. The dangers that troubled Monroe in 1823 bore no relation to conditions in 1895: the dispute involved neither the colonization of American soil by a European power nor the imposition of a European system of government on an American state. It was "simply the determination of the frontier of a British possession" in which the United States had "no apparent practical concern."

In an attempt to discredit the American contentions, Salisbury inflated Olney's simple call for arbitration of the Venezuelan boundary into a broad general corollary to the Monroe Doctrine, namely, that "if any independent American State advances a demand for territory of which its neighbour claims to be the owner, and that neighbour is the colony of a European State, the United States have a right to insist that the European State shall submit the demand, and its impugned rights, to arbitration." To this, the prime minister declared, Britain could not accede.

Nor, Salisbury continued, did Britain adhere to the "political maxims" known in America as the Monroe Doctrine. The doctrine "must always be mentioned with respect" because of the "distinguished statesmen" and the "great nation" who had adopted it, but international law rested on "the general consent of nations." "[N]o statesman, however eminent, and no nation, however powerful," was competent to insert into the corpus of international law "a novel principle which was never recognized before, and which has not since been accepted by the Goverment of any other country." The United States had the right to involve itself in any controversy where its interests were at stake, he declared. That right, however, was in "no way strengthened or extended" by the fact that the dispute included "some territory which is called American."

Salisbury emphatically denied that permanent ties between Britain and her American possessions were "inexpedient or unnatural," or that the interests of the United States were involved "in every frontier dispute" that might arise in the Western Hemisphere, or that the United States by right could insist upon arbitration of disputes between European and American states. He ended with the hope that the Anglo-Venezuelan controversy would "be adjusted by a reasonable arrangement at an early date."

In his second note, Salisbury traced the long dispute, arguing that the British claim had undergone no change over the years. Far from trying to extend its sovereignty, Britain repeatedly had expressed readiness to arbitrate "large tracts of territory which from their auriferous nature" were known to be "of almost untold value." That the concessions offered diminished over the years was because the British government, in justice, could not abandon settlers who meanwhile had moved into the contested zone. Similarly, Britain could not agree to an arbitration that might result in the "transfer of large numbers of British subjects," who for years had "enjoyed the settled rule of a British Colony," to rule by "a nation of different race and language, whose political system [is] subject to frequent disturbance and whose institutions as yet too often afford very inadequate protection to life and property."[14] Salisbury apparently regarded his remarks as conclusive; without waiting to see if the United States wished to respond, he asked Pauncefote to sound out Olney with regard to immediate publication of the note of 20 July and the British reply.[15]

Salisbury's absolute intransigence surprised and angered Olney. So certain had he been that Britain would yield—at least in part—that he had devised no plan for meeting a flat refusal. At once Olney began drafting a message for Cleveland to consider upon his return. The problem was what course to pursue. Olney never considered retreat. Falling back meant ruin for the administration; beyond that, Olney by nature was incapable of seeing his note as a blunder. To back down would be weakness and folly. At the same time he was not prepared to recommend going to war.

Olney's friends subsequently credited (and Cleveland's friends blamed) the secretary of state for the message that the president sent to Congress on 17 December. Neither group was wholly right. In his draft, Olney recommended abandoning all reliance on the Monroe Doctrine as justification for American intervention. Salisbury, he said, had either misapprehended the position of the United States regarding the doctrine, or was "inexcuseably trifling" in his reply. Contrary to the prime minister's interpretation, the note of 20 July neither argued that conditions in 1895 were the same as in 1823, nor claimed that the Monroe Doctrine enjoined upon England any duty to accept arbitration of the dispute. The United States had "most explicitly stated" its position: The Monroe Doctrine embodied a "living principle" as applicable to the Venezuelan boundary dispute as to conditions seventy years before. That principle gave the United States an interest in the controversy that it was "bound to protect and defend." The note of 20 July had simply asked whether Britain would submit the dispute to arbitration. The proposal was made *"not by virtue of anything in the Monroe Doctrine,"* but because of the disparity in strength between Venezuela and Great Britain and because of the "inherent propriety and reasonableness of such an arbitral adjustment."

Olney proposed that Cleveland undermine Britain's claim of undoubted right to all lands east of the Schomburgk line by citing evidence showing that from the very beginning it had never been anything more than a line of convenience. As for settlers in the disputed zone, Olney contended that lust for gold motivated them more than concern for the benefits of British rule. Only a plebiscite could determine the degree to which British governance had attracted them. Moreover, they must have known that British title to the region was contested and that at any time a treaty or arbitration award might place them under Venezuelan jurisdiction. Settlers offered no block to arbitration in any event, Olney argued: "any properly framed agreement of arbitration would expressly provide for them and would secure the rights and quiet the titles of all *bona fide* settlers and investors within the disputed territory."

Despite the threat he had made in the note of 20 July, Olney did not propose to turn the affair over to Congress. Instead, he resorted to that time-honored device for temporizing, the investigative commission. The president should name such a body to determine the "true boundary line" between British Guiana and Venezuela. After careful study, giving "due weight" to all "legitimate considerations bearing on the claims of both parties," the commission should report its findings. If the president found the report "satisfactory," he should notify Britain of the true boundary and warn that any appropriation of territory or exercise of jurisdiction beyond it would be regarded by the United States as "wilful aggression upon rights and interests which this government is bound to protect and defend . . . "

By no means did Olney propose forcing Britain to recognize or accept an expanded Monroe Doctrine. In fact he was anxious to drop all reference to the doctrine so long as Britain recognized that American interests gave it the right to insist upon a resolution of the dispute. Although Olney demanded a final ruling on the ownership of all lands in question, he did not champion Venezuela's claim to the line of the Essequibo, and he did not deny the rights of British settlers in the disputed zone. His objective in December was essentially what it had been in July: to bring the dispute to a conclusive settlement without depriving Venezuela of a full hearing on its entire claim.

Tactically, Olney was careful not to box in the administration or to commit it irrevocably to any course of action. He suggested, for instance, that Britain and Venezuela might still negotiate a mutually acceptable solution. The proposed commission would buy time for working out other possible solutions, and its findings were subject to presidential approval, which left yet another loophole, if needed.[16]

Upon his return, Cleveland read Salisbury's notes and Olney's draft message to Congress. He also read, but was not impressed by, a cheerful note from Bayard, hailing Salisbury's reply as "in good temper and moderate in tone," and laying blame for the difficulties on "the wholly unreliable character of the Venezuelan Rulers and people. . . . "[17] For two days the president worked on his message. Although he borrowed heavily from Olney's opening and closing paragraphs, he disagreed completely with the secretary's handling of Salisbury's bold rejection of the Monroe Doctrine. Political realist that he was, Cleveland knew that that challenge could not be allowed to stand. Rather than skirting around the doctrine as Olney proposed, the president brought it to the fore. "[T]he doctrine upon which we stand is strong and sound," he declared, "because its enforcement is important to our peace and safety as a nation and is essential to the integrity of our free institutions and the tranquil maintenance of our distinctive form of government." The doctrine "was intended to apply at every stage of our national life," and could not "become obsolete while our Republic endures." Just as the balance of power was important to England and "a subject for our absolute non-interference," so was the Monroe Doctrine "of vital concern to our people and their Government."

To Salisbury's argument that the Monroe Doctrine was not a part of international law, Cleveland replied that it involved a principle that had "peculiar, if not exclusive, relation to the United States." Although the doctrine had not been admitted "in so many words to the code of international law," the principle that every nation was "entitled to rights belonging to it," and should have those rights protected, allowed the United States to claim a place for the doctrine within the corpus of international law "as certainly and as securely as if it were specifically mentioned."

Cleveland also decided against any acknowledgement of the rights of British settlers in the disputed area. He insisted that the whole district at dispute be subjected to international arbitration to determine "in a satisfactory and conclusive manner" whether Britain was using the uncertain boundary "to extend her possession on this continent without right," or was merely seeking "possession of territory fairly included within her lines of ownership. . . . "

Although he rejected most of Olney's arguments, Cleveland recognized in the proposed commission a formula by which he could outmaneuver his jingoist opponents in Congress. He also paraphrased a passage from Olney's draft that implied a readiness to fight for the principles at stake. "In making these recommendations," Cleveland wrote, "I am fully alive to the responsibility incurred and keenly realize all the consequences that may follow."[18] With a presidential election only eleven months away, Cleveland took so firm a stand on Venezuela that only a request for war could have gone further. The language he used was as bold as any jingo's, but the actions he proposed paved the way to a solution less drastic than war. It seems safe to conclude that Cleveland anticipated—with a little luck—that both his domestic and foreign opponents would back down before a resort to force became necessary.[19]

On 29 December, Cleveland wrote at length to Bayard, explaining his reaction to Britain's reply and the rationale behind his message to Congress. Salisbury's unwillingness to arbitrate had been "intensely disappointing," because he could not "see the force of the reasons given for refusal." "After a little hesitation," he added another reason for his "disappointment and chagrin," though insisting that it had had "absolutely nothing to do" with the action he had taken. It would have been "exceedingly gratifying and a very handsome thing for Great Britain to do," he said, "if in the midst of all this Administration has had to do in attempts to stem the tide of 'jingoism,' she had yielded or rather conceded something . . . for our sake." His administration had been "open, honest and fair" in its relations with Britain and he could not see why Salisbury could not have acquiesced "in arbitration when not obliged to do so, in aid of the ascertainment of facts which a friendly power felt should be developed to relieve it from embarrassment." Put another way, Cleveland believed that out of good will, Britain should have acceded to arbitration so as to have let his administration off the hook with the domestic jingoes.

The British refusal, Cleveland complained, presented him with a problem. The matter could not be dropped—"far from it"—simply because Britain insisted that she was right and that she would not arbitrate. His proposal for an investigative commission was designed to avoid extreme action or action upon mistaken facts. "[I]nstead of threatening war for not arbitrating, we simply say inasmuch as Great Britain will not aid us in finding the facts, we will not go to war but do the best we can to discover the true state of facts for ourselves. . . . " Of course, if the investigation revealed that England had "seized the territory and superseded the jurisdiction of Venezuela," that would be a "different matter."[20]

There seems to be little justification for regarding the message as taking the United States to the edge of war. Had Cleveland reported Salisbury's blunt refusal to arbitrate and turned the question over to Congress, war might well have followed. But Olney and Cleveland substituted the commission as a way to prevent war and apparently made no move whatever to alert the armed forces for either offensive or defensive action. The British ambassador, unlike the American press, saw through the bombast to the real intent of the message. Writing to Salisbury's private secretary, Sir Julian referred to the president's message as "very pale and washy." He noted that the commission offered a way out of the deadlock and was a fine "safety valve."[21] Had war come, it would had to have come by act of England. That country would have had no reason to attack the United States unless and until the United States attempted to enforce an arbitrary boundary line in Guiana.

President Cleveland's Venezuela message stunned the nation. Many people, latching onto the closing paragraphs, thought war imminent. "This is all tremendously serious," Sigourney Butler wrote Olney; "Drop me ten words & tell me if you think it means a fight."[22] A goodly number of men, including many Civil War veterans, offered their services in the event of hostilities. Theodore Roosevelt was ecstatic: "I earnestly hope our government do'nt [sic] back down. If there is a muss I shall try to have a hand in it myself! They'll have to employ a lot of men just as green as I am even for the conquest of Canada. . . . "[23]

Others, ever politicians, thought only of the impact of events on party. "I am full of joy to think that the Democratic party by its latest act has won the almost unanimous approval of the American people," wrote an assistant treasurer of the United States from Boston. A United States attorney and Democratic leader from Iowa declared that the administration's policy might bring "the discordant and dissatisfied elements in our party together" and bury "the free silver heresy and anything else."[24] To the embarrassment of many of Cleveland's usual supporters who opposed the Venezuelan policy, the Republicans seemed united behind the president. Even the enemy press, led by the *New York Tribune* and the *New York Times,* backed Cleveland. Whitlaw Reid, editor of the *Tribune,* in a public address touched on another theme of those who supported the president's policy. "This," he said, "is the golden opportunity of our merchants to extend our trade to every quarter of Central and South America."[25] The administration was strongly backed by chamber of commerce resolutions, letters, and other messages from the business community, particularly in the Midwest, South, and West.[26]

But there were significant sour notes, too. Many of the president's oldest and strongest supporters held their tongues in public while shaking their heads in private. Secretaries Carlisle and Morton both blamed the bristling language of the message on Cleveland's failure to consult in advance with his whole cabinet.[27] In the scholarly community, John Bassett Moore, Albert B. Hart, John W. Burgess, Frank W. Taussig, and Thomas M. Cooley, among other friends of the administration, were taken aback at the message.[28] James B. Angell, president of the University of Michigan, was surprised that the work confided to the commission had not been done beforehand. Olney "was a pupil of mine in college," he wrote Moore, "and I never before knew him to do a thing backend foremost."[29] A minority of newspapers, including the *New York Evening Post* and *New York World* (ordinarily Cleveland supporters), regarded the message as a serious blunder.

In eastern banking and commercial centers—especially in New York and Boston—the thought of hostilities was chilling. Henry Lee Higginson wrote Olney urging caution.[30] Meanwhile, he and a group of Boston businessmen petitioned Cleveland to name foreigners to the proposed commission "to obviate the possibility of accusations of prejudice. . . . "[31] On 19 and 20 December, the New York Stock Exchange panicked. "While on the surface there is general approval of the President's message," Peter Olney wrote from New York, "there is an undercurrent of sentiment among bankers and business men of considerable strength" that the talk of war would "render it more difficult for the government to obtain gold . . . to maintain the gold reserve."[32] Secretary Lamont, with close ties to Wall Street, received many complaints. "[T]he 'war' has struck us first in the Stock Exchange," one broker wrote. The president of Hanover National Bank, noting that "we have had a 'parrot and monkey' time here," complained that he was "sick of these troubles. . . . " Andrew Carnegie suggested several possible solutions that he thought Lamont might want to relay to Cleveland for ending the crisis. "The Money question," he added, was "far more serious than this of Venezuela!"[33] Henry Villard, a strong backer of Cleveland, warned that the message had "reduced to naught" the president's "great efforts to save the country from financial collapse."[34]

The eager support of their jingo enemies, the negative reaction of their staunchest supporters, and the brief collapse of the stock exchange dismayed both Olney and Cleveland but did not alter their course. Olney became defensive, arguing that underlying weaknesses, not the president's message, were the cause of the panic on Wall Street.[35] Other backers of the president's policy offered different explanations. Henry Cabot Lodge asserted that the British had manipulated the market, and Olney's cousin, Sigourney Butler, blamed the "Jews" for rigging both the New York and London exchanges.[36] Given the complexity—if not irrationality—of stock-market fluctuations, the impact of Cleveland's message can only be guessed. There is no doubt, however, that the men in the eastern business centers who had tutored and supported the administration in its currency policies were unhappy at the turn of events. The administration, in turn, questioned the patriotism of men who put profit and speculative gain above principle.[37]

In December the president might well have been willing to allow the commission to proceed exactly as stated in his message—whatever Olney's views—and back its findings with force if need be. In a high temper over the British reply and annoyed by the clamor following his message, Cleveland seems to have been at odds with everyone. Even Olney, perhaps seen as the chief architect of his woes, was temporarily out of grace. Cleveland named his commission, for example, without regard for Olney's opinions and included at least one member whom Olney disapproved of.[38]

Except for appointing the commission, however, Olney bore responsibility for all that followed. New though he was to diplomacy, the secretary conducted himself with considerable skill. From the first Olney placed no faith in the commission as the vehicle for resolving the controversy; his goal was direct Anglo-Venezuelan negotiations if possible, Anglo-American if necessary, to settle the question once and for all. He did not abandon the commission until the dispute was ended, however, using it as a prod whenever the British lagged. The speedy conclusion that he wanted he could not achieve. Salisbury, believing that domestic politics caused the outburst from Washington, prescribed delay and would not be hurried. But Olney, like a dog worrying a bone, kept gnawing away. He would not let Salisbury rest, and he would not abandon the principle of complete and unrestricted arbitration. Tactically, however, he remained flexible and imaginative. When relations were at their worst during January and February 1896, Olney turned to unofficial channels for negotiating. These conversations became tangled and eventually broke down, but not before they had lubricated the way to settlement by conventional means.

The president had not yet finished naming his commission when Olney began his first foray into informal diplomacy. On New Year's Day 1896, Olney held the first of several meetings with Henry Norman, a special correspondent and subeditor of the *London Daily Chronicle*.³⁹ Ostensibly, Olney sought to assure the British of the American desire for a peaceful and reasonable solution to the controversy. But he also hoped to accomplish through Norman and his column what he had failed to induce Cleveland to do in his Venezuela message: destroy the validity of the Schomburgk line and remove the Monroe Doctrine from the discussion. For Norman's first inspired column, Olney supplied direct quotations from high British officials of 1840 and 1841 showing that when the Schomburgk line was first drawn, they regarded it as merely "preliminary" and a "talking point."⁴⁰ In his second column Norman declared that the intent of Cleveland's message had been "amicable," whatever its results. As for the Monroe Doctrine, that was not worth discussing. If it had not originally brought such matters as the Venezuelan dispute within its "four corners," the "new Olney doctrine," supported "overwhelmingly" by the American people, had. Norman reported that the president was aware of the domestic political value of his message, but the British government could make "no greater mistake" than to regard the message "as a mere party manoeuvre." The United States demanded arbitration "as a sacred right" and would fight, if necessary, to get it. Norman outlined four ways—all presumably suggested by Olney—for reaching arbitration, but noted that Washington preferred a direct Anglo-Venezuelan agreement, and to that end was prepared to put pressure on the Latin republic.⁴¹

Norman's third column declared that "everybody here worth considering desires peace," and that if Salisbury would suggest a way, any advances that he made would be "received with wide-open arms." The issue went beyond either the validity of the Schomburgk line or "any promiscuous discussion of the Monroe Doctrine." The United States was "perfectly willing—indeed, glad—to see England secure any amount of Venezuelan territory" so long as her claims were "capable of historical and diplomatic proof."⁴² Norman overreached himself. Olney complained that the column did "great harm" by representing the American people as "sighing for peace" and "wanting peace at any price." The correspondent replied that his pieces were doing great good, indeed, had "demolished the chief argument" of his own government.⁴³ Unmoved, Olney declined further interviews. He had gotten his message through and won a victory. On the day of the break with Norman, the *London Times* declared editorially that there was "no particular sanctity in the Schomburgk line"; it had served only to mark off settled from unsettled districts. So long as all British and Venezuelan settlements were excluded, arbitration should be possible without any reference whatever to the controversial line. "I trust Boston people are still loyal to the Schomburk [*sic*] line," Olney remarked sarcastically to Sigourney Butler, "notwithstanding London has thrown it over."[44]

Cleveland's message had produced widespread shock and disbelief in England. A quick succession of events elsewhere in the world, however, jarred British complacency even more profoundly. Longbrewing troubles in South Africa bubbled over at year's end when a British filibustering expedition failed in an attempt to seize Johannesburg and topple the Boer Republic. Britain's chagrin at the ill-fated Jameson raid was compounded on 3 January when Kaiser Wilhelm telegraphed congratulations to Boer President Paul Krugar, implying German support of the Afrikanders. Britain suddenly found herself alone in a hostile world. Already at odds with France over control of West Africa, the Nile Valley, and parts of Siam, and with Russia over Turkish matters, England now saw the vague hope of working with the German-dominated Triple Alliance dashed by the Kaiser's telegram.[45] A chilling sense of isolation, coupled with growing awareness that its claim in Guiana was far less certain than Salisbury had suggested in November, wrought a rapid change in the attitude of the British public.

In early January, Salisbury still advocated stalling on the Venezuelan question, at least until the United States replied formally to his notes of 26 November. Given time, he believed, "material interests" in the United States would tend to "outweigh sentiment," especially when "superficially held." Besides, Venezuela at any time might blunder.[46] Chamberlain, too, regarded the American threat as less serious than it sounded and saw little chance of war. Opposed to arbitrating any land east of the Schomburgk line, he talked vaguely of "other ways" to settle the controversy peacefully.[47]

At the first postholiday cabinet session on 11 January, Salisbury and Chamberlain found themselves in the minority. Recent events convinced the others that Britain could not afford to risk war with the United States. To Salisbury's disgust, they voted to open negotiations.[48] The prime minister would not be rushed, but a slow retreat, beginning with recognition of the Monroe Doctrine, got under way. On 15 January, Arthur Balfour (leader of the Tory party in Commons, First Lord of the Treasury, and Salisbury's nephew) declared in a public address that Britain had supported the doctrine in Monroe's time and had never altered its stand. Nor was England using the dispute with Venezuela to enlarge its holdings. Britain had no "forward policy" in South America: "we have never desired, and we do not now desire, either to interfere in the domestic concerns of any South American State or to acquire for ourselves any territory that belongs to them." The prospect of an Anglo-American war, Balfour added, carried with it "something of the unnatural horror of civil war. . . . We should be fighting our own flesh and blood (*hear, hear*), speaking our own language, sharing our own civilization (*Cheers*)." The day would come, he predicted, when "some statesman of authority" would "lay down the doctrine that between English speaking peoples," war was "impossible."[49]

Pursuant to the ministry's decision, Salisbury authorized Chamberlain to open unofficial conversations ("amateur diplomacy," the prime minister called it) with the United States.[50] And so, through Lyon Lord Playfair, a friend of the American ambassador, who met with Bayard, Chamberlain raised a number of exploratory questions with Olney. Unfortunately, Bayard was too eager an advocate of Anglo-American friendship and cooperation, and too much a critic of the administration's Venezuelan policy, to function effectively. Olney's note of 20 July had appalled him, and he could only believe that it did not reflect the president's thinking. Cleveland's message of 17 December killed that illusion, and—coupled with the Jameson raid— Bayard wrote, "sent my heart down to its very depths and I cannot raise it."[51] Cleveland, he believed, had made a "grave and great error of judgment." The clash might have been avoided, he admitted, if Britain had not "most unwisely disregarded" appeals "to heal this *Venezuela* sore." Instead of putting American fears to rest, Salisbury had evinced "a disposition to press forward without abatement" in India, Central America, Guiana, and Africa. "If Dr. Jameson had made a successful entry into Johannesburg," he observed, "I can scarcely doubt the govt would have sustained him and his act would have been equally *without law*."[52]

The exchange with Playfair gave Bayard new hope. The British made two proposals: that a conference be called to discuss adding the Monroe Doctrine to international law, and that Britain and the United States agree to submit all lands in dispute in Guiana—excluding districts already settled by Venezuela or Britain—to a tripartite British, American, and Venezuelan commission. The conference appealed to Bayard. It might "save trouble" in the future "if open public notice to all trespassers" were "posted on the European side of the Atlantic."[53] Olney promptly shot down the scheme. The United States, he cabled, was "content with existing status of Monroe Doctrine, which, as well as its application to said controversy, it regards as completely and satisfactorily accepted by the people of the Western Continents."[54]

Having had trouble enough with the doctrine, Olney preferred not to see it bruited about at an international conference and then rejected, however England might vote. Even if it were approved, any subsequent action taken by the United States under the doctrine would be subject to review or interpretation by the other powers. Olney's firm veto won another victory: it effectively removed the Monroe Doctrine from further consideration.

As for tripartite arbitration, excluding settled districts, Olney proposed instead that England and the United States sign a convention providing for the submission of all controversies arising between them—including the Venezuelan question—to arbitration by dual Anglo-American tribunals. As for the Venezuelan dispute, explicit provision should be made that "long-continued occupation of territory" would be "considered" and "given all the weight belonging to it in reason and justice, or by the principles of international law."[55] When Bayard inquired if Venezuela had agreed to its exclusion from the tribunal, Olney testily asked who wanted to know. Learning that Bayard's inquiry was in anticipation of Britain's asking, Olney instructed him to wait until the point was raised. When Playfair subsequently did ask, Olney, who of course had not consulted Venezuela, made no reply.[56]

Chamberlain did not object to general arbitration, but insisted that settlements in Guiana must be excluded, not just taken "into account." He also believed that Venezuela should be represented on the tribunal. Bayard reported, however, that Britain would probably accept stipulation by the United States of Venezuelan concurrence. Once more Britain had yielded; the right of the United States to speak for Venezuela was not raised again.[57]

Bayard repeatedly pressed Britain's case with Olney. The "apparently undefined, unexplained, and ever-progressive extension of British jurisdiction" over disputed lands could "now be assumed" to be absolutely halted, he wrote, thanks to the strong stand taken by the administration. Having abandoned the Schomburgk line, Britain was prepared to arbitrate all territory in question if only districts already settled were excluded. Olney refused to budge. "With sincerest purpose to do so," he cabled, "am unable to comprehend the justice or pertinency of the proposition that mere occupation shall be decisive of title." The time, character, and circumstances of occupation all had to be taken into consideration. Putting his finger on one of the chief blocks to agreement, Olney predicted that defining settled areas would be difficult. Even if accepted in principle, each specific instance would lead to debate and probably end in disagreement, and Venezuela would have to be consulted at every step, thereby causing "interminable" delay.[58] From this exchange, Bayard somehow concluded that Olney had no objection to excluding bona fide settlements and misled the British by tacitly—if not explicitly—conveying the idea to them. Chamberlain suggested that perhaps "five years *bona fide* occupation would be a fair definition."[59]

Bayard's statement to Olney that the British were "quite ready to meet us half-way and I trust we can make up the other half," characterized his sentiments throughout.[60] Not surprisingly, Olney decided near the end of January that he could no longer work with Bayard. Since the president would not recall him, Olney moved quietly behind the scenes to transfer the negotiations to Washington. James R. Roosevelt, secretary to the American legation in London, then home on leave, became Olney's willing accomplice. Roosevelt called at the State Department and filled Olney's ears with gossip that confirmed his suspicions that Bayard not only was unsympathetic to the administration's policy, but was trying to thwart it. Roosevelt may also have been the source of the story that Bayard, in conveying the note of 20 July, had suggested that Olney did not speak for the president. At any rate, Roosevelt agreed, upon his return to London, to sound out the ambassador's reaction to transferring the talks to Washington. To the surprise of both Roosevelt and Olney, Bayard did not object, though he was unwilling himself to initiate the move. Disappointingly, Bayard gave no indication that he was thinking of resigning.[61]

Meanwhile, to circumvent Bayard, Olney opened a second informal channel of communication with the British government. George W. Smalley, long-time London correspondent of the *New York Tribune* and recently appointed American correspondent for the *London Times*, like Norman before him, offered to convey the secretary's views in his columns. In return, George Earle Buckle, editor of the *Times*, after consulting with Salisbury, was to reply on the editorial page. Smalley repeated the points made earlier by Norman: The administration was not playing politics, it wanted a settlement that would not discredit England, it was open to suggestions, and it hoped agreement could be reached before the report of the Venezuela commission. Smalley also resurrected the various alternatives for reaching arbitration that Olney had suggested to Norman.[62] Then, on 24 January, Smalley cabled Buckle a new set of proposals from Olney. The United States would withdraw its present commission and substitute a commission consisting of two Englishmen and two Americans. After careful examination of the facts (not seeking to establish the "true" boundary line), the commissioners would report to their respective governments.

In the event of disagreement, a fifth commissioner, named by a neutral personage, would be added. The commission's findings were not to be binding "unless perhaps" on matters of fact. Once the facts were determined, "all parties concerned" would enter into direct negotiations to draw a mutually acceptable boundary. "If preferred," the matter could be submitted to a tribunal consisting of the chief justices of England and the United States, and, if necessary, a third neutral jurist.[63]

Salisbury and his colleagues accepted the proposal at once. Unfortunately Olney saw the text of Smalley's communication only after it was sent and insisted that three "alterations" be sent at once. (1) The commissioners were to act as a body, not as two separate groups. (2) Findings of fact were to be conclusive. And (3), if direct negotiations failed, both parties were to accept binding arbitration by the proposed tribunal. Salisbury was upset at Olney's apparent reneging on his own proposals, but accepted the first two alterations with the proviso that findings of fact, to be binding, must be unanimous. Conclusive unrestricted arbitration he rejected. Smalley accepted blame for having "misunderstood" Olney, and the British tried to save the agreement by accepting "ultimate binding arbitration" if districts "bona fide settled for say ten years" by either party were excluded.[64]

In spite of complaints from Buckle that Britain alone had made concessions—on the Schomburgk line, on the Monroe Doctrine, on the United States' acting for Venezuela, and on ultimate arbitration so long as settled districts were excluded—Olney held firm. The Smalley-Buckle-Salisbury channel closed in early February when Smalley confessed that unless the settled-districts issue could be resolved, the two sides were "reduced to mere argumentation."[65] Smalley stayed on, however, and was used by Olney from time to time to prod London.

Not long after, the Chamberlain-Playfair-Bayard line collapsed when Olney sent over it the same proposal already conveyed through Smalley and Buckle. Although settlements could not be excluded because mere occupation did not confer title, he wrote, Bayard should ask the British for their definition of settled districts. Chamberlain, assuming from earlier conversations that Olney long since had agreed to the principle of excluding bona fide settled districts, now demanded explicit assurance. When Bayard evaded the issue, Chamberlain called off the conversations.[66]

Steps to transfer the negotiations to Washington were already under way. As a first step, Olney persuaded the British to move the still-festering Uruan incident to the United States because Venezuela had no representative in London, while both Venezuela and Britain had envoys in Washington.[67] When the *London Times*, on 21 February, declared that the newspaper discussions had reached a turning point and that protocol required the United States to take the next step, Olney inquired through Smalley if the editorial reflected Salisbury's thinking. Assured that it did, he at once proposed transfer of the talks to Washington. Salisbury concurred.[68] Roosevelt at the London embassy was cheered. "We were daily losing ground," he reported. "[T]here was a deplorable lack of 'grip' and energy here." Bayard had "worried and fretted" so much that he no longer seemed well. Roosevelt believed that the ambassador was "now really *glad* to have matters moved to Washington."[69]

Despite the transfer, Olney insisted on humiliating Bayard, for whom he now had only contempt. The ambassador must correct the impression that the United States (meaning Olney) had even temporarily conceded exclusion of settled areas from arbitration. "Nothing emanating from this side of the water" gave the "slightest countenance to the idea," Olney declared, and he instructed Bayard to state to Chamberlain the "true position of the United States which I am sure you apprehend. . . . " The reason, he said, was that Chamberlain's misconceptions were prejudicing negotiations in Washington. Two weeks later, Olney wired for a report on steps taken. "Mr. B. has been rather shaken up by your cable," Roosevelt wrote. The secretary agreed with Olney (he always did) that the matter should be cleared up, but admitted that Chamberlain "understands our position pretty well now."[70]

Bayard, in response, questioned the need to reopen communications only to repeat what already had been stated in previous contacts. Since informal conversations had ended, he doubted the propriety of approaching any department of the British government except the Foreign Office. Olney ordered Bayard to reopen the channel with Chamberlain or to go directly to Salisbury. Whichever, he was to correct the misimpression. The order gave Roosevelt "great satisfaction," but "brought Mr. B. up with a round turn and fairly made him jump!" Bayard would "have agreed to almost *anything*, rather than be obliged to show either [Chamberlain or Salisbury] your letter," Roosevelt declared.[71] Olney scored his point, but negotiations were in no way speeded.

By the end of February 1896, the Anglo-American dispute over Venezuela had passed its crisis. The stupidity of possible war with the United States over an unfamiliar piece of South American jungle, coupled with mounting concern for the balance of power in Europe and the problems of Turkey and South Africa, produced the backdown. In the United States, Olney and Cleveland willingly assisted Britain in retreating gracefully. The detente, though unofficial, completely altered the tone and substance of the discussion. Bold assertions and haughty disdain gave way to an earnest effort to find common ground. Britain no longer questioned the right of the United States to concern itself with the boundary dispute or to act as surrogate for Venezuela. In turn, the United States dropped the prickly issue of the Monroe Doctrine as soon as Britain acknowledged adherence to its principles (albeit not with specific application to Venezuela). Both sides now favored impartial investigation. Only whether arbitration was to apply to all parts of the disputed zone, including settled districts, and whether the award would be binding and final, remained to be resolved.

14

Arbitration

Informal diplomacy had narrowed differences over Venezuela, but remaining issues kept Olney and Pauncefote sparring through the spring and summer. As his opening thrust, Olney asked Pauncefote to submit officially the investigation-negotiation-arbitration scheme already put forward through Smalley and Buckle and rejected. When Pauncefote observed that the plan was unacceptable because it provided for final and binding arbitration, Olney replied that Smalley had "positively informed" him that the formula was acceptable to Salisbury. Olney must have been bluffing. Smalley had positively informed him that Salisbury would accept only the original version cabled to Buckle, not the corrected one. As predicted, Salisbury rejected the plan because, in effect, it ultimately empowered a single "foreign jurist" (the neutral judge, voting with the Americans) to evict British colonists from lands long occupied. Instead, Salisbury suggested, the first step should be an authoritative investigation of the facts, "leaving to subsequent discussion" how a settlement based on those facts would be reached.[1]

The prime minister confused matters by reviving Olney's earlier proposal of an Anglo-American general arbitration treaty. Since the two powers could not agree on how far to carry arbitration in the Venezuela conflict, Salisbury suggested that they determine the practical limits of arbitration through experimentation. As a "modest beginning," he proposed that all questions of national honor or territorial integrity be excluded. Other differences, however, would be submitted to a tribunal consisting of an English, an American, and a neutral jurist (the last being chosen in advance but used only if the first two could not agree). Awards involving claims of private citizens of either country would be final. Where "the territory, territorial rights, sovereignty, or jurisdiction" of one of the signatories was at stake, awards would not be conclusive if either government protested within three months. A protested award would go into effect only if subsequently affirmed by a majority of no less than five to one, of a court of review made up of three judges each from the highest courts of Britain and the United States.[2]

Olney suspected the move to be dilatory, but went along in the hope that some good might result. The definition of subjects for arbitration was too imprecise, he believed, the exclusion of disputes involving national honor too all-inclusive, and allowing two judges on the court of review to overturn the whole proceeding, rendered the plan "illusory and abortive." "[A]rbitration which does not end in a final award," he said, "is no arbitration at all."[3] When Olney learned that the Venezuelan dispute was not to be included, he told Pauncefote that he was sorry he had wasted time on the proposal. General arbitration would "keep," Venezuela would not.[4] The plan had seemed to offer the means for resolving both future controversies and the Venezuelan dispute, but the latter now seemed "further off than ever." Congress was about to adjourn, the presidential campaign would be getting under way, the report of the investigative commission (which would tie the administration's hands) would soon appear, and Salisbury's response seemed "to put an end to the negotiations."

For one party to assert terms at the outset and to refuse to modify them, Pauncefote replied, did not constitute negotiations. Why not simply begin with a joint commission to establish the facts? Olney, "his tone one of despondency, not unmixed with irritation," replied that the United States would not accept any plan that did not provide ultimately for a conclusive decision. Perhaps, he threatened, his only recourse was to stir up the press. Since the intervening discussions had been private, Pauncefote suggested that a formal reply to Salisbury's most recent note would be more appropriate.[5]

An official exchange brought agreement no closer. Olney tried to broaden the subject matter of general arbitration by suggesting that any controversy be arbitrable unless specifically withdrawn by act of Congress or Parliament as too deeply touching national honor. Awards should be conclusive in all cases, Olney insisted. Even a protested award should go into effect if affirmed by a simple majority of the joint court of review. If that body should divide evenly, three (not one) neutral jurists, whose vote would be final, should be added.[6]

Again Salisbury rejected the proposal. Impartial arbiters would be difficult to find, and international law neither defined the process nor specified the time required for establishing title to land by prescription. If adopted, the plan would give rise to a flood of cases. Unlike war, arbitration involved no risk for claimants, so they had nothing to lose by advancing exaggerated claims. As the number of cases increased, he added, so would opportunities for mistakes. Olney disagreed. International law was quite specific in the matter of title by prescription. Occupation must be "open, exclusive, adverse, continuous, and under claim of right." A precise time limit was inexpedient because such conditions as rate and degree of settlement and the amount of investment and development had to be taken into account. As for Salisbury's fears of a rash of claims and injustices, Olney suggested that would be true only if the treaty were multilateral. Since it was limited to the United States and Britain, he envisioned few territorial claims, boundary disputes, or problems of prescriptive rights of settlers living in unoccupied lands in the Western Hemisphere.[7]

In an effort to salvage general arbitration, Pauncefote proposed simplifying the courts of review. Could not a protested award be reviewed by five judges of the highest court of the protesting power? he asked. Unless they rejected an award, he argued, it should go into effect. Salisbury accepted the modification and added that if the United States would stand in Venezuela's place (by naming one of the three members of the arbitral tribunal, and, if the award were protested, allow five members of its Supreme Court to review the decision) Britain would submit the Venezuelan dispute to arbitration under the proposed treaty.[8] Olney favored the plan, Pauncefote reported, but was overruled by the cabinet. Since Olney and Cleveland kept the cabinet entirely out of the matter, Olney must have used that excuse to cover his objection. At any rate, Olney agreed that the modification was a "step in the right direction" for a general arbitration treaty, but declined to submit the Venezuelan dispute under the new plan. The two matters thereafter were kept separate.[9]

Venezuelan negotiations once more turned to the question of settlers in the disputed zone. In winding down the London negotiations, Olney had instructed Bayard to press the British for a definition of settled districts, which they had promised. Possibly they were using the term in "some special or extraordinary sense" which, if known, could be helpful. It was Olney's "abiding conviction," however, that if a definition were made, "no more convincing exposure of the preposterous character of their claim could be desired." On that point he might have been right. Despite repeated promises, Salisbury never defined the term.[10]

In June, Salisbury offered to accept Olney's investigation-negotiation-arbitration formula (with minor modifications) providing no bona fide settlements of either party as of 1 January 1887 were awarded to the other. Olney's response was cutting. The proviso was manifestly unjust because it helped only the British while hurting Venezuela. Britain, he pointed out, had not proclaimed the Schomburgk line to be the provisional boundary of British Guiana until October 1886. Prior to that date British settlers could not have believed that they were establishing bona fide settlements on British soil. Quoting British officials in Guiana, Olney demonstrated that after June 1887, all settlers going into the disputed zone were warned of Venezuela's claims. Only between October 1886 and June 1887 could settlers have justifiably believed themselves settling undisputed lands. The question involved not so much the bona fides of the colonists as the bona fides of the British government. All territory at dispute must be submitted to arbitration, though the stipulation should be added that the rights of settlers should be given "such weight and effect" as "reason, justice, the rules of international law, and the equities of the particular case may appear to require." Salisbury, in response, pointed out that Venezuela's extreme claim to the Essequibo threw into doubt British titles that had run unquestioned "for many generations." The problem was how to separate those areas from districts recently settled or as yet unsettled.[11]

By this time both sides were anxious to break off discussions for the summer. Believing that publication of the correspondence to date might win public support, each side tried to end on a strong note. When the prime minister sent a parting salvo, Olney refused to let him have the last word. "If Salisbury's note takes you sudden," Cleveland observed, "why don't you respond with a kind of waiting, promising suggestion despatch, indicating more to follow?"[12] The "promising suggestion," according to Pauncefote, came from James J. Storrow, a Boston lawyer hired by Venezuela (on Olney's recommendation) to prepare its case. Salisbury's most recent communication indicated that Britain's chief concern was for settlements that had been unquestioned for generations. Would England accept conclusive, unrestricted arbitration of the entire area at dispute, Olney asked, if the rule were adopted that territory in "exclusive, notorious, and actual use and occupation for even two generations, or, say, for sixty years" was excluded? With that question—which proved to be the ultimate key to the matter—left dangling, official negotiations ended until October.[13]

As the two sides maneuvered for advantage before publishing, passages in notes were excised or altered, replies were made to previously unanswered points, and letters were drafted to secure the best position. "Undoubtedly all this backing and filling is true diplomacy," Olney wrote Cleveland. "There may be something very profound in it. But my impression is that it is a sort of pettifogging which accomplishes nothing and which is in truth not in keeping with the serious character of the grave issues involved." In spite of his impatience for results, Olney had held his own. He also derived considerable pride from Salisbury's request that a portion of the correspondence, in which Olney demolished one of the prime minister's arguments, not be published.[14]

Throughout, Olney acted without consulting Venezuela, as if he held blank power-of-attorney for that country. His every move was related to what he thought best for the United States, though he probably thought that he did Venezuela full justice. He allegedly told one British visitor, however, that if Britain had but agreed to "our arbitration," he and the president, whose "predilections were English," would have favored their cause. Once arbitration was accepted, he added, England could keep it going "for ten years" if it wished. Venezuela, he added, must do exactly what the United States told her.[15]

Although the Caracas government had appointed a commission of its own to prepare its case and had employed the pamphleteer Scruggs, among others, to assist, Olney urged Venezuela to hire Storrow also. The two had been acquainted since their days together at Harvard Law School, but Olney had not known of Storrow's interest in Venezuela until he published an article on the dispute in January 1896. Much taken with it, Olney gave a copy to Pauncefote, who forwarded it to London. Storrow had applied the Monroe Doctrine to the dispute much as Olney had. The doctrine, he wrote, was a statement of fact, not of law. The fact that it stated was that any European expansion in the New World constituted a threat to the security of the United States. That threat, in turn, justified United States intervention. In his treatment of the substance of the controversy, Storrow made a strong case for the Moroco River line—first proposed by Lord Aberdeen in 1844—as the just frontier between British Guiana and Venezuela.[16]

Learning that Storrow was on a business trip to Venezuela, and knowing him to be a "first rate lawyer," Olney urged the Venezuelan government to secure his services. Despite his inclination to refuse because of poor health, Storrow accepted. A preliminary investigation convinced him that up to about 1885 there had been little settlement in the disputed zone. With the discovery of gold in the area that year, a rush developed. Even so, the influx of settlers did not begin in earnest until 1887 when the British began a "system of deliberate invasion . . ."[17] Within a month, Storrow returned to the United States to prepare a refutation of a bluebook on the dispute that the British had published in March 1896.

Two other incidents illustrated Olney's attitude towards Venezuela. The Uruan affair, as already noted, had been transferred at Olney's suggestion to Washington for direct conversations between Pauncefote and the Venezuelan minister, Don Jose Andrade. Before those discussions reached a conclusion, a British surveyor was arrested by Venezuelan officials in the disputed zone. When this came to Olney's attention, he urged upon Andrade the wisdom of releasing the man. "[I]t is most unwise," he commented, "by springing new questions and adding to existing grievances, to embarrass and impede the settlement of issues already pending between Venezuela and Great Britain and in respect of which Venezuela has solicited and obtained the good offices of the United States." Although Venezuela on its own released the Englishman before Olney's intervention, the British ambassador commended Olney's "promptitude & good will."[18] On 23 September, Andrade informed Olney that when his government agreed to pay a £1,500 indemnity, the British government regarded the Uruan incident as closed. On the other hand, the British had just sent a demand for payment of £1,000 for the arrest of the surveyor. "Is Venezuela to yield also in that case?" he asked.[19]

During the summer, two influential young Republican visitors to England lent their support to ending the dispute. Olney met the first, Henry White, at a dinner party given by Senator Lodge in May. A former secretary of legation in London, White was knowledgeable about English affairs and endorsed Cleveland's Venezuelan policy. Unlike present embassy staff members, he had direct social access to ruling circles in England. Learning that White was soon to leave for Britain, Olney enlisted his services unofficially. At a round of dinner parties and weekends at the country houses of the mighty, White talked with the "Powers that be" (Salisbury, Balfour, and Chamberlain), "leaders of the opposition" (Sir William Harcourt and Herbert Asquith), and a leading financier, Baron Rothschild. The ministry, he learned, favored delay, hoping the November elections in America would bring a more pliable administration to power. Salisbury regarded compulsory arbitration as "a dangerous precedent" for the empire, one that would give rise to innumerable claims from every quarter of the globe. Canada, too, opposed retreat, lest the United States next turn northward. Cleveland's first-term secretary of war, William C. Endicott of Boston (Chamberlain's father-in-law), and other American businessmen counseled delay, insisting that the Venezuelan issue was dead in the United States.

White also learned that unidentified Americans had persuaded Salisbury that Olney was an extreme Anglophobe, seeking only personal acclaim or party advantage, who, as a lawyer rather than diplomat, was more interested in winning a legal case than in reaching accord. To the extent that he could, White countered these impressions. He also expressed doubt that any new administration would offer easier terms. Olney was impressed. White's reports showed how the United States was "handicapped" by having as its representative in London a man not in sympathy with its policy, who, "through sentiment, self-conceit, physical infirmity or otherwise," had been "practically disabled from rendering the services rightfully expected of him."[20]

The second visitor, John Hay, was close to the Republican presidential candidate William McKinley. Invited to give his views on the election and its impact on the Venezuelan dispute, Hay told Salisbury, Chamberlain, Harcourt, and others that he expected McKinley to win. Britain should expect no backward step in Venezuela, however, because the American people were nearly unanimous in their support of Cleveland's policy. Should Bryan win, no one could predict what might happen. Reporting afterwards to Olney, Hay noted that many Englishmen now believed Salisbury's reply of 26 November a mistake, and that on the whole the United States was acting reasonably. All favored settlement of the matter if it could be reached without damage to Britain's prestige.[21]

In September, Joseph Chamberlain and his wife visited her parents in Boston. "A frank and unofficial talk on the subject [of Venezuela] between two men of business," he wrote Olney, "might assist the amicable settlement" both desired. White had warned of Chamberlain's coming and pointed out that the colonial secretary was "the chief obstacle" to submission of the settled districts to unconditional arbitration. If Olney would not yield on that point, Chamberlain had told White, he was prepared to await the next administration. When White replied that a new administration would not change course, Chamberlain shot back, "Well, then, I am afraid, that, sickening as is the prospect, we shall have to look forward to war." White interpreted Chamberlain's visit as an indication that the ministry had "practically decided" on terms of settlement. The colonial secretary apparently wanted to have "a hand in it" and would probably try to get Olney to modify his stand on settled districts.[22]

Content to work with Pauncefote, Olney asked Chamberlain point-blank if he had special instructions from Salisbury. Learning that he did not, the secretary gave him little attention beyond the requirements of courtesy. The two did discuss settled districts, however. Since both Britain's and Venezuela's extreme claims were "monstrous," Chamberlain suggested laying down reasonable intermediate lines between which an arbitral commission could draw the final boundary. Olney granted that no court would uphold Venezuela's extreme claim, but declined to draw a line that he would have to press on the Caracas government. When Olney noted his proposal to Salisbury—that all settlements occupied for sixty or more years be exempted from arbitration—Chamberlain replied that thirty years would be better.[23]

Anticipating a second meeting, Olney discussed the issue of settled districts with Storrow. Was a forty-year exemption feasible? he asked. Storrow saw no objection from a practical point of view because British settlement had not begun until the 1880s. However, Salisbury in his note of 26 November had said that Venezuelan advances in the disputed zone subsequent to the pledges of 1850 were invalid. The same point should apply with equal force against British encroachments, Storrow argued. Although sixty years was the classic period for establishing a claim by prescription, rather than lose the arbitration, the United States could afford to move as far as fifty years without waiving or impairing the agreement of 1850.

Olney and Storrow agreed that it would be "dangerous to go far" in dealing with Chamberlain. At the same time they wished to keep him "in a good frame of mind" by letting him believe his mission had "accomplished something."[24] The opportunity came when Chamberlain sent a note proposing a second meeting and inviting Olney to comment on the possibility of Anglo-American cooperation in Turkey. The world had just learned of another slaughter of Armenians on the streets of Constantinople, followed by similar massacres throughout Anatolia. British public opinion was astir. While the ministry preferred not to intervene unilaterally, no European power was willing to engage in joint action with Britain.[25]

Olney decided to substitute a letter for a second meeting and discussed with Cleveland what he should write. It was "hard to restrain one's self" on the "cursed Turkish question," Cleveland admitted, but he "supposed we must." Olney ought not to repel Chamberlain's call for cooperation "any more than necessary," and should stress "protecting our people very distinctly indeed." The president did not want to give the British the excuse that the United States was unmindful of its duty, even if England was.[26]

In his letter to Chamberlain, Olney noted that the spirit manifested in the United States after Cleveland's Venezuelan message still prevailed "in all its original intensity." "The college presidents, pseudo-diplomats, disgruntled office-seekers, and cranks of all sorts," who assumed that this reaction was due to "deep seated and chronic hostility" toward England, completely misread popular sentiment. Far from hating the mother country, Americans were proud of their Anglo-Saxon heritage. Nothing was more un-English, however, than fawning and toadying, and when American representatives abroad engaged in such behavior, however much it amused Englishmen, Americans were humiliated. The purpose of the note of 20 July had been to end such toadying. London's rude reply had aroused the American people because it seemed to indicate that Britain thought that the United States had no policy, or, if it did, that it did not matter because the United States could not defend it.

As for Armenia, Olney declared, the American people would be gratified to stand side by side with England as an ally in defending human rights and Christian civilization. The traditional policy of the United States, however, confined it to duties within the Western Hemisphere, and to noninterference in European affairs. Nonetheless, the United States stood ready, as its growing navy attested, to protect its citizens and their rights anywhere. If Britain should decide to put the "Armenian charnelhouse" in order, the United States would consider the "moment opportune for vigorous exertion on behalf of American citizens and interests in Turkey," and would support those demands with "physical force."[27] Whether Olney suspected that Britain would never act without the support of the other European powers or was encouraging Britain to act by offering cooperation is not known. In light of Cleveland's instructions, however, the former seems the more likely.

In late October, Pauncefote returned to the United States with drafts of two treaties: one for settling the Venezuelan dispute, the other providing for general arbitration of disputes between Britain and the United States. The British accepted Olney's investigation-negotiation-arbitration formula for settling the Venezuela controversy, but modified it with a rule that districts settled for a specified period were to be excluded. Chamberlain had muddied that issue by reporting that Olney would accept a thirty-year rule. Following the advice of Andrade and Storrow, Olney refused to consider any date later than the Anglo-Venezuelan agreement of 1850.[28] As negotiations proceeded, the plan was simplified. Investigation and Anglo-Venezuelan negotiations were dropped in favor of arbitration by a five-man tribunal consisting of two each from the supreme courts of England and the United States, and a fifth neutral jurist. The negotiators adopted a fifty-year rule on settled districts because it was less complicated than reference to the agreement of 1850 would have been. Finally, to circumvent the necessity for approval of the treaty by the United States Senate, they agreed that Great Britain and Venezuela should be the signatory powers.[29] On 12 November, Olney and Pauncefote initialed a memorandum containing the heads of treaty. As soon as Venezuela and Britain restored diplomatic relations, they would formally sign the treaty. Olney promptly suspended the work of the commission appointed eleven months before, and so far as the public was concerned, the long controversy was at an end. Olney believed that he had won a great victory.[30]

What sort of triumph, if any, had Olney won? However much historians have deplored the Venezuelan affair, most have conceded that it was a major event in the rise of the United States to world-power status. From the dispute emerged a stronger and expanded Monroe Doctrine. The affair revealed a dramatic increase in American interest in the Caribbean and, coupled with the Spanish War, marked the onset of American expansionism in the area. The Venezuelan controversy also divided the era of American Anglophobia and British indifference to the United States from the period of Anglo-American cooperation in world affairs. How much of this was planned and intended by Cleveland and Olney and how much was fortuitous is uncertain. So, too, were the motives and goals of the administration which have been seen variously as strategic, economic, or political. There can be, of course, no conclusive answer. Olney put it well in 1903 when asked to supply evidence to disprove the statement that "Cleveland, playing for the vote of the Anti-British Democrats of the Southern and Western States, issued his Venezuelan Message, which was tantamount to a threat of war." Olney had "not the slightest doubt" that the statement was "absolutely unfounded," but, he observed, "in asking me for proof of what was *not* in Mr. Cleveland's mind, you are asking for something which no mortal being, unless it be Mr. Cleveland, himself, can possibly furnish."[31] Determining what *was* in Olney's or Cleveland's mind is no easier.

If the goal of the administration was strategic—to use the Venezuelan dispute as a pretext for enhancing the Monroe Doctrine, thereby strengthening and extending the influence of the United States in the Western Hemisphere—it was achieved.[32] In the light of subsequent developments, the powers, led by Britain, became more respectful of the doctrine after 1896 and interpreted Olney's 20 July note as an assertion of United States domination over the hemisphere. The evidence indicates, however, that such had not been the administration's objective. Cleveland and Olney invoked the doctrine not to enlarge its scope, but to remind Britain of existing American policy regarding political or territorial expansion by European powers in the New World. Far from holding that all boundary disputes between European powers and American states, because of the Monroe Doctrine, had to be submitted to arbitration, the administration had concerned itself only with the quarrel in Guiana, the only important territorial dispute then pending in the hemisphere between an American and a European state.

The unintended broadening of the Monroe Doctrine was more the result of Salisbury's attempt to discredit Olney's arguments than anything Olney said in his note. Significantly, scholars referring to the Olney Corollary have drawn on Salisbury's exaggerated statement rather than on Olney's own words. When Cleveland overruled Olney on the point of repudiating Salisbury's interpretation, and when Britain subsequently yielded to American demands, the "Olney Corollary" as characterized by Salisbury, in effect was validated. Olney, quick to see the advantage of the strengthened doctrine, blocked all subsequent efforts to curtail or weaken it. He was to recommend, not long after, that it be invoked in Cuba against Spain.

From the beginning, many persons interpreted the Venezuelan contest in economic terms, assuming that surface appearances cloaked the material interests at stake. At the time, these explanations were crude. Many Americans, including Cleveland and Olney, suspected that Britain's objective was to grab gold fields along the Guiana frontier, or to gain control of the Orinoco and its trade.[33] Some British officials obviously were interested in gold, but the refusal to accept unrestricted arbitration stemmed chiefly from concern for the empire as a whole. As for control of the Orinoco, Britain in 1844, 1881, and 1886 had offered to surrender the land at the river's mouth to reach accommodation with Venezuela. During the crisis, many Englishmen and some Americans believed that Venezuela's grants of mining concessions to United States citizens in the disputed area lay behind the trouble. If Cleveland and Olney were not deliberately acting on behalf of those interests, they were believed to have been duped by them.[34] The concessions were real enough, but no evidence links them with Cleveland or Olney or to the formulation of policy. At most the mining concessions and land grants aroused the interests of speculators.

In recent years the economic explanation has been revived. The Venezuelan crisis, it is asserted, was part of the Cleveland administration's program to end the depression of 1893 by acquiring overseas markets in which to dispose of American overproduction. Specifically, the administration was concerned that the Orinoco and its commerce would fall to the British. More generally, to expand exports within the hemisphere it was necessary to break Europe's hold over the trade of the area. By vigorously asserting the Monroe Doctrine, the United States sought to establish commercial domination over all of Latin America. The timing of the note to Britain (which coincided with the trough of the panic) and the lack of American concern for the views of Venezuela allegedly confirm the economic thesis.[35]

It is true that in the 1890s much attention focused on the Orinoco and its commerce. But Cleveland's and Olney's concern for ownership of land at the river's mouth, though real, was not the primary factor guiding their policy. The commerce in question was at best potential. The Orinoco had no port of consequence; its basin was largely unsettled and undeveloped, its trade negligible. A glance at the map reveals that if Britain were granted her extreme claim (the small tip of land on the right bank of the river's principal, but not only, mouth) her "control" of the Orinoco would not have been greatly enhanced. Similarly, if she were denied that land, her influence in the area would not have been hampered. Whatever her frontier with Venezuela, Britain would possess land very near the Orinoco's mouth to the southeast, as well as the busiest harbor in the region at Port of Spain on the island of Trinidad, just north of the Orinoco's delta.

If the administration's goal was commercial, it was generally unsuccessful. The percentage of American exports to Latin America did not rise appreciably for over a decade and the percentage of British trade with Latin America, though lower in the late 1890s than before the crisis, rose significantly between 1900 and 1913.[36] The timing of Olney's note was geared to politics rather than to economic stringency. Whatever is known today about the trough of the Panic of 1893, in June 1895 the Cleveland administration believed the situation had turned for the better.[37] It was not sickness of the economy in July 1895 that led Cleveland and Olney to make demands on the British, but concern that if affairs were not in order by December when Congress returned, the Republicans would crucify the administration for failing to uphold the Monroe Doctrine. Olney's failure to consult with Venezuela illustrated only how little he and the administration regarded the views of any small power. The State Department had not consulted with either side in formulating policy for Hawaii in 1893, for Brazil during the revolt of 1893–94, or for Nicaragua at the time of the occupation of Corinto. For that matter, in domestic affairs the administration had not consulted with the governor of Illinois before sending troops into Chicago to suppress the Pullman Strike.

Olney and Cleveland obviously favored expansion of the nation's overseas trade, but at no point did either man suggest publicly or privately that a bold assertion of the Monroe Doctrine would reduce European trade with Latin America or lead the southern republics to buy more goods from the United States. Moreover, the administration was shrewd enough to know that saber-rattling would never reverse the channels of world trade in time to correct the economic ills besetting it between 1895 and 1897. At most, Cleveland and Olney were blocking what seemed to them a possible extension of British colonialism (with both its political and its economic implications) in Latin America, and that, of course, squared with the intent of the Monroe Doctrine.

Political explanations of the Venezuelan crisis have also persisted through the years. Worried Democrats in 1895 believed that the administration's policy was a clever move to reunite the party by diverting attention from domestic differences.[38] Others saw Cleveland bidding for a third term or at least seeking to avert disaster for his party. A few close supporters of the president suspected that Olney was grasping for the nomination.[39] In England, Salisbury and the men around him, who had observed previous outbursts of Anglophobia during American elections, wrote off Olney's note and the president's message as but "another move in the sordid game of American domestic politics . . . , and a party bid for the Irish American vote."[40] To varying degrees, successive generations of scholars have accepted political explanations, even those favoring multiple rather than single causation.[41] It appears, however, that neither Cleveland nor Olney was seeking the nomination in 1896 (though either probably would have accepted it if offered). Both men failed to take advantage of the political opportunities that the crisis provided. Both would also have regarded any blatant move to win popular acclaim as unthinkable demagoguery.

Recent scholars who see political motivation as the principal factor in Cleveland's policy doubt that the president was seeking either a third term or to reassert control over his divided party. They have seen him rather as trying simply to quiet political controversy. Disturbed at the rising tide of jingoism, Cleveland sought to defuse it in advance of an election campaign.[42] This seems reasonably close to the mark and is consistent with both Cleveland's expressed political philosophy and his previous behavior in the realm of foreign policy.

Much of the confusion over the administration's motives has sprung from treating the affair and its aftermath as a unit in which final results were the product of original intentions. But the various stages of the affair, for largely political reasons, forced changes in tactics and objectives. The decision to send the note in July was prompted by the desire to have the Venezuelan question under control before the opening of Congress in December. When Salisbury's reply dashed that hope, the president's message was formulated to outmaneuver the jingoes at home while bringing Britain to terms. When the message produced a war scare, Olney sought an accommodation that would allow both powers to preserve their self-respect without surrendering the demand to settle the boundary dispute once and for all. When the Monroe Doctrine emerged from the crisis stronger than ever, it was incorrectly assumed that Olney had intended that result from the start.

In the end Olney won a significant victory, achieving the basic objectives of the administration—quieting the Venezuelan dispute as a domestic political issue and halting any possible British encroachments in Guiana that, if allowed to continue, might eventually lead to war. Along the way he fumbled badly. Expecting his note of 20 July to produce an immediate British back-down, he instead reaped a risky confrontation. But Olney recovered quickly, skillfully mixing firm insistence upon ultimate, conclusive arbitration with flexibility over precise means and an appreciation for British sensitivities. Salisbury retreated slowly, but conceded nearly all of Olney's points. In securing an end to the Venezuelan dispute, Olney achieved something that had eluded his predecessors for two decades. It was no mean accomplishment for the novice who had taken on one of Europe's ablest diplomats.

Once Olney initialed the memorandum containing the heads of treaty between Britain and Venezuela, the United States technically was no longer involved. In Venezuela, however, the treaty ran into strong opposition. The Caracas government, to win public support, asked that instead of the United States Supreme Court's selecting two of the five arbiters, the president of Venezuela be allowed to name one. Pauncefote told Olney that Britain objected to any Venezuelan on the tribunal and had agreed to the proposed treaty only because it assumed that the United States Supreme Court would choose its own members as arbiters. Irritated by Venezuela's "offensive" attitude, which was blocking negotiations, Olney urged Caracas to restore relations with Britain at once. Would a stipulation that Britain name no British Guianan to the tribunal and the United States no Venezuelan help? he asked obtusely.[43]

Unhappy with Olney, Venezuela turned to Britain, arguing that unless it was permitted to designate one arbiter, popular resentment would prevent ratification. The concern of the Caracas government apparently was genuine. If allowed to select one member of the tribunal, the president of Venezuela promised not to name a Venezuelan and to allow Britain to approve the nominee in advance. Further, Caracas offered to "facilitate the conclusion of a commercial treaty on advantageous terms to Great Britain," an ironic offer for those who regard Olney's note as a warning to both Latin America and Europe that the trade of the hemisphere was a practical benefit of the Monroe Doctrine accruing to the United States.[44]

In the end Venezuela won the concession it sought, but "decided" in advance that its nominee would be a member of the United States Supreme Court.[45] Venezuela chose Chief Justice Fuller, the Supreme Court selected Justice David J. Brewer, and Lord Chief Justice Charles Russell and Lord Justice Sir Richard Collins represented Great Britain. The fifth member and president of the tribunal was the well-known Russian writer on international law, Professor Fëdor F. Martens.

While preparing to argue Venezuela's case, Storrow suddenly died. Among others, Cleveland and Olney (by then out of office) were asked to fill the vacancy. Both declined on grounds of propriety, but Olney assisted in securing the services of former president Benjamin Harrison as chief counsel for Venezuela.[46] The tribunal began work in Paris in June 1899, with argument running until the end of September. After six days of deliberation, the arbiters handed down their ruling. Venezuela was awarded all territory west of the Schomburgk line as well as Point Barima and nearby land at the mouth of the Orinoco, and several thousand square miles of land in the interior east of the line. The tribunal gave no statement on its reasoning or other explanation.[47]

A common interpretation holds that Britain's claim had been largely upheld. The assumption seems to be that after careful examination, the tribunal found that right, justice, and international law were all on the side of the British and that this should have been obvious from the very beginning.[48] It should be remembered, however, that in 1895 Britain refused to arbitrate her extensive claims west of the Schomburgk line unless Venezuela first renounced claim to all land east of that line. The final award, in fact, gave Britain less than her minimum claim, not most of her maximum claim.

More recently, evidence has come to light which suggests that the tribunal reached its decision by less than strictly judicial means. Shortly before his death in 1949, the distinguished expert in international law, Severo Mallet-Prevost, who assisted Harrison in presenting Venezuela's case before the tribunal and who was the last survivor of the Paris proceedings, drafted a sworn statement. After argumentation of Venezuela's case, he charged, he had been called to the quarters of Justices Fuller and Brewer. It was useless to keep up the "farce" that the proceedings were judicial, Brewer excitedly told him. The president of the tribunal, Martens, had informed Fuller and Brewer that the British judges were "ready to decide in favor of the Schomburgk line, which starting from Point Barima on the coast would give Great Britain the control of the main mouth of the Orinoco. . . . " If the American judges continued to insist on the Moroco River line, he, Martens, would side with the British and declare the Schomburgk line to be "the true boundary." Because he was anxious for a unanimous award, however, he proposed the line ultimately adopted and undertook to "secure the acquiescence" of the British if the Americans would agree. Fuller and Brewer, certain that the boundary should begin at the Moroco, were willing to issue a dissenting opinion. However, since that would result in adoption of the Schomburgk line, they were prepared, if Venezuela's counsel approved, to accept the compromise.

After a stormy session, Mallet-Prevost and Harrison agreed to Martens's line, largely because, as Harrison argued, "if it should ever be known that we had it in our power to secure for Venezuela the mouth of the Orinoco and failed to do so we should never be forgiven." Once the Americans accepted his plan, Martens apparently used the same tactic to secure British agreement—that is, threatened to vote for the Moroco line unless they accepted his compromise.[49]

Embittered, Mallet-Prevost upon his return conferred with Olney and Cleveland. "I asked him to dine," Olney reported, "with the result that he consumed less food than time and that the feast was not so much a flow of solid and liquid refreshment as of intense wrath and bitterness of soul at the course and decision of the arbitral tribunal. . . . " The worst outcome, Olney concluded, was not the loss of territory by Venezuela, "but the general discrediting of the cause of arbitration." Both Fuller and Brewer, he learned, had returned home "pretty sick of arbitration." Olney later learned that Fuller did "not fully concur" with Mallet-Prevost's views, which included a belief that the British had bribed Martens.[50]

Chief Counsel Harrison, too, was upset at the Paris proceedings. Writing to his Indianapolis law partner, William H. H. Miller, he noted that in view of British claims prior to United States intervention, the findings of the tribunal were good. However, "judged from the standpoint of strict right," the award was "far from good." British jurists were "as always aggressive advocates," not judges. "Law is nothing to a British judge it seems when it is a matter of extending British dominion." As for the settlement, he thought securing the mouth of the Orinoco very important and derived satisfaction that "the British flag must come down from three (3) stations." In explanation of the American judges' acceptance of the decision, he said it was " 'lest a worse thing befall you'."[51] Writing in December, he observed that the chief difficulty of arbitration proceedings involving American questions arose from the European refusal to accept arbiters from any American state except the United States. "The result is that the ultimate decision of every American question is in the hands of a European umpire." Europeans, he declared, were all committed to the seizing and appropriating of territory belonging to weak nations, which meant that Latin American states "could hardly secure fair treatment." The British judges in the Venezuelan case, he said, were "as distinctly partisans as the British Counsel."[52] The umpire, too, "was a disappointment . . . "[53] If there was any truth in the sworn statement of Mallet-Prevost and the supporting comments of Harrison, it cannot be argued that the decision of the tribunal, however practical and expedient, established the legality or the right of the British claim.

Once the memorandum ending the Venezuelan controversy was signed, Olney resumed talks with Pauncefote on general arbitration. Just as the Pullman strike had opened his eyes to the need for machinery to forestall major railway tie-ups and he became a champion of compulsory arbitration of such disputes, so the Venezuelan controversy revealed to him the need for devices to avoid international crises and he became the advocate of international arbitration. In both instances Olney sought to establish institutionalized channels for handling these matters so that his successors would not have to face Pullman strikes and Venezuelan disputes. Perhaps his proposals in both instances were merely the response of a good lawyer to problems that were not adequately covered by law or precedent, or perhaps Olney feared that lesser men in future crises might not respond as wisely or as well as he had. In retrospect he might even have had some regrets at his own rash acts under pressure and was making reparation in the form of insurance against future acts of the sort. Whatever his motivation, as he wrote for President Cleveland's final message to Congress, the general-arbitration treaty aimed not only at reducing the possibility of war between the United States and

Britain, but also at "precluding those fears and rumors of war which of themselves too often assume the proportions of a national disaster."[54]

Fortunately for the cause of arbitration, British officials also wished adoption of such a treaty. Pauncefote saw an arbitration agreement as a fitting capstone to his career as ambassador to the United States. In England, Lord Salisbury accepted general arbitration for practical political reasons. He distrusted the device in principle and had misgivings about its use, but recognized that public opinion favored it and wanted credit for the treaty to go to his party rather than to the opposition when next they came to power.[55]

As in the case of compulsory railway labor arbitration, Olney wanted too much. He believed, first, that all disputes between the United States and Britain should be treated as arbitrable so that arbitration would become the accepted means for settling Anglo-American differences. If there were to be exceptions, they should be specific cases withdrawn by act of Congress or Parliament. The executive or "political" branch of government, he feared, was too apt to mistake party advantage for national welfare in deciding whether to turn to war instead of arbitration. Olney also insisted that in all cases the process must ultimately end with a binding settlement.[56]

Salisbury disagreed on each of these points. He favored restricting cases to limited and not-too-important issues, at least until arbitration became more familiar and trusted. Cases involving territorial claims, sovereignty, jurisdiction, or national honor he would exclude altogether. He also sought to devise ways around binding awards by proposing judicial review of arbitral findings, and even rulings of these review courts were not to be binding in all cases.[57]

The negotiations produced a number of compromises and once again Olney won more than he conceded. In its final form the treaty excluded no cases from arbitration. Instead, controversies were divided into three categories, each to be handled differently. Cases involving individual or collective pecuniary (but not territorial) claims of less than £100,000 were to be submitted to a three-man tribunal consisting of one American, one British, and one neutral jurist, for conclusive settlement by majority vote. The second category, involving pecuniary claims in excess of £100,000 "and all other matters in difference"—except territorial—where either party had rights "under treaty or otherwise," were to be handled as in the first category except that awards to be binding must be unanimous. A majority award was subject to review by a court of "five jurists of repute"—two each from the United States and Britain and the fifth from a neutral nation. The finding of the review court, whether unanimous or by majority vote, was to be binding. Controversies involving territorial claims, a "principle of grave general importance," or "national rights" were to be submitted to six-man tribunals to which the United States and Britain each named three jurists from their highest courts. Unanimous or five-to-one decisions were to be final. Four-to-two decisions were to be binding only if not protested by either party within three months. A protested award had no validity, but both parties pledged not to take "recourse to hostile measures of any description" until the mediation of one or more neutral nations was invited. At Salisbury's insistence the treaty was limited to a trial period of five years "and further until the expiration of twelve months" after notice to terminate was given by either party.[58]

As Olney noted, the treaty fell short of the goals of "advocates of immediate, unlimited and irrevocable arbitration of all international controversies." At the same time, it made "a long step in the right direction" and embodied "a practical working plan" by which Anglo-American disputes would "reach a peaceful adjustment as matter of course and of ordinary routine."[59]

President Cleveland, his successor elected and awaiting inauguration, submitted the treaty, negotiated by a lame-duck secretary of state, to the closing session of a Senate controlled by his opponents. Critical senators argued that the phrase making "all matters of difference" arbitrable might lead to an arbitration of the Monroe Doctrine. That, Olney protested, was "all wrong." Only where the parties had "*rights* against the other under treaty or otherwise" would arbitration be required. The "express object" of the phraseology used, he insisted, was to exclude all questions of policy such as the Monroe Doctrine from arbitration.[60]

Chances for ratification dimmed as the Cleveland administration neared its close. There were hints that the treaty was being "talked over to the next session" when Republicans could claim credit for it. Olney feared (correctly, as it turned out) that the treaty was being talked to death. He proposed that friends of arbitration hold public meetings throughout the country, "especially in the large cities of the west," to urge "immediate ratification."[61] Although Great Britain ratified the treaty, the United States Senate, early in the McKinley administration, rejected it. The defeat, Olney wrote Henry White in England, placed the United States in "a most humiliating and mortifying position." Defeat was not due to public disapproval of arbitration or to hatred of England, he said, but to Cleveland's lack of popularity in Congress, to the work of a group of senators led by Lodge who hoped to badger England into a scheme of international bimetallism, and to senatorial encroachment on presidential prerogatives. Subsequently Olney added to the list an address by Lord Russell before the American Bar Association which proved "an arsenal" from which foes of the treaty drew their "most powerful weapons."[62]

Olney remained a friend of international arbitration for the rest of his life and frequently offered advice and guidance to those seeking its adoption. However, immediately after the Senate vote, when attempts were made to resurrect the issue in a new treaty, Olney advised against it. The Senate, "weary of the subject," would "resent being called upon to consider it again so soon. . . . " The cause of arbitration would be better served, he suggested, if a second treaty on the subject were not defeated.[63]

The Venezuelan crisis and the attempted treaty of general arbitration marked a watershed in relations between the United States and Great Britain. From that time forward, despite occasional differences, Anglo-American relations were generally friendly and cooperative. In the subsequent rise of the United States, Britain saw no threat to its interests in the Western Hemisphere and increasingly entrusted those affairs to the care of the United States.[64] Some have attributed the improved relations after 1895 to British tact, aimed at winning America's friendship and support. Olney, however, believed himself entitled to at least part of the credit. "You are quite right, in my judgment," he wrote A. Maurice Low in 1899, "in ascribing the present Anglo-American *entente* to the year 1895 and the administration's course as respects Venezuela." At the time many people were crediting Bayard for the improved relations. "As you know," Olney declared, "nothing could be farther from the truth. You cannot bring two nations into relations of regard and friendship if, while greatly gratifying the *amour propre* of the one, you greatly wound and offend that of the other." Bayard's "sentimental speeches lauding everything English, comparing things English with things American always to the disadvantage of the latter . . . made his countrymen . . . without distinction of party excessively angry." Olney believed that after his note of 20 July and the president's message, "Englishmen at once began to conceive that respect for us which is the foundation and essential prerequisite of all real regard."[65] Olney obviously belonged to the school of diplomacy which held—as one historian has put it—that the best way to reach a friendly understanding with John Bull is "to begin by giving him a stiff punch in the nose."[66] In this instance at least, Olney might have been right.

15

Cuba and China

Revolt erupted in Spain's troubled "Pearl of the Antilles" in February 1895. No problem that Olney faced as secretary of state proved more persistent, more annoying, or less soluble. In the beginning the Cleveland administration viewed the revolution in Cuba as only another worry. Fighting there fired up the jingoes and expansionists at home; Cuban-born naturalized citizens and their sympathizers supplied the rebels with money, guns, and information in defiance of the neutrality laws; Spanish demands for greater vigilance against gun-running forced expensive surveillance of the coast opposite Cuba; and the arrest of Cuban-Americans for revolutionary activities in the island complicated relations with Spain. Even so, aside from the *Allianca* incident (when a Spanish gunboat fired on an American merchantman near the coast of Cuba) and occasional demands for protection from Americans arrested in Cuba, the administration was able to ignore the first six months or so of the troubles.[1]

For two years the Cleveland administration worked with the problem. Sometimes it changed tactics, but its objectives remained the same: peace must be restored under Spanish rule and the harassment of American citizens, property, and commerce in Cuba must end. Independence was out of the question, Cleveland and Olney believed, because the Cubans were incapable of self-government. Transfer of the island to another power was unacceptable, and annexation would involve empire-building, which Cleveland opposed. When guerilla warfare in Cuba became more savage and public sympathy for the rebels increased, the administration refused to alter course. Cleveland and Olney repeatedly searched for new solutions, only to return to the same point: pacification under Spanish rule. They mistakenly believed (or perhaps only hoped) that Spain would be able to buy off the independence movement by granting substantial reforms. Given the forces at work in Spain, Cuba, and the United States, that goal was doomed from the start.

Two days after Olney was sworn in as secretary of state, Cleveland issued a proclamation that acknowledged the disturbances in Cuba, declared the neutrality of the United States, and admonished American citizens to in no way assist or promote the revolt against the government of a friendly neighbor.[2] In these early months, the administration apparently believed that Spain would be able to suppress the rebellion with force. It raised no objection to the repressive methods employed and so far as possible helped by enforcing the laws against gun-running. When a Texas bank inquired if it could lawfully accept deposits from men known to be supporting the revolution, Olney replied that only a court of law could answer authoritatively. If, however, the bank published its acceptance of such deposits "to the world," he would feel duty-bound to test whether the act was criminal or grounds for forfeiture of the bank's charter.[3]

What Olney knew of Cuban affairs he learned chiefly from pro-Spanish informants such as his fellow-Bostonian, Edwin F. Atkins, who looked to Spain for protection of his extensive sugar plantations in Cuba, and de Lôme, the Spanish minister.[4] According to de Lôme, the rebels were the "lowest order" of Cubans, representing neither the property, intelligence, nor "true interests" of the island. They were "the ignorant and vicious and desperate classes marshaled under the leadership of a few adventurers." If successful, they would be "incapable of founding or maintaining a decent government" and would reduce Cuba to "anarchy and a repetition . . . of the worst experiences of other West India Islands."

Olney's first doubts that Spain would put down the revolt came in late September 1895, when Paul Brooks, an American citizen and consular agent resident in Cuba, called at Falmouth. Olney reported to Cleveland that Brooks, a man of great wealth who owned thousands of acres in Cuba and employed some eight hundred people on his estates, was "a businessman first and all the time," who cared little for forms of government so long as they secured "the peace and order of the community." Olney regarded him as an objective source of information. Brooks's views were "utterly at variance" with everything Olney had previously heard: the rebels were not "the scum of the earth," "hardly a prominent Cuban family" was without one or two members in the movement, and although many Cubans did not openly support them, nine-tenths of the population was in sympathy with the insurgents. "To a man," the propertied class was disgusted with Spanish misrule, which burdened the island with debts and taxes but failed to fulfill "the primary functions of government by insuring safety to life and security to property." If the insurgents succeeded,

Brooks predicted, the propertied class would be on hand to establish and maintain a "regular and permanent" government.

Most alarming to Olney was Brooks's assessment that the insurrection was "more formidable" than the ten-year revolt of 1868–78 and that Spain would never wholly quash it. According to the planter, Spain was rapidly running out of money and would soon make a desperate attempt to "utterly smother the insurrection in its own blood." If that failed, Cuba would be "for sale to the highest bidder."

The administration must no longer base its policy on inadequate information, Olney told the president. Increased fighting in Cuba would enlist the sympathies of more Americans behind the Cubans, rebel emissaries would soon be demanding recognition of their belligerency or independence, and congressmen returning to Washington in December could be expected to set "their sails . . . so as to catch the popular breeze. . . . " Also, many Americans traveled back and forth to Cuba, Olney pointed out. Commerce with Cuba was "large and important," and much American capital was invested there. Since hostilities would seriously affect all those interests, the United States would "surely . . . and rightly" be called on to protect the lives and property of Americans in Cuba and to "exact indemnities for injuries actually inflicted upon them."

The United States should continue to enforce its neutrality laws strictly, Olney believed. But it should also inform itself whether the insurgents were "merely gangs of roving banditti," or "a substantial portion of the community revolting against intolerable political conditions and earnestly and in good faith seeking the establishment of a better form of government." If the movement were significant, and "perhaps in any case," the United States could properly protest resort by either party to "cruel and inhuman modes of warfare." So that the administration could "intelligently" deal with the questions that were bound to arise—such as recognition of the belligerency or even the independence of the insurgents—Olney proposed sending a special agent to Cuba to investigate the situation and report to the president.[5]

Cleveland had also talked with Brooks and was annoyed that the planter had concealed his earlier meeting with Olney. His information, nonetheless, impressed the president. Cleveland, too, saw the wisdom of a fact-finding mission to Cuba and suggested a military man ("in dealing with such countries as Spain a military title helps"). Olney, Lamont, and Cleveland discussed the merits of various army officers for the job, but Spain vetoed the project.[6]

As Brooks predicted, fighting intensified when Spain appointed a new governor for Cuba, General Valeriano Weyler, a man notorious "for venality and cruelty."[7] The stepped-up warfare, in turn, produced a rash of resolutions when the Republican-dominated Fifty-fourth Congress assembled on 2 December. Senator Lodge called for formal congressional sanction of the Monroe Doctrine, while other senators proposed recognition of Cuban belligerency or independence. Fervor over Cuba subsided briefly when Cleveland's Venezuela message suddenly stole the jingoes' thunder. By early January, however, the resolution mills began grinding once more. For weeks the House and Senate disputed the relative strengths of two resolutions and finally, on 6 April, adopted the Senate version which asked the president to recognize Cuban belligerency and to offer good offices to Spain for "recognition of the independence of Cuba."[8] Olney and Cleveland watched disapprovingly, seeing it all as mere politics. There was little they could do, however, except hope that the deadlock might never be broken.

While Congress debated, Olney explored various courses of action. With Adee he weighed the consequences of recognizing Cuban belligerency. At most that would "imply a moral sentimental belief in the capacity of the Cuban insurgents to establish self-government," Adee pointed out. Undoubtedly the move would "*prejudice*" claims against Spain for damages inflicted by rebels on American property prior to the date of recognition, and would "virtually *debar*" subsequent claims. So long as the United States remained neutral, such recognition in no way would change the rules regarding protection of Americans. The United States would continue to hold each side responsible in the areas it controlled for observing the rights of American citizens.[9] Belligerency status apparently would in no way benefit the United States. A gratuitous insult to Spain, it would not materially aid the rebel cause, while it would lift from Spain all responsibility for damages wrought to American property by rebels.

Recognition of Cuban independence was even less attractive. The insurgents failed to establish competent civil government in districts they controlled. Olney doubted that they ever would. If the Cubans defeated Spain (and that would not be done easily or quickly), he expected racial warfare and anarchy to follow. Far from ending agitation for American intervention and annexation, such troubles would serve only to increase it. Moreover, recognition would almost certainly lead to war—if not by Spain's initiative, then because the United States would be obliged to act. Any attempt by Spain to "reimpose" colonial status on Cuba once the United States recognized it as one of the independent American republics would clearly violate the Monroe Doctrine.[10]

Olney despaired of protecting the property of Americans in the island. Since it was "their misfortune to reside and have invested their capital in a country in which a rebellion has broken out," he wrote Cleveland, he did not see how the United States government could protect them "from the inevitable consequences." In conversation with Paul Brooks, Olney suggested that the best solution might be to buy Cuba. He was certain, however, that under prevailing conditions, Spain would not sell.[11]

The remaining alternative, which would have little or no support in Congress or with the public, was to assist Spain in quelling the rebellion. This, Olney believed, would require extensive administrative reform of the island by Spain. Informal conversations with the Spanish government on that subject were discouraging. If the United States wished to help pacify the island, thereby protecting American property and interests, the Spanish foreign minister observed archly, "the most sure and efficacious proceedings would be to deprive the insurgents of all hopes of moral and material aid, and to prevent the territory of the United States of being the center and basis of the organization of expeditions and resources."[12]

Ignoring the rebuff, Olney and Cleveland pushed forward. In a forceful note to Spain, Olney observed that the insurrection, now in its second year, was "more formidable than ever." Although the rebels did not yet qualify for status as belligerents, they did exercise control over much of Cuba. Spain, on the other hand, ruled only in the seaports and larger towns of the interior. The flow of development capital to Cuba had stopped and investors were withdrawing funds, apparently foreseeing only "the complete devastation of the island, the entire annihilation of its industries, and the absolute impoverishment . . . of its inhabitants . . . " Unable to suppress the rebellion, Spain sooner or later would be forced to abandon the fight, and Cuba would be left to the horrors of interracial strife. The concern of the United States was not merely humanitarian or Christian. Conditions in Cuba posed a threat to American property there. The United States contemplated no intervention but, Olney warned, so long as the island was wracked by war, that possibility would exist.

Olney proposed that Spain at once grant the Cubans "all such rights and powers of local self-government as they can reasonably ask." Spain would retain full sovereignty over Cuba, but the United States would use its good offices and influence to secure acceptance of the reforms by the insurgents. This done, most grievances in Cuba would be removed. If hostilities continued, at least "the moral countenance and support" that the rebels enjoyed in the United States would be largely lost.[13]

In its reply the Spanish government agreed that the rebels did not deserve recognition as belligerents and that a Cuban victory was unthinkable, and expressed gratification that the United States had no plans to intervene. Cuba, it declared, suffered no tyranny, as was frequently charged, but enjoyed "one of the most liberal political systems in the world." Even so, reforms were planned and would be instituted just as soon as the insurgents laid down their arms. Spain regretted that fighting inflicted losses on American property-holders. If the rebels succeeded, however, American interests would not "merely suffer," they would "entirely and forever disappear amid the madness of perpetual anarchy." Thanking the United States for the "kind advice it bestows on Spain," de Lôme assured Olney that good offices would be of no effect. Pacification would come only with the "actual submission" of the rebels. Meanwhile, certain that the "high moral sense" of the United States would "undoubtedly suggest to it other more effectual means" for halting the flow of supplies to the rebels, Spain would "do more every day . . . to correct the mistakes of public opinion in the United States," and to expose "the plots and calumnies of [Spain's] rebellious subjects."[14]

The administration's second measure—appointment of General Fitzhugh Lee as consul general in Havana—was even less successful. Since Spain refused to permit an inquiry into conditions in Cuba, Cleveland and Olney hoped that Lee might assess the situation there in conjunction with his consular duties. Despite impressive credentials—he was a nephew of General Robert E. Lee, a distinguished Confederate cavalry officer in his own right, and a former governor of Virginia—Lee was not the ideal man to secure objective information. He did not speak Spanish, knew nothing of Spain or Cuba, and had no diplomatic experience. His hot temper, self-importance, and penchant for striking dramatic poses attracted newspaper headlines. He delighted in stealthy conspiracies and Machiavellian politics, and, among other things, found opportunities to use his new post to advance his personal political and economic fortunes.[15]

From his arrival in Havana onward, Lee trumpeted for annexation. The administration's hope for an autonomous Cuba under Spanish sovereignty was futile, he reported. Members of the old autonomist party now favored independence, followed by a vote on annexation to the United States. Lee did not hide his sympathies. The fertile island with but one-and-a-half million inhabitants could easily support a population of from five to six million. "Cuba will become an immense garden, supplying the United States with its earliest vegetables & fruits & be its richest and most prosperous possession. . . . In its splendid harbors can conveniently float American vessels, charged with defending American interests and promoting American commerce." He anticipated no racial difficulties: "the native Cubans and negroes live in harmony and are most peaceably disposed toward each other." Although Spain could not "conquer a peace," neither could the insurgents compel Spain to withdraw. He doubted that the Cubans would accept mediation by the United States, but thought they might be willing to purchase their independence by taking over the Cuban debt from Spain. Once Cuba was free, annexation should be considered. If the United States took over, Spanish capital that otherwise would leave with the Spanish army, would stay.[16]

Lee's reports to the secretary of war lacked specific military data just as his reports to Olney provided little useful political information. The time "for action" had come, he told Lamont, and outlined a three-step program. In the interest of "peace—to preserve commerce & protect her citizens," the United States should offer mediation. Spain would decline, and unless "coupled with independence," so would the insurgents. The United States should then propose specific reforms in Cuba. Again, both sides would probably refuse, even if the United States guaranteed the reforms. The third and "only solution practicable" was purchase of the island for its debts. A republic could then be organized under American guidance—because "treaties of trade & all that" had to be arranged so as to pay the interest and principal of the Cuban debt. If Spain declined to sell, the United States would have "done everything in her power & if war comes from the effort to protect her commerce and defend the interests of her citizens, *she must meet it.*"[17]

Olney thanked Lee for his report, but clearly was more interested in the status of the rebel government than in converting the island into the nation's choicest truck patch. Did the rebels have a de facto civil government or a fixed seat of government? Olney asked. Were legislators and other civil officials elected and did a legislative body convene regularly to enact laws? Were the insurgent forces under civilian control? Did the rebel government protect life, liberty, and property? Had it established courts to administer justice? Did it levy and collect taxes, provide mail service, issue currency, build roads, or provide educational facilities? "In short, what of the ordinary functions of civil government, if any," did the "so-called Cuban Republic exercise?" or was it "a mere government on paper?" From Lee's reply, Olney concluded that Cuba as yet had no established civil government.[18]

By late June and early July, the administration's attention focused less on the insurrection in Cuba than on the revolution occurring within the Democratic Party at its national convention in Chicago. In the early months of 1896, state conventions one by one had fallen to the silverites. When Cleveland failed to declare his own intentions, eastern Democrats talked of nominating Governor William E. Russell of Massachusetts, or William C. Whitney. A few mentioned Olney. The president's silence, however, blocked booms for any of his followers.[19] It mattered little because western and southern rebels promptly took charge at Chicago. They drew up a platform damning the administration and its works, virtually read Cleveland out of the party, condemned the administration's monetary policy, adopted a plank calling for the free and unlimited coinage of silver at 16 to 1, denounced "government by injunction," and selected William Jennings Bryan as the nominee.[20]

In the midst of this upheaval, Cleveland and Olney, repudiated and dumbfounded, suddenly found it necessary to restrain Lee. About 1 July, Lee began filling routine reports with gratuitous and provocative remarks about the situation in Cuba. "[T]he condition of the inhabitants . . . is growing worse day by day"; "This is another evidence of the want of confidence in the authorities here"; "the cigar manufacturers . . . are afraid to trust the Government"; new taxes added "greatly to the many disturbing elements already in force . . . which must sooner or later produce disaster . . . "; Havana and Cuba were like "a huge volcano within whose limits fierce fires were raging, which must in the near future produce an eruption"; "No one" expected Spain to grant reforms or the "rebels to accept them if tendered"; the consular office was filled daily with "property owners who complain of arson, pillage and murder" by Spanish troops; Spaniards increasingly saw but two courses, "war with the United States or an ignoble surrender . . . of the two the former will be chosen, because, as they say, they can then lose the Island with honor."[21]

Lee's barrage turned out to be the prelude to a more aggressive move. Feelings between Spaniards and Americans were growing more intense and "matters are daily converging to a certain focus," he wrote on 8 July. The long-promised reforms would not be forthcoming, nor would they any longer "enter into the solution of the Cuban question." Again Lee suggested purchase of the island. If that failed, "a declaration of its independence should promptly follow, something after the order of President Jackson's treatment of the Texas question in 1836." The war with Spain that would "almost certainly follow" would be "short and decisive." As an immediate "precautionary measure," he recommended stationing a warship at Key West "under a discreet officer, with a full complement of Marines." The officer would be in direct communication with the consul general, "and at my request" would "drop anchor in this harbor" if needed to protect the consulate and the lives of American citizens from "mob violence."²²

Lee's proposal raised the shade of Minister Stevens at Honolulu in 1893. "General Lee's suggestion does not at first blush strike me favorably," Olney wrote Secretary Herbert. Herbert agreed. Noting that the consul general seemed "to have fallen into the style of rolling intervention like a sweet morsel under his tongue," Cleveland thought the reference to Jackson and Texas "not fortunate." Purchase was "perhaps worth thinking of," but leading interventionists opposed incorporation of Cuba into the American system. Any other course— such as permanent colonial status—would be "entering upon dangerous ground." To buy the island only to turn it over to its inhabitants seemed absurd. Cleveland thought "prudent measures" to protect American lives and property wise, but objected to putting a man-of-war at Lee's disposal. "I do not want *now* anything of that kind made a convenient excuse for trouble with Spain." Olney had already notified Lee that the ship would not be sent to Key West.²³

Disappointed, Lee admitted to Olney that his purposes were political. Given Bryan's nomination, Democrats who abhorred "anarchical success" had a choice of voting for McKinley, not voting, or calling a second convention to nominate their own candidate. To have "the chance to win," they must endorse the accomplishments of the Cleveland administration, recognize the "helplessness of the struggle in Cuba," and call for an end to the "devastation of the Island, the shooting, arrest and imprisonment of American citizens . . . , the abatement of American commerce and the destruction of American interests." Democrats should pledge to offer American mediation in Cuba, "or, if necessary, American intervention." Such a program would give Cleveland and "Sound Democrats" credit for stopping "wholesale atrocities" in Cuba and for acquiring the island "by purchase or by fighting a successful [war], if war there be." Warming to his theme, Lee pointed out the domestic advantages of war. "[T]he enthusiasm, the applications for service, the employment of many of the unemployed, might do much towards directing the minds of the people from imaginary ills, the relief of which, is erroneously supposed to be reached by 'Free Silver!' "²⁴ Olney never replied.

Convinced that Lee's reports were hopelessly biased and that he was trying to use his post for political gain, Olney and Cleveland no longer trusted anything that Lee said. Removing him from office was impossible. His bravado and patriotic stance had won him a considerable reputation among the jingoes. He had also justly won acclaim for his vigorous and well-publicized handling of cases involving American citizens arrested in Cuba.

In Cuban matters, Olney never hesitated to make demands on, or to recommend courses of action to the Spanish government. In private communications to de Lôme he was frequently blunt. When, for example, the Spanish arrested a bishop named Diaz, Olney urged de Lôme to make public at once the grounds for arrest, if "clear and satisfactory." If the arrest was on mere suspicion, detention would stir up religious sentiment in the United States. Two days later, with Diaz still in custody, Olney became peremptory. "If you realize where your interests and mine lie, you will have Diaz and his brother landed in the United States within the next twenty-four hours. It makes little difference what they have done or what they have not done. A more troublesome and dangerous hornets' nest could not have been stirred up . . . " Although Spanish authorities had "not the slightest doubt" that the Diaz brothers were agents of the revolution, they released the men.[25]

De Lôme was discouraged. While the United States continually urged Spain to end the fighting, the struggle was kept alive only by help from American sympathizers. In recent incidents, de Lôme complained, he had served as "a second Minister of the United States, not the Minister of Spain." Fearing that his "influence for good" was wasting as quickly as his health, he thought it might be wise to resign. His government still trusted him, he believed, but "how long can it last if I go on asking favors for the United States and not giving equal proofs of friendship in return?"[26]

In July, Spain sent a note asking President Cleveland to issue a strong proclamation modeled after one that President Zachary Taylor had issued in 1849, warning Americans then engaged in filibustering that their citizenship would not shield them from punishment if they were captured by the Spanish.[27] Taken aback at Spain's presumptuousness, Olney advised de Lôme not to leave the communication in its original form. The Spanish foreign minister had a right to state facts that aggrieved his government, but it "was hardly within his province to suggest to the President what specific remedies should be applied. . . . " After all, the president "could hardly appear to be acting in the discharge of [his] official duties" under the advice of the Spanish minister. The note was rewritten and on 27 July Cleveland issued a new and stronger proclamation, but one that fell far short of what Spain wanted.[28]

Spain's request was part of a renewed determination to suffocate the revolt "by force of Arms alone without any political concessions whatever." If the United States helped, well and good; if the policy led to war, the Spanish ministry was "determined not to shrink" from it. Against that contingency, Spain sought to enlist the European powers in "a moral alliance" opposed to American interference or intervention in Cuba.[29] The plan was for Spain to issue a circular letter stating reasons why the United States had no right to involve itself in Cuban affairs, and to ask the European powers to endorse the statement. In exploring the possibility informally, the Madrid government received only guarded responses. The British ambassador, H. Drummond Wolff, expressed hope that the letter would be "very carefully worded" so as not to include proposals that would conflict with "the settled policy of the United States."[30] Prime Minister Salisbury, already burned in the Venezuelan affair, warned the Austrian government of the "risk of extravagant and violent action (especially during the excitement of the Presidential campaign) which an uncontrollable democracy might adopt in regard to a question of foreign policy on which public opinion in the United States is undoubtedly very sensitive."[31]

Discovery of the scheme by Hannis Taylor, and the cautiousness of the powers, defeated the plan. When Taylor confronted the Spanish foreign minister, demanding an explanation for the contemplated affront, he was promised that the circular letter would not be sent. Taylor, in turn, let it be known throughout the diplomatic corps that the letter would have been "a signal infringement of the Monroe Doctrine." If acted on by the powers it would have excited "the greatest indignation in the United States." Spanish diplomats later delivered the content of the circular letter orally to the courts of Europe, but none of the powers was willing to support Spain.[32]

In early October, de Lôme, taking a new tack, asked specifically how the United States might cooperate with Spain in guaranteeing reforms in Cuba. Olney replied that the reforms could be set forth in the preamble of a new commercial agreement between Spain and the United States, "as part of the inducement to the United States to make the treaty." De Lôme apparently regarded the plan as feasible, but insisted that the treaty include provisions on naturalization so as to end fraudulent abuse of that right by Cubans. Such provisions, however badly needed, Olney warned, would prevent Senate ratification.[33]

Meanwhile, in Madrid, the British ambassador learned from Taylor that after the election in November, the Cleveland administration would devote the balance of its time to cooperating with Spain to restore peace. "What the United States required for Cuba," Wolff reported, "was 'peace with commerce.' Any combination securing these two objects under the sovereignty of Spain would be welcomed by the U.S."[34] The diplomats were right. In early November, Olney and Cleveland began work on the Cuban portion of the president's final annual message. They decided on a forceful statement for two reasons: Spain must be pushed into granting substantial reforms as quickly as possible, and the administration must appear to have the situation under control. Meant chiefly for domestic consumption, the message was designed to undercut the Republicans who, having swept to victory on a platform sympathetic to Cuban independence, would probably harass the administration as much as possible on the issue.

In effect, Cleveland repeated the analysis sent to Spain in April. No progress had been made in suppressing the revolt. Rebels roamed at will over two-thirds of the island. Civil government and the protection of property had all but been abandoned. Americans were disturbed as they watched the "utter ruin" of a near neighbor. Their concern was not "wholly sentimental or philanthropic"; American investment and trade in Cuba was second only to Spain's. Efforts to halt the flow of supplies from sympathizers were costly and "inevitably involved" the United States in the conflict. Cleveland reviewed and once more ruled out recognition of Cuban belligerency or independence, transfer of the island to another power, or purchase by the United States. "[G]enuine autonomy," guaranteed by the United States but "preserving the sovereignty of Spain" should "satisfy all rational requirements" of the Cuban people. He added a note of urgency. The patience of Americans was limited. Their "hitherto expectant attitude" could not be "indefinitely maintained." When it became evident that Spain could not "deal successfully with the insurrection," that Spanish sovereignty in Cuba was "extinct," and that the struggle had been reduced to a "useless sacrifice of human life," United States obligations to Spain would be "superseded by higher obligations." The ways and means for meeting those new obligations Cleveland left until the time for action arrived.[35]

Olney's notes for the message indicated that he favored an even more aggressive stance. In early drafts he suggested giving Madrid less than a month to bring Cuba under control. "If by the coming of the New Year, no substantial progress" had been made, "either by force of arms or otherwise," the United States might well conclude that Spain was incompetent to deal with the problem.[36] Olney subsequently dropped the ultimatum in favor of the warning that American patience was limited. In one draft, Olney recommended invoking the Monroe Doctrine—both to forestall interference by other powers, and to justify direct American intervention. Foreshadowing the Roosevelt Corollary, Olney proposed to remind Spain that America's "traditional policy" not only "asserts rights but entails correlative obligations—not merely declares the right of the United States to regulate the affairs of Cuba to the exclusion of European powers, but requires it to do so whenever such outside regulation becomes imperative."[37]

Certainly Olney contemplated no intervention, but he was willing to use the doctrine to goad Spain into granting reforms. Perhaps Olney realized that he had erred a year before when he suggested to Cleveland that he abandon the doctrine in his Venezuela message. Invocation then had rallied public support behind the administration, giving it the strength necessary to force a British retreat. How much more effective such a threat should be against Spain! In the end, however, Olney—or Cleveland—decided against the assertion.

The president's message did not impress critics in Congress. Despite strong protestations from the State Department, Senate leaders introduced a resolution calling for recognition of Cuban independence.[38] Because such a resolution could lead to war, Wall Street's nerves were on edge. Fearing that "another financial panic would be precipitated," Olney acted quickly and, since the president was not in Washington, on his own initiative.[39] Summoning the press, Olney explained that if the Cameron Resolution passed, it would be nothing more than "an expression of opinion by the eminent gentlemen who voted for it. . . . " Only the executive was empowered to recognize Cuba as an independent state. Resolutions of Congress, adopted by whatever majorities, were "inoperative as legislation." Thus deflated, the resolution never came to a vote.[40]

Eastern bankers and businessmen rushed to congratulate the secretary of state.[41] Letters from Boston, Olney observed sourly, came from business associates who only a year before had vehemently denounced him for his Venezuela policy. Their praises now left him indifferent. "What I want is to succeed in what I undertake and believe to be right," he wrote Miss Straw. "In Venezuela I *have* done so—if I am to believe all the signs, I shall do so in this case of Cuba." Olney went on to connect the two affairs. "Once we had recognized Cuba as independent, the Monroe doctrine just established by this administration would require us to at once declare war against Spain—to prevent her acquiring territory on this continent by force. Neither this nor the next administration could help itself—after the pronounced stand taken in the Venezuela case." This, he suspected, lay behind the Cameron Resolution on Cuba. Accordingly, he decided to "step on it as hard as I know how and without waiting to consult or ask anybody to help share the responsibility."[42]

Even as the annual message was being prepared, Olney began to sound out Cuban reaction. Through Atkins he learned that autonomy, guaranteed by the United States, was acceptable to "the better classes" of rebels who would influence the others. The wealthy Bostonian also reported that Cuban leaders in New York found autonomy "most acceptable" and perhaps even "preferable to independence."[43] Before entering into treaty with Spain, Olney wanted direct information and so commissioned Oscar B. Stillman, former manager of the East Boston Sugar Refining Company and currently in charge of the Trinidad Sugar Estate in Cuba, to go to Cuba to determine unofficially but directly the sentiments of leaders in the field. Stillman confirmed Atkins's report. Except for Maximo Gomez, chief of the rebels, and a few others, "the great majority" of insurgents "would gladly accept any form of autonomy—always provided that it be guaranteed by the U.S."[44]

Olney's hopes rose when General Lee cabled from Havana that "some well informed persons" there thought that rebel leaders "might accept reforms" along the lines proposed by the president. If Spain would grant a twenty-day truce, a conference of interested parties could meet and draw up mutually acceptable reforms. His interest whetted, Olney waited three days for details. Finally, in exasperation, he wrote, "I assume that you would not have sent this telegram unless the situation as you judged of it at our last interview, has undergone some material change." What specific facts, Olney asked, had led Lee to send the cable? As it turned out, Lee's information had come from Stillman.[45]

Olney summoned Stillman to Washington for conferences with himself and de Lôme. At a meeting on 31 January, the three agreed that Spain should soon proclaim sweeping reforms that would "practically" give Cuba "self-government," and that General Weyler would be recalled. Coinciding with announcement of the reforms, Spain and the United States would enter into treaty, the "direct and most important object" of which would be "to secure and confirm the execution of these reforms by giving to the U.S. Govt the right to insist upon [their] fulfillment." Stillman believed peace possible on these terms. De Lôme asked Stillman to secure "an expression of opinion" directly from rebel leaders. Stillman, in turn, urged de Lôme "to undertake [an] extra-legal action in behalf of his government" to end the fighting and possibly even secure for Spain the "loyal services" of the insurgents by incorporating them into the Guardia Civil and offering command of that police force to Gomez, the rebel leader.[46]

Spain was slow to inaugurate reforms. A surprisingly successful national loan in November to finance the war hardened the ministry's attitude. Immediately prior to the loan, when its success was doubted, high Spanish officials talked to the British ambassador of generous concessions. Once the loan was floated, Wolff "perceived much alteration" in the language of the foreign minister, who spoke of waiting patiently for the "action of the military" in Cuba. Wolff feared the worst.[47]

In mid-January, Wolff reported that negotiation of a commercial treaty was under way in both Washington and Madrid. The American minister in Madrid seemed more interested in commerce with Cuba than in home rule for the island; so much so that on at least one occasion Olney had to disavow his language. Cynics in the Madrid rumor-mills concluded that the desire of the United States "for very extensive reforms" in Cuba had "apparently been greatly lessened in view of large commercial privileges" in the island.[48]

Whatever Taylor's interests, Olney wanted the Cuban issue resolved before he left office. Commercial advantages, though important, were secondary. Similarly, he was unwilling to trade the rights of imprisoned Americans for the proposed treaty. On 22 January he sent Taylor the names of three United States citizens held without charges and of several prisoners awaiting trial whose cases had been unreasonably delayed. Olney requested that charges be filed against the three and "immediate trial or release" of the others. Taylor regarded the demands as "opportune" and tried to use them to pressure Spain into acting more quickly on the larger negotiations. The prime minister promised a decree within two weeks "conceding real self-government to Cuba." Spain would retain control of Cuba's tariff schedules, but "very favorable commercial arrangements certain with us," Taylor reported. "May I now use reasonable discretion in pressing your last damand?"[49] Olney instructed Taylor to proceed "with all reasonable discretion of course." But, he added, "the rights and liberty of American citizens" were "paramount objects of care of this Government," and "Spain's action or proposed action for her own best interest in the way of reforms in Cuba should not be allowed to prolong unlawful imprisonment of American citizens."[50]

Rumors persisted in Madrid that a highly advantageous commercial treaty would soon be signed and that Spain would adopt "a plan of autonomous Government for Cuba proposed by Mr. Olney. . . . " At the end of January, Wolff reported a credible, though unverified, story as to why no treaty was signed. President Cleveland, who "disliked the Insurrection altogether and was opposed either to the annexation or the independence of Cuba . . . refused to take cognizance of the reforms in detail." In effect he told the Spanish that they knew "the nature of the concessions required to reconcile Cuba." When they took shape, the United States, if it considered them sufficient, would use "its undoubted power to put an end to the Insurrection." As for the commercial agreement, Cleveland was "opposed in principle to all reciprocity treaties" and would leave that for his successor.[51]

Early in February, Spain announced the long-awaited reforms. The foreign minister confided to Wolff that Cleveland, Olney, and McKinley all regarded them as "even more than was necessary."[52] Whether such assurances were given mattered little. General Lee charged that the reforms did not give genuine home rule and that the rebels saw the plan "as a clever move to prevent action by the United States."[53] Even Atkins and Stillman confessed that Cuban leaders would "not touch reforms," though Stillman hoped the scheme might "serve as a medium for arrangement." The administration in Washington, now in its last days, allowed the matter to pass over to McKinley.[54]

Possibly the view reported by Lee—that Spain only toyed at reform to stall action by the United States—was accurate. A year later, upon reading the celebrated de Lôme letter of 9 February 1898, Olney was less disturbed at the minister's characterization of McKinley than at his suggestion that Spain should "agitate the question of commercial relations, even though it would be only for effect. . . . " He had had "much confidence" in de Lôme, he wrote Cleveland, "and thought him able, sincere, and patriotic." Olney confessed, however, that "some expressions of his letter stagger me, and if they bear the interpretation the President has put on them and mean that Spain has been tricking us as regards autonomy and other matters incidental to it, I should have wanted the privilege of sending him his passports before he had any chance to be recalled or resign."[55]

Olney was not to leave office without weathering a final attempt by Fitzhugh Lee to force intervention. In part Lee hoped to make money.

> Some one told me—it matters not when or where—[he wrote privately to Lamont] that you were interested in street railways. So—it has occurred to me to say to you—that here in Habana is a gold mine—Picture in your mind a city as large as Washington—with no modern travelling facilities—The car *lines* are limited to *three* in number—short old fashioned cars—drawn each

by thin little poor horses & this in a city where from March to November everybody rides & the remainder of the year large numbers of persons—Not a cable—not a trolley—no open or summer cars—attractive suburbs—beautiful places—within close range—on the Ocean &c &c &c. I have an excellent well posted man looking over the field now with a view of getting options— buying out the old lines & acquiring ocean property outside—so that when peace is declared the business can be proceeded with. Now all can be purchased *low* when the war is over everything will be high.

In case of a change of flag here no one can estimate the possibilities. I see no chance of the Cubans driving the Spanish from the Island or of the Spanish quelling the present insurrection. . . .

Now if you & Mr. [William C.] Whitney (I understand he too is interested in N.Y. city lines)—, or either would like to look over the "*bonanza*" here, send me a man in whom you have confidence to examine & report . . . You had better run down here after 4th March & see for yourself unless you have no use for more money. . . . ⁵⁶

A few days later, once more lacing his reports with inflammatory comments, Lee began a campaign to change Cuba's flag. There was "no change here in the situation and no . . . prospect of peace unless the United States stops this *horrible* war." Cuba could be "captured in two weeks by a blockading fleet, without firing a gun or landing a soldier." One cable after another carried reports of new provocations. The Spanish had searched ladies aboard an American steamer anchored in Havana harbor—"twice ashore before women employed to do it." Was he to allow "such proceedings in future *whether Americans or not?*" he asked. A new issue of paper money gave concern because it was not redeemable in coin. "Trouble and violence at any time in consequence," he warned. Another report told how rebel officials passed from one part of Cuba to another through Spanish lines. "No provinces pacified, no peace in sight."⁵⁷

Then came the death of Richard Ruiz, a naturalized citizen who had returned to his native Cuba to practice dentistry. Arrested and confined incommunicado for 315 hours, Ruiz, according to rumor, either went mad and killed himself or was beaten to death by his captors. Lee urged the State Department to authorize him to demand the immediate release of all Americans "suffering and lingering in the prisons and jails" of Cuba. When Lee discovered a second American, Charles Scott, held incommunicado for 264 hours, he cabled, "Cannot stand another Ruiz murder and have demanded his release. How many war vessels, Key West or within reach, and will they be ordered here at once if necessary to sustain demand?"⁵⁸

Olney promptly took charge of cooling down the badly overheated consul general by flooding him with questions that implied neglect of duty. "It being your duty to protect [Ruiz] before death as well as afterwards," Olney wrote, why had Lee done nothing between 4 February, when he reported the dentist's arrest, and the man's death thirteen days later? Was Ruiz, indeed, an American citizen? And why, after saying on the nineteenth that the facts in the case were difficult to obtain, did Lee on the twentieth refer to Ruiz's death as murder? As for Scott, how did Lee know he was a citizen? When, where, and under what circumstances had he been arrested, what was Lee doing to protect his rights, and why had the confinement been reported only after 264 hours? Olney also questioned Lee's reasons for insisting upon the release of all imprisoned Americans. "Is it the idea that such demand, which must be refused, can be made the basis for hostile intervention or demonstration?" The United States made demands "only when prepared to enforce them, and therefore only on assured grounds . . . " Given the uncertainty about the facts, Olney said, Lee's suggestion as to warships was "most surprising."⁵⁹

The stratagem worked. Lee fumed that Olney questioned his handling of the Ruiz case. Over the next few days he repeatedly wrote, trying to answer the questions, trying to prove Ruiz's citizenship, and trying to show that he had done everything possible to save the dentist. He continued also to press for orders to demand the release of all Americans. As for the suggestion that he was provoking an incident, Lee was evasive. "Deprecate war," he wrote on 22 February, "seen too much of it. Actuated only by desire to serve the President and you and American interests." If Olney disapproved of his proposals, the "remedy" lay in Olney's hands and he "should not hesitate to employ it." The next day Lee again urged Olney to support him. "If you do not, I must depart."⁶⁰

Ignoring Lee's invitations to recall him, Olney continued to prod the consul general. "This Department is entitled to a clear statement of your views on this point for its information and guidance," he wrote. "I desire to ask therefore, a distinct answer to the question whether, in the case of a prisoner claiming American citizenship, your idea of duty is that nothing is to be done in the way of inquiry, or protest, or in way of insuring immunity from maltreatment, because the prisoner's confinement is aggravated by his being kept incommunicado?"⁶¹

On 24 February, Lee admitted in part what he was up to and why. In a cable to Olney, marked "confidential," he asked, "Cannot the President see way clear before leaving office to demand capital punishment for all persons concerned Ruiz murder if such fact be properly proved. Nothing can prevent Cuban matter very soon settling itself. I am deeply interested that administration should participate."[62]

Far from seeking to participate in the overthrow of Spanish rule in Cuba, Cleveland and Olney were struggling to avoid intervention. The president was sufficiently disturbed at Lee's machinations to call upon Frederic R. Coudert, an international lawyer of considerable reputation, to undertake a mission to Spain to avert war. War would come, the president warned, because of the activities of Americans in Cuba whose "ringleader" was General Lee. When Coudert declined, the matter dropped. Four days later at the inauguration of McKinley, Cleveland advised his successor that Lee was not to be trusted.[63] With that warning the Cleveland administration's responsibility for the Cuban question ended. Olney and Cleveland had won few of their objectives—only the most important. They had avoided war.

American commerce with China also needed protection between 1895 and 1897—not from warfare, but from the machinations of the imperialist powers as they vied with one another for the trade of the Celestial Empire. Japan's surprisingly easy victory in the Sino-Japanese War of 1894–95 had revealed China's essential helplessness. In the Western World, opinion differed whether China would collapse and be carved up by the powers, or like a sleeping giant, arouse itself and modernize. Americans with an interest in such matters believed that China would pursue modernization. Industrialists laden with surpluses and merchants eager for customers saw China as a limitless market. Railroad-builders who had already spanned North America yearned to try their hand in Asia. Seeking new areas for investment, financiers increasingly looked to the far Pacific, while shipbuilders, armaments manufacturers, and munitions makers assumed in the wake of Japan's recent triumph a ready market in China for their wares.[64]

Chief caretaker of American interests in China between 1885 and 1898 was the United States minister, Charles Denby. A lawyer by profession and a long-time promoter of railroads, Denby throughout his tour of duty worked diligently, assisting entrepreneurs in forwarding their schemes and stirring up the interest of businessmen at home who seemed unaware of the rich markets available if only they would act.[65] Unfortunately, a long-standing instruction of Secretary of State

Bayard prevented Denby from freely assisting American interests in the race for prizes. In his first years at Peking, Denby had tried without success to promote a railroad-building project. Learning of the scheme, Bayard had instructed the minister to abstain "from the furtherance of individual plans and contracts connected with foreign Government until they have been submitted to the Department and received its approval."[66]

In the spring of 1895, Denby sought to have the restraint lifted. "if . . . by any possibility your Administration could get the glory of greatly increasing and spreading American interests in China," he wrote Secretary Gresham, "it would be a grand consummation." Not long after, he cabled for advice on the request of an American syndicate for help in arranging a large loan to China. Acting Secretary Edwin F. Uhl instructed Denby to limit himself to making formal introduction of the Americans to Chinese officials. He was not to use his official position to further their projects. Denby replied that the distinction was meaningless in China; the introduction of a businessman by a diplomat implied the support of the government involved.[67]

Gresham's death left responsibility for answering Denby to Olney. So far as he changed the order at all, Olney restricted rather than widened the minister's discretion. Bayard's 1887 instruction, Olney believed, was misleading, especially if "construed to assume that such assistance is to be rendered as a part of your ordinary and regular official duties as Minister. . . . " Denby could properly introduce and vouch for American citizens of satisfactory character and responsibility, but he should "carefully abstain" from using his position to promote their financial or business enterprises. "[O]nly in an extraordinary case—to be first submitted to this Department with all the facts and reasons pertaining thereto"—was any different course to be followed.[68]

Unhappy with the revisions, Denby complained that his work on behalf of American businessmen in China was not properly understood at home. Some of his counterparts in Peking used their diplomatic positions to demand favors for their countrymen "in the boldest and most truculent manner." Although Chinese officials acknowledged owing more to the United States than to any other power, he was "precluded," because of his instructions, from taking advantage of the situation. So far as possible, he said, he served American businessmen; "except that I do not take China by the throat and demand concessions—everything else that is possible is done." Many Americans came to China ill-prepared to transact business, "with no knowledge of procedure, no interpreters, no translation of their papers into Chinese, and without staff or advisers of any kind." Most stayed only a brief time and had no resident agent. In serving these men, Denby listened to their schemes and helped to revise and amend them with advice. Nor were the projects modest: They embraced laying thousands of miles of railroad track, lending millions of dollars to China, taking over and operating the country's arsenals, and selling great quantities of guns and munitions. Whatever the State Department's views, businessmen expected such services. "My house, my vehicles, my time and that of my subordinates have been fully put at the disposal of my fellow citizens." Not only did he arrange interviews with high officials, he also tried to educate those officials in advance by supplying them with articles prepared at the legation and translated into Chinese, on "the advantages of the American system of railways" and its "peculiar adaptation" to China's needs.[69]

Denby's appeal led to no relaxation of the rules. On the other hand, subsequent reports showed that he did not allow the restrictions to hamper his promoting of American interests. In January 1896, he wrote of assisting the Bethlehem Iron Works to secure contracts for ships. "I have encouraged the Chinese Government to look to America not only for men-of-war and armament but also for railroad rolling stock and other supplies in the production of which the factories of the United States hold the preeminence." China was "sure to become" a great field of industrial enterprise, he explained. Securing "an early entry" was important and worthy of "greater attention than the manufacturers of the United States have so far given it."[70] In May he again reported on the Bethlehem project and noted the activities of two other firms, the American Trading Company of New York, in which J. P. Morgan was interested, and the American-China Development Company, made up of prominent politicians, railroad builders, and bankers. International competition made "some recognition" of these firms by his office "essential to prevent unjust discrimination against American enterprise." Scrupulously avoiding "official endorsement" of their projects, he authorized his staff to make translations for them and himself introduced their agents to Chinese officials, giving "unofficial assurances of the firms they represent."[71] Denby clearly was stretching his instructions.

The low priority which the Cleveland administration assigned to Chinese matters was illustrated by the pro forma reception given to the visit of Li Hung-chang in late August 1896. Li, the most distinguished official of his country to visit the United States, for a quarter-century had simultaneously held several of the highest posts in the Chinese government, having important or chief responsibility for foreign policy, international commerce, and defense. Designated to represent the Emperor of China at the coronation of Czar Nicholas II, Li announced that he would afterwards make a leisurely tour of Western Europe and the United States. Although his visit would be unofficial after leaving Russia, he would carry letters from his emperor to the heads of the various states he would visit.

Businessmen and news reporters in Western Europe and the United States preferred to believe that the mission to Russia was mere cover for more important transactions in the West. They speculated that Li would be shopping, letting contracts, and granting concessions for armaments, ships, railroads, and all the other goods needed for the defense and modernization of China. Despite lavish receptions by both heads of state and leading businessmen in Germany, France, and England, it was evident that Li had placed few if any contracts.[72] American entrepreneurs, nonetheless, nursed hope that Li's visit to the United States would have a different result. Uniting with missionary societies, former diplomats, and other "old China hands," they planned an extensive itinerary for the distinguished guest.[73]

The promoters sought to enlist the United States government in their plans to at least match the receptions given Li in Europe. Neither Cleveland nor Olney, who were vacationing on Cape Cod, displayed much interest. "I suppose we will have to do something by way of entertaining Esquire Li Hung Chang," the president wrote Olney. "How would it do to light a bunch of fire crackers?" Olney thought the suggestion novel and "brilliant," but since the Kaiser had given Li a breakfast, "something a little more conventional," such as "entertaining him at an afternoon tea," seemed more appropriate.[74] In Washington, the War, Navy, and State Departments—urged on by Li's business-minded friends—fell to wrangling over plans for the reception. Secretary Lamont and officials at the State Department questioned the propriety of the president's going to New York to meet Li and suggested that Li should go to Buzzard's Bay. General Miles, nominating himself as escort, worked out an elaborate tour.[75] The president agreed to a military escort, but objected to "our highest general" being assigned to an unofficial visitor. Since he planned to be in New York "about the time the great Chinaman arrives," Cleveland decided to meet Li there. He declined, however, to participate in any of the banquets or other ceremonies being planned.[76]

Because the army was to escort Li, the navy insisted on putting on a display in New York harbor. Assistant Secretary William Mc-

Adoo pestered Olney about the propriety of a nineteen-gun salute. "[U]nder all the circumstances of this peculiar case and as it will be all the navy will do," Olney suggested to the president that it "might not be amiss to direct the salute to be fired. . . . " It would be "sure to gratify McAdoo (his name might well be Much Ado), if not Earl Li."[77]

When the great day arrived, Li was greeted by ten warships, "the most formidable fleet . . . ever assembled in American waters." J. P. Morgan's yacht and other private vessels added to the celebration. The navy fired its salute, but Li's ship unfortunately passed to one side of the formation rather than sailing between the two rows of warships as planned. The army then took over, officially welcoming Li and escorting him with a parade of soldiers to the Waldorf. The next morning Olney and Li exchanged brief ceremonial calls at one another's suites in the hotel. The two then rode in an open carriage up Fifth Avenue to the residence of William C. Whitney. There, in a brief, formal ceremony, Cleveland accepted the Emperor's letter and made a brief speech of greeting. Li replied, pleasantries were exchanged, and in less than an hour Li was enroute back to the hotel. Olney and Cleveland both left the city that same afternoon.[78]

The administration's role in welcoming Li could hardly be called extravagant. The letter from the emperor had made a formal meeting necessary, and for his own convenience the president met Li in New York. There is no evidence that pressures from the business community induced the administration to alter its program in order to impress the visitor. Neither does it appear that the visit in any way changed Cleveland's or Olney's thinking about the role of the government in promoting American ventures in China.[79]

The businessmen involved were disappointed with the ten-day visit. They found few opportunities to engage in serious negotiations, and the visitor's banter, at least as reported in the press, could hardly have encouraged them. Shipbuilding magnate Charles H. Cramp's interview with Li in Philadelphia was perhaps typical. Not having time to visit the shipyards as planned, Li agreed to talk with Cramp in his private car for fifteen minutes before it left for Washington. Cramp told newsmen afterwards that he doubted Li was in the United States to place any contracts for ships.[80]

While Li was still in the United States, Denby reported from Peking that the Baldwin Locomotive Works had recently made the lowest bid on a contract to supply China with eight locomotives. The bidding was about to be reopened, however, and Denby feared that foreign governments were pressuring Chinese officials to deny the contract to the American firm. Writing to the Tsungli yamen, Denby expressed hope that "no underhand means would be permitted to defraud the American manufacturers of a contract they had fairly earned." Whatever the effect of Denby's letter, Baldwin won the contract.

Two months later, Denby again hinted that the rule against official assistance to business projects should be relaxed. Affairs in Peking "touching material American interests" had reached "an important phase." The "instructions, consultations, advice and writing and translating papers" now appeared to be about to pay off. "Great plans" for railroad construction, mining, and related activities were hopefully "on the eve of becoming assured." The one concrete evidence that he cited was approval by the Director General of Chinese Railways of preliminary plans for a large loan from an American syndicate (apparently the American-China Development Company) to finance the construction of a major railroad.

Another project under consideration involved "in its correlative branches and outcroppings, mines, banks, manufactures, the furnishing of arms, armor and ships—in fact—the whole field of progress." Whether American capitalists would consider only immediate returns from one transaction or would "look to great results, whose fruition, though it may be delayed, is not doubtful," remained to be seen. If the plans awaiting decision were consummated, the "almost limitless field of financial and industrial operations" in China would be "occupied, dominated and controlled by Americans." If not seized, the opportunity might well pass to other countries.[81]

Olney relented, in effect giving Denby nearly a free hand. Denby was not to "assume directly or impliedly in the name of the government any responsibility for or guarantee of any American commercial or industrial enterprise trying to establish itself in China." However, he could use his "personal and official influence" and "lend all proper countenance" to securing for reputable American businessmen "the same facilities for submitting proposals, tendering bids, or obtaining contracts as are enjoyed by any other foreign commercial enterprise in the country." It was not practicable, Olney continued, "to strictly define" Denby's duties in such matters, nor were past instructions to be "too literally followed. . . . " Giving due weight to his own judgment and experience and to the standing of the firms and agents involved, Denby, "broadly speaking," was to "employ all proper methods for the extension of American commercial interests in China, while refraining from advocating the projects of any one firm to the exclusion of others." So that the department might be in a position to "understand the scope of the 'great plans' of Americans" in China, Olney instructed him to keep the department "thoroughly advised" on "this most interesting and important subject."[82]

Olney's instruction was meant to free Denby to use such diplomatic influence as might be necessary to protect American businessmen from losing contracts because of pressures by other governments on China. As a subsequent report revealed, however, Denby again stretched his instructions. Efforts to prevent Chinese officials from yielding to pressures and reneging on bids fairly won by American firms clearly came within his new instructions. Some of the arguments that he presented to the Tsungli yamen, however, did not. Instead of limiting himself to demands that American companies be dealt with honestly when they bid on specific contracts, Denby insisted that American firms were entitled to a fair share of all contracts being let. This, he said, was because the United States had performed more services for China than any other power (particularly with reference to ending the war with Japan) and had asked for nothing in return. The other powers had all demanded and received rewards for their services on China's behalf.

Further, Denby argued, Americans were entitled to railroad contracts because they were the best at building railroads. Allowing Americans to help develop China was also safer for China because, unlike the leading European powers, the United States "had and could have no ulterior designs on Asiatic territory . . . " Denby took Li Hung-chang to task for refusing to help secure a railroad contract for representatives of the American-China Development Company, whose agents were then in Shanghai. The leader of the group had come to China at Li's "instance," Denby declared, and at a meeting of the Tsungli yamen he "made Li understand" that he knew of the incident and held him responsible. The session would "exercise a beneficial influence on American interests in China," Denby believed. He only hoped that Olney would not think he had exceeded his instructions.[83]

Olney left office without answering Denby. His successor, John Sherman, raised no objection to what Denby had done, but questioned his endorsement of the American-China Development Company as being composed of men who were "worth several hundred millions of taels." According to Sherman's information, the company was a limited-liability corporation with "a very little capital." The worth of the persons in the company, under those circumstances, had "little to do with the matter."[84] In the end the syndicate did not build the railroad line Denby had worked so hard to get for it; not because they were cheated out of the contract, but because they themselves rejected it. As Denby feared, they were more concerned with immediate returns than in winning the right to develop all of China.[85]

In relaxing the rules, Olney betrayed no desire to push beyond assurance of equal treatment for American merchants in China. As a later instruction showed, he did not envision American businessmen setting up factories in China. When the Shanghai Chamber of Commerce sought State Department support for a program to encourage foreign manufacture of cotton cloth in China for sale to the Chinese, Olney demurred. Treaties with China did not give the United States "just claim to embark in competition with native factories to supply the native markets," he pointed out.[86] In permitting Denby to give assistance to Americans doing business in China, Olney had not been converted to expansionism. Rather, the hands-off policy was inadequate for protecting Americans against the unfair tactics of their European counterparts. As a practical matter it is difficult to see how he could have done less.

Olney left Washington in March 1897, never to return to public office. He shared, as would be expected, some of the opprobrium that fell on the departing administration, particularly since a change of political party was involved. His performance in office, nonetheless, was generally regarded as successful. Even those who disagreed with him saw Olney as a strong secretary of state. Henry Lee Higginson welcomed him back to Boston with a heartfelt note. "Never did man take up new & heavy responsibilities & duties more unwillingly than you & rarely has a man fulfilled them better—perhaps never—I know of no public officer during my sixty years who has so entirely satisfied me or my neighbors." He could not help adding, "We did not agree with your Venezuelan course at the time, but see that it has led to excellent results."[87]

Untrained and inexperienced though he was in diplomacy, Olney had done a creditable job. He had blundered on occasion, most noticeably in his Venezuelan note to Britain. His adroit recovery in the negotiations that followed, however, justly earned him the praise of even his critics. His bluntness—in the Venezuelan affair, the Mora claim negotiations, and the Cuban question—showed that he was no diplomat in the classic sense. At the same time, bluntness coupled with skillful, pragmatic maneuvering and patience brought results. The Cuban revolution in many ways had been the greatest challenge and the most frustrating problem that he faced. Encumbered by his own and Cleveland's predispositions, badgered by congressional and jingoist clamor, poorly served by General Lee in Havana, and perhaps deceived by the suave de Lôme, Olney steered a course that avoided war with Spain. In the process he displayed mastery in short-circuiting mischievous congressional resolutions and the artificial crises stirred up by Consul General Lee.

True to his beliefs, Olney's foreign-policy objectives ranged no farther than protecting American lives and property abroad, assuring businessmen of fair treatment in world markets, and quieting foreign incidents that threatened to produce political or economic turmoil at home. Olney did not use foreign policy, as some have suggested, either to divert attention from domestic ills or to expand overseas markets as a means to check economic depression.[88] Other conditions remaining unchanged, it is difficult to believe that Olney would have behaved differently in the absence of domestic depression. His response to annexation of Hawaii, to British encroachments in the New World, to revolution in Cuba, to attacks on missionaries in Turkey and China, and to the loss of contracts by American businessmen because of foreign intrigue would have been no different in an era of prosperity. Similarly, given his and Cleveland's adherence to laissez-faire doctrine, it seems unlikely that the administration, in the absence of foreign problems and opportunities for expansion, would have dealt with the problem of depression at home by instituting broad social reform or undertaking a restructuring of the economic order.

Appreciation for Olney grew as the nation stumbled toward war with Spain under his successors. De Lôme, writing to Olney about the new minister from Spain, expressed hope that McKinley would listen to him. "The fruit is ripe, I hope it will not be left to rotten by lak [*sic*] of true statesmanship. Were you in Washington!" Similarly, Edwin F. Atkins and Henry Lee Higginson besought Olney's help in averting hostilities as the war drew near.[89] At the same time, advocates of a firm stand in Cuba—at least the female contingent—showered Olney with notes. "Oh! if you could know how we have longed for you during the last month . . . ," Alice Lee wrote from Washington. "Oh! for an hour of you & Mr. Cleveland." Senator Cameron's wife agreed: "It is seldom that I want any thing as much as I have wanted to see you these last weeks. . . . Why could you not have remained in the State Dept. another year—or four? I have just returned from Washington. Such an old fuddy wudge of a Cabinet I have never seen." Once war broke out, Mrs. Henry Cabot Lodge paid her respects. "We are living in tremendous days, & I truly wish you were at the helm. You don't know how often this thought comes . . . your grasp & courage & determination would carry us through it triumphantly."[90]

However strong a leader he might have been, however wise his judgments, however well thought of by admirers from both parties, Olney after 1897 spoke only as a critic, not as a shaper of policy. For the next sixteen years Republicans, not Democrats, ruled in Washington. Until the Democrats again controlled the White House, Olney was relegated to the role of elder statesman in the minority party. After 1913 he would be too old to do more than offer advice.

16

Presidential Boomlet

Olney busied himself at the State Department on Inauguration Day 1897, avoiding the formal ceremonies that marked the transfer of power from Cleveland to McKinley. A few days later he moved home to Boston. Offered a chair of international law at Harvard, he declined. Life in Washington, he told President Eliot, had made inroads into his finances that would require all of his remaining energies to repair.[1] Olney need not have been concerned. His regular clients—the Boston & Maine and Burlington railroads, the Old Colony Trust Company, Henry Lee Higginson, and others—all welcomed his full-time attentions once more. At the same time, new clients, eager to retain so prestigious an attorney, flocked to his door. Among the many corporations that he served after 1897 as attorney, or director, or trustee, were the American Sugar Refining Company, American Telephone & Telegraph, the Amoskeag textile mills, Champion Copper, General Electric, the Massachusetts Electric Companies, the National Surety Company of New York, the New England Gas & Coke Company, the Old South Building Trust of Boston, and the St. Mary's Mineral Land Corporation. As trustee for the Cheney estate, Olney served on the boards of the St. Louis & San Francisco and the Mexican Central railroad companies between 1897 and 1902.[2]

When Olney and Miss Straw closed down his law office in 1908, they saved little of his business correspondence. A remaining exchange with Higginson perhaps suggests why so many people wanted Olney to act as trustee of their properties. The banker, hoping to unload some securities, wrote, "We happen to have a good sized bunch of Calumet & Hecla Mining Co. for sale." The mine had never looked better: it was paying "$40 a year and earning more—perhaps a good deal more." The "safest and steadiest property" he had "ever known," he thought Olney might like some shares for the Cheney estate. Higginson also offered Boston Terminal bonds which were paying about three per cent and taxes. Despite his close ties to Higginson, Olney refused to buy. He and a co-trustee of the estate had "not had much luck with the securities you have been so good as to mention," he replied. In fact, he had heard that the stock was "a wasting investment and present prices so high as to make the duty of a trustee rather to sell than to buy more." As for the bonds, he believed the estate should earn more than three per cent on its investments.[3]

Olney found that he could practice law at his own pace. He was relatively free to take or refuse clients or cases as he chose, without worry over fees. He soon abandoned courtroom appearances altogether—partly as a matter of preference, but also because of his sense of what was proper for a retired cabinet officer. After 1897 Olney's work consisted chiefly of consultation with other lawyers and the arranging and drafting of agreements, appeals, legal briefs, and legislation for his clients. In his practice he was completely successful, at least to the extent that he could live well and very much as he pleased. Without enslaving himself to his work, he amassed an estate officially inventoried at nearly $1,400,000. Except for real estate valued at $22,350, he held his wealth in the form of stocks, bonds, and cash.[4]

Besides serving his clients, Olney devoted part of his time to charitable, philanthropic, and civic organizations. Elected president of Boston's Franklin Foundation, he presided over the building of the Franklin Union—a trade school where young workingmen were enabled to complete their educations. Until his death in 1917, Olney regularly visited the Union and addressed its students at the annual commencement exercises.[5] Between 1905 and 1914, when Progressive forces were trying to reform Boston's city government, Olney headed the Citizen's Municipal League. Although the League successfully pushed through a new charter over the opposition of Mayor John F. "Honey-Fitz" Fitzgerald, it could not prevent the machine, led by James M. Curley, from resuming control of Boston in 1914.[6] In the same period, Olney accepted appointment as one of five trustees committed to making the *Boston Herald* a "clean, wholesome, and progressive" newspaper.[7]

At the national level Olney served as a regent of the Smithsonian Institution between 1900 and 1908. He was also a trustee of the Peabody Education Fund, which worked to improve education in the South, especially for young blacks.[8] Olney's most difficult public service came as counsel for the American Red Cross. Clara Barton, Oxford, Massachusetts's most famous daughter, prevailed upon her fellow townsman to accept the post in 1900. Olney did not know that the organization was about to tear itself apart in a contest for control. Miss Barton, nearing eighty, had run the Red Cross almost as a one-woman operation since 1882. But in 1900, Mabel Boardman, of Washington, D.C., led a group determined to modernize the organization, broaden its base, and make it more responsible and efficient. Caught between two strong-minded women and their followers, Olney strove to preserve and strengthen the Red Cross while protecting—so far as possible—the reputation and feelings of Miss Barton. In the end the modernizers took charge under a new charter that Olney had helped to prepare and Miss Barton went into retirement.[9]

Having once tasted public life, Olney found that his busy but quiet law practice no longer satisfied. "I have resumed business at the old stand—and am running in the old ruts with many of the old clients," he complained to former President Cleveland, "but must confess to a little slowness in getting very much interested." Perhaps "the greater profit" would "atone for the smaller excitement."[10]

Suitable opportunities for speaking out on public issues rarely presented themselves in 1897. Popular interest in anything that Cleveland or one of his cabinet officers might say was at a low. The Democratic party, defeated and in disarray, remained under Bryan's spell, while the interest of the nation at large focused on the new administration. Occasionally, sound-money cliques extended invitations, but Olney believed addresses before such groups did more harm than good. Gotten up by "bankers, brokers, financiers, etc." for their own glorification, such affairs only emphasized the differences between the sponsors and the masses of working people. Instead of weakening the free-silver malady, they made it "more obdurate and more virulent." Like measles or mumps, the easy-money craze would simply have to run its course.[11]

Olney's return to public debate began in the field of foreign relations. Prior to becoming secretary of state, he had had little inclination or reason to think about the role of the United States in the world. In office, the press of immediate problems monopolized his attention. In retirement, however, he found time to reflect on the broader issues of international affairs. Freed from restraints imposed by official responsibility and deference for Cleveland's views, Olney drifted away from positions he had taken as secretary of state. Briefly he swept along on the tide of expansionism.

Although a vigorous defender of American rights and interests within the Western Hemisphere while secretary of state, Olney had opposed the acquisition of possessions or colonies, the assumption of new obligations, or intervention in the affairs of other countries in the New World. Outside the hemisphere his policies rarely went beyond insistence upon the strict fulfillment of treaty obligations and the extension of customary protection to American lives and property. He said little about expansion of trade. Perhaps he had favored such commerce, but if so, he made no strong statements on the subject and undertook no obvious program to encourage trade.

Once he left public office, Olney spoke out publicly on foreign policy on three occasions between 1897 and 1900: in a speech opening the Philadelphia Commercial Museum on 2 June 1897, in an address at Harvard on 2 March 1898 (published in the May issue of *Atlantic Monthly*), and in an article in the March 1900 issue of *Atlantic Monthly*.[12] On each occasion Olney called upon the United States to assume a greater political and commercial role in the world at large.

Of the three, Olney worked hardest in' preparing the Harvard address and it attracted the most attention. Speaking only two weeks after the sinking of the *Maine*, he urged the United States to abandon its traditional isolationism and to take up the responsibilities of a world power. For too long, he argued, the nation had clung to principles derived from a misunderstanding of Washington's Farewell Address. The first president, despite strictures against permanent entangling alliances, had actually sanctioned temporary alliances when expedient. He certainly had not suggested that the nation should shrink from protecting its citizens and their interests "wherever in the world" they needed protection. Properly understood, Washington expected the United States to guard the "natural development" of its commerce against fraudulent, forcible, or unfair blockage. If it chose, Olney pointed out, the United States might even colonize "uninhabited or unappropriated portions of the globe" without going against the advice of the first president.[13]

But the Farewell Address, however interpreted, was outmoded and inadequate as a safe guide to foreign policy. The United States could no longer allow its overseas interests to suffer rather than assume responsibilities outside the hemisphere. Olney illustrated his contention by noting events in Africa, Turkey, and China. In 1884, for example, the United States had refused to sign an international agreement to preserve freedom of commerce in the Congo Basin because it might be obligated to help enforce that neutrality. This in spite of the fact that the United States some day might very well want to establish a colony—"a second Liberia"—in the region. More recently, Americans had demanded that the Turks stop butchering Armenians, but tendered only "moral support" to any power willing to "send its fleet through the Dardenelles and knock the Sultan's palace about his ears. . . . " Desiring the same trading privileges in China as the other powers, the United States had "loudly hark[ed] Great Britain on to the task" of assuring equal access for all nations, but came "to the rescue" itself "with not a gun, nor a man, nor a ship, with nothing but . . . 'moral support.' " Was it any wonder that the United States stood without a friend among the great powers or that it impressed other countries "as a nation of sympathizers and sermonizers and swaggerers—without purpose or power to turn [its] words into deeds" and not above "the sharp practice" of accepting advantages for which it refused to pay its share of the cost?[14]

American political isolationism, Olney observed, had led to commercial isolationism. Confining their industrial and commercial development to domestic demand, American businessmen refused to "enter the world's market or to trade over the world's counter." Relying on the " 'home market' fallacy," the United States government erected tariff barriers against outside competition. Foreign merchants, unable to sell their goods in the United States, in turn could not afford to buy American goods. The same exclusivist notions that resulted in the protective tariff system also brought decay to America's once-powerful merchant fleet and laws to shut off the migration of foreign workmen to the United States.[15]

At Philadelphia in 1897 Olney declared that "The Anglo-Saxon in America has lost none of the qualities which have for centuries made the race predominant in the history of the world's trade and commerce." American business interests wanted and were entitled to "a fair field and no favor" for their enterprise, "free and full access to all the markets of the world," and a merchant marine capable of carrying the nation's overseas commerce "under the American flag."

Olney suggested that Latin America offered the best prospects for expanded trade. The southern republics were "natural allies" of the United States commercially and politically, and "intimate commercial intercourse" among the nations of the Western Hemisphere was "one of those things . . . ordained by natural laws."[16] By 1898, Olney's interest had turned to the China market. The United States would be entirely justified, he said, in resisting attempts by the powers to divide up China and exclude Americans from its trade. In 1900 he wrote, "Nothing will satisfy us in the future but free access to foreign markets—especially to those markets in the East. . . . " He endorsed the recently proclaimed Open Door policy and supported an enlarged navy to uphold it.[17]

America's attempt to seclude itself politically and commercially from the world, Olney declared, was a "pitiful ambition." It was no longer enough for the once-poor pioneer country that had become a powerful millionaire to "vaunt its greatness and superiority and . . . call upon the rest of the world to admire and be duly impressed." The United States must take up its mission, foregoing "no fitting opportunity to further the progress of civilization practically as well as theoretically, by timely deeds as well as by eloquent words."[18]

The most startling of Olney's proposals called for the United States to cooperate closely and perhaps even to ally itself with Great Britain. Olney's conversion from seeming Anglophobe to ally of Britain came by stages. In 1897 his sentiments were mixed: Americans resented one power's "sequestering the highways of the ocean for itself," he told his audience. At the same time he attributed the desire of Americans for a strong merchant fleet to "the people from whose loins we have sprung . . . whose constant steadfast grasp of sea-power" had made them "second to none in dominion upon the land."[19]

At Harvard in 1898, Olney argued that the United States should consider temporary alliances with Britain—"our best friend as well as most formidable foe." Not only might such ties be useful for protecting American rights in Turkey and China, but more generally would promote American commercial ends and the advancement of civilization. Given the "present crying need" for more and larger markets overseas, Olney could think of no agency through which Americans could more easily "gain new outlets" than that empire "whose possessions girdle the earth" and whose ports were open equally to the flags of all nations. Appealing to "a patriotism of race as well as of country," Olney predicted that Anglo-Americans were "as little likely to be indifferent to the one as to the other." He dismissed "family quarrels" of the past as mere "liberties of speech which only the fondest and dearest of relatives indulge in" and pictured Britain and the United States standing together against any "alien foe" and working in harmony to erase the scourge of war.[20] Although he had disapproved of American acquisition of the Philippine Islands following the war with Spain, in 1900 Olney declared that "except for Great Britain's countenance, we should almost certainly never have got the Philippines; except for her continued support, our hold upon them would be likely to prove precarious, perhaps altogether unstable."[21]

It would be a mistake to take Olney's expansionist pronouncements between 1897 and 1900 too literally, however. He seems to have entertained simultaneously two conflicting visions of America's future. On the one hand he saw the United States as another Britain—perhaps even a second Rome—with world-wide commitments and responsibilities and an imperial destiny to fulfill. On the other, he clung to the practical advantages of the United States remaining unallied and uncommitted, free to pursue its own interests. By restricting itself to the Western Hemisphere, it avoided the dangers of overextension, embroilment in the affairs of others, and commitments beyond the scope of its powers. Olney was also torn between his emotional preference for vigorous, daring moves to establish American superiority in every competitive situation, and his intellectual commitment to restrained and responsible behavior as a civilized power. Unable to resolve these inconsistencies, he simply glossed them over with forceful rhetoric.

Olney's attack on isolationism in 1898 almost immediately became an embarrassment to him. It brought fulsome praise from jingoes but only noncommital comments from friends such as Cleveland.[22] To Olney's chagrin, after the battle of Manila Bay, expansionists cited his 1898 article favorably in support of permanent occupation of the Philippines. He immediately drew back. Following the logic of his remarks, he admitted to one correspondent, there was "nothing in the nature of things, in right reason or traditional policy" to prevent acquisition. But, he asked, was "the game worth the candle?" If the United States kept the Philippines, it would be responsible for furnishing "good government for seven or eight millions of savages living at an immense distance from our own shores." In administering the islands, if the United States extended the "American System" and excluded the other powers from trade, it would give offense. To administer the Philippines on the "open door" plan, on the other hand, would give the United States "a gratuitous trusteeship" under which it would bear all the burdens of empire while sharing the benefits with others.[23]

Making the same points to Beatrice Chamberlain (daughter of the British colonial secretary, Joseph Chamberlain), Olney added that permanent occupation of the Philippines would throw the United States "into the arms of Great Britain." However desirable "a cordial Anglo-American understanding or even alliance" might be, he suggested that it would be a mistake for the United States to "sacrifice its freedom of action" at this time. Would not the voluntary evolution of Anglo-American cooperation be more beneficial than an involuntary union forced because one party "got into a position of dependence upon the good will and aid of the other . . . ?"[24] When the issues of colonies and alliances became practical rather then theoretical, Olney, like those Americans he criticized in his Harvard address, quickly shrank from both the responsibilities and the opportunities of great-power status.

In his 1900 article Olney devoted considerable attention to why the United States should have annexed Cuba but not acquired the

Philippines. For all practical purposes Cuba already was an integral part of the United States, he argued. Its proximity and strategic location at the entrance to the Gulf of Mexico, and the long-standing interest of the United States in Cuba, made the connection "natural" and inevitable. The sooner Congress recognized that fact by law, the better. Not only did the wealth and intelligence of Cuba favor annexation, but until annexation, Americans would hesitate to migrate to or invest in the island, thereby delaying its industrial, political, and commercial development. Acquisition was but part of the "instinct and impulse" of "national growth and expansion," the lack of which would be a "sure symptom of national deterioration." Nations, like individuals, never stood still; if not advancing, they surely retrogressed. Although Olney did not explicitly advocate statehood for Cuba in his article, he did believe that to be the ultimate objective.[25]

At the same time, Olney disapproved of too much national growth and expansion. When the United States "came out of its shell," it had been neither wise nor expedient to become "a colonizing power on an immense scale." To his thinking, neither the promise of commercial advantage, nor anything in the way of duty, honor, or maintaining the flag once hoisted, justified the United States in keeping the Philippines. Since the United States was not overpopulated, and the climate of the islands was unsuited to white settlers, the Philippines were neither needed nor practicable as outlets for American migration. Without whites to develop the islands' resources, trade between the Philippines and the United States would always be negligible.

The vast China market beyond—to which many advocates of acquisition pointed—could better be protected with a single naval base in the Philippines (not the whole archipelago) and an enlarged navy, Olney argued.[26] To those who insisted that the United States was obligated to carry "the blessings of good government and civilization" to the Filipinos, Olney replied that charity should begin at home. America's first care should be the welfare of the slum-dwellers of New York and Boston, not civilizing "the Kanakas and Malays of the Orient." No power, however great, he insisted, could afford "to regard itself as a sort of missionary nation charged with the rectification of errors and the redress of wrongs the world over."[27]

But, again, the vision of imperial sway would not down. Only a few paragraphs later in the same article, Olney argued that "however bad the blunder," the Philippines had been acquired. The United States, alas, was no longer a purely American empire—it was an Asiatic power as well. Hereafter, relations with Europe and Latin America would continue to be governed by the old fundamentals: The United

States would not meddle in the domestic affairs of Europe, and "in things purely American" it would continue to "claim paramountcy." In Asia, on the other hand, the United States would find itself contending with the other powers. As for the world at large, where the United States asserted "interests and sympathies . . . as wide as civilization," there was no reason whatever why it "should not act for the relief of suffering humanity and for the advancement of civilization wherever and whenever such action would be timely and effective."[28]

Speaking at a dinner in honor of Admiral William T. Sampson in February 1899, Olney talked of America performing its "just international part in the policing of the seas and of the waste places of the earth."[29] However, McKinley's war to suppress the Philippine Insurrection and the advent of Theodore Roosevelt's "strenuous policy" of Americanizing the Filipinos and brandishing the "big stick" in the Caribbean, quickly cooled Olney's ardor for rushing to the relief of suffering humanity. In private, unpublished memoranda, he criticized the McKinley administration for getting into war with Spain, for failing to grasp Cuba when the chance was offered, and for acquiring the Philippines, which would never be of benefit to the United States.[30]

Once the nation had blundered by taking over the Philippines, and again by fighting a four-year war to hold them, Olney did not see how the United States could simply abandon the islands as some advocated. Instead the Filipinos should be prepared for complete independence as quickly as possible.[31] Much could be learned from Europe's long experience with colonies, Olney suggested. The United States should give the islanders the fullest possible self-government; it should make no attempt to Americanize them (we could no more "eradicate" their racial characteristics and replace them with Anglo-American characteristics than we could "change the color of their skins"); and the United States should avoid the temptation of trying to exploit the islands commercially.

Roosevelt's Philippine program was wrong on all three scores. The islands were to be subjected to between fifty and a hundred years of American tutelage before their ultimate disposition would be decided; American-style local government, courts, and schools (complete with American teachers giving instruction in English) were being forced upon the islanders; and the tariff laws were so set up as to facilitate the sale of American products in the Philippines while blocking the movement of Philippine products into the United States. No policy, Olney concluded, could be better calculated to alienate the Filipinos and to convince them that they were not so much a part "of the American empire as mere tributary appendages."[32]

Olney was especially critical of Roosevelt's Caribbean adventures. He charged that the president defined the Monroe Doctrine too narrowly in the case of the Venezuelan crisis of 1902–03. Roosevelt had said that the European powers were free to punish Venezuela for its misdeeds so long as they did not occupy any of its territory. Olney pointed out that that doctrine also prohibited European political control of an American state and for the powers to have pressed their demands at a time when Venezuela was torn by revolution in effect was to aid one side, and ought not to have been permitted.[33]

Acquisition of the Panama Canal aroused Olney even more thoroughly. "The construction of the Isthmian Canal with all practicable speed is, of course, in the interest of the American people," he wrote Senator John Daniel. "But it is much more in their interest . . . that the means to the end should be legitimate; that the honor of the country should be kept without stain; and that treaty stipulations and the rules of international law should be scrupulously observed."[34]

In a letter to his brother, Peter, Olney was even more outspoken. The course of the administration struck him "as both legally and morally indefensible—as a gross outrage upon a feeble sister republic and an even greater injury to the American people." With nations as with individuals, "no loss is to be compared to the loss of character." Under the McKinley-Roosevelt "regime," the nation's character was greatly, if not irreparably, injured. "[W]e now stand before the world as a bullying, land-grabbing, treaty breaking power, all the more offensive for the unctuous and pharisaical professions of the public functionaries who represent us." In spite of his disgust, Olney hesitated to speak out publicly. "I have been proud of my country," he said, "and it is still my country, and I dislike to indulge in any utterances however justifiable which will give aid and comfort to its enemies." It was always possible, he added, that some undisclosed circumstances existed that might give different color to what had been done.[35]

Meanwhile, Olney also lost interest in close Anglo-American cooperation, whether to further civilization or to exploit the world's markets. After 1900 he never again spoke of alliances with Britain and by 1904 was mocking the theory that "the 'saints' should enjoy the earth and that the conglomeration of races, miscalled the Anglo-Saxon, is the 'saints' . . . "[36] By 1908, although still favoring expanded trade with China, Olney criticized the conduct of the Western powers in East Asia. Assuming the superiority of their civilization, Westerners believed that the force of their arms justified them in treating Eastern peoples as "negligible factors." The Open Door policy, for example, ignored the fact that the door in question belonged to China and that China had as much right to open or close it as England had to open wide its doors or as the United States had to block its doors by high tariffs. "[W]ith trade in mind and solely to prevent any one of them from 'besting' any other," the Western powers prescribed the Open Door for China with no thought whatever "of her welfare or her wishes." Pluming themselves on their moderation, they boasted at not helping themselves "to slices of China's territory." Olney noted a growing concern in the West over the "yellow peril" and frequent predictions of war between East and West. If the West continued "to treat Oriental countries simply as fields for commercial exploitation and their inhabitants as inferiors without rights entitled to respect," that danger sooner or later would become "credible," he said.[37]

McKinley's and Roosevelt's application of principles not unlike his own soon soured Olney on both the men and the principles. The undesirable consequences of colonialism and vigorous diplomacy were becoming all too evident to him. No doubt his devout partisanship played a part in his changed attitude: almost any act of a Republican administration was apt to draw his scorn. Finally, there was the matter of increased talk of Olney as the Democratic nominee for president in 1904. Consciously or unconsciously, Olney might have shifted his position so as to sharpen the contrast between himself and Roosevelt.

Suggestions that Olney was of presidential caliber had first appeared in the wake of his victory over the Chicago strikers in 1894. The tide of Bryanism two years later, however, swept everything before it. The Great Commoner's continued hold on the party after 1896 gave rise to proposals for a new political grouping. Olney's 1898 attack on isolationism brought him a spate of letters for and against such a move. One correspondent proposed a new party based on rejection of both the free-silver craze of the Democrats and the protectionist folly of the Republicans. The new alliance would commit itself to ending isolationism, expanding overseas trade, enlarging the navy and diplomatic corps, strengthening ties with Britain, and adopting most of the other suggestions in Olney's article. Olney was interested enough to suggest additional planks, but stopped writing when his correspondent urged him to take command of the movement.[38]

About the same time, Don M. Dickinson, leader of conservative Democrats in Michigan, warned Olney against schismatic moves. Democrats should concentrate on beating out the fires of Bryanism in the fall elections. Once that was done, the resurrected party would be ready for a "radical change—a right about" on foreign policy. Democrats should then commit themselves to open ports for trade throughout the world and to a peaceful alliance with Britain that would promote and protect Anglo-American commerce everywhere. "You yourself," he said, referring to Olney's article, "have sketched the platform."[39]

The Spanish-American War later that year spawned a handful of heroes, some of whom became Democratic presidential hopefuls. One, General Nelson A. Miles, called on Olney in March 1899. Reporting to Cleveland, Olney feigned disappointment that the general, noted for his vanity, had come "in plain clothes & not in his gold uniform." Exactly what he wanted, Olney added, was not clear, but "I think I found out that the Presidential bee in his bonnet has swelled to the size of a full grown peacock."[40] The next year, Admiral George Dewey expressed interest in the nomination and said that if elected he wanted Olney to be his secretary of state. He regarded the Bostonian as "one of the greatest men in the country," and would not seek the nomination himself if Olney were to run. When Olney failed to declare, Dewey entered the contest.[41]

Neither conservative Democrats nor war heroes made much progress in denying Bryan a second nomination. As early as February 1900, Olney wrestled with the problem of supporting the Nebraskan. His concern was not free silver: on that issue Bryan was simply "wedded to an economic error" only slightly less objectionable than McKinley's attachment to the protective tariff. The chief obstacle was Bryan's continued adherence "as a whole and in every detail" to the 1896 platform which had attacked the courts and "government by injunction"—issues of deep concern to the former attorney general.[42]

Bryan easily won renomination, but as his campaign chugged along towards certain defeat, conservative Democrats took heart for 1904. Their immediate practical concern was the stance to take in the present contest. Would it be wiser to make a show of party loyalty by supporting the doomed candidate, or to avoid contamination by remaining silent? The choice was difficult and conservative leaders chose different courses. Olney professed no interest whatever in the 1904 nomination. He was fully aware of the conservatives' lack of leadership and suitable candidates, however, and from mid-1900 on did nothing that would impair his availability should the nomination come his way. In June he firmly rejected a feeler from Governor David R. Francis of Missouri to head a third-party ticket, and in August he issued a public letter reluctantly supporting Bryan. The Nebraskan had not been his choice, he admitted, and he dissented from certain planks in the Kansas City platform. Nevertheless, he called upon the electorate to choose Bryan, however distasteful, as a lesser evil than McKinley.

The Republican candidate, Olney charged, was a "syndicated" president, bought up and controlled by the moneyed interests. McKinley's foreign policy blunders—the failure to annex Cuba, acquisition of the Philippines, the war to suppress Aguinaldo, and joining the "ranks of the international land-grabbers" in China after the Boxer Rebellion—drew Olney's sharpest fire. To support McKinley meant supporting America's setting up "in business as an Asiatic Power" and welcoming a large standing army, an increased navy, an enlarged and costly diplomatic corps, onerous taxes, and international complications and entangling alliances—indeed, most of the things that Olney himself had urged upon the nation in his *Atlantic* article in May.[43]

John Hay rightly condemned Olney for not "squarely" coming out and saying that he was "homesick" to rejoin his party. It was "a mean thing" for him to tell "a lot of lies to justify his going over to Bryan. . . . His Atlantic Monthly article contradicts every line of his letter."[44] Former President Cleveland also thought it strange that Olney, who was "largely responsible through his Atlantic article, for the doctrine of expansion and consequent imperialism, should now be so impressed with the fatal tendency of imperialism as to be willing to take Bryanism as an antidote." Earlier that summer, Olney had told Cleveland of his inclination to vote for Bryan and had suggested that those who did so "might better secure the confidence of the party in the future." Olney possibly was right, Cleveland conceded, *"as there may have been something more in his mind than there was in mine."* The former chief executive, whose own presidential aspirations were not wholly dead, had decided to remain unsullied until the rank-and-file of the party returned to their senses. Then, he predicted, they would "welcome the counsel of those who have never yielded to disastrous heresy."[45]

As soon as the votes were counted, the Cleveland wing of the Democratic party moved to reassert control. Hoke Smith, writing to Olney on political matters, suggested that if the nomination were made at once, "no name would be so strong or so available as yours." Olney had no illusions about being nominated. "[I]f age were not a sufficient obstacle," he replied, he lived "much too near the North Star and in a region much too firmly joined to Republican idols." He proceeded, nonetheless, to outline a platform designed to show that the party was "up-to-date," "alive to present conditions," and both "progressive and patriotic." To rebuild public confidence, particularly among businessmen, the Democrats must accept the free-silver issue as settled. Abuses by trusts must be prevented and punished by new legislation. At the same time, concentrations of capital must be recognized as "as much an economic evolution as the division of labor" and as "absolutely essential to cheap production and to American competition in the markets of the world."

Still in his expansionist phase, Olney urged the party, "now as always," to stand for "all territorial expansion demanded by the national welfare," including annexation of Cuba. As for the Philippines, he suggested that the Democrats try to minimize and mitigate the consequences of acquisition so far as possible. The army should be enlarged so that the war against Aguinaldo—if it must continue—could be made "as short, sharp and decisive as possible." A larger navy was needed to insure the primacy of the United States in the Western Hemisphere and to protect "the lives and property and industrial interests of American citizens throughout the world."[46]

After 1900, Charles S. Hamlin, a leading young conservative Democrat in Massachusetts, began actively to promote Olney for the 1904 nomination. Invited to campaign with Bryan across Maine in 1902, Hamlin tried to advance Olney's cause with the Nebraskan. Bryan, who neither expected nor wanted the nomination himself, was determined that it go to no one who had failed to support him in 1896. Bryan thought Olney's candidacy impossible because of his close connections with the trusts. Hamlin suggested that Olney was not a contender, that he "even shrank" from being considered, and would allow his name to be advanced only in response to the "overpowering wishes of the people." Hamlin "begged" Bryan to remember in such an event that Olney had done more than any man in the country by coming out for him in 1900. Bryan asked how Olney had voted in 1896. Hamlin, not knowing, supposed he had voted for Bryan because Olney once said that he would never leave his party over an economic doctine. Bryan was not appeased. Olney's single vote in 1896 had not offset the thousands he could have influenced by supporting him openly. No member of Cleveland's cabinet could have done that in 1896, Hamlin countered, because the convention had refused to endorse the administration's honesty.

Turning to the trust issue, Bryan recalled that during the Cleveland administration he had given Olney evidence of a violation of the antitrust law and that Olney had done nothing. If elected president, would he enforce the law? Hamlin declared that Olney would "break every trust in the country if he accepted office on such a platform." Believing that he had made a "great impression" on Bryan, Hamlin was certain the Nebraskan would "not violently oppose" Olney's name if it ever came before him for approval.[47] Hamlin reported the conversation to Olney.

Realizing that he was vulnerable on the antitrust issue, Olney offered an unconvincing defense when Republicans attacked his record as attorney general. The federal courts between 1890 and 1897, he insisted, had consistently refused to apply the Sherman Act to cases brought before them. Citing as examples the Whiskey and Sugar Trust cases, Olney mentioned neither his personal role in either case nor the fact that he had applauded both decisions. Considerably stretching the truth, he asserted that Cleveland's Department of Justice had done "everything in its power to give the law a fair chance," and had persevered despite "great discouragement and many adverse decisions."[48]

Even as he was explaining his failure to enforce the Sherman Act while attorney general, Olney became involved in the celebrated Northern Securities antitrust suit. As counsel for the Burlington Railroad, he had "actively participated" in setting up the Northern Securities holding company, which had bought up control of the Northern Pacific, the Great Northern, and the Burlington. When the United States Circuit Court ruled against the combine in the spring of 1903, Olney offered to contribute whatever he could "in aid of the defendants' contention" on appeal to the Supreme Court.[49]

When appeal was taken, President Perkins of the Burlington hoped that Olney would appear before the high court. Daniel S. Lamont, another defendant, sought Olney's services as his personal counsel.[50] Olney declined both assignments, but did prepare a summary of his views in the case. Perkins suggested that the piece be published in some influential magazine such as the *North American Review*. Olney refused. His screed "was not and is not for the public eye." He had written it for C. W. Bunn and other counsel for the defendants to use in "any way" they "saw fit." Subsequently both Bunn and Francis Lynde Stetson borrowed from Olney's argument in preparing their briefs.[51]

Shortly before the case was to be argued in court, two New York attorneys, Lewis Cass Ledyard and James C. Carter, read and praised Olney's "most lawyerlike and thoughtful paper." Olney's pride of authorship surged to the fore. Although he had refused to allow his statement to be submitted to the court or to be published under his name, he now complained that "disconnected extracts" had been taken from what was intended to be "a continuous piece of reasoning." Whatever merit it had was "very much impaired, if not lost . . . " If Bunn and Stetson had not used it at all, Olney added petulantly, he could "easily have it published in some law magazine" such as the *Harvard Law Review*.[52] Again, Olney was being less than candid. Concern for his public image was the chief reason he had not gone into print. Early in the affair, the *Boston Globe*, unaware of Olney's role in the matter, invited him to prepare a statement about the case for their readers. Because of his various connections, he replied, he was afraid that any statement he might make would "easily" put him in "a false position."[53]

Throughout 1902 and 1903, Olney played a familiar role in American politics—that of the pleasantly annoyed noncandidate who modestly rebuffs those who urge him to seek the presidency. He steadfastly refused to speak at political gatherings where his presence might be "misconstrued" as office-seeking. He declined to have his picture taken for the newspapers. He wrote well-wishers that he did not expect "presidential lightning" to strike in his direction and would do all that he "decently" could to ward it off.[54] When a Memphis Democrat invited him to speak at the founding of an Olney-for-President Club in Tennessee, he politely refused. "Not being a candidate for the Presidency, I cannot, of course, encourage the formation of the proposed Club." He did not ask the group to disband, however. "I ought to be . . . frank in saying," he wrote, "that the favorable sentiments of yourself and those you represent are highly appreciated and give me sincere pleasure."[55]

A strong indication that Olney meant to be prepared in the event the nomination was offered was his preparation of a series of papers on leading national issues. Partisan but thoughtful, they ranged over domestic and foreign problems in detail. Suitable for publication as articles in opinion-shaping magazines, none were published until 1906 and 1907, when part of the material on trusts and labor unions appeared in revised form in *Inter-Nation* magazine.[56]

As Theodore Roosevelt's hold on the presidency grew firmer and his renomination more certain, Olney privately showered criticism on the man and his party. How much the shift was due to a genuine dislike of the brash young president, his policies, and his style, and how much to Olney's growing sense of rivalry, cannot be known. During the Cleveland administration, when Roosevelt was a member of the Civil Service Commission, the two attended many of the same social functions, and Olney frequently invited Roosevelt to play tennis—a privilege not accorded frivolously. In 1897 Olney warmly congratulated Roosevelt upon his appointment as assistant secretary of the navy—a position that promised both "distinction for yourself" and "usefulness to the country."[57]

When Roosevelt acceded to the presidency, Olney wrote most graciously: "not as you are President, but a friend whom I value and in whose fortunes I am much interested." He congratulated Roosevelt upon the "radical change" in his life—"upon your escape from a purely decorative office to one in which every faculty will have room for the fullest exercise. You come to the presidency under more favorable auspices than any one before you; in the very heyday of manhood, with health and strength such as few can boast; with talents of a high order disciplined and developed by all the educational opportunities which modern life affords; with a prestige and hold upon the admiration and affection of the people at large without regard to party lines such as no other man in public life to-day enjoys. The titular head of the American people, you may easily be their real head as well—their real leader at a time of all others when wise leadership is most needed. . . . "[58] Not ordinarily given to flattery, Olney seems to have been sincere.

Olney was soon sniping at Roosevelt's hyperactivity, however, particularly in foreign affairs. "Are they not having a splendid picnic at Washington?" he wrote Cleveland. "Isn't the flirtation between Willie [Kaiser Wilhelm] and Teddie amusing?"[59] And, as noted, Olney disapproved of Roosevelt's handling of the 1902 Venezuelan crisis and his role in the acquisition of the Panama Canal.

Under increasing pressure in 1903 to announce himself a candidate, Olney wrote to his brother Peter in apparent candor, "As for my supposed candidacy, there is absolutely nothing in it. A draft might of course fetch me—it would, I suppose, any man—but nothing else." Judge Alton Parker seemed "the best and most available candidate in sight," and Olney frequently advocated the New Yorker's nomination.[60] When interest revived in a third term for Cleveland, Olney became an enthusiastic supporter, publicly proposing Cleveland's name at a dinner for distinguished Democrats in New York City on 4 January 1904.[61] Olney's support of his former chief was probably genuine. He must have known, however, that the more delegates committed to the former president, the greater his own strength if Cleveland were to fail. Boosting Cleveland was one of the tactics adopted by Olney supporters in the months before the 1904 convention.[62]

Massachusetts Democrats, led by Hamlin and the Mayor of Boston, Patrick A. Collins, began an Olney boomlet early in 1904. In January the state central committee unanimously urged Olney to run. Pleased, but fearful of being regarded an avowed candidate, Olney asked the committee for a signed statement that he was in no way committed by their action. Support continued to build in Massachusetts and around the country as political and business acquaintances and admirers, many of whom were Republicans, rallied to his support.[63] By the end of March the contest for delegates to the Massachusetts state convention began. Olney preferred not to be involved. His friends urged that unless his name was offered, Massachusetts Democrats would support William Randolph Hearst, whose journalistic exploits and political views were anathema to Olney. On 12 April, Olney delegates swept the caucuses, defeating the controversial editor by a three-to-one margin.[64]

"I am much gratified that your friends have 'wallopped' the Hearst contingent in Masstts.," Peter wrote from New York. It was a "scandal," however, that there should be "any Hearst 'boomers' " in the state. If Parker's drive should fail, he predicted, the nomination would go to Richard. Cleveland, Peter reported, was telling his friends that Olney was his personal first choice for the nomination.[65]

Competition with Hearst left Olney "feeling uncommonly cheap." Any contest with that man, however successful, was "inevitably demeaning of itself," he wrote. If Hearst could have been stopped in any other way, he would have declined to let his name be used. As for Peter's prediction, he had "never taken the idea seriously" and did not wish to now. If he could have the presidency for the asking, he would "refuse it unless considerations of duty made that course impossible." The thought of campaigning was loathsome to him: "I don't know any one less suited to such an ordeal." Having gone through four years of public life "without marked discredit," it seemed to him to be tempting Providence to risk the "little record" already made by seeking higher office. Olney suspected, too, that the Democrats, whoever their nominee, would lose because the party had no "stirring and vital and moral issue," and because of Roosevelt's influence with organized labor—a group traditionally in the Democratic camp.[66]

On 21 April, the Massachusetts convention endorsed Olney for president and instructed its delegates to the national convention to nominate and support him until a nominee was chosen or until his name was withdrawn. Olney was upset. He would have preferred a simple endorsement without specific instructions. When Hamlin assured him that he was absolutely free to withdraw his name at any time, Olney agreed to allow the delegation to do as it saw fit for the time being.[67]

On 24 May, Olney wrote to Collins, chairman of the Massachusetts delegation, asking that his name not be placed in nomination at St. Louis. Collins conferred privately with Olney and afterwards persuaded Hamlin that they should continue to work for Olney's nomination. One month later, the reluctant candidate sent Hamlin written suggestions for the party platform. Then, as the delegation embarked for St. Louis, he asked Hamlin to have Collins read his letter of declination to the Massachusetts delegates and to withdraw his name. Giving "a rather evasive answer," Hamlin departed for the West.[68]

Just as Olney had alternated between accepting and rejecting Cleveland's invitation to join the cabinet in 1893, so in 1904 he was torn between withdrawing his name and allowing his supporters to press for his nomination. Had Olney really wanted his name withdrawn, it is easy to imagine the forceful way in which he would have acted. His feeble protestations indicated a willingness to let the nomination come to him if fate so decreed.

As matters turned out, the Democrats at St. Louis decreed otherwise. The overwhelming majority was committed to a conservative course, but already had its candidate: Alton Parker. The rest leaned towards Hearst. At the all-night session to select the nominee, the names of Parker and Hearst touched off lengthy demonstrations. Then the weary delegates listened as favorite sons were placed in nomination— former Senator George Gray of Delaware, Senator Francis M. Cochrell of Missouri, General Miles, and others. Finally, at 2:30 A.M., Mayor Collins rose to place Massachusetts's favorite son before the convention. He "shouted 'Olney' in clarion tones from the platform and then waited for the expected burst of applause," a newsman from the *Chicago Tribune* reported. "But it hung fire. Hand claps and faint cheers, but it was all over in less than a minute." Men bearing an Olney banner stood poised outside the delegate area, but never came onto the floor. A shower of confetti and "long, snakey streamers of tissue paper" were tossed into the air, "but the atmosphere was too damp and they fell flat. So did the boom of Richard Olney." His supporters "decently hurried" his banner "out of sight." Later that morning, Parker won on the first ballot. Of nearly 1000 votes, Olney got 38: 32 from Massachusetts, 4 from Maine, and 1 each from Nebraska and Oklahoma.[69]

Conservative Democrats rejoiced that the party had returned to first principles. Cleveland, Olney, and other leaders in the previous Democratic administration heartily endorsed the candidate. If Olney regretted the selection of Parker, he gave no indication. During the campaign he delivered at least two important addresses on the candidate's behalf.[70] In defeat, Parker carried fewer states than Bryan in 1900 and lagged behind the Nebraskan's popular vote by nearly one and a half million. Conservative Democrats could hardly claim the right to choose the party's 1908 standard bearer. Olney, by then seventy-three years old, followed events closely, but wielded little influence. Judson Harmon, his successor as attorney general, was "A. No.

1," he believed, but he feared the Ohioan had little attraction for the "plain people."[71] Clutching at straws in hope of warding off a third Bryan nomination, Olney urged the candidacy of Governor John A. Johnson of Minnesota. But Johnson, hardly known outside his own region, made a poor showing even in nearby states in the contest for delegates.[72]

When Bryan once more became the nominee, Olney dutifully supported the party's choice. William Howard Taft's victory in 1908 consigned the Democrats to another four years in the political dustbin. Olney's slight political influence now quickly ebbed. After 1908 he was a relic of the past, honored, but without influence, even among Democrats.

17

Reflections of an Elder Statesman

Olney's experiences in Washington in some ways had broadened and mellowed him. Freed from the need to drive himself relentlessly, he gave over more time to relaxation and socializing. He spent long afternoons at tennis, golf, fishing, and hiking. Summers at Falmouth increasingly stretched on into the fall. He read more and ranged widely in biography and history. Paintings became a new interest, and he and his widowed daughter, Agnes Minot, frequented exhibits and art shops. In his last years Olney collected—in a small way—the works of some of the French impressionists, L'Oiseau, Maufra, and Moret, among others. When bridge became popular, he took it up with zeal.[1]

New inventions, whether for pleasure or convenience, won Olney's quick favor. Edison's "vitascope," which he first saw in 1896, was "a wonderful thing which must be seen to be appreciated," he wrote Mrs. Olney. As early as 1907 he and his family were using automobiles.[2] The telephone, however, was the exception. When, for convenience sake, the Boston & Maine installed a private phone on his desk in 1898, Olney objected. He preferred to continue using the party-line phone in a nearby office still listed in the name of his deceased cousin, Sigourney Butler. The arrangement avoided public listing of Olney's name and cost but one-fifth as much as a private line. Although he relented, he was soon annoyed by intrusions into his privacy. Someone appeared to be giving out his private number, he complained. "This morning I was called up by a total stranger in Worcester. The same thing has happened once or twice before." He also found fault with the operator. Service was "inefficient" and the girl seemed "slow and unfamiliar with her business and inclined to be inattentive."[3]

Olney's prestige and advancing age made it possible for him to indulge his idiosyncrasies more than ever. He resented mention of his birthday in the newspapers and each year Miss Straw was careful to warn editors against noting the event.[4] No one and no thing were permitted to break into his appointed rounds on the tennis lawns or golf links. Within his family he became ever more autocratic and no one contradicted him on any point, however wrong he might be. Over the years he continued to summon the family to Thanksgiving and other holiday dinners. For a few young members of the family these ceremonial affairs were something of an ordeal. On one occasion, nephew Wilson Olney and grandson Francis Minot fortified themselves in advance with alcohol. When the turkey arrived in customary splendor, Wilson made the mistake of saluting it with a hearty, "Hello, Mr. Turkey." Looking his twenty-five-year-old nephew straight in the eye, Olney ordered him to leave the table.[5]

In his later years—as before—Olney was plagued by the "servant problem." "Your boy John has been giving me a good deal of trouble by absenting himself during office hours and being late both in the morning and at noon," he wrote the father of one of his office boys. "Unless he can be relied upon to keep the office hours which I desire, I shall have to get another boy."[6] Patrick Flannery, Olney's gardener and general handyman, frequently crossed him. "I have already warned you several times against running up large bills without consulting me," Olney complained upon receipt of a large bill for begonias. "If you persist . . . I shall have to find a way to protect myself." After nearly twenty years of service, Flannery asked Olney to fill out a reference form for another position. Olney's responses were frank if not flattering:

Implements kept in proper place?	Not particularly.
Manages help successfully?	Yes.
Neat and clean in appearance when at work?	Not particularly.
Temperate?	Yes, as far as I know.
Honest?	Yes, as far as I know.
Obliging?	Tolerably so.
What failings?	The customary failing of a man employed so long in one place as to think himself indispensible.[7]

Olney's disdain for the residents of Falmouth and their dislike of him hardened over the years. It flared into the open at the time of President McKinley's assassination in 1901. The day the president was

shot, Olney's coachman, Michael Conway, went to his favorite drinking place and, after a few glasses, observed that "it was good enough
for the President" and that "he ought to have been killed long ago."
Shocked, the people present assumed that Conway was joking until
he refused to retract his remarks. Word of the incident spread quickly
through the devoutly Republican village, but since McKinley appeared
to recover, nothing happened. When, a few days later, the president
died, a crowd of over a hundred formed and decided to tar and feather
Conway. When he failed to make his customary appearance for mail
at the post office, the mob marched on Olney's house to demand their
man. Some seem to have suspected that the staunchly Democratic
Olney shared his coachman's sentiments and was harboring him. Olney
sat alone in his darkened house, stubbornly refusing to come out and
speak to the mob. When, at length, they learned that Olney had
dismissed Conway and sent him out of town just before their arrival,
they cheered and left.[8] Olney promptly put his house up for sale.
Apparently unable to find a buyer at that time of year, he decided
to keep the place and returned each summer until his death.[9] He
and the townspeople never spoke, however, and even as Olney lay
dying in 1917, no one from Falmouth inquired of the family as to
his condition.

The collapse of the movement to make him president in 1904 in no
way diminished Olney's interest in national and international problems.
He continued to write and speak on foreign and domestic issues to
within a few months of his death. Whatever might have been true
earlier, after 1904 Olney's views were not conditioned by the chance
that he might be seeking public office, and time had largely erased
any need to justify his administration of the Justice or State Departments. Olney's public utterances between 1904 and 1916 were the
careful distillations of the experiences and reflections of his lifetime.
Nearly all of his speeches and articles in those years were informative
and thoughtful. A few were prophetic.

In the realm of foreign policy, Olney strenuously objected to the
so-called Roosevelt Corollary, particularly when the administration
attempted to link it with his own Venezuelan policy of 1895.[10] Until
Roosevelt's time, the Monroe Doctrine had never been seen as em-
powering the United States to use force in the affairs of an American
state, Olney insisted, "except against its enemies and to aid it in defending its political and territorial integrity against European aggression."[11] The new corollary perverted the Monroe Doctrine by asserting

a protectorate over Latin America and by guaranteeing foreign creditors against any default on debts, by taking possession, if need be, of the ports of the delinquent nation and receiving and disbursing its revenues. Such a policy would become increasingly burdensome, Olney predicted. Since American intervention would be without foundation in international law, it would be purely arbitrary, and if either the debtor or creditor nation in question objected, the United States might have to resort to force. Moreover, although many Latin American states were deeply in debt and already in arrears, foreign lenders, confident that the United States would guarantee repayment, would have "fresh impetus" to make new loans with "less care and caution than ever before."

If Roosevelt's reasoning were right, Olney declared, the Monroe Doctrine had found in him "its worst enemy." Europe had long argued that if the United States protected Latin American states from chastisement for wrong-doing, it must also guarantee their good behavior. It was not that the Europeans hoped the United States would agree. Instead, they expected the United States to abandon the Monroe Doctrine rather than assume such heavy responsibilities. Roosevelt's acceptance of these obligations, Olney warned, might well result in the American people's demanding a disavowal of the Monroe Doctrine in its entirety.

Olney regarded the assumption of such broad responsibilities as unnecessary. He doubted that the punishment of American states for defaulting on debts posed any immediate threat of European territorial encroachment in the hemisphere. It would be sufficient, he suggested, for the United States to remain watchful and possibly to reaffirm its position that "coercion of an American state . . . to obtain pecuniary satisfaction must stop at any permanent occupation of territory."

In the past the Monroe Doctrine had always rested on self-interest, not on altruism, Olney observed. The United States prevented European aggression in the New World simply to protect its own interests. That the policy benefited the Latin American nations was wholly incidental. Because the United States did not meddle in their affairs, the southern republics gave the Monroe Doctrine their "sympathy and perhaps . . . active support." Under the new corollary, although the weak states of Latin America might be grateful for protection against foreign powers, they would also be humiliated that the United States no longer treated them as equals, but "put on airs of an over-lord" who took their affairs out of their own hands. Without "conciliating Europe," the new policy would alarm America's neighbors to the south, undermine their friendship, and wound their pride.[12]

When it became clear that the United States was not going to abandon the corollary, Olney advocated giving it standing in international law and putting its enforcement on a multilateral basis. In an address before the first session of the American Society of International Law (of which he was a vice president from 1906 until 1917) Olney called for making the principles of international law consistent with actual practice. "[I]ndividualism as the essence of relations between states," he said, had been modified by internationalism, and "state independence as the basis of international law" had been "radically qualified by state interdependence." In recognition of these facts, Olney proposed the formation and recognition of regional concerts of nations empowered to act on the needs of their members. The already functioning Concert of Europe, he suggested, might be matched by a Concert of American states. Under this arrangement the United States would no longer assume the role of American "boss"—as under the Roosevelt Corollary—but would work with the other American powers. The "American concert of purely American states . . . would tend to avert wars between states as well as insurrections and revolutions within states, . . . would do much to further trade and intercourse of all kinds between the various American states, and . . . the United States, as a leading member of the concert, might be counted upon as an agency for good even more potent than if acting in the invidious role of sole and supreme dictator" of the Western Hemisphere.

As a concrete example of how the concert might work, Olney suggested that in building the Panama Canal, the United States had "practically appropriated" the property of a sister state, claiming to act as "the mandatory of civilization." Under his proposal, if the general good required the expropriation of property of a member state, the concert, not the United States, would act, and as beneficiary the concert would compensate the victim.[13]

Over the years Olney watched as first Roosevelt's "Big Stick" policy, then Taft's "Dollar Diplomacy," and finally Wilson's attempts to guide the Latin American states to American-style democracy led to repeated armed interventions in the Caribbean and Central American states. None of these developments met his full approval. "The United States," he wrote Lyman Abbott, editor of *Outlook*, in 1915, "is no longer regarded as the big benevolent brother, playing the simple role of protector and friend and in no way interfering with the autonomy of the South American peoples." In the Latin view, the United States had taken upon itself far-reaching police powers over the hemisphere. It not only guaranteed the obligations due to European creditors but, in order to make good that guarantee, claimed the "right to preserve order in such states, to nip in the bud what it deems causeless revolutions, and to seize ports and sequester customs revenues for the benefit of foreign creditors." Either these extensions of the Monroe Doctrine "must be reversed" (which Olney doubted would happen) or they "must be regarded as an integral part of the Monroe Doctrine." In the latter event, he accurately predicted, the United States' relations with Latin America "would long continue to be unfortunate."[14]

Writing in the February 1916 *North American Review*, Olney suggested even broader hemispheric duties for his proposed concert of American states. Instead of the United States unilaterally enforcing the Monroe Doctrine and Roosevelt Corollary, Olney urged the concert to undertake these obligations as a joint venture. "The Concert would put all American states behind the Monroe Doctrine, so enlarged as to mean the protection of every American State not only against European aggression, but against foreign aggression from whatever quarter." At its own discretion the concert would decide "when in the common interest it was necessary and proper to so far invade the independence of any particular state as to compel it to recognize and perform its international duties, and would also determine by what state or states the decision of the Concert should be enforced." Similarly, the concert might well "make appropriate and adequate provision" for the security and defense of the Panama Canal, whether against military or economic assault.[15]

Over the years Olney wasted little time in fighting against accomplished facts in American foreign relations. The distorted interpretation of his own Venezuelan policy, American acquisition of the Panama Canal Zone, and Roosevelt's mischievous corollary, among other matters, he hoped could somehow be made legitimate and brought within the framework of a larger developing international order. The basis of this order broadened in Olney's mind over the years. While secretary of state he had seen the United States as sole guardian of the Western Hemisphere against outside aggression and protector of American citizens in their rights around the world. Later he envisioned an Anglo-American alliance securing law and order in the channels of world commerce. By the end of his life he appreciated the need for even broader bases—regional concerts, perhaps, or even a world-wide league to insure peace.[16]

In domestic matters after 1904, Olney's chief interest was the trust problem. Borrowing heavily from one of his 1902 position papers, he published a comprehensive article on the subject in 1907. Defining a trust as "simply such a concentration of capital upon an industry as minimizes or tends to minimize the cost of production," he observed that by nature they restricted competition. "So long as there are two plants which can be combined in one, there is a duplication of both capital and labor which prevents the lowest cost of production being reached."

Attempts to eliminate trusts were wrong-headed, he believed. Only by radically limiting the fundamental basis of "civilized society," that is, "the right of private property, the right of every man honestly to get, hold, and use the natural and just rewards of his industry, probity, and skill," could trusts be destroyed. Olney doubted that any political party or substantial group of citizens would advocate so drastic a step. Similarly, he doubted that government would undertake to control trusts by regulating the prices that they charged.

In part the problem stemmed from the public's misunderstanding of both the benefits and the disadvantages of trusts. Trusts were an "economic evolution" not unlike "the division of labor" or the use of "machinery as a substitute for manual labor." The failure "by demagogues or by statesmen, by the state or by the nation, by courts or by the legislatures" to suppress them indicated that they were "natural." So did the fact that they appeared in all nations in the same stage of economic development as the United States.

Because they minimized production costs, trusts produced far-reaching benefits to all American society: successful competition for foreign markets, the rapid industrial progress of the United States in recent years, a higher standard of living for everyone because goods became less expensive, and increased job and wage security for those who worked for the trusts. Unless the United States was prepared to halt its industrial progress, "or even go backward," it "must continue to excell in cheap production." This meant, in effect, that it could not do away with any instrumentality vital to the reduction of costs.

Olney admitted that trusts had faults, but the question was not how to abolish combines, but how to secure the benefits they offered while preventing abuses by them. Many of the evils attributed to trusts—overcapitalization, rebates, and illicit favors—were not peculiar to them, but could exist with any form of business. Only three abuses were inseparable from the trust form: They discouraged "the development of human character of a superior type" by tending "to divide the community into a few employers on the one side and a vast multitude of wage-earners on the other," they menaced free institutions by creating an "oligarchy of capitalists" in what should be a republic, and they injured all consumers by making possible "excessive prices and exorbitant profits."

The first charge, Olney observed, was more fancied than real. Presumably trusts destroyed the middle class by driving small merchants, farmers, producers, and employers into the ranks of labor, thereby depriving society of desirable character traits found in these groups—"self-reliance and independence of thought and action." But trusts in turn created a new middle class, the "class of superintendency" (the superintendent, the overseer, and the foreman) which fostered such important character traits as fidelity and trustworthiness. Since both sets of characteristics were needed by society, the state should not favor one over the other.

The concentration of economic and political power in the hands of a few capitalists and employers, Olney admitted, constituted a threat to republican institutions. However, clergymen, lawyers, doctors, scientists, teachers, and others who belonged to and were controlled by neither capitalists nor wage-earners acted as a moderating influence. So did the rising new superintendency. "[I]ndispensable to the employer," these men could not be dealt with arbitrarily; "naturally recruited" from the wage-earning class, their sympathies were more with labor than with capital.

As a further protection against the power of the employing class, however, Olney urged the government to strengthen labor unions by extending to them charters similar to those that had proved so beneficial to corporations. Unions, which had done much to secure an "equitable share" of the benefits of production for workers, might also prove useful in protecting the "free exercise of their right of suffrage" and in guaranteeing "truly republican institutions." Unions, for example, could prevent their members from being discharged for holding political views or voting contrary to the interests of the employer.

To correct the third abuse of trusts—overcharging and garnering to themselves excessive profits—Olney proposed relying on competitive forces rather than on governmental regulation or some form of socialism. Labor unions, for example, could act as a countervailing influence; when profits of trusts became exorbitant, the unions would demand and get for the workers a larger share of the earnings. This raised the specter of conspiracy between unions and trusts to raise both wages and profits while passing the cost onto the consuming public in the form of higher prices. Where railroads, public utilities, and other natural monopolies engaged in such practices, Olney saw no objection to governmental price-fixing. For other businesses, however, excessive prices would result in fewer customers and more competitors eager to share in the high profits. Since intelligently managed trusts sought above all else to avoid competition, their pricing policies would tend to be moderate.

Government could assist competitive forces in several ways to prevent excessive prices and profits, Olney pointed out. Reduced tariff rates, for instance, would lower the price of goods in the United States while creating greater markets abroad. Public carriers and utilities could be forced by law to serve all customers fairly and without rate discrimination. Patent laws could be amended to reward inventors in some way other than giving them monopolies over the use of their inventions.

To benefit both capital and labor, Olney recommended a revision of antitrust policy "to conform to the dictates of common sense and to the practical requirements of business." The Sherman Act, as it stood, discouraged enterprise and restricted the free use of capital necessary to efficiency and cheaper production. At the same time, "no matter how peaceful or law-abiding," combinations that restrained interstate commerce were illegal under the act. Intelligent revision would concede to both capital and labor the right to combine and organize. Only if "the operation of natural laws, unhampered by artificial restraints" proved ineffective, should other measures be adopted.[17]

Olney's opposition to the Sherman Act never changed. Not only did he regard the law as unenforceable, he fought against court interpretations and legislation designed to make it so. In 1902, for example, he objected to legislation that would sanction "reasonable" combinations while outlawing "unreasonable" ones. The attempt to make an unworkable law workable, he argued, would throw upon the courts the legislative duty of determining what were acceptable practices in business. It would also cause great uncertainty for businessmen because the courts were limited to disposing of cases one by one as they arose and to ruling only on the specific points raised in each particular case. Consequently, they could hand down no uniform, comprehensive rules. Even more unsettling, federal judges could be expected to differ considerably as to what each would accept as "reasonable."[18]

Although Congress refused to fasten such responsibility on the judiciary, the Supreme Court in its 1911 American Tobacco and Standard Oil decisions assumed the very responsibilities that Olney had warned against. Writing in the *Boston Herald*, Olney repeated his objections to the rule of reason and suggested that it would have been wiser for the court to have invalidated the obviously unenforceable

Sherman Act. That would have forced Congress to rewrite the measure, incorporating into the new statute the knowledge gained from a quarter-century of experience with the problem. "Congress could not have helped seeing that the problem before it was not how to squelch big business altogether, but how to retain its advantages while at the same time safeguarding the public against its possible abuses. . . . " Large industrial combinations, Olney declared, could well be regarded as in "the same class with the public service corporation," and be subjected to "like supervision and regulation." An agency similar to the ICC might well be employed to regulate large industrial combinations.[19]

Olney felt vindicated when the initially enthusiastic response of the business community to the rule of reason gave way to "general skepticism." Increasingly, businessmen realized that no uniform rule on reasonableness could be expected from federal courts scattered around the country, and the result of varied decisions would be "not merely confusion and perplexity in business circles, but great loss of prestige by the national judiciary." Only Congress, he suggested, could "effectually and permanently lift business out of the slough of despond in which it is now plunged."[20]

All the while that Olney discussed publicly the need to prevent abuses by the trusts, he was working with his private clients to thwart governmental regulation of big business. His role in the Northern Securities case has already been noted. Olney also continued to work to reduce the ICC's authority over railroads and their rates. To Olney's delight, a bill that he had drafted in 1892 to weaken the ICC by giving its functions over to a special interstate commerce court (or courts), or by subjecting its rulings to review by such a court, was revived. Olney described the measure to Massachusetts Congressman Samuel W. McCall as a golden mean between the extremes of socialism and rampant laissez faire, aimed at "preserving the private ownership and management of railroads and yet establishing such governmental control of rates as to insure their reasonableness in the public interest."[21] The proposal got around the problem of inexpert judges ruling on matters beyond their competence, he told Senator Stephen B. Elkins, by creating two tribunals to act in each controversy—"one, viz., the Commission, which is well qualified to reach correct conclusions but is powerless to enforce them, and the other, viz., a United States court of ordinary jurisdiction, which has the power to enforce correct conclusions but is not well qualified to reach them."[22]

To Daniel S. Lamont, vice-president of the Northern Pacific, Olney explained his bill more candidly. Its "whole object" was "a judicial enforcement of the provisions of the Interstate Commerce Act as they stand." The bill did away with the ICC and substituted for it a court that had "no power over rates at all except as it may decide in regular suits that a charge by a railroad is or is not reasonable or on other grounds unlawful."[23] Defeated in 1902 and 1904, an interstate commerce court was established in 1910. Until dissolved three years later, it repeatedly overruled ICC decisions.

When Congress in 1905 began consideration of governmental rate-making for interstate railroads, President Tuttle of the Boston & Maine asked Olney to prepare a statement on the subject. Greatly pleased with the result, Tuttle urged Olney to publish the document as an article in the *North American Review*. It would carry weight there, Tuttle believed, because readers would think it written from a "disinterested and quasi-judicial point of view." Olney had doubts. "[P]repared as a brief or argument for the railroad side," it "no doubt" had "the bias usually inherent in briefs and arguments" and would not fool the public. If it were noted at all, the public would probably see it "as the production of a railroad director or lawyer." He was prepared to do all that he fairly could for the railroads, but posing "as not specially concerned with them" would put him "in a false position without really advancing the railroad cause."[24]

Despite his reservations, Olney allowed the article to be published. Its essential burden was threefold: If Congress had the authority to fix railroad rates, its power could not be delegated to other agencies such as the ICC; the Constitution, in granting power to the federal government to regulate commerce, did not authorize Congress itself to conduct that commerce; and, if Congress did not have the power to operate railroads, neither could it prescribe their charges for services because rate-making was "the very essence of the ownership of the transportation business."[25] The article attracted considerable notice, but whatever its influence on the public, President Roosevelt characterized it much as Olney had feared. "Mr. Olney is a good fellow and a strong man," the president allowed, "but he is one of the most extreme pro-corporation men in the entire country, . . . and his article struck me as simply a brief in behalf of the ultra-reactionaries among the great financiers."[26]

Between 1907 and 1914, Olney was deeply involved in the merger of the Boston & Maine and New Haven systems and in the dissolution proceedings that followed.[27] Throughout he played his usual role of broker—working with both companies and having an interest in both as well as some influence with government officials. His goal was to protect so far as possible all railroad interests involved.[28] When, in the spring of 1914, the companies and the Justice Department reached an impasse over the terms of dissolution, Olney interceded directly with President Wilson. He had been careful, he observed, not to intrude suggestions or views on the president despite an often-personal "lively interest" in matters under consideration. He was obliged to break this rule, however, in the case of union of the two great railroads. The merger had always seemed to him to be in the public interest, bringing under a single management one continuous trunk line from New York to the maritime provinces of Canada. When the matter was questioned by the Justice Department, he had hoped that the consolidation might be preserved while trolley lines, steamship companies, and "other excrescences" acquired by the combine "were lopped off." Since the attorney general and the New Haven management thought otherwise, a decree of separation had been entered into. Olney offered suggestions to Wilson about how best to effect the dissolution with a minimum of difficulty for the railroads. Subsequently he helped to work out an agreement through conferences with Colonel Edward M. House, Wilson's personal advisor.[29] It was Olney's last service for the Boston & Maine.

Olney's second major domestic concern was organized labor. Like many progressive contemporaries, he saw the need for unions but was troubled by their potential for evil. Borrowing once more from his 1902 position papers, he published a number of observations on the labor question. Olney favored the recognition and acceptance of unions on the grounds that they were inevitable, that labor must be given equal treatment with capital before the law, and that unions were needed to counterbalance the power of big business.

Continued economic progress, he believed, required that businessmen be left free to pursue their self-interest, expanding and combining as that interest dictated. In fairness, and for their own protection, individual workingmen must be accorded an equal right to organize and to bargain collectively. However, Olney was less interested in unions as devices for securing justice or higher wages, shorter hours, and better working conditions for workers, than as a means for offsetting the growing economic and political power of the trusts. As noted, he saw unions as a check against overpricing by trusts because they would demand for workers a greater share of the profits in the form of higher wages.

But unions would also tend to prevent the degeneration of the American government into rule by a moneyed oligarchy. They would protect workmen from employers who were apt to regard a vote against policies or candidates they favored as "sufficient cause for depriving the employee of work." The danger that political activity by unions would "array the poor against the rich" caused Olney little concern. Class antagonism already existed and would continue whether unions became politically active or not. Olney also evoked unions in hopes that they would prove useful in battling his own pet political worries—the drift of government towards centralization, paternalism, lawlessness, militarism, and higher taxation. Big businesses could not be counted on to oppose these "pernicious" trends because they benefited too greatly from a strong, money-spending government favorable to business enterprise. Professionals such as lawyers and clergymen were ineffective because they sharply divided over most controversial issues. Only the workers, with their interest in the preservation of free institutions, offered hope.

The matter of labor leadership did trouble Olney. Since workmen "inevitably" depended upon others for political guidance, he thought it better that they secure it from their own leaders—men "in touch and sympathy" with labor interests—than from "demagogues and partisans" who would seek only to use workers to further their own ends.[30] When, at last, workers "came into their kingdom," Olney feared that they might try to reduce or eliminate inequality among men by confiscating property outright or by levying unjust, confiscatory taxes. Workers, he warned, must choose between paternalistic government with its tendency towards despotism, and government that made individual freedom "the great end of its existence." The "true freedom" that workers coveted and needed, he said, was not so much the right to vote or to be voted for, as the right "to all the self-development" of which they were individually capable.[31]

To protect against some of the abuses of unions, Olney advocated their incorporation under federal law. Unions would thus become responsible in law for all of their acts and would be empowered to make contracts binding on their members. Their charters should provide for the arbitration of disputes under governmental auspices whenever unions and employers were unable to reach agreement. Where disputes involved transportation, communications, or public utilities, the public would be protected against strikes by court injunctions, while the corporations involved would be placed in receivership until the dispute was resolved.[32]

When the Supreme Court in 1908 struck down as unconstitutional the clause of the Erdman Act prohibiting yellow-dog contracts, Olney, who had helped draft the law, lashed out. Public policy, he argued, favored the organization of workers into unions, as demonstrated by the 1886 statute authorizing the federal incorporation of unions, and by the Erdman Act which recognized unions as legal parties in the arbitration of labor disputes. Having recognized and promoted unionization, Congress in the Erdman Act had undertaken the "next logical, almost necessary, step" of trying to protect railroad employees against discrimination or loss of work for belonging to unions. To invite railwaymen to organize and then to permit their employers to deny them jobs for accepting the invitation made little sense.

The complaint of the court that the Erdman Act invaded the liberty of contract of both workers and employers, Olney charged, was an "archaic . . . long step back into the past." No longer could labor relations be regarded as between single individuals. "Cooperation and combination are the characteristics of modern industrialism, and associations of capitalists and employers in the form of partnerships and corporations long preceded any similar organizations on the part of employees and laborers." Unions had arisen to protect wages, hours, and working conditions, and "to shut a man from work" because he belonged to a union was "an attack upon labor unions of the deadliest character." If such attacks could not be prevented by law, unions, "their very existence at stake," could hardly do other than respond by striking. Olney denied that constitutional protection of the liberty of the individual overrode and controlled the government's powers to regulate commerce. In "civilized society," he declared, "there is no such thing as absolute liberty—either liberty of conduct or liberty of contract. It is necessarily liberty regulated by law."[33]

Speaking before the Merchants Club of Boston on 21 January 1913, Olney made what turned out to be his last major public address. Reminiscing would have been forgiven a man of seventy-eight; instead he called upon his listeners to understand the age in which they lived. The world was in transition, he noted, "with the old order passing and the new order on the way but not yet arrived." Worldwide unrest was bringing about far-reaching political, economic, and social change. These stirrings, which came from below—"a sort of revolt of the masses against bad living conditions"—were in progress in all civilized nations without regard to race, nationality, or form of government.

In the United States a general spirit of lawlessness, domination of government by wealth, and "tremendous inequalities of living conditions" between rich and poor were the chief causes of discontent. Lawlessness among the ignorant masses took the form of lynchings. At the highest levels a recent administration had incited revolution in a sister republic in order to appropriate part of its territory, and had vigorously prosecuted some law-breakers while allowing others to go free. The "trail of money," Olney declared, ran through the operations of government from the nominating and electing of public officials to tariff favoritism for wealthy business interests to "dollar diplomacy" that shaped the nation's foreign policy.

As for the inequality of living conditions, "in no country and at no age" had the "extremes of wealth and luxury on the one hand, and of poverty and misery on the other, been more pronounced and conspicuous . . . " It was not enough to point out that the masses had never been "better fed, better housed, better paid, or better educated." Every gain in standard of living created the desire for yet higher standards. Similarly, the argument that wealth did not bring happiness carried little weight. Riches obviously brought power, and the envious lower classes concluded that riches, power, and happiness were linked.

Two major movements aimed at meeting the problem. One, essentially political, sought to restore to the masses the powers of government that in fact had been subverted by the wealthy few in their own interest. All that could be said with certainty of this movement's chief reforms—the initiative, referendum, recall, and direct primary—was that they had not yet proved themselves. The second movement, both political and economic in nature, held that individualism had been carried too far in the United States, that limited, inactive government, aimed at preserving the greatest possible individual freedom, was no longer adequate, and that hereafter government must become an "active agency for the betterment of society," even at the expense of curtailed individual freedom. This "practical socialism," unlike "doctrinaire socialism," respected individual rights and private property. At the same time, it sought "the greater equalization of opportunity for the masses of mankind through better and stabler industrial conditions, made possible by the regulating action of government."

Citing social security programs already enacted in Britain and Germany, Olney predicted similar attempts to pacify popular unrest in the United States. The government, "slowly, perhaps, but surely," would "engage in various enterprises for the social benefit of people." It would so regulate contracts between employers and employees as "to prescribe a living wage, to charge industries with casualties and the pecuniary consequences of sickness and old age, and to compel sanitary living conditions. . . . " In business, Olney observed, the old competition was "discredited" and dying. Under the new order, competition would be regulated by law so "as to be fair," and would be "restricted to practices and methods that [were] open and honest and succeed only through superior merit."

Conservatism, within limits, was admirable, Olney told his audience. But regard for the past must never be so strong that it produced an "inability—and perhaps unwillingness—" to appreciate the present. It must be realized that political and economic concepts of the eighteenth century were not "necessarily or naturally" fitted to conditions in the twentieth, that all statesmanship was not centered "in the men of 1789," and that all economic insights were not "vested in Adam Smith and his school."[34]

Olney's remarks constituted a fitting valedictory to his thinking on domestic problems. But given his private remarks to clients and his valuable services to the nation's greatest corporations, were his public utterances sincere? Apparently Olney compartmentalized his thinking, discreetly separating long-range philosophic opinions from the immediate practical expedients recommended to his clients. Since his livelihood depended on satisfying those who hired his services, his statements to them were calculated to please. His public remarks, however, especially after 1904 when they could do him little good or harm, seem to have been genuine attempts to contribute to the solution of important contemporary problems.

As early as 1907, Olney approvingly noted the rising star of Woodrow Wilson. "I have always been much taken with . . . Wilson," he wrote his brother, Peter, in September 1910. "He rarely if ever makes a public utterance that is not worth listening to or reading."[35] From 1908 on, Olney wavered between supporting Judson Harmon for political reasons and Wilson whom he preferred. "Intellectually I think he has no superior now actively engaged in politics," and practical contact with the presidency would make Wilson "a perfectly sane and safe Executive," he predicted.[36]

When Wilson became the Democratic nominee, Olney enthusiastically rendered all possible aid. He spoke on Wilson's behalf in Boston, contributed to his campaign fund, and brought pressure to bear on the *Boston Herald* when it attacked Wilson in a manner Olney thought unfair. He warmly congratulated Wilson on his election in November, and on his inaugural address and cabinet selections in March. He only wished, he said, that he were able "to substantially aid in the success of an administration which starts off so auspiciously."[37]

Shortly after Wilson's inaugural, rumor reached Boston that Olney was being considered for appointment as ambassador to London. "[I]n your heart of hearts," Olney asked Bishop Lawrence, who had sent congratulations, "which do you think would be the greater fool—the President to offer Mr. Olney the post or Mr. Olney to accept it?"[38] There are conflicting stories about why Olney declined the offer when it came. His wife was not well and Olney himself from time to time had medical problems. Because of "obstacles of a personal and family nature," he wrote Wilson, and because the assignment required living abroad, he could not accept.[39]

But Olney also told friends that the ambassadorship was "a show place—all the real work being done in Washington." "An ambassador is nobody in these days," he reportedly remarked; "he sits at the end of a cable and does what he is told."[40] On that score Olney should have known, having himself done much as secretary of state to reduce the influence of ambassadors. A year later Olney repented his decision. "Confession being good for the soul," he wrote Wilson, "I may as well add that if my foresight had been equal to my hindsight, I should have gone to England last Spring. A physical upset, accentuated by medical opinion which turned out 'to be not so,' made me panicky—and I now see that I might have been of use in London in other ways than in doing social stunts, for which I have neither fancy nor vocation."[41]

Wilson took the letter as an indication that Olney was now available for public service. Needing men to serve on the recently created Federal Reserve Board who would reconcile suspicious bankers and businessmen to the new banking system, he offered a two-year appointment to Olney. "[T]he whole country might feel secure," Wilson wrote, and the "whole business world would be greatly heartened." Olney, though honored, again declined. The law required board members to devote full time to their duties. "In the course of a long life," he explained, he had "assumed duties" and "undertaken trusts" that could not "properly be devolved upon others."[42]

Olney's relations with the new administration remained cordial despite the president's failure to accept the Bostonian's recommendations on appointments. Although Olney played no part in enactment of Wilson's "New Freedom" legislation, he warmly endorsed it in a letter written for publication just ahead of the 1914 congressional elections.[43] When the First World War began to intrude on the nation's consciousness, Olney generally supported Wilson's neutrality policy, though possibly he would have favored a firmer stand against German depredations.[44] When Secretary of State Bryan suddenly resigned in 1915 rather than make stronger demands against Germany over the sinking of the *Lusitania*, Olney drafted a note to be sent to Germany and offered to forward it to Wilson if he wished to see it. Wilson, who previously had answered every letter from Olney, made no reply. Since the president was courting his second wife and was on vacation at the time, it is possible that Olney's letter never got past his secretaries.[45]

In April 1916, Olney vigorously endorsed Wilson's ultimatum to Germany following the sinking of the *Sussex*. Wilson's "Peace Without Victory" speech in January 1917 drew Olney's warm and open approval. "The fundamental idea," he wrote in a letter to the *New York World*, was "nothing less than a stroke of genius. If any statesman of any other country has conceived of it, he has lacked the courage to proclaim it—if any statesman of any other country has been endowed with the necessary courage he has lacked the wisdom to realize that only through 'peace without victory' is any peace possible."[46] War, not peace, was in the offing, however. Only a week later, Germany resumed the unrestricted warfare that she had abandoned after the *Sussex* affair. Step by step in the weeks that followed, the United States moved to war. Like the president himself, Olney had long favored the Allied cause over that of the Central Powers. But also like the president, he favored America's staying out of the conflict. When German policy made noninvolvement impossible on terms consistent with American honor—as Wilson and Olney understood it— Olney saw war as unavoidable.

Olney enjoyed remarkably good health and vigor until his seventy-fourth year. In January 1909 he complained of an "ugly throat" that kept him "constantly hoarse." Not long afterwards, in March, he underwent a "slight operation" to remove a "carbuncle" from the back of his neck. The operation left a sizeable hole that refused to heal. Olney was not the best of patients. Only a few days after surgery he insisted on traveling to New York City to attend memorial services for his ex-chief, Cleveland, and a special meeting of the Peabody Fund trustees. His doctor, who disapproved of the trip, accompanied him to change the dressings on his neck at frequent intervals.[47]

By the next January, Olney again was in the hospital for removal of another growth from his neck. The second operation, he complained, was to "undo some of the mischief caused by the first." Again the wound healed slowly, requiring nearly three months' hospitalization. By mid-March Olney was himself once more. "I take pleasure in paying the enclosed bills and recognize with gratitude the care, skill, and attention I received at the Cory Hill Hospital," he wrote the head nurse. "Nevertheless," he added, "I realize the object of your recent vacation. I am sure it was to acquire the vigor necessary to enable you to make out a bill of such dimensions."[48]

For the next six years the growth on Olney's neck lay dormant, allowing him to resume his writing and speaking, to continue serving on a few boards of directors, and to enjoy the role of sometime adviser to President Wilson. At eighty he still played lawn tennis and golf and took long walks. In 1916 he spent his last summer at Falmouth. That autumn when he returned to Boston, the malignant growth was again active and this time would not be checked. Operations in late September and October revealed that he had incurable cancer. "I've never named his trouble to him, and he has never named it to me," his doctor declared, "but I am sure that he knows." Unknown to his family, Olney went out to Mount Auburn Cemetery and selected a burial site among the Proper Bostonians he had served so long. On 6 December he made out his will.[49]

Despite increasing pain, Olney continued to dress formally for dinner and to go through daily rituals adopted decades before. To ease his suffering, he was heavily drugged. Even so, his mind stayed clear and his interest in public affairs remained high as the end drew near. In particular he closely followed the approaching entry of the United States into the Great War. To a friend who urged him not to worry about such matters until he was better, Olney replied that the war was on everyone's mind. Members of his family sought his opinion "of this or that bellicose episode," callers—whether bent on business or pleasure—soon plunged into the war question and would talk of nothing else, and "even the doctor" summoned to treat his ailment dismissed it with a few sentences and turned to lengthy discourses on the conflict in Europe.[50] As a matter of fact, Olney's callers probably turned with relief to the subject of the war rather than dwell on their host's worsening condition. "I am keeping up the fight as vigorously as I know how," he wrote a friend, "but dare not prophesy what the temporary issue may be. How it will end permanently there is, of course, no doubt."[51] Within a month, on 8 April 1917, Olney's death ended the matter.

To the end only the outer Olney was knowable, not the inner man. His philosophy—what he thought of life, of death, of beauty, of the meaning and purpose of human existence—Olney kept to himself. He was outwardly cold, unfeeling, and indifferent; his love for wife, children, family, and friends can only be inferred from scattered remarks and deeds. Few attended the private services at his apartment on the Fenway, and the press made little note of his passing. Tributes poured in on his invalid widow, but most were acknowledgements of gratitude for long years of service well performed, not of warm admiration and friendship. Olney's eulogists spoke primarily of the competent attorney and public servant who had gone to his reward.

It was Bishop Lawrence who wrote in his diary after the funeral that Olney "had elements of a great man. . . . "[52] The bishop, no doubt, was thinking of Olney's role in quenching the Chicago Strike, bringing the Venezuelan dispute to a successful resolution, skirting war with Spain. But Olney's handling of these affairs was controversial at best, not evidence of greatness. To be sure, suppressing Debs and the American Railway Union required firmness and determination, but many public officials of the era would have responded in the same way. His contentious note to Britain was more rash than great, however skilled his subsequent maneuverings to achieve diplomatic victory.

Olney's particular genius lay in his ability to learn from mistakes and in his capacity for continuous intellectual growth. He had entered public life, for example, late in his career, with narrow interests, experience largely confined to a specialized law practice, and a view that good government consisted of protecting life and property and enforcing the obligations of contract. But once in office, Olney developed quickly. Where the ordinary government official might have been content to bask in the glow of victory over the Chicago strikers, Olney insisted on wrestling with such prickly issues as the right of workmen to organize, to strike, and to be protected in their rights when the nature of their work made striking impossible. Similarly, many statesmen, finding that they had blundered, as in the case of the Venezuelan note, might have retreated or stumbled on into war. Olney, avoiding both, not only settled the matter creditably but undertook negotiation of a general arbitration treaty designed to forestall such crises in the future.

Had Olney had more time in public life, or been elevated to the presidency, he might have developed into a good, if not great, national leader. Energetic and imaginative, with an urge to put matters right (once convinced that something needed doing), he might well have introduced the reforms that he formulated in his 1902 position papers. In that event, many of the programs later identified with Theodore Roosevelt might have been credited to an Olney administration. But unfortunately Olney lacked many of the essentials for greatness in public life in America. He was often petty and mean-spirited, and too intolerant of the shortcomings of others. He was incapable of the necessary give and take of political life. Cold and impersonal, Olney was too disdainful of ordinary men and women to seek out and win the popular support necessary to be elected or to carry out a program when in office. Cleveland's lethargy prevented repeated thwartings by Congress from crushing him; Olney's vigor, quick temper, acid tongue, and combative spirit would have made working with an unresponsive Congress intolerable to him. All in all, it was perhaps fortunate that Olney did not go on to higher office.

Retirement and advancing age did not lure Olney into stagnant reminiscing. Rather, he thought and rethought the current issues of the day. Militantly anti-imperialistic while in office, Olney reassessed America's role in the world after 1898 and concluded that the nation should both take advantage of new opportunities overseas and assume the responsibilities imposed by power. When McKinley and Roosevelt drifted too deeply into the quagmire of foreign adventure and colonialism, however, Olney called for restraint and responsible retreat.

Essentially conservative, Olney was not given to advocating broad programs of social, political, or economic reform. On the other hand, he was neither a stand-patter nor a reactionary. He yielded to change reluctantly, but recognizing its inevitability and necessity, preferred to join and direct it rather than merely be dragged along. Originally suspicious of labor unions and hostile to strikes, Olney came to see labor organizations as legal and beneficial and finally as vital countervailing balances to the burgeoning power of the great trusts. Completely opposed to governmental regulation of business—especially of the railroads—Olney by 1913 held views at least as advanced as those of Theodore Roosevelt and Woodrow Wilson.

In his valedictory address before the Boston Merchants Club in January 1913, Olney concluded with a statement of his matured political philosophy:

> The advent of a new era is not to be ignored. It can not fairly be condemned by applying to it the standards of a bygone age. True conservatism dictates that what it stands for be examined with an open mind and be determined by such actual merits, if any, as are found to exist. If none are found, condemnation will of course be in order. But if merits are found, if government ought to be made in fact what it is in theory, namely, government of the people; if government ought to be utilized for the general welfare of society to a greater degree than ever before; if business enterprises and the mutual relations of business men ought to be

regulated in the interest of fair play, justice, and equality of opportunity and treatment,—such assuredly meritorious objects are not to be refused recognition because not within the conception of the men of past generations. On the contrary, the ends in view being found worthy, good sense and good citizenship require them to be supported even if the cherished ideas and sentiments of a life-time must go to the scrap heap.[53]

If nothing else, Olney throughout his life was alive to the reality and necessity of change. What he urged upon others, he practiced himself. No article of faith, however old or cherished, was too dear to discard once he became convinced that new circumstances had rendered ancient belief untenable. To that extent, at least, Olney possessed some of the elements of greatness.

Notes

1   Making His Mark

1. *Memorial Exercises of the Boston Bar Association Before the Supreme Judicial Court in Memory of Richard Olney* (Boston, 1919), p. 19 (hereafter cited as *Olney Memorial Exercises*). See also *Boston Globe*, 10 Apr. 1917; Matthew's correspondence with Antoinette M. Straw (Olney's long-time private secretary and executrix of his papers), Richard Olney Papers, Massachusetts Historical Society, Boston (hereafter cited as OP,MHS).

2. 9 Apr. 1917 (italics supplied).

3. Editorial, 10 Apr. 1917.

4. *Proceedings of the Massachusetts Historical Society*, 50 (Apr. 1917): 218–21.

5. William Lawrence, *Memories of a Happy Life* (Boston and New York, 1926), p. 383.

6. George Fisher Daniels, *History of the Town of Oxford, Massachusetts* (Oxford, 1892), pp. 418–19; D. Hamilton Hurd, *History of Worcester County, Massachusetts*, 2 vols. (Philadelphia, 1889), 2: 1306–7.

7. James H. Olney, *A Genealogy of the Descendants of Thomas Olney* (Providence, 1889), pp. 11–12.

8. Daniels, *History of Oxford, Mass.*, pp. 198–200, 634–35.

9. Henry James, *Richard Olney and His Public Service* (Boston, 1923), p. 8.

10. Except where otherwise indicated, this account of Wilson Olney is based on a MS. sketch in OP,MHS; Daniels, *History of Oxford, Mass.*, p. 635; Hurd, *Worcester County*, 2: 1318–19.

11. James, *Olney*, p. 9.

12. Will and inventory of estate, Richard Olney (1770–1841) Papers, Antiquarian Society of America Library, Worcester, Mass. (hereafter cited as ASA Library).

13. *Boston Herald*, 14 July 1895; Hurd, *Worcester County*, 2: 1319.

14. *Boston Globe*, 7 July 1893; Mary B. Douse to Olney, 21 Mar. 1893, Richard Olney Papers, Library of Congress (hereafter cited as OP,LC).

15. *Catalogue of the Trustees, Instructors and Students of Leicester Academy, Massachusetts* (Andover, 1848; Worcester, 1849–51), ASA Library; Emory Washburn, *Brief Sketch of the History of Leicester Academy* (Boston, 1855), pp. 16, 27–29, 31. For Olney's living arrangements and academic record I am indebted to his niece, Catherine Olney, whom I interviewed at Leicester on 23 Dec. 1957. For Olney's recreation, see George Henry Sargent to Olney, 23 Feb. 1893, and James W. Brooks to Olney, 11 June 1895, OP,LC; and *Centenary of Leicester Academy* (Worcester, 1884), pp. 43, 83–84.

16. Olney to John E. Kimball, enclosing $1,000 in his father's memory as a contribution to a new library for Oxford, 22 June 1904, OP,LC.

17. *Boston Herald*, 14 July 1895.

18. Records of Admission, 1827–56, Brown University Archives, John Hay Library, Providence (hereafter cited as Brown Archives); *Catalogue of Brown University, 1852–1853*, 2d ed. (Providence, 1852), p. 24.

19. Meeting of 27 Sept. 1851, Records of the Philermenian Society, 1842–59; Student Records, Classes of 1848–59 (Olney was in the class of 1856); Library Record Book, 1850–54, Brown Archives. For Olney's intermission see Charles P. Greenough, "Memoir of Richard Olney," *Proceedings of the Massachusetts Historical Society*, 51 (Dec. 1917): 204; interview with Francis Minot, Sr., Hatchville, Mass., 3 Jan. 1958. Minot, who was Olney's grandson, lived in the Olney household after his father's death in 1895. He observed that his grandfather played tennis to the age of eighty without needing eyeglasses.

20. Robert W. Carpenter to Ira C. Hersey, enclosing extract from *Foxboro Public Documents*, 2: 18, town reports, 1848–67, 9 Apr. 1924, OP,MHS.

21. Junior and Senior Exhibition Programmes, p. 285, Brown Archives; Robert P. Brown et al., eds., *Memories of Brown* (Providence, 1909), pp. 125–32.

22. Comments of classmates Charles Blake and John Peirce, *Boston Globe*, 7 July 1895.

23. Lewis H. Bowen to Olney, 20 Oct. 1898, OP,LC; Erlunia Smith, quoted in *Boston Herald*, 14 July 1895.

24. William G. Dearth, "Praeterita: Journal of Acts and Thoughts, 1854–1855," unpublished diary, Brown Archives, entries for 19, 27 June 1855. Dearth was one year ahead of Olney at Brown.

25. According to Walter C. Bronson, *The History of Brown University 1764–1914* (Providence, 1914), p. 344, organized athletics were introduced at Brown sometime after 1855. John Peirce quoted, *Boston Globe*, 7 July 1895.

26. Minot interview.

27. Samuel F. Batchelder, *Bits of Harvard History* (Cambridge, Mass., 1924), pp. 229–32; Samuel Eliot Morison, *Three Centuries of Harvard 1636–1936* (Cambridge, Mass., 1936), pp. 336–37; Charles Warren, *History of the Harvard Law School and of Early Legal Conditions in America* (New York, 1908), 2: 95, 354.

28. Parsons to Thomas, 11 Apr. 1859, OP,LC.

29. Hurd, *Worcester County*, 1: xlv–xlvi; James, *Olney*, p. 10.

30. George W. Smalley, *Anglo-American Memories* (London, 1910), pp. 65–66.

31. Agnes Abbot (Olney's granddaughter) to Eggert, 3 Apr. 1958; Minot interview.

32. "Attorney-General Olney," *Green Bag*, 5: 258–59; James, *Olney*, pp. 14, 17–18.

33. James W. Brooks (quoting Olney) to Olney, 11 June 1895, OP,LC.

34. Cleveland Amory's *The Proper Bostonians* (New York, 1947), is a delightful account of the Proper Bostonians and their habits. Several of Olney's clients are discussed in the book.

35. For a list of cases and copies of briefs prepared by Olney, see OP,MHS.

36. For accounts of the Eastern's difficulties, see Charles J. Kennedy, "The Eastern Rail-road Company, 1855–1884," *Business History Review*, 31 (1957): 186–87;

Edward Chase Kirkland, *Men, Cities and Transportation* (Cambridge, Mass., 1948), 2: 4–12; and George Pierce Baker, *The Formation of the New England Railroad Systems* (Cambridge, Mass., 1949), pp. 152–63. Accounts of creditors' meetings appear in the *Boston Transcript*, 8, 15 Jan. 1876.

37. *An Act for the Relief of the Eastern Railroad Company, and the Securing of Its Debts and Liabilities*, chap. 366, Acts of Mass. General Court, 1876, OP,MHS.

38. *Boston Transcript*, beginning 14 Mar. 1876, carried accounts of the investigation. For Olney's role, see *Olney Memorial Exercises*, pp. 26–27, 33; Olney to Geo. H. Olney, 6 Jan. 1917, OP,LC.

39. The Albert R. Hatch Papers, New Hampshire Historical Society, Concord, have several Olney letters dealing with Eastern Railroad litigation, 1876–82.

40. Kennedy, "Eastern Rail-road Company," p. 206; *Olney Memorial Exercises*, p. 27; *Railroad Gazette*, 15 (30 Mar. 1883): 198.

41. *Boston Transcript*, 27 June 1882. See also 16 Mar., 24 June 1882.

42. For reports and comments on lease, see *Boston Transcript*, 13, 15 Dec. 1882; 13–15, 26, 29 Mar. and 12, 13 Dec. 1883; *Railroad Gazette* 15 (30 Mar. 1883): 198.

43. Loring to Straw, 27 Nov. 1924. See also letter of 7 Nov., OP,LC.

2   Railroad Lawyer

1. For Jones's background, *Dictionary of American Biography*, 10: 168; *Portsmouth Herald*, 22 June 1948; *Biographical Directory of the American Congress, 1774–1949* (Washington, 1950), p. 1385. Except where otherwise indicated, this account of Jones's management of the Boston & Maine is based on Kirkland, *Men, Cities and Transportation*, 2: 14–25; Baker, *New England Railroad Systems*, pp. 166–71.

2. *Boston Transcript*, 5, 6, 20 Oct., 17 Dec. 1885; Olney, *Argument . . . in Favor of Ratifying the Lease of the Worcester, Nashu & Rochester Railroad to the Boston & Maine Railroad* (Boston, 1886), pp. 6–7, State Library, Boston.

3. *Forty-fourth Annual Report of the Railroad Commissioners of the State of New Hampshire* (1888), pp. 5–7. The reports for 1889 and 1890 were also useful.

4. New Hampshire, *Proceedings and Testimony . . . in the Investigation of Charges of Bribery of Members of the Legislature* (Concord, 1887), 3, part 2: 257–58. Copy, State Library, Concord.

5. *Annual Report of the New Hampshire Railroad Commissioners*, 1890, 1895.

6. Olney to John W. Sanborn, Gen. Mgr., Boston & Maine, 23 Jan. 1893, OP,LC.

7. *Boston Transcript*, 9, 10 Dec. 1885; 9 Jan. 1886.

8. Olney to Higginson, 4 Jan. 1887 [1888], Henry Lee Higginson Collection, Baker Library, Cambridge (hereafter cited as Higginson Collection). Apparently Olney misdated the letter at the beginning of the new year. It is filed in 1888, which seems consistent with later developments.

9. Olney to Jones, 21, 22 Feb.; Olney to President and Directors, Boston & Maine, 21 Feb. 1890, OP,LC.

10. *Boston Journal,* 26 Feb.; Olney to Wm. W. Clapp, editor, 28 Feb., 1 Mar. 1890, OP,LC. For the editorial, see *Boston Journal,* 1 Mar. 1890.

11. Olney to William D. Sohier, 3 Mar.; Olney to James T. Furber, 4 Mar. 1890, OP,LC.

12. *Boston Journal,* 10, 11 Dec. 1891. Maverick affairs filled Boston newspapers throughout the last half of 1890 and early 1891.

13. *Boston Journal,* 21 Feb.; *Boston Transcript,* 12 Oct. 1893.

14. Haven to Whitney, 2 Dec. 1891, William C. Whitney Papers, Library of Congress; *Boston Journal,* 10 Dec. 1891; 14 Dec. 1892; *Boston Transcript,* 14 Dec. 1892; *New York Tribune,* 10 Dec. 1891.

15. *Boston Transcript,* 1–27 Oct., 14 Dec. 1892; *Boston Journal,* 27 Oct. 1892. Accounts of McLeod affair will be found in Stuart Daggett, *Railroad Reorganization* (Cambridge, Mass., 1924), pp. 118–34; E. G. Campbell, *The Reorganization of the American Railroad System, 1893–1900* (New York, 1938), pp. 109–128; Jules I. Bogen, *The Anthracite Railroads* (New York, 1927), pp. 66–71; Kirkland, *Men, Cities and Transportation,* 2: 28–31; Baker, *New England Railroad Systems,* pp. 65–68, 98–99, 173–74.

16. United States Industrial Commission, *Report of the Industrial Commission on Transportation* (Washington, 1901), 9: 567, 574; *Boston Transcript,* 14 Dec. 1892; Clarence W. Barron, *More They Told Barron,* ed. Arthur Pound and Samuel Taylor Moore (New York, 1931), quoting Prince, pp. 121–22, 135, 138.

17. Olney to William C. Whitney, 19 Oct. 1892, OP,LC; Kirkland, *Men, Cities and Transportation,* 2: 28, 69; *Boston Journal,* 27 Oct. 1892.

18. Baker, *New England Railroad Systems,* pp. 173–74; *Boston Transcript,* 16, 20 Dec.; *Boston Herald,* 17 Dec. 1892.

19. Olney to Prof. Chas. Sargent, 28 Jan. 1893, OP,LC.

20. Quoted by Baked, *New England Railroad Systems,* p. 174.

21. Daggett, *Railroad Reorganization,* pp. 120–27.

22. Prince statement, 7 Apr. 1893, quoted in Barron, *More They Told Barron,* pp. 121–22.

23. *New York World,* 7 Mar 1893; Baker, *New England Railroad Systems,* pp. 94–95; Kirkland, *Men, Cities and Transportation,* 2: 31.

24. *New York Tribune,* 26 Jan.; *Boston Journal,* 28 Feb. 1893.

25. Butler to Olney, 16 Mar. 1893, OP,LC.

26. Butler to Olney, 8, 12, 29 Mar., 23 May 1893, OP,LC.

27. Olney to Haven, 21 May 1893. See also Olney to Prince, 31 May 1895, OP,LC. *Boston Transcript,* 27 June 1893.

28. Olney to Lewis Cass Ledyard, 9 Aug. 1893, OP,LC.

29. *New York Tribune, Boston Journal, Boston Transcript,* 12 Oct. 1893; Olney quoted, *Concord* (N.H.) *Evening Monitor,* 11 Oct. 1893.

30. William Z. Ripley, *Railroads, Finance and Organization* (New York, 1920), pp. 462–66.

31. Kirkland, *Men, Cities and Transportation,* 2: 475.

32. Olney to Charles E. Perkins, 2 Feb. 1891, Perkins file, Burlington Archives, Newberry Library, Chicago (hereafter cited as BA), used with permission.

33. *Wabash, St. Louis & Pacific Railroad* v. *Illinois,* 118 U.S. 577 ff. (1886).

34. Olney to Perkins, 28 Jan. 1889, Perkins file, BA. For the Munn Case, see 94 U.S. 113 (1877).

35. Olney to Perkins, 8, 20 July 1890; 10 Feb. 1891, Olney file, BA; *Chicago, Milwaukee & St. Paul Railroad Co.* v. *Minnesota*, 134 U.S. 418 (1890).

36. Gabriel Kolko, *Railroads and Regulation 1877–1916* (Princeton, 1965), argues that by the mid-1880s the railroad community overwhelmingly supported a federal commission that could fix and maintain rates because their own pools and joint-rate associations had failed to enforce rate agreements. However accurate Kolko's thesis, he considerably overstates the argument and suggests a degree of unanimity among railroad leaders that is not borne out in their papers. He also seems to take at face value many self-serving and face-saving statements of railroad lawyers and officials. Many railroad executives might have favored such a commission, but only if they were free to determine the rates that the commission would enforce. Whatever might have been true of railroad officials generally, Olney's employers, the Santa Fe, the Burlington, and the Boston & Maine, opposed such legislation.

37. Olney and others, "Memorandum of Advice of Counsel Concerning the Construction of Certain Sections of the Inter-State Commerce Act," 17 Feb. 1887, BA; Olney to Edward C. Perkins, 18 Feb. 1887, Charles E. Perkins Papers, Overton-Cunningham Collection, formerly in the possession of Richard C. Overton but now in the Burlington Archives, used with permission (hereafter cited as Perkins Papers, O-C).

38. Olney to T. S. Howland, 6 May 1889; Olney to Perkins, 3 July 1890, Olney file, BA.

39. Leon Burr Richardson, *William E. Chandler, Republican* (New York, 1940), pp. 428–36; Chandler to ICC, 11 July 1891, case 308, ICC Records, National Archives (hereafter cited as Free Pass Case file).

40. James T. Furber, Vice-Pres., Boston & Maine, "Answer to Informal Complaint"; Olney's brief, Free Pass Case file.

41. *Report and Opinion of the ICC* (Washington, 1891), p. 4, copy, Free Pass Case file; Olney to Perkins, 20 Jan. 1892, Olney file, BA.

42. Olney to Charles J. Paine, 21 Apr. 1897, OP,LC. See also Thomas C. Cochran, *Railroad Leaders 1845–1890* (Cambridge, Mass., 1953), pp. 198–99; Olney to Perkins, 28 Jan. 1889, Olney file, BA.

43. Perkins to Olney, 22 Dec. 1892, OP,LC.

44. Olney to Perkins, 28 Dec. 1892, OP,LC.

45. Perkins to Olney, 2 Jan. 1893, OP,LC.

46. Perkins to "Mr. Coolidge"; to John Murray Forbes, 20 Nov. 1890; to Sen. Wm. B. Allison, 31 Aug.; to Forbes, 21 Sept.; to "Hatton," 2 Oct. 1891, Perkins Papers, O-C; John Ely Briggs, *William Peters Hepburn* (Iowa City, 1919), p. 93; James C. Olson, *J. Sterling Morton* (Lincoln, Nebr., 1942), p. 326.

47. Perkins to "Mallory," 12 Mar.; to Morton, 17 Mar. 1894, Perkins Papers, O-C.

48. Perkins to Olney (two letters), 27 Jan. 1892, Perkins Papers, O-C; Perkins to Olney, 2 Jan.; Olney to Perkins, 6 Feb. 1893; 5 Mar. 1894; Olney-Stephen B. Elkins correspondence, 22 Jan.–6 Feb. 1902; Olney to Daniel S. Lamont, 17 Dec. 1904, OP,LC. For the Commerce Court, Felix Frankfurter and James

M. Landis, *The Business of the Supreme Court* (New York, 1928), pp. 153–74; I. L. Sharfman, *The Interstate Commerce Commission* (New York, 1931), 1: 52–70.

49. Perkins to Olney, 11 Jan. 1893, OP,LC.

50. Olney to Perkins, 17 Jan. 1893, OP,LC.

51. Olney to Perkins, 16, 17 Jan., Olney file, BA; Perkins to Wolcott, 17 Jan. 1893, Perkins Papers, O-C; *National Cyclopaedia*, 8: 397–98.

52. Peck to Olney, 19 Jan.; Olney to Peck, 21 Jan.; Peck to Olney, 22 Jan. 1893, OP,LC.

53. Olney to Perkins, 21 Jan. 1893, OP,LC.

54. Perkins to Olney, 30 Dec. 1892; Butler to Olney, 4 Feb. 1895 OP,LC.

55. Olney to Butler, 11 Feb. 1895, OP,LC.

3   *The Measure of Success—1893*

1. Barron, *More They Told Barron*, p. 146; Olney to Wm. C. Endicott, 27 May 1886, Endicott Papers, Massachusetts Historical Society; John J. McCook to Olney, 3 Jan. 1894, OP,LC.

2. Straw to Greenough, 21 Aug. 1917, OP,MHS; Straw to James, 24 Feb. 1922, OP,LC; Robert T. Swaine, *The Cravath Firm and its Predecessors: 1819–1947* (New York, 1946), 1: 461–62; Greenough, *Proceedings of the Massachusetts Historical Society*, 51: 204–05.

3. Straw to Greenough, 21 Aug. 1917, OP,MHS.

4. Olney to P. B. Olney, 5 May 1905, OP,LC.

5. James, *Olney*, p. 14 n.

6. *Boston Herald*, 10 Apr. 1917.

7. Ibid.; unidentified newspaper clipping, Catherine Olney scrapbook; James, *Olney*, pp. 14–15.

8. Olney to Howard Stockton, 11 July 1893, describes a case in which Olney acted as referee; Straw to James, 24 Feb. 1922, OP,LC; *Green Bag*, 5: 258–59.

9. Olney to Edward W. Hutchins, 14 Feb. 1893, OP,LC, quoted in full.

10. *Boston Journal*, 24 Feb. 1893.

11. Typewritten MS., commencement address, Columbian University Law School, June 1894, OP,LC.

12. For example, see Olney's testimony before a Massachusetts legislative committee investigating employers' liability, OP,MHS.

13. Olney, "To Uphold the Honor of the Profession of Law," *Yale Law Journal*, 19 (Mar. 1910): 342–43.

14. Ibid., p. 344.

15. Olney to B. F. Yoakum, Pres., St. Louis & San Francisco Railroad, 12 Oct. 1902, OP,LC. As an example of Olney's handling of press questions about business matters, see *Boston Transcript*, 26 Oct. 1892.

16. *Boston Transcript, Post, Herald,* and *Journal,* 20 Mar.–2 June 1875. Olney's

summation has been published in *American Journal of Legal History*, 13 (Jan. 1969): 68–84.

17. Bradley Gilman to Olney, 14 Dec. 1888, OP,LC; *Proceedings of the Massachusetts Historical Society*, 50: 219; George Arnold Torrey, *A Lawyer's Recollections in and out of Court* (Boston, 1910), pp. 142–43.

18. Straw to James, 24 Feb. 1922. See also Straw to James, 13 Feb. 1922, OP,LC.

19. Forbes to Hugh McCulloch, 1 Jan. 1894, OP,LC.

20. Forbes to Perkins, 7 Mar., Forbes file, BA; Perkins to Forbes, 8 Mar.; Perkins to Dexter, 17 Apr. 1889, Perkins Papers, O-C.

21. Robert Grant to Olney, 8 Oct. 1892; Straw to James, 24 Feb. 1922, OP,LC.

22. Both quoted in *Boston Journal*, 24 Feb. 1893.

23. Typewritten copy, address in memory of Judge Wm. C. Endicott, 24 Nov. 1900, OP,LC.

24. Social item from unidentified Falmouth newspaper clipping, supplied by Agnes Abbot, Olney's granddaughter (hereafter such clippings are cited as Olney news clippings).

25. James, *Olney*, p. 10.

26. Abbot to Eggert, 25 Aug. 1959; Olney to John Hitchcock, 14 Mar. 1896, OP,LC.

27. Abbot to Eggert, 25 Aug. 1959; unidentified item, Olney news clippings.

28. James, *Olney*, pp. 13–14, attributes the drying-up of Olney's humor and high spirits to years of discipline and hard work. According to Olney's grandson, he regarded most of his fellow men as "fools" or "second-raters." Minot interview.

29. James, *Olney*, p. 13.

30. *Boston Journal*, 5 Mar. 1896.

31. James, *Olney*, pp. 11–20, 196; Abbot to Eggert, 3 Apr. 1958; Minot interview. Through the years, according to Minot, Olney increasingly "froze out" those who offended him. To Olney, such persons, like Mary, thereafter were "dead" to him.

32. Olney to Frederick W. Whitridge, 6 Jan. 1899, OP,LC.

33. Olney to Geo. F. Edmunds, 8 Feb. 1895, OP,LC.

34. Olney to Holmes, 9 Apr. 1904, OP,LC.

35. Olney to Higginson and Burnett, 9 Apr. 1904, OP,LC.

36. Last Will and Testament of Richard Olney, Suffolk County Courthouse, Boston.

37. Olney to "The Operating Surgeon," Mass. Gen. Hospital, Boston, 15 Feb. 1908. For another example, see Olney to Walter M. Hatch & Co., 23 Mar. 1904, OP,LC.

38. Olney disliked anything that he regarded as "cheap," "vulgar," or "common," and the list, according to his grandson, was quite long. Included were hurdy-gurdy music, a sister-in-law of lowly origins, dandelions, and people with large families of children. Minot interview.

39. Ibid.; Catherine Olney interview; James, *Olney*, pp. 13–17; Abbot to Eggert, 3 Apr. 1958.

40. James, *Olney*, p. 12; illustrations opposite pp. 12, 78.

41. Ibid., pp. 10–12.

4 Serving Two Masters

1. Olney to Whitney, 27 Jan.; Whitney to Olney, 29 Jan. 1893, OP,LC.

2. Charles E. Perkins to Olney, 27 Jan. 1893, OP,LC.

3. Memo, 4 Jan. 1893, Daniel S. Lamont Papers, Library of Congress.

4. George F. Parker, "The Return to the White House and the Second Cabinet," *McClure's Magazine*, 32 (Mar. 1909): 472.

5. For Cleveland's cabinet making, see memoranda dated 7, 9 Dec. 1892, 4, 16 Jan. and 22 Feb. 1893, Lamont Papers; Cleveland to Gresham, 9 Feb., Grover Cleveland Papers, Library of Congress; to Lamont, 19 Feb. 1893, Lamont Papers; Allan Nevins, *Grover Cleveland, A Study in Courage* (New York, 1932), p. 511.

6. James, *Olney*, p. 7, n.; Frank Jones to Cleveland, 27 Apr. 1888; incomplete autobiographic memorandum dictated by Olney in Feb. 1901, covering the period when he was attorney general (hereafter cited as Olney Memoir); Olney to Whitney, 1 July; Chas. S. Fairchild to Olney, 1 Nov.; Olney to Adams, 12 Aug.; to John Murray Forbes, 1 Nov.; to Josiah Quincy, 2 Nov. 1892, OP,LC.

7. Russell to [Geo.] Olney, 31 Jan., OP,LC; Butler to Cleveland, 7 Feb. 1893, Grover Cleveland Papers, Burton Historical Library, Detroit Public Library.

8. Diary entry, 8 Mar. 1893, Charles S. Hamlin Papers, Library of Congress. In Olney Memoir, Olney credits Butler with bringing his name to Cleveland's attention. For Butler's visit to Cleveland, see *New York Times*, 16 Feb. The *Boston Herald*, 22 Feb., noted that Olney had been appointed without Quincy's knowledge. See Quincy to Cleveland, 27 Feb. 1893, Cleveland Papers, Library of Congress.

9. Memo, 22 Feb. 1893, Lamont Papers; Geo. F. Parker, "Cleveland's Second Administration as President," *Saturday Evening Post*, 9 June 1923, p. 42.

10. P. B. Olney to Olney, 16 Feb. 1893, OP,LC.

11. Olney Memoir.

12. Straw to James, 24 Feb. 1922, OP,LC. *Boston Journal*, 24 Feb. 1893, estimated Olney's income at between $50,000 and $60,000 per year.

13. P. B. Olney to Olney, 16, 17 Feb. 1893, OP,LC.

14. Cleveland to Lamont, 19 Feb. 1893, Lamont Papers.

15. P. B. Olney to Olney, 18 Feb. 1893, OP,LC.

16. Olney to Perkins, 16 Feb. 1893, OP,LC.

17. Perkins to Olney, 17 Feb. 1893, OP,LC.

18. Forbes to Olney, 20 Feb. 1893, OP,LC.

19. Straw to James, 24 Feb. 1922, OP,LC.

20. Statement of Amounts Charged to Boston Office Expenses, 1891–1903, BA; Straw to James, 24 Feb. 1922, OP,LC. James P. Reinhold, Asst. to the Pres., Atchison, Topeka & Santa Fe Railway System, to Eggert, 13 May 1957, reported no extant records showing Olney in the pay of that company.

21. Edgar J. Rich to James H. Hustis, 8 June; Hustis to James, 12 June 1922; Boston & Maine to Olney, 1 Jan. 1894, OP,LC.

22. Memo, 22 Feb. 1893, Lamont Papers; Parker, *Saturday Evening Post*, 9 June 1923, p. 42. Cf. Olney Memoir.

23. Olney to Cleveland, 22, 23 Feb. 1893, Cleveland Papers, Library of Congress; Olney Memoir.

24. *New York World*, 18–22 Feb. 1893. See also telegram, W. H. Merrill to Cleveland, 17 Feb. 1893, Cleveland Papers, Library of Congress.

25. *New York Press*, 23 Feb. 1893.

26. *New York World*, 24 Feb. 1893.

27. Assorted incoming letters, 22 Feb.–4 Mar. 1893, OP,LC.

28. Perkins to Olney, 23 Feb. 1893, OP,LC.

29. Nevins, *Grover Cleveland*, pp. 449–52; Cleveland to Benedict, 6 Feb. 1898, *Letters of Grover Cleveland, 1850–1908*, Allan Nevins, ed. (Boston and New York, 1933), pp. 492–93 (hereafter cited as *Cleveland Letters*). For earlier letters on stock transactions and the joint account, see pp. 345, 373, 376, 391–93; also unpublished letters, Cleveland to Benedict, 3 Dec. 1896, 10 Jan. 1897; and Benedict to Cleveland, 8 Jan. 1897, Cleveland Papers, Library of Congress.

30. Olney's correspondence with both Higginson and Coolidge was extensive during his four years at Washington. On his remaining a director of the Old Colony Trust, see Straw to James, 24 Feb. 1922; notification of board meeting, 1 July 1893, OP,LC.

31. Gerald G. Eggert, *Railway Labor Disputes: The Beginnings of Federal Strike Policy* (Ann Arbor, 1967), pp. 87–88. See also pp. 36–38.

32. Mark D. Hirsch, *William C. Whitney, Modern Warwick* (New York, 1948), pp. 466–67. Also, *New York Times*, 5 Mar. 1893. On 24 Feb. 1893, Lamont resigned as a director of the Continental National Bank and on 4 Mar. from the Pennsylvania Steel Refining Co. On 30 Mar. he was notified of a board meeting of the New York Loan & Improvement Co. to be held at "Mr. Whitney's House." Lamont Papers.

33. A. A. McLeod to Olney, 24 Feb., OP,LC; *New York Times*, 19 Feb. 1893; Henry V. & H. W. Poor, *Poor's Manual of the Railroads of the United States* (New York, 1895), p. 588.

34. Olson, *Morton*, pp. 192, 291.

35. Dewey W. Grantham, Jr., *Hoke Smith and the Politics of the New South* (Baton Rouge, 1958), is the best biography of Smith. For Smith's dealing with clients while in office, see *New York World*, 16 Nov. 1893; Smith to Cleveland, 3 Nov. 1894, Cleveland Papers, Library of Congress.

36. C. Vann Woodward, *Origins of the New South, 1877–1913* (Baton Rouge, 1951), p. 271.

37. *A Compilation of the Messages and Papers of the Presidents, 1789–1897*, comp. James D. Richardson (n.p., 1899), 9: 389–93 (hereafter cited as *Messages and Papers*).

38. For example, see Olney's typewritten address, Harvard Commencement Dinner, 28 June 1893, OP,LC.

39. *The Cabinet Diary of William L. Wilson, 1896–1897*, ed. Festus P. Summers (Chapel Hill, 1957), pp. 8, 56 (hereafter cited as *Wilson's Cabinet Diary*); Hilary A. Herbert, "Grover Cleveland and His Cabinet at Work," *Century*

Magazine, 85 (Mar. 1913): 740–41; Gresham to D. A. Woods, 4 Aug. 1893, Walter Q. Gresham Papers, Library of Congress.

40. See *Wilson's Cabinet Diary*, pp. 4, 8, 14, 25, 26, for but a few of many such comments. Parker, *Saturday Evening Post*, 9 June 1923, p. 44, referred to it as "the Cabinet without a friction."

41. Harmon to James, 17, 24 May 1922; Olney to Paul Morton, 16 Oct. 1905, OP,LC; *Wilson's Cabinet Diary*, pp. 56, 70; Bissell to Cleveland, 8 Sept. 1900, Cleveland Papers, Library of Congress.

42. Cleveland to Don M. Dickinson, 20 Mar. 1895. See also Cleveland to Benedict, 9 June 1895, *Cleveland Letters*, pp. 382, 397.

43. Cleveland to Lamont, 2 Oct. 1894, Cleveland Papers, Library of Congress. For the comment on Carlisle, see Robert McElroy, *Grover Cleveland, the Man and the Statesman* (New York, 1923), 2: 6.

44. Nevins, *Grover Cleveland*, pp. 618, 627; Sigourney Butler to Olney, 14 Jan. 1894, OP,LC.

45. Minot interview.

46. James, *Olney*, p. 27; Straw to James, 14 Sept. 1921, OP,LC.

47. Minot interview. Olney's complaints of financial sacrifice are scattered through his letters between 1893 and 1897. See, for example, Olney to Sen. Geo. F. Hoar, 23 Oct. 1894, OP,LC.

48. Minot interview.

49. Olney to Geo. S. Dexter, 11 Apr. 1893, OP,LC.

50. Olney to John J. McCook, 12 Feb. 1897, OP,LC.; James, *Olney*, pp. 77–79; James A. Barnes, *John G. Carlisle: Financial Statesman* (New York, 1931), p. 212.

51. Olney to Straw, 9 Dec. 1893, quoted in Straw to James, 12 Aug. 1922, OP,LC.

52. Olney to McCook, 12 Feb. 1897, OP,LC.

53. *Register of the Department of Justice* (Washington, 1895), pp. 5–6, 28–29.

54. Harmon to James, 17 May 1922, OP,LC.

55. Such letters are scattered through the Olney Papers and the Justice Department Records, 1893–95. Olney to Lamont, 30 Oct. 1894, OP,LC.

56. See below, pp. 103–5.

57. Olney to Sen. Hoar, 23 Oct. 1894, OP,LC.

58. Ibid. Olney himself, years before, had been employed by the government as counsel in a case and then had his fee slashed. He refused to serve again. Olney to John W. Mason, 4 Nov. 1889, OP,LC.

59. James, *Olney*, pp. 25–27; letters, Mar.–Dec. 1893, OP,LC.

60. Olney to Rep. Wm. Everett, 25 Feb. 1895; to W. O. Hamilton, 9 Aug. 1894, OP,LC.

61. C. F. Morse to Charles Merriam (forwarded to Olney), 7 Sept. 1893; Peck to Olney, 20 Mar. 1893, OP,LC.

62. Barlow to Olney, 16 Mar.; Olney to Barlow, 17 Mar. 1893, OP,LC.

63. P. B. Olney to Olney, 20 Mar.; Olney to P. B. Olney, 22 Mar., OP,LC; P. B. Olney to Cleveland, 25 Mar. 1893, Cleveland Papers, Library of Congress.

64. Butler to Olney, 12 Mar. 1893; 14 Jan. 1894, OP,LC.

65. Samuel E. Kercheval to Olney, 8 May 1893, Year file 3825–93 (hereafter cited as Jackson file); General Records of the Justice Department, Record Group 60, National Archives (hereafter cited as RG 60 NA).

66. Olney to Jackson, 11 May 1893, Instruction Book 30: 43–45; Jackson to Olney, 6 June 1893, Jackson file.

67. Olney to Jackson, 6 June 1893, Instruction Book 30: 377–79.

68. Jackson to Olney, 12 June 1893, Jackson file.

69. Sen. Vest to Olney, 21 June; Jackson to James J. McAlester, marshal, Indian Territory, 15 July; McAlester to A. H. Garland, 19 July 1893, Jackson file.

70. Sherman Hoar to Olney, 29 Jan., Year file 1298–94; Olney to Hoar, 31 Jan. 1894, Instruction Book 36: 491.

71. Olney to O. J. H. Summers, 27 Feb. 1894, Instruction Book 37: 296. See also Olney to Judge Albert B. Fall, Judges & Clerks Book (hereafter cited as J&C) 41: 531.

72. *Boston Journal*, 5 Mar. 1896.

73. Olney to Higginson, 12 July 1893, Higginson Collection; Higginson to Olney, 2 Apr. 1895, OP,LC.

74. Several letters enclosing passes were received by Olney between 1893 and 1895. For Olney's request for a pass, see Olney to Butler, 9 Feb. 1894, OP,LC.

75. G. B. Roberts to Olney, 2 Aug.; Olney to Roberts, 10 Aug. 1893, OP,LC.

76. Coolidge to Olney, 3 May 1893, OP,LC.

77. Olney to Herbert, 6 May; Herbert to Olney, 9 May 1893, OP,LC.

78. Coolidge to Olney, 1, 8 Oct. 1894, OP,LC.

79. Olney to Herbert, 10 Oct.; Herbert to Olney, 10 Oct.; Coolidge to Olney, 25 Oct. 1894, OP,LC.

80. Tuttle to Olney, 23 Feb.; Olney to Bissell, 26 Feb.; Bissell to Olney, 26 Feb. 1894, OP,LC. See also Edward T. Fairbanks, *The Town of St. Johnsbury, Vt.* (St. Johnsbury, 1914), p. 451.

81. Forbes to Perkins, 8 Mar., Forbes file, BA; Perkins to Forbes, 12 Mar. 1893, Perkins Papers, O-C.

5 Panic Problems

1. Typewritten copy of address, OP,LC.

2. For examples of the monetary explanation, see William Jett Lauck, *The Causes of the Panic of 1893* (New York, 1907); Alexander Dana Noyes, *Forty Years of American Finance*, 2d ed. (New York, 1909). For more recent works, see Frank P. Weberg, *The Background of the Panic of 1893* (Washington, 1929); Charles Hoffman, "The Depression of the Nineties—An Economic History" (diss., Columbia University, 1954). For a very brief summary, see Harold U. Faulkner, *Politics, Reform and Expansion 1890–1900* (New York, 1959), pp. 143–47.

3. Davis Rich Dewey, *Financial History of the United States*, 12th ed. (New York, 1934), pp. 372–78, 405–7, 436–38; Barnes, *Carlisle*, pp. 224–25; U.S., *Statutes at Large* 26: 289–90.

4. Barnes, *Carlisle*, pp. 231–32; various letters from bankers and businessmen to Cleveland, 1893, Cleveland Papers, Library of Congress.

5. William Endicott, Jr., to Olney, 23 Apr. 1893, OP,LC.

6. Higginson to Olney, 19, 21 Apr., 13 May 1893, OP,LC.

7. Hoffman, "Depression," pp. 40–55, 250–73; Nevins, *Grover Cleveland*, pp. 523–28; Barnes, *Carlisle*, pp. 250–73.

8. Butler to Olney, 5 July; Olney to Carlisle, 5 July; Carlisle to Olney, undated [6 July 1893], OP,LC.

9. Nevins, *Grover Cleveland* pp. 528–33; *New York World*, 8 July 1893.

10. In Olney Memoir, Olney states that he first saw Cleveland a fortnight after the operation. He apparently was mistaken. The *Boston Globe, Boston Herald*, and *New York Times*, 9 July 1893, all reported his visit on 8 July.

11. Higginson to Olney, 11 July, OP,LC; Olney to Higginson, 12 July 1893, Higginson Collection.

12. Perkins to Olney, 15 July 1893, OP,LC. Perkins sent Forbes a copy of the letter and suggested that he too contact Olney. Perkins to Forbes, 14, 15 July 1893, Perkins Papers, O-C.

13. Olney to Cleveland, 17 July 1893, OP,LC.

14. Forbes to Olney, 20 July 1893, OP,LC.

15. Draft of message, dated 21 July; Forbes to Olney, 25 July; Olney to Forbes, 25 July 1893, OP,LC. *Boston Globe*, 23 July 1893, reported that the *Wild Duck* stopped at Buzzard's Bay and that Mrs. Olney and her nieces chatted with the president. It seems likely that Olney and Forbes talked with him on the same occasion.

16. Forbes to Olney, 25, 26 July 1893, OP,LC.

17. Second draft, dated 26 July; Forbes to Olney, 29 July 1893, OP,LC. *Boston Globe*, 29 July 1893, reported the stop and noted that Forbes paid a social call on Cleveland.

18. Forbes to Olney, 30 July, 1 Aug.; Olney to Forbes, 3 Aug. 1893, OP,LC.

19. Forbes to Olney, 26, 30 July 1893; drafts of message dated 21, 26, 31 July 1893, OP,LC.

20. *Boston Globe*, 1–5 Aug. 1893; compare Olney drafts with Cleveland's message, *Messages and Papers*, 9: 401–5; Olney Memoir.

21. Nevins, *Grover Cleveland*, pp. 533–48.

22. Olney to Higginson, 27 Oct., Higginson Collection; Higginson to Olney, 4 Nov. 1893, OP,LC. For the disastrous effects of the battle on the unity of the Democratic Party, see J. Rogers Hollingsworth, *The Whirligig of Politics, The Democracy of Cleveland and Bryan* (Chicago and London, 1963), pp. 15–21.

23. Olney to John L. Gardner, 27 Oct. 1893, OP,LC.

24. Nevins, *Grover Cleveland*, pp. 596–99; Barnes, *Carlisle*, pp. 287–319.

25. Nevins, *Grover Cleveland*, pp. 652–58; Barnes, *Carlisle*, pp. 359–60, 363.

26. *Messages and Papers*, 9: 561–65.

27. Nevins, *Grover Cleveland*, pp. 658–61; Barnes, *Carlisle*, pp. 372–83.

28. Barnes, *Carlisle*, pp. 384–85; Herbert Lee Satterlee [Morgan's son-in-law], *J. Pierpont Morgan, an Intimate Portrait* (New York, 1939), p. 286. See also

James Brown Scott, *Robert Bacon, Life and Letters* (Garden City, N.Y., 1923), pp. 69–79.

29. Olney to Satterlee, 15 Apr. 1914, OP,LC.

30. This account is based on Carl Hovey, *The Life of J. Pierpont Morgan* (New York, 1911), pp. 176–80; Satterlee, *J. Pierpont Morgan*, pp. 288–91; and bond sales investigation testimony, *Senate Document No. 187*, Fifty-fourth Congress, Second Session (Washington, 1896). Satterlee relied heavily on the Hovey account, indicating that it was in accord with the story given him by his father-in-law, J. P. Morgan. Olney also wrote Satterlee that Hovey's account seemed accurate to him. Olney believed that both Lamont and Belmont had been at the meetings on the evening of 7 Feb. and the morning of 8 Feb. Lamont denied being present and Belmont was unable to get to Washington until the afternoon of 8 Feb. because of a severe blizzard. Olney to Satterlee, 15 Apr. 1914; Olney to Lamont, 13 May 1904; Lamont to Olney, 17 May 1904, OP,LC.

31. Cleveland to Lamont, 19 Feb. 1893, Lamont Papers. See also Matilda Gresham, *Life of Walter Quintin Gresham, 1832–1895* (Chicago, 1919), 2: 712.

32. Barnes, *Carlisle*, pp. 388–91; Olney to Satterlee, 15 Apr. 1914, OP,LC.

33. According to Satterlee, *J. Pierpont Morgan*, p. 299, Morgan made no profit whatever. Nevins, *Grover Cleveland*, p. 644, states that "a hard bargain had unquestionably been driven." Barnes, *Carlisle*, p. 395, asserts that the profit was insignificant compared to the losses that would have followed had the United States left the gold standard. Lewis Corey, *The House of Morgan. A Social Biography of the Masters of Money* (New York, 1930), p. 189, sets the syndicate's profit at between seven and twelve million dollars. Frederick Lewis Allen, *The Great Pierpont Morgan* (New York, 1949), p. 124, had access to the records of the American syndicate and found that it made $1,534,516.72, exclusive of interest, which had to be shared by sixty-one banks belonging to the group. Of that amount, $131,932.13, exclusive of interest, went to the House of Morgan. If Morgan's share of the commission for handling the bonds is included, the total comes to almost a quarter of a million dollars.

34. Barnes, *Carlisle*, pp. 399–424; Nevins, *Grover Cleveland*, pp. 663–66, 684–88. Paul Studenski and Herman E. Kroose, *Financial History of the United States* (New York, 1952), p. 231, assert that Cleveland was able to keep the country on a de facto gold standard only by putting "a straight jacket on the economy" and limiting expansion.

35. E. Ellery Anderson et al., *Report of the Government Directors of the Union Pacific Railway to the Secretary of the Interior* (Washington, 1893); *New York World*, 15 Oct. 1893. In addition to the five government appointed directors, there were fifteen directors representing the stockholders.

36. Daggett, *Railroad Reorganization*, pp. 236–40; *New York World*, 14 Oct. 1893.

37. Daggett, *Railroad Reorganization*, pp. 220–21, 238–42.

38. Attorney General to Speaker of the House, 20 Oct. 1893, Executive & Congressional Book (hereafter cited as E&C), 15: 89–91, RG 60 NA.

39. Olney to Hoar, 16 Oct. 1893, OP,LC.

40. Perkins to Forbes, 20 Sept.–28 Dec. 1893; passim, Perkins Papers, O-C; Julius **Grodinsky**, *The Iowa Pool, a Study in Railroad Competition, 1870–1884* (Chicago,

1950), discusses the Chicago-to-Omaha roads, and in *Jay Gould, His Business Career, 1867–1892* (Philadelphia, 1957), the rivalry between the Burlington and Union Pacific. See especially pp. 225–49.

41. Perkins to Olney, 3 Nov. 1893, Perkins Papers, O-C, marked "not sent."

42. Perkins to Forbes, 4 Nov. 1893, Perkins Papers, O-C.

43. Perkins to Forbes, 17 Nov. 1893, Perkins Papers, O-C.

44. Conclusion of letter, Forbes to Olney. The first pages with the date are missing, OP,LC. In the last sentence Forbes apparently referred to Olney's role in reorganizing the Union Stockyards in Chicago, 1890–91.

45. Higginson to Olney, 4 Nov. 1893, OP,LC.

46. Olney to Hoadly, 30 Oct. 1893, OP,LC.

47. Olney to Higginson, 30 Oct., Higginson Collection; Lee, Higginson & Co. to Olney, 30 Oct. 1893, OP,LC.

48. Hoadly, *Testimony Before House Committee on Pacific Railways, April 27, 1894* (n.p., n.d.), copy, Union Pacific bundle, OP,LC.

49. Perkins to Forbes, 16 Nov. 1893, Perkins Papers, O-C.

50. Perkins to Forbes, 20 Sept., 16, 17, 20 Nov., 22, 28 Dec. 1893, Perkins Papers, O-C.

51. Daggett, *Railroad Reorganization*, pp. 245–46; A. A. H. Boissevain to Higginson, 6 Mar. 1894, Higginson Collection.

52. Olney to Hoadly, 4 Nov. 1894, OP,LC.

53. *Congressional Record*, Fifty-third Congress, Third Session, 30 Jan. 1895, p. 1539 ff.: Daggett, *Railroad Reorganization*, pp. 241–44.

54. "Letter from the Attorney General . . . April 11, 1894," *House Executive Document 194* (Washington, 1894), Fifty-third Congress, Second Session.

55. Olney to Hoadly, 7 Apr. 1894, OP,LC.

56. Forbes to Perkins, 30 Apr., Forbes file, BA; Perkins to Forbes, 3 May 1894, Perkins Papers, O-C.

57. Perkins to Forbes, 9 May 1894, Perkins Papers, O-C.

58. Daggert, *Railroad Reorganization* pp. 242–48.

59. *Congressional Record*, Fifty-third Congress, Third Session, 30 Jan. 1895, pp. 1539–40; Henry Kirke White, *History of the Union Pacific Railway* (New York, 1895), p. 97; Olney to Hoadly, 19 June 1894; to David B. Culberson, 23 Jan. 1895, OP,LC.

60. Daggett, *Railroad Reorganization*, pp. 249–50, 256; Nelson Trotter, *History of the Union Pacific, a Financial and Economic Survey* (New York, 1923), pp. 270–72; Campbell, *Reorganization of American Railroad System*, pp. 243–44; H. R. Meyer, "The Settlement with the Pacific Railways," *Quarterly Journal of Economics*, 13 (1889): 427–44; *Congressional Record*, Fifty-third Congress, Third Session, 30 Jan. 1895, p. 1557.

61. This undated letter appears to be in Hoadly's hand, Union Pacific bundle, OP,LC.

62. Stuart Daggett, *Chapters on the History of the Southern Pacific* (New York, 1922), pp. 3–82, 395–424. For a detailed account of Huntington, Stanford, Crocker, and Hopkins, see Oscar Lewis, *The Big Four* (London, 1938).

63. Solomon to Cleveland, 8 June 1893; Year file 7622-92 (hereafter cited as Stan-

ford Case file), various Justice Department officials to Solomon, Miscellaneous Book 11: 313, 447, 474–75; Solomon to various Justice Department officials, 22 July, 19, 25, 26 Aug., 13, 27 Sept. 1893, Stanford Case file, RG 60 NA.

64. Solomon to Attorney General, 22 July, Stanford Case file; Attorney General to Solomon, 25 Oct. 1893, Miscellaneous Book 12: 197.

65. Thomas to Olney, 3 Oct. 1893, Union Pacific bundle, OP,LC.

66. Olney to Wm. H. Clopton, 9 Apr., Instructions Book 38: 315; Clopton to Olney, 12 Apr. 1894, Stanford Case file.

67. *St. Louis Republic*, 22 Apr. 1894.

68. Resolution, 28 Apr. 1894, copy, Stanford Case file; Olney to Speaker, 1 May 1894, E&C 17: 222.

69. Olney to Hoadly, 12 May 1894, OP,LC. Empty folders in Stanford Case file show that Olney sent Hoadly nine letters from Solomon dated 11, 12, 13, 16, 22, 27 Apr. and 5, 7, 11 May 1894. Apparently they were not returned.

70. Olney to Charles A. Garter, 15 May 1894, Instructions Book 39: 407, and passim, Instructions Books 39, 43; Olney to Special Counsel L. D. McKesick, passim, Miscellaneous Books 17, 18; *United States* v. *Stanford*, 161 U.S. 412 (1896).

71. Olney to Hoar, 8 June 1894, OP,LC.

6   Battling the Trusts

1. The income tax cases and the Debs case are discussed in chapters 7 and 10.

2. Hans B. Thorelli, *The Federal Antitrust Policy* (Baltimore, 1955), pp. 376–77; William Letwin, *Law and Economic Policy in America, the Evolution of the Sherman Act* (New York, 1965), pp. 106–116.

3. Thorelli, *Antitrust Policy*, pp. 376–77; *Boston Transcript*, 1, 12, 30 Mar., 15 Apr., 13 May 1892.

4. Olney's brief, *U.S.* v. *Greenhut*, OP,MHS.

5. *United States* v. *Greenhut*, 50 Fed. 469 (1892). Since he had been attorney in the case, Olney, as attorney general, declined to recommend dropping the case. He did discuss the matter with the U.S. attorney in Boston, however. Sherman Hoar to Olney, 1 Feb. 1894, Year file 1890–8247 (hereafter cited as Antitrust file); Olney to Hoar, 3 Feb. 1894, Instructions Book 36: 534, RG 60 NA.

6. *In re Corning*, 51 Fed. 205; *In re Terrell*, 51 Fed. 513; *In re Greene*, 52 Fed. 104 (1892).

7. *Annual Report of the Attorney General of the United States for the Year 1893* (Washington, 1893), pp. xxvi–xxviii; Olney to President of Senate, 22 May 1894, E&C 17: 412–15; answers to inquiries from various U.S. attorneys regarding the antitrust law, Instructions Books 29–50 (1893–95); Olney to Cleveland, 19 Apr. 1895, OP,LC. Whether Judge Jackson saw Olney's Greenhut brief is not known.

8. 52 Fed. 104; *Cincinnati Commercial Gazette*, 12 June 1892.

9. *New York World*, 18–22 Feb., 3–15 Apr. 1893.

10. G. G. Haven to Olney, 7 Apr. 1893; Olney to W. H. Corbin, 23 Feb. 1894, OP,LC. See also *National Cordage Co.* v. *Pearson Cordage Co.*, 55 Fed. 812 (1893).

11. *New York World,* 10 Apr. 1893.

12. Olney to Phillips, 20 Apr.; Maxwell to Phillips, 4 July 1893, Miscellaneous Book 10: 419; 11: 178.

13. Thorelli, *Antitrust Policy,* p. 378; *United States* v. *E. C. Knight Co.,* 156 U.S. 1 (1894).

14. Thorelli, *Antitrust Policy,* pp. 386–87; Ingham to Attorney General, 27 Mar. 1893, and throughout Antitrust file.

15. Ingham to Phillips, 15 Nov. 1893, Antitrust file.

16. Maxwell to Ingham, 23 Dec. 1893, Instructions Book 35: 506.

17. *Annual Report . . . Attorney General, 1893,* pp. xxvi–xxviii. In a letter to Miss Straw, 7 Dec. 1893, Olney said that he had not written some parts of the report and was not completely satisfied with it. The section on the trust problem reads very much as if written by Olney.

18. 8 Dec. 1893.

19. Ingham to Maxwell and Phillips, 14 Sept. 1893; 3 Jan. 1894; to Olney, 6 Jan. 1894, Antitrust file.

20. Benjamin R. Twiss, *Lawyers and the Constitution: How Laissez Faire Came to the Supreme Court* (Princeton, 1942), pp. 206–12; Ingham to Olney, 20 Jan. 1894, Antitrust file.

21. 60 Fed. 306 (1894).

22. Olney sent four letters to Ingham between 31 Jan. and 3 Feb. 1894, Instructions Book 36: 498, 499, 512–13, 549.

23. Phillips to Maxwell, 6 Mar. 1894, Antitrust file.

24. 60 Fed. 934.

25. The brief, on file, Supreme Court Library, Washington, does not resemble the hundred or so briefs by Olney on file in OP,MHS. It is rambling and lacks Olney's usual conciseness and organization.

26. *New York World,* 25 Oct. 1894.

27. 156 U.S. 1, 9–46 (1894).

28. Olney to Straw, 22, 23, 24 Jan. 1895, OP,LC.

29. Gresham, *W. Q. Gresham* 2: 652–53, concluded that Ingham (later convicted of counterfeiting) had sold out to the sugar trust and suppressed evidence. William Howard Taft, *The Anti-Trust Act and the Supreme Court* (New York, 1914), pp. 58–59; Matthew Josephson, *The Politicos* (New York, 1938), p. 608; Nevins, *Grover Cleveland,* p. 671; George Shiras III, *Justice George Shiras, Jr. of Pittsburgh* (Pittsburgh, 1953), p. 147; and Thorelli, *Antitrust Policy,* pp. 598–99, all relieve the Court of blame for the government's defeat on grounds that it could have reached no other conclusion given the weak case presented to it. Thorelli cites later cases to prove his point. However, those cases (Trans-Missouri Freight Association and Addyston Pipe & Steel) involved pools operating over state lines, not outright mergers of competing companies as in the sugar trust case. Carl B. Swisher, *American Constitutional Development* (Boston, 1943), p. 429, and Edwin S. Corwin, "The Antitrust Acts and the Constitution," *Virginia Law Review,* 18 (Feb. 1932): 357, are of the opinion that at least part of the blame for the sugar trust case must rest on the courts.

30. Olney certainly so construed the ruling. On 22 Mar. 1895, he wrote a U.S. attorney: "Unless the facts show a contract, combination or conspiracy in itself operating upon interstate commerce and not merely indirectly in restraint of

interstate or international trade or commerce, the Court would have no jurisdiction even though such trade be affected and a practical monopoly be the result of the transaction between the parties." Instructions Book 49: 340–47.

31. *Washington Post*, 22 Jan. 1895.

32. For example, see Olney to Sec. of Treas., 24 Nov. 1894, E&C 19: 470–71; Olney to Wm. K. Tubman, 11 Dec. 1893, Miscellaneous Book 12: 484.

33. Olney to D. S. Alexander, 12 May 1893, Instructions Book 30: 69–72.

34. For example, see Olney to John T. Ensor, 1 Nov. 1893, Instructions Book 24: 305. An exception was made in the Trans-Missouri Freight Association case. Special counsel was not employed because of a lack of funds. "An examination of your very full and exhaustive brief," Olney wrote the U.S. attorney, "satisfies me that you have presented the case of the Government for all its worth." Instructions Book 29: 563–64. The case, which included among its defendants a branch of the Burlington, was won by the government in 1897.

35. Passim, Instructions Books 29–50 (1893–95).

36. Glenn to Olney, 6 Aug., 10, 16 Oct., 3 Dec. 1894, Antitrust file; Glenn to Olney, 18 Jan. 1895, OP,LC; Olney to Glenn, 11 Aug., 12 Oct., 12 Dec.; 1894, Instructions Book 42: 96; 44: 9; 46: 81.

37. Glenn to Olney, 14 Mar., Antitrust file; Olney to Glenn, 16 Mar. 1895, Instructions Book 49: 214.

38. Olney to Glenn, 22 Mar., Instructions Book 49: 340–47; Glenn to Olney, 28 Mar 1895, Antitrust file.

39. Olney to Denis, 14 Aug. 1895, OP,LC, has copies of the wires exchanged.

40. Copy of brief against Southern Pacific, OP,LC.

41. Olney-Tweed correspondence, 23 July–8 Aug. 1894, OP,LC.

42. Olney to Denis, 1, 14 Aug. 1894; Olney Memoir, OP,LC.

43. Thorelli, *Antitrust Policy*, pp. 384, 389; Olney to U.S. Attorney Hoar, 16 Oct. 1893, Instructions Book 34: 40–41.

44. Letwin, *Law and Economic Policy*, pp. 100–106, 117–130. The quote is from p. 102. On p. 118, Letwin says that Olney in 1893 worked to have the antitrust law repealed–proof that he was above board in his opposition to the act. Letwin is in error. The Sherman Act that Olney worked against in 1893 was the Sherman Silver Purchase Act.

45. Quoted in Letwin, *Law and Economic Policy*, p. 117. See also pp. 85–87.

46. Finley Peter Dunne, *Mr. Dooley in the Hearts of his Countrymen* (Boston, 1899), pp. 145–46.

7   Defending the Income Tax

1. Typewritten copy of address, OP,LC. This chapter in slightly different form appeared in the *Mississippi Valley Historical Review*, 28 (June 1961): 24–41, and is used here with permission.

2. U.S., *Statutes at Large*, 28: 553, 556.

3. Swisher, *American Constitutional Development*, pp. 440–45; Randolph E. Paul,

Taxation in the United States (Boston, 1954), pp. 32–39; Nevins, *Grover Cleveland*, pp. 666–68.

4. Olney to Ellen Hammond, 22 May 1894, OP,LC.

5. Louis B. Boudin, *Government by Judiciary* (New York, 1932), 2: 206–7.

6. Sidney Ratner, *American Taxation, Its History as a Social Force in Democracy* (New York, 1942), p. 195; Swaine, *Cravath Firm*, 1: 518–21.

7. Maxwell to Cleveland, 5 Feb. 1895, Cleveland Papers, Library of Congress.

8. Olney to Maxwell, 29 Jan. 1895, OP,LC.

9. Maxwell to Olney, 30 Jan. 1895, E&C 20: 382¾, RG 60 NA. Copies of the original *Congressional Directory* and Maxwell's revisions are in OP,LC.

10. Maxwell to Cleveland and to Henry T. Thurber, presidential secretary, 30 Jan.; Cleveland to Maxwell, 30 Jan. 1895, handwritten draft in pencil by Cleveland on back of Maxwell's note to Thurber, Cleveland Papers, Library of Congress.

11. *New York Sun*, 9 Feb. 1895; Henry M. Bates, "Lawrence Maxwell," *Michigan and the Cleveland Era*, ed. Earl D. Babst and Lewis G. Vander Velde (Ann Arbor, 1948), p. 145; Swaine, *Cravath Firm*, 1: 521–22. See also diary, Index & Digest, p. 387, Hamlin Papers, Library of Congress.

12. Olney to Straw, undated correspondence [3 Feb. 1895], OP,LC.

13. Butler to Olney, 4 Feb. 1895, OP,LC.

14. See above, p. 95.

15. *Springer* v. *United States*, 120 U.S. 586 (1881). See also Swisher, *American Constitutional Development*, p. 447; Nevins, *Grover Cleveland*, p. 668; Ratner, *American Taxation*, p. 201; Theron G. Strong, *Joseph H. Choate* (New York, 1917), p. 164; Olney to James C. Carter, 18 Mar. 1895, OP,LC.

16. Edward B. Whitney, "The Income Tax and the Constitution," *Harvard Law Review*, 20 (Feb. 1907): 285.

17. Olney to Straw, 24 Feb. 1895. "I have run out of the Income Tax cases," Olney wrote Charles H. Tweed, 15 Mar. 1895, "only to run into the Debs case—in which my own personal interest (apart from my pecuniary interest) is much greater." See also Olney to Geo. R. Peck, 12 Apr. 1895, OP,LC.

18. Whitney, "The Income Tax and the Constitution," p. 290.

19. Herbert B. Turner, William Jay, Flamen B. Candler, and William C. Gulliver appeared on briefs in defense of the income tax, while Benjamin H. Bristow, David Willcox, Charles Steele, Victor Morawetz, Samuel Shellabarger, Jeremiah M. Wilson, and Charles F. Southmayd prepared briefs for the plaintiffs. Carter, who was paid by Seward, Guthrie, Morawetz & Steele, reportedly received $5,000 for his services while the Seward firm netted $25,600 for its part in the two hearings. Swaine, *Cravath Firm*, 1: 519–20. Choate claimed to have received $34,000 for his two appearances, Strong, *Choate*, p. 232. Olney and Whitney received no fees.

20. The oral remarks of Guthrie, Seward, Whitney, and Edmunds are reported in 157 U.S. 429 (1894), pp. 442–52, 452–69, 469–82, and 482–99, respectively.

21. Ibid., pp. 499–513.

22. Ibid., p. 499.

23. Ibid., p. 513.

24. Seward to Olney, 18 Mar. 1895, OP,LC.

25. 157 U.S. 513–32.

26. Ibid., pp. 532–53.

27. Strong, *Choate*, pp. 164–65.

28. Olney to Carter, 18 Mar. 1895, OP,LC.

29. Guthrie to Whitney, 27 Feb. 1895, OP,LC.

30. 157 U.S. 553–86. For analyses of the arguments and opinions at both hearings, see Boudin, *Government by Judiciary*, 2: 206–261; Ratner, *American Taxation*, pp. 195–214; Paul, *Taxation*, pp. 40–64; Willard King, *Melville Weston Fuller* (New York, 1950), pp. 193–221; Edwin R. A. Seligman, *The Income Tax* (New York, 1911), pp. 531–89. The dissent of Justice Edward White at the first hearing (157 U.S. 608–52) was particularly thorough in pointing out the historical and legal errors of the plaintiffs and of the Court's opinion. It is possible that the vote at the first hearing was 5 to 3 on the issues decided rather than 6 to 2. This account follows the views of Boudin, *Government by Judiciary*, 2: 252; Nevins, *Grover Cleveland*, p. 669; Ratner, *American Taxation*, p. 202; and King, *Fuller*, p. 195. Years later, Olney was uncertain as to the vote. Olney to James Ford Rhodes, 12 Dec. 1904, OP,LC.

31. Olney to Straw, 8 Apr. 1895, quoted in Straw to James, 12 Aug. 1922, OP,LC.

32. *Washington Post*, 9 Apr. 1895. *Washington Star*, 8 Apr. 1895, declared that Olney in his oral remarks had suggested that rents and municipal and state bonds might be exempted from the income tax without harming the measure. Olney protested that he had *not* suggested exempting *rents*. *Washington Star*, 9 Apr. 1895. See Olney's remarks, 157 U.S. 502–4.

33. 158 U.S. 601 (1894), especially pp. 602–6.

34. Olney to Carter, 26 Apr.; Wm. C. Gulliver to Olney, 29 Apr.; Carter to Olney (two letters), 29 Apr., OP,LC; Olney to Carter, 30 Apr. 1895, Miscellaneous Book 17: 579.

35. Carter to Olney, 27 Apr. 1895, OP,LC.

36. Olney to Straw, 18 Apr. 1895, OP,LC.

37. Josephson, *The Politicos*, pp. 608–12. Had Olney wanted to defeat the income tax he might well have pursued the course followed in the sugar trust case: allow subordinates to handle the case and trust the conservative views of the Court to accomplish the desired end. By temperament, Olney was a fighter who exerted every effort to win every case he undertook. Since he was generally candid, and especially to Miss Straw, I see no reason for not taking him at his word. The Court, having in his opinion decided incorrectly at the first hearing, should be persuaded to reverse itself. If he failed, of course, all was lost. Even the most severe contemporary critic of Olney as attorney general, the *New York World*, which openly accused him of having deliberately lost the sugar trust case, grudgingly admitted the forcefulness of his arguments in the income tax case and accused him of nothing more than fighting without enthusiasm.

38. *Boston Herald*, 8 May 1895. Olney wrote Miss Straw on 9 May: "The view of the Herald reporter is very intelligent—If I can't get the rents back into the law, perhaps it had better go by the board." See also Olney to Carter, 26 Apr. 1895, OP,LC.

39. *U.S. Reports* did not include the oral remarks at the second hearing. They were thoroughly reported in the 7–9 May issues of the *New York World, Tribune,* and *Times,* and the *Boston Herald,* among other newspapers.

40. Olney to Carter, 11 May 1895, OP,LC. "I stuck closely to the rent question for the reason that unless the Court can be induced to reconsider that question what remains of the law is hardly worth preserving. That, of course, is between us."

41. *New York World,* 9 May 1895. Brisbane's account of the whole rehearing, though extremely prejudiced, and on occasion inaccurate (as when he referred to Whitney as Olney's son-in-law), was the most graphic newspaper account.

42. Ibid., 8 May 1895.

43. Based on accounts in the *New York World* and *Tribune,* 9 May 1895.

44. 158 U.S. 601ff.

45. In 1933, Sidney Ratner, in an appendix to Nevin's *Grover Cleveland,* pp. 778–79, fixed on Brewer as the justice who switched. In his 1942 book *American Taxation,* Ratner changed, accepting Edward S. Corwin's thesis in *Court Over Constitution* (Princeton, 1938), p. 201, that it was Justice Gray who changed. Boudin, *Government by Judiciary,* 2: 249–52, asserts that both Brown and Shiras shifted, but gives no proof. Olney expressed a similar view to James Ford Rhodes in 1904. "Looking at his [Brown's] dissenting opinion in the second case, it seems to me that he must have coincided with the minority in the first case. But it was certainly said at one time that Brown as well as Shiras, changed his original views and that the first case was decided by 6 to 2—both Brown and Shiras concurring in the opinion of the Court." 12 Dec. 1904, OP,LC. Shiras, in the biography of his father, the justice, presents a strong but unproven contention that it was not his father who shifted. King, *Fuller,* pp. 218–21, concludes that it is impossible to determine from the available evidence how most of the justices voted at the first hearing.

46. Olney to Straw, 21, 23 May [1895], OP,LC. When I used this quote in my article in the *Mississippi Valley Historical Review,* I had not located the original, but quoted from Straw to James, 12 Aug. 1922. Miss Straw substituted blanks for the amounts of tax.

47. Olney to A. C. Griscom, Jr., 16 May 1898; Olney to F. S. Sorrenson, 29 July 1910, OP,LC.

8   Coxeyites and Strikers

1. Charles Hoffman, "The Depression of the Nineties," *Journal of Economic History,* 16 (June 1956): 138.

2. Benton to Olney, 15, 26 Mar.; U.S. Attorney John W. Judd to Olney, 7 July 1893, Year file 2704-93 (hereafter cited as Eureka file), RG 60 NA.

3. Olney to Benton (two telegrams), 15 Mar., Instructions Book 28: 545–46; Benton to Olney, 15 Mar. 1893, Eureka file. Benton cited the Edmunds-Tucker Act of 1887.

4. Benton to Olney, 18, 26 Mar. 1893, Eureka file.

5. Benton to Olney, 6 May; Judd to Olney, 7 July 1893, Eureka file.

6. Duggan to Olney, 2 Apr., 10 Dec. 1893, Eureka file.

7. *St. Paul Daily Globe*, 25–27 Oct.; *St. Paul Pioneer Press*, 26 Oct. 1893.

8. *St. Paul Daily Globe*, 27 Oct. 1893.

9. *St. Paul Pioneer Press*, 27 Oct. 1893. Transit company officials used the term "agitators" while the chief of police described the strike-breakers.

10. "Laban" to Washburn, 26 Oct. 1893, Year file 11192–93, RG 60 NA.

11. Olney to Donahower, 26 Oct. 1893, Instructions Book 34: 220. Olney reported directly to Lowry, "Have wired instructions to Marshal Donahower." Miscellaneous Book 12: 204.

12. *St. Paul Daily Globe*, 27, 31 Oct. 1893.

13. Donald L. McMurry, *Coxey's Army* (Boston, 1929), chap. 3; *Washington Star*, 1, 2 May; *Washington Post*, 2 May 1894.

14. Olney, "The Scholar in Politics," address, Brown University, reported in *Philadelphia Daily Evening Telegram*, 20 June 1894. The theme of world-wide labor unrest and possible revolution recurred in Olney speeches and articles after 1893. In later years he foresaw peaceful rather than violent revolution in America. For Gresham's views, see memo dated 4 May 1894, John Bassett Moore Papers, Library of Congress.

15. *Boston Journal*, 25 Apr.; *Washington Star*, 23 Apr.; Office of Commissioners, District of Columbia, to Henry Thurber (Cleveland's private secretary), 15 Apr.; Various letters 1–30 Apr. 1894, Cleveland Papers, Library of Congress.

16. Olney Memoir.

17. McMurry, *Coxey's Army*, chap. 10.

18. Eggert, *Railway Labor Disputes*, pp. 35, 37–40, 232–33.

19. S. H. H. Clark, Oliver W. Mink, E. Ellery Anderson, and Frederic R. Coudert to Attorney General, 21 Apr. 1894, Year file 4017–94 (hereafter cited as Coxey file).

20. Hoadly to Olney, 21 Apr. 1894, Coxey file.

21. Acting Attorney General to Sec. of War, 21 Apr., E&C 17: 155; Sec. of War to Acting Attorney General, 21 Apr., Coxey file; Maxwell to Hoadly, 22 Apr. 1894, Miscellaneous Book 14: 21.

22. W. M. McDermott to Attorney General, 21 Apr., Coxey file; Olney to McDermott, 23 Apr. 1894, Instructions Book 38: 589.

23. McNaught to Olney, 23 Apr. 1894, Coxey file.

24. Judge Hiram Knowles (countersigned, U.S. Attorney Preston Leslie) to Olney, 24 Apr., Coxey file; Olney to Knowles, 24 Apr., J&C 6: 102; Knowles to Olney, 24 Apr. 1894, Coxey file.

25. McDermott to Olney, 24 Apr., 1 May; McNaught to Olney, 24 Apr. 1894, Coxey file.

26. *Washington Post*, 26 Apr. 1894.

27. Schofield to McNaught, 24 Apr. 1894, Letters Sent, IV: 2: 452, Headquarters of the Army, Early Wars Branch, Record Group 108, National Archives (hereafter cited as Army Headquarters, RG 108 NA).

28. Gov. John E. Rickards to Cleveland, 25 Apr. 1894, Cleveland Papers, Library of Congress.

29. McMurry, *Coxey's Army*, pp. 202–205.

30. McDermott to Olney, 27 Apr.; McNaught to A. H. Garland, 26 Apr., Coxey file; Olney to McDermott, 28 Apr. 1894, Instructions Book 39: 93.

31. Judge Cornelius Hanford to Olney, 24 Apr.; U.S. Marshal J. C. Drake to Olney, 26 Apr. (two telegrams), Coxey file; Olney to Drake, 24 Apr. 1894, Instructions Book 39: 39.

32. *New York Tribune*, 29 Apr.; Grady to Olney, 27 Apr. (two telegrams); Judge Chas. Bellinger to Olney, 28 Apr. 1894, Coxey file.

33. *Washington Star*, 26 Apr.; *New York Tribune*, 29 Apr.; Grady to Olney, 29 Apr. 1894, Coxey file.

34. Drake to Olney, 29 Apr., Coxey file; *New York Tribune*, 29 Apr. 1894; McMurry, *Coxey's Army*, p. 220.

35. Troops were sent, for example, on 14 May to Spokane to prevent seizure of a train, on 15 May to recapture a train stolen at Montpelier, Idaho, and on 19 May to the Coeur d'Alene district to maintain order. J&C 6: 151; Army Headquarters to Gen. Brooke, 14 May, Coxey file; Letters Sent, IV: 2: 506–507, Army Headquarters, RG 108 NA.

36. Hanford to Olney, 2 May; McNaught to Olney, 12 May; McDermott to Olney, 7 June; U.S. Attorney Henry V. Johnson to Olney, 7 June 1894, Coxey file.

37. Olney to Judge Elmer S. Dundy, 13 June; to Judge Hanford, 14 May; to Judge John A. Riner, 15 May 1894, J&C 6: 151, 153, 198.

38. Olney to Leslie, 23 May, Instructions Book 39: 556; W. H. Rossington to Olney, 11 May; McDermott to Olney, 28 Apr.; Leslie to Olney, 20 Apr., Coxey file; Olney to Neely, 11 May 1894, Instructions Book 39: 370; McMurry, *Coxey's Army*, pp. 210, 214–15; Hanford to Olney, 12 May; Hanford and Drake to Olney, 13 May 1894, Coxey file.

39. Olney to Lamont, 11 May, E&C 17: 331–32; Olney to Lamont, 6 June 1894, OP,LC.

40. Olney to A. J. Sawyer, 21 June 1894, Instructions Book 40: 426–27. See also Olney to McDermott, 20 Apr.; Olney to Neely, 11 May 1894, Instructions Book 39: 104, 370.

41. Anderson to Olney, 19 May; McNaught to Garland, 26 Apr., Coxey file; John F. Dillon, Winslow S. Pierce to Olney, 24 May 1894, OP,LC.

42. Olney to Forney, 19 May 1894, Instructions Book 39: 498.

43. Beatty to Olney, 3 May 1894, Coxey file.

44. Olney to McNaught, 26 Apr. 1894, Miscellaneous Book 14: 51.

45. McMurry, *Coxey's Army*, pp. 205, 224, 226; Frank E. White and A. J. Sawyer to Olney, 21 June 1894, Coxey file.

46. Neely to Olney, 31 Oct. 1894, Coxey file.

47. Beatty to Olney, 23, 24 May 1894, Coxey file.

48. Schofield to Lamont, 18 May 1894, Letters Sent, IV: 2: 504–505, Army Headquarters, RG 108 NA.

49. Beatty to Olney, 24 May 1894, Coxey file.

50. Olney to Beatty, 29 May, J&C 6: 173; Olney to Pinkham, 18 May, Instructions Book 39: 503; Olney to Murphy, 29 May 1894, Instructions Book 40: 52.

51. Beatty to Olney, 5 June 1894, Coxey file.

52. Olney to Lamont, 6 June 1894, OP,LC. Notation on wire, Beatty and Pinkham to Olney, 7 June: "received from the Attorney General after he had conversed with the President on the subject," Coxey file; Olney to Pinkham, 7 June 1894, Instructions Book 40: 177.

53. Olney to Carlisle, 25 June 1894, E&C 18: 46–49.

54. J. C. Musgrove to Attorney General, 8 Oct.; James Blackburn to Attorney General, 31 Oct.; Frank P. Bradley to Olney, 7 Nov. 1894, Coxey file.

55. Olney to Musgrove, 17 Oct. 1894, Instructions Book 44: 48.

56. Olney to Blackburn, 9 Nov.; Olney to Bradley, 13 Nov. 1894, Instructions Book 45: 6, 85; Olney to S. Guthrie, 14 Nov. 1895, Miscellaneous Book 20: 326; Olney to H. H. Baldridge, 15 Jan. 1895, Miscellaneous Book 16: 321.

57. Ray Ginger, *The Bending Cross, a Biography of Eugene Victor Debs* (New Brunswick, N.J., 1949), pp. 102–7; *Minneapolis Tribune,* 15 Apr. 1894.

58. Hill to Olney, 19 Apr. 1894, Coxey file. All letters relating to labor disturbances on railroads in the spring of 1894—including the Great Northern Strike and Illinois Coal Strike—were filed with the Coxey correspondence.

59. Eggert, *Railway Labor Disputes,* pp. 41–45, 90–98, 148–50. See also James E. White, *A Life Span and Reminiscences of Railway Mail Service* (Philadelphia, 1910), pp. 17–18, 200–2.

60. White, *Reminiscences,* pp. 207–8. Since by law the attorney general could only advise the president and cabinet members, the request was over the postmaster general's name and was addressed to the attorney general, 21 Apr. 1894, Coxey file. For Maxwell's railroad connections, see *Washington Post,* 4 Feb. 1895; Poor, *Railroad Manual, 1895,* pp. 427, 754.

61. *Opinions of the Attorney General* (Washington, 1895), 21: 542–43.

62. Ginger, *Bending Cross,* p. 103; Bissell to Olney, 21 Apr. 1894, Coxey file.

63. Hill to Cleveland, 24 Apr., Cleveland Papers, Library of Congress, and 28 Apr. 1894, Coxey file.

64. Olney to Lamont, 20 Apr. 1894, OP,LC.

65. W. B. Brinton to Olney, 15 June 1894, Coxey file.

66. Olney to W. J. Allen, 16 June 1894, J&C 6: 203.

67. Clinton, Clark & Ingram to D. S. Alexander, 1 May, Antitrust file; Olney to Alexander, 12 May 1893, Instructions Book 30: 69–72.

68. *Philadelphia Daily Evening Telegraph,* 20 June 1894.

9   *The Pullman Strike*

1. The standard account is Almont Lindsey, *The Pullman Strike: The Story of a Unique Experiment and of a Great Labor Upheaval* (Chicago, 1942). A more recent study of the company town is Stanley Buder, *Pullman: An Experiment in Industrial Order and Community Planning, 1880–1930* (New York, 1967). Much useful first-hand information about the company town and the strike will be found in the testimony gathered by the United States Strike Commission appointed by President Cleveland after the disorders. See U.S. Strike Commission, *Report on the Chicago Strike of June–July, 1894* (Washington, 1894). Hereafter cited as *Strike Comm. Report.*

2. Resolution, 25 June; minutes for 26–28 June 1894, General Managers Association, *Minutes of Meetings* (Chicago, 1894), pp. 94–107. Only twenty-five copies of these secret minutes were printed. One is in the John Crerar Library, Chicago. For the companies' attitude toward the ARU, see Lindsey, *The Pullman Strike*, p. 137; Eggert, *Railway Labor Disputes*, pp. 156–57. For the GMA, see Donald L. McMurry, "Labor Policies of the General Managers' Association of Chicago, 1886–1894," *Journal of Economic History*, 13 (Spring 1953): 160–78.

3. Pullman joined Olney as a director of the Boston & Maine in 1892. Olney's ties with the others have already been discussed. When Olney died in 1917, the single most valuable block of stock in the inventory of his estate was five hundred shares of Pullman stock valued at nearly $80,000. I have been unable to determine when Olney purchased this stock. Although it might have been after the strike, it is also possible that he bought it in 1892 when the Boston & Maine gave Pullman a sleeping-car monopoly over the line and invited him to sit on its board.

4. Eggert, *Railway Labor Disputes*, pp. 84–90, 111–15.

5. Postmaster General Bissell to Olney, 25 June 1894, Letters of the Postmaster General, Record Group 28, National Archives (hereafter cited as Letters PMG).

6. Acting Postmaster General Frank H. Jones to Olney, 28 June; Olney to U.S. Attorney, Thos. M. Milchrist, 28 June 1894, *Appendix to the Annual Report of the Attorney General of the United States for the Year 1896* (Washington, 1896), pp. 55, 245–46. Hereafter cited as *Strike Correspondence*.

7. *Chicago Daily Tribune*, 29 June; GMA, *Minutes*, 1 July; *New York World*, 2 July; *New York Times*, 3 July 1894; *Strike Comm. Report*, p. 65; Clarence Darrow, *The Story of My Life* (New York, 1931), p. 61. The postmaster general found it necessary to remind several railroad companies of their duty as mail carriers. See Bissell to various officials, 10–11 July 1894, Letters PMG.

8. GMA, *Minutes*, 29 June, p. 113; *Chicago Times*, 30 June 1894.

9. Testimony of ARU Vice President Geo. Howard, *Strike Comm. Report*, p. 18; *Chicago Daily Tribune*, 30 June, 1 July; *New York Evening Post*, 2 July; Bissell to Charles F. Mayer, 10 July 1894, Letters PMG.

10. Eggert, *Railway Labor Disputes*, pp. 12–15.

11. GMA, *Minutes*, 30 June–3 July 1894, pp. 124–27, 135–36; *Strike Comm. Report*, pp. 227–33; Arnold to Olney, and Milchrist to Olney, 1 Dec. 1894, file 16–1–23, RG 60 NA (hereafter cited as Pullman Strike file).

12. Olney to Straw, 2 July, OP,LC; *Washington Post* weather reports, 17 June–3 July 1894.

13. *New York Times*, 2 July 1894; *The Bench and Bar*, vol. 4, Industrial Chicago series (Chicago, 1896), pp. 449–52; *Who's Who in America, 1899–1900*, p. 760.

14. *Chicago Times*, 3 July; *New York Times*, *Washington Post*, 2 July; Gresham to Franklin MacVeagh, 12 July 1894, Gresham Papers. There is no correspondence between Olney and Walker prior to the strike in the OP,LC or RG 60 NA. Olney rarely went to Chicago on business; the Burlington Board of Directors met in Boston.

15. Lambert Tree to Gresham, 6 July 1894, Gresham Papers.

16. Olney to Walker, 30 June 1894, *Strike Correspondence*, p. 60; Olney Memoir.

17. GMA, *Minutes*, 30 June; Milchrist to Olney, 30 June 1894, *Strike Correspondence*, p. 58.

18. *Strike Correspondence,* pp. 57, 59; *Annual Report . . . Attorney General, 1893,* p. xxviii. For the precedents, see Eggert, *Railway Labor Disputes,* pp. 164–65.

19. Olney is quoted indirectly. See Eggert, *Railway Labor Disputes,* p. 165.

20. Italics supplied. Olney to Chas. A. Garter, 29 June; to Milchrist and Walker, 1 July 1894, *Strike Correspondence,* pp. 18, 61.

21. Walker to Olney, 2 July 1894, Pullman Strike file. This letter was published in *Strike Correspondence,* pp. 63–64, but with all references to the role of the judges omitted. For the injunction, see *U.S.* v. *Debs et al.,* 64 Fed. Rep. 724–27 (1894).

22. *New York World,* 4 July; Olney to Milchrist and to Walker, 1 July 1894, *Strike Correspondence,* p. 61.

23. *New York Evening Post,* 2 July 1894.

24. Arnold to Olney; Olney to Walker, 1 July; Walker to Olney, 2 July 1894, *Strike Correspondence,* pp. 61–62.

25. Arnold to Olney, 2 July; Olney to Milchrist, 3 July 1894, *Strike Correspondence,* pp. 62, 65.

26. Olney to Walker; Walker to Olney, 3 July 1894, *Strike Correspondence,* pp. 66–67.

27. Arnold to Olney, 3 July 1894, *Strike Correspondence,* p. 66. Nevins, *Grover Cleveland,* p. 621, points out the errors in Arnold's telegram.

28. *Chicago Times,* 8 July 1894; Olney Memoir.

29. Nelson A. Miles, *Serving the Republic* (New York, 1911), p. 253.

30. Olney conversation reported in Diary, Index & Digest, p. 461, Hamlin Papers; Olney Memoir.

31. Schofield to Martin, 3 July 1894, Army Headquarters, Letters Sent, IV: 2: 566, RG 108 NA; Cleveland quoted in Nevins, *Grover Cleveland,* p. 628.

32. *Boston Herald,* 5 July 1894.

33. Theodore Roosevelt to Anna Roosevelt, 12 Aug. 1894, *Letters of Theodore Roosevelt,* ed. Elting E. Morison and John M. Blum (Cambridge, Mass., 1951), 1: 393; James, *Olney,* p. 172.

34. Miles to Adj. Gen., 18 July 1894, "Chicago Strikes" file, Office of Adjutant General, Early Wars Branch, Record Group 94, National Archives (hereafter cited as Army Chicago Strikes file).

35. For Altgeld-Cleveland correspondence, see *Documents of American History,* ed. Henry Steele Commager, 8th ed. (New York, 1968), 2: 609–12. Governors Davis H. Waite of Colorado and J. S. Hogg of Texas took stands similar to Altgeld's; Waite to Cleveland, 5 July, Lamont Papers; Hogg to Cleveland, 11 July 1894, Cleveland Papers, Library of Congress. For Altgeld's prompt use of militia during strikes, see Waldo R. Browne, *Altgeld of Illinois* (New York, 1925), pp. 128–40; Harry A. Barnard, *"Eagle Forgotten"–The Life of John Peter Altgeld* (Indianapolis, 1938), pp. 290–93; Altgeld, *Biennial Message to the 39th General Assembly* (n.p., n. d.), pp. 40 ff. In June Olney had refused to approve the use of federal troops to protect railroads in receivership from coal strikers, because Altgeld stood ready to use the Illinois militia.

36. Columnist Alfred Henry Lewis attributed authorship of both replies to Olney

(*Chicago Times,* 10 July 1894). Olney might have assisted, but a copy of the second reply in Cleveland's own hand is in the Cleveland Papers, Library of Congress.

37. *Washington Post,* 7 July 1894.

38. For 1877 precedents, see Eggert, *Railway Labor Disputes,* pp. 26–27, 37–38.

39. Miles to Adj. Gen., 18 July 1894, Army Chicago Strikes file.

40. Miles to Adj. Gen., 4 July 1894, in Schofield, *Forty-six Years in the Army* (New York, 1897), p. 498; Olney Memoir; Miles to Adj. Gen., 5 July 1894, *Strike Correspondence,* p. 70.

41. Miles to Adj. Gen., 5 July (two telegrams), Schofield, *Forty-six Years,* pp. 499–500; Miles to Lamont, 6 July 1894, quoted in Grover Cleveland, *Presidential Problems* (New York, 1904), p. 104.

42. Lindsey, *The Pullman Strike,* pp. 203–9.

43. Alfred Henry Lewis column, *Chicago Times,* 9 July 1894.

44. Roosevelt quoted by Margaret Leech, *In the Days of McKinley* (New York, 1959), p. 200. Since no one questioned Miles's bravery as such, it might have been that his reluctance to fire stemmed from political ambition which such an act would have endangered. See Leech, *Days of McKinley,* p. 200, on Miles's political connections.

45. Miles to Adj. Gen., 5 July 1894, quoted in Schofield, *Forty-six Years,* p. 500.

46. Lewis, in *Chicago Times,* 6 July, described Cleveland's and Lamont's attitudes. For Schofield's order to Miles, 5 July 1894, see Schofield, *Forty-six Years,* p. 500.

47. Lewis column, *Chicago Times,* 6, 8, 9 July; General Order No. 23, 9 July 1894, Schofield, *Forty-six Years,* pp. 504–5.

48. Lindsey, *The Pullman Strike,* pp. 222–29, 239–70.

49. Olney to Walker, 11 July 1894, Miscellaneous Book 14: 454, RG 60 NA.

50. Walker to Olney, 2 July; Olney to Walker, 3 July 1894, *Strike Correspondence,* pp. 64, 66.

51. Walker to Olney, 2 July; telegram, 5 July; 6 July 1894, *Strike Correspondence,* pp. 68, 70–72.

52. Olney to Walker; Walker to Olney, 8 July 1894, *Strike Correspondence,* pp. 74–75.

53. *Messages and Papers,* 9: 499–500; Walker to Olney, 9 July 1894, *Strike Correspondence,* p. 77.

54. Olney to Walker, 11 July 1894, *Strike Correspondence,* p. 80.

55. Walker to Olney; Olney to Walker, 12 July 1894, *Strike Correspondence,* pp. 80–81.

56. Walker to Olney, 14 July; Olney to Walker, 16 July 1894, *Strike Correspondence,* pp. 83–85.

57. Walker to Olney, 20, 26 (two letters) July 1894, *Strike Correspondence,* pp. 91–95.

58. Olney to Walker, 28 July 1894, OP,LC.

59. P. B. Olney to Olney, 6, 9 July 1894, OP,LC.

10 Changing Views and Vindication

1. *New York World,* 4, 5 July; *Chicago Times,* 3, 8, 9 July 1894. After 5 July the *World* suddenly switched position and became a supporter of the administration's strike policy.

2. Twenty-four petitions arrived between 21 July and 28 Aug. 1894. *Congressional Record,* Fifty-third Congress, Second Session, 26: 7799 f.

3. Ibid., p. 7544.

4. On 26 July, the Senate passed a resolution calling for all correspondence and the next day reconsidered and recalled the resolution. Ibid., pp. 7868, 7879, 7921. Explanation was made on 10 Dec. (ibid., Third Session, 27: 153–154). The correspondence, made public in Jan. 1897, contained nothing sensational. Some items were published with elisions and some were not published at all, but remained in the Pullman Strike file, RG 60 NA, or were kept by Olney and are now in OP,LC. It is possible, but not certain, that some letters were lost or destroyed.

5. Statement of Amounts Charged to Boston Office Expenses, Jan. 1891–June 1903; Charles E. Perkins to J. W. Blythe, 4 Feb. 1895, Perkins file, BA. See also Perkins to Olney, 7 [or 9] Mar. 1897, OP,LC.

6. Olney to George R. Peck, 4 Aug. 1894, OP,LC. The volume of correspondence with clients in OP,LC and BA fell off after the summer of 1894. Olney's daughter, who lived with him after 1893, declared that after a year or so in the cabinet he did relatively little for his clients, Straw to James, 2 Mar. 1922, OP,LC.

7. Agnes Abbot to Eggert, 3 Apr. 1958.

8. OP,LC.

9. *Farmer's Loan & Trust Co.* v. *Northern Pac. R. Co., et al.,* 60 Fed. Rep. 803–821 (1894). For a more detailed account, see Eggert, *Railway Labor Disputes,* pp. 130–35.

10. Olney to Harlan, 26 Aug. 1894, OP,LC.

11. Olney to Charles E. Perkins, 4 Oct. 1894, OP,LC.

12. *Arthur et al.* v. *Oakes et al.,* 63 Fed. Rep. 329 (1894).

13. Walker to Olney, 14 Sept.; Olney to Walker, 24 Sept. 1894, OP,LC.

14. Walker to Olney, 29 Sept. 1894, OP,LC.

15. Olney to Charles S. Hamlin, 10 Aug. 1899; Olney Memoir, OP,LC.

16. Olney Memoir. James, *Olney,* p. 63, says Wilkinson "took Olney in" with an exaggerated story.

17. Olney to Moseley, 1, 3 Oct. 1894, OP,LC.

18. Olney to A. C. Griscom, Jr., 16 May 1898, OP,LC.

19. Olney to Hamlin, 10 Aug. 1899, OP,LC.

20. Olney to Judge Dallas, 6, 11 Oct., 6 Nov. 1894; copy, *Thomas C. Platt v. Philadelphia & Reading Railroad Co. et al., Some Suggestions Submitted by Richard Olney, esq.* . . . (n.p., 1894).

21. *Philadelphia Ledger,* 9 Nov. 1894.

22. Debs's statement, *New York World,* 15 Nov.; Brown to Olney, 15 Nov., OP,LC; Nimmo to Perkins, 19 Nov. 1894, Perkins file, BA.

23. *Platt* v. *Philadelphia & R.R. Co. et al.,* 65 Fed. Rep. 660–66 (1894).

24. Olney to Straw, 28 Nov. 1894, OP,LC.

25. *Strike Comm. Report,* pp. xxvii, xxi, xxxviii–xxxix, xlvi, xliv–xlv.

26. Olney to Perkins, 22 Nov., Perkins file, BA. Carroll D. Wright described Olney's reaction in letters to Nicholas E. Worthington (24 Nov.) and John D. Kernan (26 Nov. 1894), Letters of the U.S. Strike Commission, Record Group 31, Labor and Transportation Branch, National Archives (hereafter cited as Strike Comm. Letters), 1: 350–51, 358. That Olney objected to railroads paying deputies, see *Strike Correspondence,* pp. 107–8; that he ordered repayment prior to the Strike Commission's report, see pp. 178–79; that he authorized marshals to borrow from railroad companies, see pp. 65, 68, 120–21. See also pp. 130, 131; Olney to Charles R. Pratt, 21 Sept. 1894, Instructions Book 43: 211–12, RG 60 NA.

27. Arnold to Olney, 20 Nov., Pullman Strike file; Olney to Milchrist and Walker, 26 Nov., Miscellaneous Book 16: 54–55, 58–59; Walker to Olney, 28 Nov.; Arnold to Olney, 1 Dec.; Milchrist to Olney, 1 Dec.; Grosscup to Arnold, 8 Dec. 1894, Pullman Strike file.

28. Harris to Olney, 8 Jan. 1895, OP,LC; Milchrist to Olney, 1 Dec. 1894, Pullman Strike file.

29. Olney to Walker, 26 Nov., Miscellaneous Book 16: 58–59; 31 Dec. 1894, OP,LC.

30. Instructions Book 43, passim.

31. *Strike Comm. Report,* pp. lii–liv; James Morgan, *The Life Work of Edward A. Moseley in the Service of Humanity* (New York, 1913), p. 149; Olney Memoir; Wright to Olney, 15 Dec. 1894; McGann to Olney, 14 Jan. 1895, OP,LC. Compare copy of bill, HR 8259, Fifty-third Congress, Third Session, OP,LC, with Arbitration Act, 1888, *Statutes at Large,* 25: 501–2.

32. Olney to McGann, 17 Jan. 1895: Cleveland's handwritten comments, copy of bill, OP,LC; Olney Memoir.

33. Wright to Kernan, 25 Feb. 1895, Strike Comm. Letters, 2: 46–47; *Congressional Record,* Fifty-third Congress, Third Session, pp. 2789–2805, 2819, 2881, 2961–2, 3025.

34. Perkins to W. W. Baldwin, 18 Feb., Perkins file, BA; Perkins to Forbes, 1 Mar. 1895, Perkins Papers, O-C.

35. Leonard A. Lecht, *Experience under Railway Labor Legislation* (New York, 1955), pp. 16–17.

36. Walker to Olney, 2 Nov. 1894, OP,LC.

37. *United States* v. *Debs et al.,* 64 Fed. Rep. 724–65 (1895), especially pp. 739–47.

38. Olney to Walker, 26 Nov. 1894, Miscellaneous Book 16: 58–59; Olney to Cleveland, 14 Jan. 1902, OP,LC.

39. Walker to Olney, 17, 22, 29 Dec. 1894; 2, 7, 8, 9, 16 Jan. 1895, Pullman Strike file; Olney to Walker, 20, 22 Dec. 1894; 12 Jan. 1895, Miscellaneous Book 16: 167–69, 178, 306.

40. Olney to Walker, 7 Jan. 1895, OP,LC.

41. Accounts of the criminal proceedings will be found in Lindsey, *Pullman Strike,* pp. 300–4; Ginger, *Bending Cross,* pp. 181–82. See Walker to Olney,

21 May, 9 Feb., 27 Apr., Pullman Strike file; Walker to Olney, 20, 22 Feb. 1895, OP,LC.

42. *Chicago Daily Tribune*, 28 Apr. 1895.

43. Olney to John Fish, 9 Feb., Miscellaneous Book 16: 498; to Joseph W. House, 13 Mar., Instructions Book 49: 90; to Henry S. Foote, 18 Apr. 1895, Instructions Book 50: 435.

44. F. B. Earhart to Olney, 3 Nov., Source Chronological, Year file 12953/94; Olney to Earhart, 5, 10 Nov. 1894, Instructions Book 44: 539; 45: 31; T. McCants Stewart to Cleveland, 12 Mar., Cleveland Papers, Library of Congress; Earhart to Olney, 12 Mar.; Executive Committee, Merchant Conference Committee on Labor Troubles to Olney, 22 Mar., Source Chronological, Year file 12953/94; *New Orleans Picayune*, 28 Mar. 1895.

45. Only little more than two years before, Onley had said to Charles E. Perkins that the ICC's supervision of the railroads was "almost entirely nominal."

46. Olney brief, printed copy, OP,LC.

47. *In re Debs, Petitioner*, 158 U.S. 582, 583, 600 (1895).

48. Olney to Straw, 27 May 1895, OP,LC.

49. Walker to Olney, 21 May 1895, Pullman Strike file.

11 The Shaping of Foreign Policy

1. Butler to Olney, 28 May; Olney to Straw, 3 June 1895, OP,LC.

2. Undated memo, Lamont Papers.

3. Montgomery Schuyler, "Richard Olney," *The American Secretaries of State*, ed. Samuel Flagg Bemis (New York, 1927–29), 8: 273; *New York Tribune*, 8 June 1895.

4. Cleveland, *Presidential Problems*, p. 257.

5. James, *Olney*, pp. 14 n., 77–78.

6. Except for John W. Foster (1892–93), no secretary of state between Lewis Cass (1857–60) and William R. Day (1898) came to office with diplomatic experience. Thomas A. Bailey, *A Diplomatic History of the American People*, 6th ed. (New York, 1958), p. 866.

7. Memoranda, 4 and 8 May 1894, John Bassett Moore Papers, Library of Congress.

8. James, *Olney*, p. 79; Henry L. Bryan to Thomas F. Bayard, 31 May 1895, Bayard Papers, Library of Congress.

9. *Boston Herald*, 29 Oct. 1895; *New York Evening Telegram*, 23 Jan. 1894; unidentified newsclipping, 29 Feb. 1896, in author's possession.

10. *Wilson's Cabinet Diary*, pp. 5–6; James Olney, pp. 78–79.

11. For Cleveland's view of the Adams set, see Cleveland to Olney, 12 Sept. 1895, OP,LC.

12. Charles S. Campbell, Jr., *Special Business Interests and the Open Door Policy* (New Haven, 1951), especially pp. 1–24; Walter LaFeber, *The New Empire, an Interpretation of American Expansion 1860–1898* (Ithaca, 1963), pp. 150–96;

and Thomas J. McCormick, *China Market, America's Quest for Informal Empire, 1893–1901* (Chicago, 1967), pp. 21–52. For the influence of one economic writer who subscribed to the theory, see Tom E. Terrill, "David A. Wells, the Democracy, and Tariff Reduction, 1877–1894," *Journal of American History,* 56 (Dec. 1969), 540–55.

13. *Wilson's Cabinet Diary,* pp. 240–41. See also pp. 37–39.

14. Quoted by Gresham to John Bassett Moore, memo, 4 May 1894, Moore Papers.

15. LaFeber, *The New Empire,* pp. 197–282, especially pp. 199–203, 242–43, 255–59. LaFeber does not attempt to present a balanced account of American foreign policy in the closing decades of the nineteenth century. He has "emphasized economic forces" because he regards them as "the most important causes and results" of the diplomacy of the era. This warning in the preface, if missed, could mislead the casual reader into thinking that only economic factors determined foreign policy in that era. Earlier, William Appleman Williams in *The Tragedy of American Diplomacy* (1959) and *The Contours of American History* (1961) presented the economic interpretation as *the* and not *an* interpretation of most of America's foreign policy, including that of the Cleveland administration. McCormick, *China Market,* adapts the thesis to China and reaches conclusions essentially similar to LaFeber's.

16. LaFeber, *The New Empire,* p. 200, quotes from two Gresham letters to establish the secretary's views. LaFeber's elisions, here italicized, I believe show that Gresham saw tariff reduction—not vigorous foreign policy—as the solution to the problem: "Sparse as our population is, compared with that of other countries, we can not afford constant employment for our labor. *This is owing, in part, to the rapid increase of labor-saving machinery, but in greater measure to high protective tariffs.* Our mills and factories can supply the demand by running seven or eight months out of twelve. It is surprising to me that thoughtful men do not see the danger in present conditions." Gresham to John S. Cooper, 26 July 1894, Gresham Papers.

"There is undoubtedly an element of danger in the present condition of society. . . . Our manufactures of all kinds should have free raw materials,—*that is to say, all such imported materials as they need in their business should come in free.* This would lower the cost of the manufactured article and enable our people to compete in foreign markets with Great Britain. Sir Julian Pauncefote said to me the other day that he feared it would be an evil day for Great Britain when the United States changed its economic policy. . . . *P.S. We have gone too far in protecting special interests. If men can be protected by the tariff against foreign competition and by trusts against home competition, they can do about as they please.*" Gresham to Judge Charles E. Dyer, 2 May 1894, Gresham Papers.

The first quotation, LaFeber says, set forth the problem, the second indicated the solution. It should be noted that the second letter was written before the first. For further details, see Paul S. Holbo, "Economics, Emotion, and Expansion: An Emerging Foreign Policy," *The Gilded Age,* rev. ed., ed. H. Wayne Morgan (Syracuse, 1970), especially pp. 201–11; and Holbo, "A View of *The New Empire,*" mimeo., read at the Organization of American Historians, New Orleans, 16 Apr. 1971.

17. Gresham, *W. Q. Gresham,* 2: 802–4 and 1: 383–401; Gresham to "Tom," 1 Aug. 1877, Gresham Papers.

18. For example, see Cleveland to Thos. C. Catching, 27 Aug. 1894, Cleveland Papers, Library of Congress. For recommendations about the panic, see Cleveland's special message of 8 Aug. 1893, and his third annual message, 2 Dec. 1895. For his first-term views, see his annual messages for 1885, 1886, 1887, 1888, *Messages and Papers,* 9: 401–5, 640–41; 8: 339–41, 508–11, 580–91, 774–76. McCormick, *China Market,* p. 27, says that Wells, who believed in the overproduction theory, influenced Cleveland's thinking on the subject. He cites no proof. Terrill, "David A. Wells," p. 554, says Wells had little influence over Cleveland. Wells's influence, little or much, came during the first term, when, if LaFeber is correct, the president had not yet subscribed to the overproduction theory.

19. *Philadelphia Evening Telegraph,* 20 June 1894; Mrs. E. S. Cameron to Olney (undated), vol. 81, OP,LC.

20. Address, Philadelphia Commercial Museum, 2 June 1897, copy, OP,LC. Later articles, calling for an end to isolation, more commerce, and increased activity in world affairs, include: "International Isolation of the United States," *Atlantic Monthly,* 81 (May 1898): 577–88, and "Growth of Our Foreign Policy," ibid., 85 (Mar. 1900): 289–301.

21. Address, Philadelphia Commercial Museum, 2 June 1897, copy, OP,LC. McCormick, *China Market,* pp. 62–63, describes Cleveland's views in essentially similar terms, but concludes that Cleveland was an "informal" expansionist—one who actively promoted economic expansion while opposing acquisition of colonies.

22. The terms are used by Williams in *The Tragedy of American Diplomacy,* and by McCormick in *China Market.*

23. For a full account of the affair, see William Adam Russ, Jr., *The Hawaiian Revolution (1893–1894)* (Selinsgrove, Pa., 1959). Merze Tate, *The United States and the Hawaiian Kingdom, a Political History* (New Haven & London, 1965), pp. 155–258, provides a brief but perceptive treatment of the role of the U.S. in the revolution.

24. Gresham to Blount, 11 Mar. 1893, quoted in Russ, *The Hawaiian Revolution,* p. 169; Tate, *The Hawaiian Kingdom,* p. 237.

25. Tate, *The Hawaiian Kingdom,* p. 238; Russ, *The Hawaiian Revolution,* pp. 245–49; Moore's memo of conversation with Gresham, 9 May 1894, Moore Papers.

26. Gresham, *W. Q. Gresham,* 2: 741, 755.

27. Gresham to John Overmeyer, 25 July 1894, Gresham Papers.

28. Olney to Gresham, 9 Oct. 1893, reprinted in Gresham, *W. Q. Gresham,* 2: 836–40, and James, *Olney,* pp. 212–16.

29. Olney to Agnes Olney Minot, 3 Dec. 1893, reprinted in James, *Olney,* pp. 217–20.

30. Gresham to Cleveland, 18 Oct. 1893, reprinted in Gresham, *W. Q. Gresham,* 2: 746–52.

31. Olney Memoir, reprinted in James, *Olney,* p. 200.

32. Gresham to Willis, 18 Oct. 1893, reprinted in Gresham, *W. Q. Gresham,* 2: 752–55.

33. The latter idea appears in Gresham to Cleveland, 18 Oct. 1893; Olney's draft of the president's special message, OP,LC; and in the president's message, *Messages and Papers,* 9: 471.

34. Willis to Gresham, 16 Nov. 1893, quoted in Russ, *The Hawaiian Revolution,* pp. 235–36. Tate, *The Hawaiian Kingdom,* p. 244, says that Willis must have misunderstood the queen because beheading was not practiced in Hawaii.

35. Quoted in Russ, *The Hawaiian Revolution,* p. 252.

36. *Message and Papers,* 9: 441.

37. Willis to Gresham, 9 Dec. 1893, Cleveland Papers, Library of Congress.

38. Russ, *The Hawaiian Revolution,* pp. 258, 266–67; Tate, *The Hawaiian Kingdom,* pp. 244–46.

39. Undated draft, Moore Papers. Olney's draft is in OP,LC. The two were carefully compared with Cleveland's final message, *Messages and Papers,* 9: 460–72. Gresham, *W. Q. Gresham,* 2: 763, implies that passages she quoted from Cleveland's message were inspired by her husband. Those passages, dealing with the morality of a great power in its relations with a small nation, appear verbatim in the Olney draft but not in the Gresham-Moore draft.

40. Olney draft, OP,LC, italics supplied.

41. *Messages and Papers,* 9: 472.

42. Tate, *The Hawaiian Kingdom,* pp. 251–58.

43. LaFeber, *The New Empire,* pp. 207–9.

12   A Heady Summer

1. Henry L. Bryan to Thomas F. Bayard, 13 Aug. 1895, Bayard Papers. Congress passed resolutions urging presidential action on Venezuela on 16 Feb., and on the Mora claim on 2 Mar. 1895. *Congressional Record,* Fifty-third Congress, Third Session, 27: 2297, 3219–20.

2. Fifty-second Congress, First Session, *Senate Executive Document 115; Foreign Relations of the United States 1894* (hereafter cited as *FRUS*), Appendix I, pp. 364–450; *FRUS, 1895,* pp. 1160–77; French Ensor Chadwick, *The Relations of the United States and Spain* (New York, 1909), pp. 423–25. Both John Bassett Moore and former Secretary of State John W. Foster regarded the Mora claim as fraudulent. As Moore wrote to Senator George Gray on 5 Jan. 1895 (Moore Papers), " . . . Mora declared his intention to become a citizen of the U.S. in 1859. He soon returned to Cuba & there he lived as a planter till 1869, when he came to the United States and was naturalized *nine days after the seizure of his property in Cuba.* . . . With a view to obtain the intervention of the U.S. in respect of an act committed against him before he was a citizen, and while he was living in Cuba as a Spanish subject, he obtained a certificate of naturalization by falsely representing to the court that he had complied with the requirement of our law touching a five years' residence in this country prior to his application for admission to citizenship. . . . " See also Foster to Moore, 20 July 1895, Moore Papers.

3. Olney to Taylor, 11 June 1895. Acting Secretary Edwin F. Uhl sent a similar instruction five days before. *FRUS, 1895,* pp. 1162–63.

4. Taylor to Olney, 20 June 1895, OP,LC (only partially published in *FRUS, 1895,* p. 1164).

5. Olney to de Lôme, 22 June, *FRUS, 1895,* pp. 1166–77; 16 July 1895, OP,LC.

6. *FRUS, 1895,* p. 1170.

7. Olney to de Lôme, "personal," 2 Aug. 1895, OP,LC.

8. *FRUS, 1895,* p. 1171; de Lôme to Olney, 4 Aug. 1895, OP,LC.

9. Copy, rough draft, Olney to de Lôme, 7 Mar. 1897, OP,LC.

10. Manuel Sanguily to Uhl, 22 July; A. A. Aguirre to Adee, 22 July; Adee to Olney (telegram and letter), 23 July; Adee to Olney, 24 July 1895, OP,LC.

11. Capt. B. J. Crowell, U.S. Navy, to Herbert, 25 July 1895, OP,LC.

12. Olney to Adee, 25 July 1895, OP,LC.

13. See *FRUS, 1895,* pp. 1232–1473, especially Olney to Cleveland, 19 Dec. 1895, pp. 1256–66.

14. Olney to Adee, 4 Aug. 1895, OP,LC. The ships originally were stationed in Turkish waters during Gresham's tenure. See *FRUS, 1895,* p. 1248.

15. For accounts of the 1895 rioting, see Marilyn Blatt Young, *Rhetoric of Empire, American China Policy, 1895–1901* (Cambridge, Mass., 1968), pp. 76–87. McCormick's *China Market,* pp. 64–65, has a shorter account that is marred by a failure to keep events in order—a task made difficult because some correspondence between China and the United States went by steamer (requiring at least a month in transit) and some by cable.

16. Denby to Olney, 1 July (received 7 Aug.), *FRUS, 1895,* pp. 88–89; Denby to Uhl, 20 June 1895, OP,LC.

17. Adee to Olney, 1 Aug., OP,LC; Adee to Denby, 10 Aug. 1895, Diplomatic Instructions to China 5: 213–15 (hereafter cited as Instructions to China) General Records of the State Department, Record Group 59, National Archives (hereafter cited as RG 59 NA).

18. Olney to Faison, 20 July 1895, OP,LC.

19. Adee to Denby, 3 Aug.; Denby to Olney, 13 Aug.; Adee to Denby, 13 Aug., *FRUS, 1895,* pp. 98, 104. McCormick, *China Market,* pp. 64–65, wrongly accuses Adee of trying to "play it safe" by "latch[ing] onto the tail of the British kite," as if the idea of the joint commission were his rather than Denby's. See Adee to Denby, 12 Aug., Instructions to China 5: 215–16.

20. Denby to Olney, 15 Aug. (received 26 Sept.) 1895, *FRUS, 1895,* pp. 108–9.

21. Denby to Olney, 28, 31 Aug.; Adee to Denby, 4, 6 Sept.; Denby to Tsungli yamen, 28 Aug. 1895, *FRUS, 1895,* pp. 121–22, 125–27.

22. *FRUS, 1895,* pp. 119–45; Olney to Denby, 20 Sept. 1895, Instructions to China 5: 247–48.

23. Olney to Denby, 19 Sept. 1895, Instructions to China 5: 243–47. An abbreviated version appears in *FRUS, 1895,* pp. 138–39.

24. Denby to Olney, 27, 28, 30 Sept., *FRUS, 1895,* pp. 145–50. For the commission's work, see pp. 156–57, 172; *FRUS, 1896,* pp. 47, 52.

25. Denby to Olney, 21 Sept. (received 8 Oct.), 24 Sept. (received 8 Nov.), *FRUS, 1895,* pp. 144–45.

26. Olney to Denby, 10 Oct. See also Olney to Denby, 21 Sept., *FRUS, 1895,* pp. 141–43, 157–58.

27. Olney to Denby, 2 Oct. (enclosing Commander's letter of 27 Aug.), Instruc-

tions to China 5: 259–60; Denby to Olney, 14 Nov. 1895, Dispatches from China, 100, RG 59 NA.

28. J. Walter Blandford to Olney, 23 Aug. 1895, OP,LC; James, *Olney,* p. 172.

29. *Messages and Papers,* 9: 627–28, 632, 637–38.

30. John A. S. Grenville and George Berkeley Young, *Politics, Strategy and American Diplomacy, Studies in Foreign Policy, 1873–1917* (New Haven and London, 1966), pp. 125–57.

31. Cleveland to Bayard, 13 Feb. 1895, *Cleveland Letters,* pp. 376–78.

32. John A. Garraty, *Henry Cabot Lodge, A Biography* (New York, 1953), pp. 156, 163, says the article was a "conscious piece of propaganda, planned as Lodge himself admitted, 'to pave the way for a stiff declaration of the Monroe Doctrine by the next Congress.'" See also Lodge to Henry White, 5 June 1895, in Allan Nevins, *Henry White, Thirty Years of American Diplomacy* (New York and London, 1930), pp. 107–8.

33. John E. Russell to Thomas F. Bayard, 8 Dec. 1895, wrote: "I am afraid this jingo Congress will get us into ~~war~~ trouble with Grt. Britain ~~if possible~~. . . . Poor Sec. Gresham told me last summer that he was in great dread of this Congress." Bayard Papers. Postmaster General Wilson noted in his diary on 3 Jan. 1896, "The Venezuelan matter has dwarfed . . . all other and lesser foreign questions on which the Republicans were getting ready to attack the administration for its 'weak and un-American' foreign policy. . . ." *Wilson's Cabinet Diary,* pp. 4–5. For the senators, see *New York Tribune,* 31 Mar. 1895. On 3 May, Pauncefote reported, "It is a remarkable feature of political life in this country that a person in the responsible position of a Senator, & Chairman of the Committee of the Senate on Foreign Relations, should be so entirely oblivious of the restraints usually imposed on an official position, as to indulge publicly in abusive language against a friendly country." Microfilm copy, British Embassy Records, Washington, Public Records Office, Foreign Office 115 (hereafter cited as Br. Emb. Records), 995: 116. On 11 May 1895, Bayard wrote Cleveland to complain of the "effusions of Senators Morgan and Stewart . . . two unrestrained and unscrupulous men." Cleveland Papers, Library of Congress.

34. Baynard to Geo. F. Parker, 25 May 1895; to Don M. Dickinson, 7 Sept. 1897, Bayard Papers; Gresham to Bayard, 4 June 1894, Instructions to the Ambassador to Great Britain (hereafter cited as Instructions to Gr. Br.) 30: 576, RG 59 NA.

35. Charles Callan Tansill, *The Foreign Policy of Thomas F. Bayard, 1885–1897* (New York, 1940), pp. 665–90; Dexter Perkins, *The Monroe Doctrine, 1867–1907* (Baltimore, 1937), pp. 40–44; LaFeber, *The New Empire,* pp. 218–19.

36. Moore to Tansill, 29 July 1939, quoted in Tansill, *Bayard,* p. 708; Nevins, *Grover Cleveland,* p. 631. See Bayard to Gresham, 5 Apr. 1895, enclosing British reply of 20 Feb. and memos of conversations on 28 Jan. and 20 Feb. 1895, Dispatches from the Ambassador to Great Britain (hereafter cited as Dispatches from Gr. Br.) 179: 404, RG 59 NA.

37. Olney gave Richard H. Dana this view of the president's thinking. See Dana to Olney, 23 Dec. 1909. Gresham told Moore that he was "anxious as to the future." If Britain occupied Nicaragua, he feared Congress would declare war when it next met. He also cited Secretary of State Seward, who had said that the United States under the Monroe Doctrine could not allow a Euro-

pean nation to acquire territory in the New World, "even as the result of a successful war." Memorandum, 23–24 Mar. 1895, Moore Papers.

38. Gresham to Bayard, 31 Mar. 1895, Bayard Papers.

39. Gresham to Moore, 11 Apr. 1895, Moore Papers. Bayard assured Gresham on 5 Apr. (Dispatches from Gr. Br. 179: 404) that Britain's intentions were good and castigated Venezuela for granting mining and land concessions in the disputed zone to United States citizens. Such conduct, he feared, would prevent the United States (the only American power that Europeans would trust as an arbiter of international disputes) from being asked to arbitrate the controversy. Moore sent Gresham histories of British Guiana by Rodman and Dalton, both British subjects. See Gresham to Moore, 11, 18 Apr.; Moore to Gray, 17 Nov. 1895, Moore Papers.

40. Acting Secretary of State Edwin Uhl to Don Jose Andrade, Venezuelan Minister to Washington, 25 May 1895, Notes to Venezuela, pp. 525 ff, RG 59 NA.

41. James, *Olney*, p. 103; diary entry, 9 June 1896, Hamlin Papers; Gresham, *W. Q. Gresham*, 2: 793–96; Moore to Gray, 17 Nov. 1895, Moore Papers.

42. Scruggs to Olney, 17 June 1895, OP,LC. I have determined Olney's preparations by comparing the note of 20 July with the sources mentioned. In several instances parallel ideas, paraphrased language, and direct quotations appear in the note.

43. For published documents on the dispute prior to 1895, see House of Commons, *Sessional Papers*, 97 (London, 1896); Fiftieth Congress, First Session, *Senate Executive Document 226* (Washington, 1888); *FRUS, 1894; FRUS, 1895*. For extensive secondary accounts, see Perkins, *The Monroe Doctrine*, pp. 43–64, 136–252; Tansill, *Bayard*, pp. 621–779.

44. Eduardo Calcano to Fish, 14 Nov. 1876, Fiftieth Congress, First Session, *Senate Executive Document 226*, pp. 3–4.

45. Evarts to Simon Camacho, 31 Jan. 1881, ibid., pp. 12–14; Alice Felt Tyler, *The Foreign Policy of James G. Blaine* (Minneapolis, 1927), pp. 86–88.

46. See for example, Frelinghuysen to Jehu Baker, 31 Jan. 1883; Bayard to E. J. Phelps, 30 Dec. 1886, Fiftieth Congress, First Session, *Senate Executive Document 226*, pp. 42–43, 67–68.

47. For example, see Frelinghuysen to Lowell, 7 July 1884; Baker to Frelinghuysen, 3 Jan. 1885; Bayard to Phelps, 30 Dec. 1886; Salisbury to Phelps, 22 Feb. 1887, ibid., pp. 47–48, 50, 67–68, 84.

48. Olney to A. Maurice Low, 20 Nov. 1899, OP,LC.

49. Cleveland, *Presidential Problems*, pp. 252–56. In particular Cleveland favored the United States acting as agent for Venezuela, pp. 258–59.

50. See Dana to Olney, 23 Dec.; Olney to Dana, 24 Dec. 1909, OP,LC.

51. Cleveland to Bayard, 29 Dec. 1895, *Cleveland Letters*, pp. 417–20.

52. For the note, see *FRUS, 1895*, pp. 545–62. In discussing the various British lines, Olney seems to have relied heavily on Scruggs's pamphlet. Compare *FRUS, 1895*, pp. 546–47, with Scruggs, *British Aggressions in Venezuela, or The Monroe Doctrine on Trial* (Atlanta, 1895), pp. 15–23.

53. *FRUS, 1895*, pp. 553–54. Scruggs, *British Aggressions*, p. 12, traced the principles of the Monroe Doctrine back to the Declaration of Independence, and said that they were "clearly foreshadowed" in Washington's Farewell Address.

54. *FRUS, 1895*, pp. 554–55; Olney to Peter B. Olney, 27 Dec. 1904, OP,LC.

55. Later (*FRUS, 1895*, p. 559), Olney used Scruggs's precise term, "American Public Law." See Scruggs, *British Aggressions*, p. 5.

56. *FRUS, 1895*, p. 555. Compare with Scruggs, *British Aggressions*, p. 14.

57. *FRUS, 1895*, pp. 555–56. Scruggs, *British Aggressions*, p. 29, credits the doctrine with "preservation of the sovereignty and territorial integrity of our sister Republics of the South."

58. *FRUS, 1895*, p. 556. President Grant in his annual message of 5 Dec. 1870, (*Messages and Papers*, 7: 99) said essentially the same thing: "the time is not probably far distant when, in the natural course of events, the European political connection with this continent will cease."

59. *FRUS, 1895*, p. 557. This statement is a paraphrase of what George W. Carter, U.S. minister at Caracas, told the president of Venezuela in 1881: "the Government and people of the United States, because of the geographical proximity of the two republics and similarity of political institutions and for commercial considerations also, entertained a sincere interest in the fortunes and success of Venezuela, and could not be indifferent to any transaction that might seriously threaten the integrity of her soil or the permanency of her free institutions, or that might materially cripple her growth or injure her prosperity." Secretary of State Frelinghuysen subsequently endorsed this statement as the correct expression of the views of the U.S. government. Fiftieth Congress, First Session, *Senate Executive Document 226*, pp. 15–17.

60. *FRUS, 1895*, pp. 557–59. Compare with Scruggs, *British Aggressions*, pp. 23–24.

61. *FRUS, 1895*, pp. 559–62.

62. For this interpretation I am indebted to Grenville and Young, *American Diplomacy*, pp. 165–66.

63. James, *Olney*, pp. 109–10 (based on testimony of Olney's daughter); report of conversation with Olney one year after the event, diary entry, 9 June 1896, Hamlin Papers.

64. Cleveland to Olney, 7 July, Cleveland Papers, Library of Congress; Olney to Agnes Minot, 10 July 1895, OP,LC.

65. Olney to Herbert, 13, 18 Apr.; Herbert to Olney, 17 Apr. 1912; Harmon to James, 17 May 1922, OP,LC.

66. Books received by Olney from the State Department library on 20 July 1895, may have indicated his new concerns and optimism about Venezuela. Two were on China, one was Max Nordau's *Degeneration*, and one was *Traite Theorique and Pratique de l'Arbitrage International*.

67. See, for example, Perkins, *The Monroe Doctrine*, pp. 147–48, 151–82; Nevins, *Grover Cleveland*, pp. 634–36; Tansill, *Bayard*, pp. 700–9.

68. Wm. H. Dunbar to Moore, 28 Feb. 1896, Moore Papers. For Bayard's and Moore's opinions of Olney, see their respective papers for Oct. 1895–Mar. 1896.

69. Nevins, *Grover Cleveland*, p. 635; Tansill, *Bayard*, p. 703.

70. Nevins, *Grover Cleveland*, p. 639; Merrill, *Bourbon Leader*, p. 202.

71. At least two scholars, Nevins, *Grover Cleveland*, p. 634, and Tansill, *Bayard*, p. 703, attribute Cleveland's acceptance of the note to his preoccupation over the birth of a daughter. Tansill speculates that "Perhaps his fatherly pride

strengthened the President's resolve to take a firm stand . . . [and] he gurgled his approval" of Olney's note.

72. Olney to E. A. Keet, Editor, *Forum*, 15 Jan. 1897, OP,LC.

73. Olney to P. B. Olney, 27 Dec. 1904, OP,LC; "The Development of International Law," *American Journal of International Law*, 1 (Apr. 1907): 423–24.

74. Olney to Hoke Smith, 15 Jan. 1912, OP,LC.

75. Grenville and Young, *American Diplomacy*, p. 166.

76. See A. E. Campbell, *Great Britain and the United States, 1895–1903* (Glasgow, 1960), p. 12.

77. Both Perkins and Tansill suggest these positions in their accounts.

78. Editorial, *London Times*, 17 Oct. 1895: "Each year adds to the value of the settlement that is taking place in the British colony, and thus, while no change takes place in the claim put forward upon historical grounds by British Governments, change is necessarily taking place in the compromise which it might be possible to accept. . . . Terms which Lord Aberdeen would have accepted in 1844 had become impossible in 1850. The agreement of 1850 was insufficient in 1880, and in 1886 it was found necessary to proclaim the absolute right of Great Britain to all territories lying within the Schomburgk line. . . . A few years hence it may be equally impossible to admit such a question anywhere within the limits which we believe to be ours of right. . . . "

79. Olney to A. Maurice Low, 20 Nov. 1899, OP,LC.

80. Olney to Sec. of State Philander C. Knox, 29 Jan. 1912, OP,LC.

13 Crisis and Detente

1. Bayard to Olney, 9 Aug. (received 19 Aug.) 1895, in James, *Olney*, pp. 222–26. See also Adee to Olney, 14 Aug. 1895, OP,LC.

2. Salisbury to Viscount Gough, 7 Aug. 1895, *Correspondence Respecting the Question of the Boundary of British Guiana* (London, 1896), p. 21.

3. Bayard to Olney, 23 Oct. 1895, with enclosures, Dispatches from Gr. Br. 181: 523, RG 59 NA.

4. Edward Wingfield (for Chamberlain) to Foreign Office, 30 Aug. 1895, Br. Emb. Records, 1018: 280.

5. Quoted in J. A. S. Grenville, *Lord Salisbury and Foreign Policy, The Close of the Nineteenth Century* (London, 1964), pp. 62–63.

6. Chamberlain to Sir C. Lees, 7 Sept. 1895, Br. Emb. Records, 1018: 294. Bayard sent clippings from the *St. James Gazette* ("a 'Jingo' paper"), and the *London Times*, 18 Oct. 1895, dealing with the ultimatum.

7. Campbell, *Great Britain and the United States*, p. 15, cites Salisbury's daughter. See Tansill, *Bayard*, pp. 714–15. Grenville and Young, *American Diplomacy*, pp. 166–67, accuse Bayard of deliberately delaying the response for his own purposes. Ernest R. May, *Imperial Democracy, The Emergence of America as a Great Power* (New York, 1961), pp. 43–46, discusses how very little U.S. policy mattered to Salisbury and Chamberlain.

8. Grenville, *Lord Salisbury*, p. 62.

9. Olney to Adee, 13 Aug., OP,LC; Olney to Bayard, 8 Oct., Instructions to Gr. Br. 31: 262 ff; enclosures, Bayard to Olney, 15, 18 Oct. 1895, Dispatches from Gr. Br. 181: 520, 522.

10. Olney to Bayard, 16 Nov. 1895, OP,LC.

11. Bayard to Olney, 18 Nov., OP,LC; Olney to Bayard, 20 Nov. 1895, in James, *Olney*, p. 226.

12. Bayard to Olney, 15 Oct., Dispatches from Gr. Br. 181: 250; 20, 22, 23, 26 Nov. 1895, OP,LC.

13. Italics supplied. Cleveland to Olney, 3 Dec. 1895, OP,LC. Cleveland was due back on 13 Dec. but did not arrive until 15 Dec. Diary entry, 11 July 1896, Hamlin Papers.

14. Salisbury to Pauncefote, 26 Nov. 1895 (two dispatches), *FRUS, 1895*, pp. 563–76. Theodore Clarke Smith, "Secretary Olney's Real Credit in the Venezuela Affair," *Proceedings of the Massachusetts Historical Society*, 65 (May 1933): 120, noted that Salisbury and Olney were very close on one point: namely, that without regard for the Monroe Doctrine, the U.S. had the right to intervene in the Venezuelan dispute if it believed its interests were involved.

15. James, *Olney*, p. 227.

16. Italics supplied. Several drafts of Olney's proposed message have been preserved in OP,LC. I have used the earliest typewritten version. Few changes were made by Olney in subsequent drafts. For the idea that Olney was temporizing, see Grenville and Young, *American Diplomacy*, p. 167.

17. Extract, Bayard to Cleveland, 4 Dec. 1895, OP,LC.

18. *Messages and Papers*, 9: 656–58.

19. Again I am indebted to Grenville and Young, *American Diplomacy*, pp. 167–68. An interview with Cleveland supporting this line of reasoning appeared in the *Boston Evening Transcript*, 8 Sept. 1908, shortly after Cleveland's death. The interviewer remarked that the message of 17 Dec. could have led to war:

> "No," said Mr. Cleveland. "The message prevented war. England had been placed in an awkward position by the carelessness of Lord Salisbury and the ignorant obstinacy of 'permanent officials' who advised him. On our side there was a strong group of men in Congress who were bent on making trouble for my Administration, but didn't wish for war. The people of neither country thought seriously about the difference over the Schomburgk line, but there were elements of great danger in allowing the British Government officials and our Congress to nag each other to a point beyond forbearance. My message took the issue out of the hands of the politicians and laid it before the people of the two countries. The anti-Administration forces in Congress were compelled by public opinion, now that the contention became really warlike, to leave the whole matter to me for settlement. I didn't want war, but I was sure it wouldn't come. The English people promptly warned their Government that they would not fight for the preservation of a very doubtful title when the means of settling the question by arbitration were freely offered. And that was the end of it. We riveted international acceptance of the Monroe Doctrine, and I had no more trouble with the jingoes."
>
> "Did you or Secretary Olney write the message?" I asked. It had been reported that the Secretary of State was the author.

"Olney?" exclaimed Mr. Cleveland, with great indignation, slamming the table with his hand. "Olney had no more to do with it than you had. I wrote every line of it myself; and Olney never saw it until I showed it to him in its complete form, just as it went to Congress. It was the best thing I ever did."

Robert L. O'Brien, editor, *Boston Herald,* sent Olney a copy of the interview for his comment. Olney said that the account erred with regard to his role, but he raised no other objections. Olney to O'Brien, 10 Sept. 1908, OP,LC.

20. Cleveland to Bayard, 29 Dec. 1895, *Cleveland Letters,* pp. 418–19. Despite Cleveland's disclaimer, that he discussed the point in such detail argues that it probably was a factor.

21. Quoted in Grenville, *Lord Salisbury,* p. 67.

22. Butler to Olney, 18 Dec. 1895, OP,LC. For a general account of public reaction, see May, *Imperial Democracy,* pp. 56–59.

23. Roosevelt to Wm. Sheffield Cowles, 22 Dec. 1895, in Morison and Blum, eds. *Letters of Theodore Roosevelt,* 1: 501.

24. Joseph H. O'Neill to Olney; Charles D. Fullen to Olney, 18 Dec. 1895, OP,LC.

25. Quoted, Jennie A. Sloan, "Anglo-American Relations and the Venezuelan Boundary Dispute," *Hispanic American Historical Review,* 18 (1938): 499.

26. Walter LaFeber, "The American Business Community and Cleveland's Venezuelan Message," *Business History Review,* 34 (Winter 1960): 393–402.

27. Diary entry, 17 Dec. 1895, Hamlin Papers.

28. Moore Papers, passim, Dec. 1895; Hart to Hamlin, 9 Jan. 1896, Hamlin Papers; Perkins, *The Monroe Doctrine,* pp. 234–35; Tansill, *Bayard,* p. 727.

29. Angell to Moore, 25 Dec. 1895, Moore Papers.

30. Higginson to Olney, 20 Dec. 1895, OP,LC.

31. 21 Dec. 1895, Cleveland Papers, Library of Congress.

32. Peter B. Olney to Olney, 20 Dec. 1895, OP,LC.

33. Geo. F. Dominick to Lamont, 20 Dec.; James T. Woodward to Lamont, 24 Dec.; Carnegie to Lamont, 22 Dec. 1895, Lamont Papers.

34. Villard to Cleveland, 21 Dec. 1895, Cleveland Papers, Library of Congress.

35. Olney to Foster, 23 Dec. 1895, OP,LC. LaFeber, *The New Empire,* pp. 273–74, whose thesis is that the business community supported imperialism, rejects the war scare as the cause of the panic.

36. *Congressional Record,* Fifty-fourth Congress, First Session, 28: 414; Butler to Olney, 29 Jan. 1896, OP,LC.

37. Cleveland, *Presidential Problems,* pp. 279–80.

38. Diary entries, 26–28 Dec. 1895, 5 Jan. 1896, Hamlin Papers.

39. For Olney-Norman conferences, see 1–8 Jan. 1896, OP,LC. For a detailed account of Olney's use of newspaper correspondents and others in carrying on informal negotiations, see Joseph J. Mathews, "Informal Diplomacy in the Venezuelan Crisis of 1896," *Mississippi Valley Historical Review,* 50 (Sept. 1963): 195–212.

40. *London Daily Chronicle,* 3 Jan. (dateline 2 Jan.) 1896. Olney had used

these quotations in his draft of the president's message but Cleveland had not used them. Why Olney concentrated on discrediting the Schomburgk line is not clear. In his second note of 26 Nov., Salisbury had said that Olney was right in characterizing the line as one of convenience and expediency. See *FRUS, 1895,* p. 570.

41. *London Daily Chronicle,* 4 Jan. (dateline 3 Jan.) 1896.

42. Ibid., 6 Jan. (dateline 5 Jan.) 1896.

43. Norman to Olney, 8 Jan. 1896, OP,LC.

44. *London Times,* 7 Jan.; Olney to Butler, 25 Jan. 1896, OP,LC.

45. Grenville, *Lord Salisbury,* pp. 66–67.

46. Minute of 6 Jan. 1896, quoted in Campbell, *Great Britain and the United States,* p. 17.

47. A. G. Gardiner, *The Life of Sir William Harcourt* (London, 1923), 2: 307.

48. Grenville, *Lord Salisbury,* pp. 68–69; May, *Imperial Democracy,* pp. 50–51.

49. *London Times,* 16 Jan. 1896.

50. Grenville, *Lord Salisbury,* pp. 67–68.

51. Samuel Bancroft, Jr. (quoting Bayard) to Moore, 11 Jan. 1896, Moore Papers.

52. Memorandum, 10 Jan. 1896, Bayard Papers, quoted in Tansill, *Bayard,* p. 733.

53. Wemyss Reid, *Memoirs and Correspondence of Lord Playfair* (London, 1899), pp. 417–20; Playfair to Bayard, private, 13 Jan., Bayard Papers; Bayard to Olney, 13, 16 Jan. 1896, reprinted in James, *Olney,* pp. 227–32.

54. Olney to Bayard, 14 Jan. 1896, in James, *Olney,* p. 229. For European views on Olney's stand on the Monroe Doctrine, see Campbell, *Great Britain and the United States,* pp. 31–33.

55. Olney to Bayard, 14 Jan. 1896, in James, *Olney,* p. 229.

56. Olney-Bayard correspondence, 15–18 Jan. 1896, OP,LC.

57. Chamberlain to Playfair, 19 Jan., in Reid, *Playfair,* pp. 419–20; Bayard to Olney, 30 Jan. 1896, in James, *Olney,* pp. 232–33. Smith, "Secretary Olney's Real Credit," p. 126, quotes Salisbury as saying in Parliament that although it was "quite unnecessary" for the U.S. to raise the Monroe Doctrine in the controversy, "it was no more unnatural that the United States should take an interest in it than that we should feel an interest in Belgium."

58. Bayard to Olney; Olney to Bayard, 22 Jan. 1896, in James, *Olney,* pp. 233–34.

59. Chamberlain to Playfair, 23 Jan. 1896, in Reid, *Playfair,* p. 420. After considerable controversy between Olney and Bayard over the point of what the ambassador told Playfair, Bayard noted in an undated memo, "The fact is *an idea of exclusion* was *not* rejected by Mr. Olney—who in reply asked for a definition of '*settlements*' . . . ", Bayard Papers.

60. Bayard to Olney, 29 Jan. 1896, OP,LC.

61. Roosevelt to Olney, 23, 28 Jan., 7 Feb. 1896, OP,LC. For Olney's effort to have Bayard recalled, see diary entry, 9 June 1896, Hamlin Papers.

62. Mathews, "Informal Diplomacy," pp. 200–209; Smalley, *Anglo-American Memories,* pp. 75–79; Smalley to Olney, 22 Jan. 1896, OP,LC; *London Times,* 22 Jan. (dateline 21 Jan.) 1896.

63. For the content of the original proposal as sent by Smalley, I am indebted

to J. J. Mathews, who found copies in the Salisbury and Chamberlain papers. Mathews to Eggert, 29 July 1961.

64. Smalley-Buckle and Smalley-Olney correspondence, 27 Jan.–5 Feb., OP,LC. Smalley offered to tell Buckle "that there was no afterthought but only a correction of a misunderstanding."

65. Buckle to Smalley, 7 Feb.; Smalley to Olney, 7 Feb. 1896, OP,LC.

66. Olney to Bayard, 8 Feb., in James, *Olney*, pp. 235–36; Chamberlain to Playfair, 1 Feb.; Bayard to Playfair, 23 Feb., Bayard Papers; Chamberlain to Playfair, 25 Feb. 1896, in Reid, *Playfair*, pp. 423–25.

67. Olney to Bayard, 11, 13 Feb., OP,LC; Bayard to Olney, 12, 15 Feb., Dispatches from Gr. Br. 183: 602, 605; Salisbury to Pauncefote, 17, 19 Feb. 1896, Br. Emb. Records, 1032: 19, 23.

68. Smalley to Olney, 26 Feb., OP,LC; Bayard to Salisbury and Salisbury to Bayard, 27 Feb. 1896, Br. Emb. Records, 1032: 24.

69. Roosevelt to Olney, 28 Feb. 1896, OP,LC.

70. Olney to Bayard, 6, 23 Mar.; Roosevelt to Olney, 24 Mar. 1896, OP,LC.

71. Bayard to Olney, 24 Mar.; Olney to Bayard, 25 Mar.; Roosevelt to Olney, 27 Mar. 1896, OP,LC.

14 *Arbitration*

1. "Paraphrase copy," secret telegrams Nos. 17, 18, Pauncefote to Salisbury, 1 Mar.; Salisbury to Pauncefote, 3 Mar. 1896, Br. Emb. Records 1033: 20, 22; 1032: 33. See also Salisbury to Bayard, 3 Mar. 1896, Bayard Papers.

2. Salisbury to Pauncefote, 5 Mar. 1896, *FRUS, 1896*, pp. 222–24.

3. Olney to Hoke Smith, 14 Feb. 1912; Olney to Cleveland, 19 Mar. 1896, OP,LC.

4. Olney to Pauncefote, 21 Mar. 1896, OP,LC.

5. Pauncefote to Salisbury, 2 Apr. 1896, Br. Emb. Records, 1024: 147.

6. Olney to Pauncefote, 11 Apr. 1896, *FRUS, 1896*, pp. 224–28. The three neutral judges were to offset Salisbury's objection to a single foreign jurist. Olney to Cleveland, 19 Mar. 1896, OP,LC.

7. Salisbury to Pauncefote, 18 May; Olney to Pauncefote, 22 June 1896, *FRUS, 1896*, pp. 228–37.

8. Pauncefote to Salisbury, 2 June 1896; Gr. Br., *Correspondence Respecting the Question of the Boundary of British Guiana* (London, 1896); "substance of telegram," Salisbury to Pauncefote, 5 June 1896, OP,LC.

9. Pauncefote to Salisbury, 23 June, Br. Emb. Records, 1026: 31; Olney to Pauncefote, 12 June 1896, in James, *Olney*, pp. 271–72.

10. Olney to James Roosevelt, 6 Apr. 1898, OP,LC. Mathews, "Informal Diplomacy," pp. 201–4, quotes Sir Richard Webster, Attorney General of Great Britain, as telling Salisbury on 4 Mar. 1896 that defining settled districts would be difficult, "very dangerous," and imprudent.

11. Salisbury to Pauncefote, 22 May, Notes from Gr. Br., 126, RG 59 NA; Olney to Pauncefote, 12 June; Salisbury to Pauncefote, 3 July 1896, *FRUS, 1896*, pp. 249–53.

12. Olney to Cleveland, 11 July; Cleveland to Olney, 13 July 1896, OP,LC.

13. Olney to Pauncefote, 13 July 1896, *FRUS, 1896*, pp. 253–54. For Storrow's role, see Pauncefote to Salisbury, 15 July 1896, Br. Emb. Records, 1033: 83.

14. Olney to Cleveland, 16 July 1896, OP,LC. The omitted passages were from Salisbury to Pauncefote, 18 May, and Olney to Pauncefote, 22 June 1896, OP,LC. See also diary entry, 19 July 1896, Hamlin Papers.

15. Sir Henry Stafford Northcote to Salisbury, 16 Mar. 1896, quoted in Grenville, *Lord Salisbury*, p. 175.

16. Olney to Lewis Stackpole, 5 June 1897, OP,LC; *Boston Daily Advertiser*, 9 Jan.; Pauncefote to Salisbury, 24 Apr. 1896, Br. Emb. Records, 1024: 321.

17. Olney to Thomas, U.S. Minister, Caracas, 17 Mar., Venezuela, Instructions Book 4: 401, RG 59 NA; Storrow to Olney, 19 Mar. 1896, OP,LC.

18. Olney to Andrade, 25 June; Olney to Pauncefote, 29 June, OP,LC; Pauncefote to Salisbury, 30 June 1896, Br. Emb. Records, 1026: 76.

19. Andrade to Olney, 23 Sept. 1896, OP,LC.

20. Nevins, *Henry White*, pp. 96–118; White to Olney, 27 May, 13, 17 June; Olney to White, 30 June, 10 July 1896, OP,LC.

21. Hay to Olney, 31 July 1896, OP,LC, and in James, *Olney*, pp. 247–48.

22. Chamberlain to Olney, 3 Sept.; White to Olney, 17 July, 27 Aug., 7 Sept. 1896, OP,LC.

23. James, *Olney*, pp. 132–33; Chamberlain to Olney, 9 Sept. 1896, summarizing previous day's conversation, OP,LC.

24. Olney-Storrow correspondence, 12–17 Sept. 1896, OP,LC.

25. Chamberlain to Olney, 19 Sept. 1896, OP,LC. For Turkish situation, see Grenville, *Lord Salisbury*, pp. 74–78.

26. Cleveland to Olney, 24 Sept. 1896, OP,LC.

27. Olney to Chamberlain, 28 Sept. 1896, OP,LC.

28. Olney to Pauncefote, 26 Oct., OP,LC; Pauncefote to Salisbury, 27, 30 Oct. 1896, Br. Emb. Records, 1033: 104; 1027: 25.

29. Olney to Pauncefote (two letters), 29 Oct., OP,LC; Pauncefote to Salisbury, 29 Oct. 1896, Br. Emb. Records, 1033: 107.

30. Olney to Brewer, 10 Nov. 1896, OP,LC. "Olney is very much elated at the success of his Venezuelan negotiations and thinks he has scored a great success, which seems true. . . . " *Wilson's Cabinet Diary*, p. 168.

31. Olney to Charles H. Dalton, 23 Nov. 1903, OP,LC; Samuel Henry Jeyes, *Mr. Chamberlain, His Life and Public Career* (London, 1903), p. 385.

32. Among those interpreting the crisis as expanding the Monroe Doctrine are Perkins, *The Monroe Doctrine*, pp. 136–252; Tansill, *Bayard*, pp. 704–7; Campbell, *Great Britain and the United States*, pp. 43–46; and George Berkeley Young, "Intervention under the Monroe Doctrine: The Olney Corollary," *Political Science Quarterly* 57: 247–80.

33. For example, former President Harrison wrote to John Hay, 22 Jan. 1900 (microfilmed Papers of Benjamin Harrison, reel 42): "What a corrupting thing the lust for gold is. . . . gold in Venezuela, gold in Alaska, and gold in South Africa seems to me to have submerged the British sense of justice."

34. The British embassy during the summer of 1895 sent clippings about concessions in the disputed territory to London from the *Washington Star*, 28 June, 1 Aug. 1895; *Boston Evening Transcript*, 28 June 1895. See also G. H. D.

Gossip, "England in Nicaragua and Venezuela from an American Point of View," *Fortnightly Review* 58 (Dec. 1895): 829–842; Gardiner, *Harcourt*, 2: 399. As noted, Bayard and Moore, among others, were concerned about the concessions.

35. LaFeber, *The New Empire*, pp. 197–283, especially pp. 199–203, 242–43, 255–59. See also Williams, *Contours of American History*, pp. 338–42.

36. U.S. Department of Commerce, *Historical Statistics of the United States* (Washington, 1957), pp. 550–53; U.S. Department of State, *Commercial Relations of the United States with Foreign Countries, 1902* (Washington, 1903), pp. 35–42; Werner Schlote, *British Overseas Trade from 1700 to the 1930s*, trans. W. O. Henderson and W. H. Chaloner (Oxford, 1952).

37. See above, p. 170.

38. For an especially rabid politician's view, see Democratic Congressman Thomas Paschal of Texas to Olney, 23 Oct. 1895, OP,LC.

39. For example, see *Nation*, 61 (19 Dec. 1895): 417; 61 (26 Dec. 1895): 455; draft letter, Moore to Bayard, 26 Nov. 1895, Moore Papers.

40. H. Whates, *The Third Salisbury Administration, 1895–1900* (Westminster, 1900), p. 65.

41. Perkins, *The Monroe Doctrine*, p. 147; Thomas A. Bailey, *A Diplomatic History of the American People*, 6th ed. (New York, 1958), p. 440.

42. For example, see Grenville and Young, *American Diplomacy*, pp. 158–66. Nevins, *Grover Cleveland*, May, *Imperial Democracy*, and Campbell, *Great Britain and the United States*, all assert that Cleveland was simply motivated by the desire to protect Venezuela, with little regard for politics. As indicated, I believe it was political stirring that first called Cleveland's attention to the problem.

43. Olney to Thomas, 12 Nov.; Storrow to Olney, 19 Nov.; Pauncefote to Olney, 12 Dec.; Olney to Storrow, 12 Dec. 1896, OP,LC.

44. "Paraphrase," Pauncefote to Salisbury, 28 Dec. 1896, Br. Emb. Records, 1033: 181.

45. Pauncefote to Salisbury, 29 Dec. 1896; 5, 7, 19 Jan. 1897, Brit. Emb. Records, 1033: 185; 1061: 4, 10, 22.

46. Olney to Cleveland, 19 May; Andrade to Olney, 22 Nov.; Olney to Andrade, 26 Nov.; Olney to Wm. H. H. Miller, 1 Dec. 1897, OP,LC.

47. Otto Schoenrich, "The Venezuela, British Guiana Boundary Dispute," *American Journal of International Law*, 43 (July 1949): 525–26; Clifton J. Child, "The Venezuela-British Guiana Boundary Arbitration of 1899," *American Journal of International Law*, 44 (Oct. 1950): 690–92.

48. Tansill, *Bayard*, p. 776; Bailey, *Diplomatic History*, p. 447; John H. Latané, *A History of American Foreign Policy* (New York, 1927), p. 488.

49. Sworn memorandum, in Schoenrich, "Boundary Dispute," pp. 528–29. In addition to what he witnessed, Mallet-Prevost speculated that the British arranged a deal with Martens during a break in the proceedings when Martens went to London. The circumstantial evidence cited by Mallet-Prevost regarding the sell-out is not convincing and Child, "Boundary Arbitration," pp. 682–93, effectively refutes most of it. The editorial comments on Child's article by William Cullen Dennis, pp. 720–27, give an excellent interpretation both of the charges and of Child's critique. Dennis states that in 1910 Mallet-Prevost told him the same story about Martens's role in settling the award, but did not mention

his suspicions of an Anglo-Russian deal. Dennis concluded from conversations with a British participant at Paris that Martens had also pressured the British into accepting the compromise line.

50. Olney to Cleveland, 27 Dec. 1899, Cleveland Papers, Library of Congress; 6 Mar. 1901, OP,LC.

51. Harrison to Miller, 7 Oct. 1899. See also Harrison to Miller, 28 Sept. 1899; Harrison to Wm. E. Dodge, 15 Jan. 1900, Microfilmed Harrison Papers, reel 42.

52. Harrison to Dodge, 12 Dec. 1899, Microfilmed Harrison Papers, reel 42.

53. Harrison to Francis B. Loomis, U.S. Legation, Caracas, 22 Dec. 1899, Microfilmed Harrison Papers, reel 42.

54. "Suggestions for General Arbitration Message—January 1897," OP,LC.

55. Olney to Cleveland, 17 July; Henry White to Olney, 29 Aug. 1896, OP,LC.

56. Olney to Pauncefote, 22 June, *FRUS, 1896*, pp. 232–37; Pauncefote to Salisbury, 17 Nov. 1896, Br. Emb. Records, 1027: 97 ff.

57. Salisbury to Pauncefote, 18 May 1896, *FRUS, 1896*, pp. 228–31.

58. For text of treaty, see *FRUS, 1896*, pp. 238–40.

59. "Suggestion for General Arbitration Message—January 1897," OP,LC.

60. Olney to Geo. F. Edmunds, 18 Jan. 1897, enclosing memo which Edmunds used almost unchanged as an article under his own name, "The Arbitration Treaty," *Independent*, 49 (4 Feb. 1897): 137.

61. Olney to Henry Loomis Nelson, editor, *Harper's Weekly*, 11 Feb. 1897, OP,LC. James, *Olney*, p. 150, said that Cleveland and Olney did "almost nothing to enlighten the public mind and to enlist popular backing" for the treaty. For a different view, see May, *Imperial Democracy*, pp. 63–65.

62. Olney to White, 8 May, 8 Oct. 1897, OP,LC; James, *Olney*, pp. 149–50; May, *Imperial Democracy*, pp. 64–65. White, in a far-fetched argument, blamed Bayard for the treaty's defeat. See White to Olney, 22 May 1897, OP,LC.

63. Olney to W. W. Rockhill, 18 May 1897. See also Olney to Wm. E. Dodge, 28 May 1897, OP,LC. Olney opposed a general arbitration treaty in 1911 because he questioned the constitutionality of the machinery it established. See "The New Arbitration Treaty with Great Britain," *Independent*, 61 (21 Sept. 1911): 622–24. The best summary of Olney's views on arbitration is "General Arbitration Treaties," *American Journal of International Law*, 6 (July 1912): 595 ff.

64. Campbell, *Great Britain and the United States*, pp. 3–10; Grenville, *Lord Salisbury*, p. 73; Nevins, *Grover Cleveland*, pp. 646–48. May, *Imperial Democracy*, p. 267, put it very well: "In effect, Cleveland and Olney startled England and the United States into one another's arms." May doubted it was intentional.

65. Olney to Low, 20 Nov. 1899, OP,LC.

66. Tyler Dennett, *John Hay, from Poetry to Politics* (New York, 1933), p. 181.

15   Cuba and China

1. For brief accounts of U.S. policy towards Cuba, 1895–97, see Grenville and Young, *American Diplomacy*, pp. 179–200; LaFeber, *The New Empire*, pp.

285–300; May, *Imperial Democracy*, pp. 69–111. For the *Allianca* incidence, see *FRUS, 1895*, pp. 1177–85; *New York Times, New York Tribune, Washington Post*, 17–24 Mar. 1895.

2. *FRUS, 1895*, p. 1195.

3. Olney to John P. Massey, 18 June 1895, OP,LC.

4. Edwin F. Atkins, *Sixty Years in Cuba* (Cambridge, 1926), p. 57.

5. Olney to Cleveland, 25 Sept. 1895, OP,LC. LaFeber, *The New Empire*, pp. 288–89, incorrectly ascribes Brooks's views to Olney. Olney was reporting the planter's views, not his own.

6. Cleveland to Olney, 29 Sept., 6, 9 Oct.; Olney to Cleveland, 8 Oct. 1895, OP,LC.

7. H. Drummond Wolff, Br. Amb., Madrid, to Salisbury, 19 Jan. 1896, Br. Emb. Records, 1018: 112. Copies of British diplomatic reports from Spain on Cuban affairs, which give a valuable perspective on what was happening, were routinely sent to Pauncefote.

8. *Congressional Record*, Fifty-fourth Congress, First Session, 28: 24, 25, 219–3627 passim. Olney did have de Lôme provide the Senate with a statement of Spain's case. See Olney to Sherman, 11 Jan. 1896, OP,LC.

9. Adee to Olney, 14 Feb. 1896, OP,LC. Adee's letter was prompted by questions raised by Atkins.

10. For Olney's views, see his various notes to Spain, communications with Cleveland, and President Grant's remarks on Cuba, *Messages and Papers*, 7: 336–40, which so influenced Olney that he read them at a cabinet meeting in February 1896. His views on the Monroe Doctrine will be developed below.

11. Olney to Cleveland, 21 Mar.; Brooks to Olney, 3 Apr. 1896, OP,LC.

12. Duke of Tetuan to de Lôme, 23 Mar. 1896, OP,LC.

13. Olney to de Lôme, 4 Apr. 1896 (not published in *FRUS*, until 1897, pp. 540–44). According to Grenville and Young, the letter—written 7 Apr.—was dated 4 Apr. so as not to appear to be in response to a resolution of Congress passed on 6 Apr. Grenville and Young are wrong about Congress adjourning after passage of the resolution. To the administration's regret, adjournment did not come until 11 June. Grenville and Young also overstate the case when they say that Olney's note proposed intervention in Cuba on Spain's behalf, if necessary, to restore peace.

14. De Lôme to Olney, 4 June 1896, *FRUS, 1897*, pp. 544–48.

15. For a fuller account of Lee's appointment and machinations, see Gerald G. Eggert, "Our Man in Havana: Fitzhugh Lee," *Hispanic American Historical Review*, 47 (Nov. 1967): 463–85.

16. Lee to Olney, 24 June 1896, OP,LC. Lee arrived in Cuba on 6 June.

17. Lee to Lamont, 21, 22 June 1896, Lamont Papers.

18. Olney to Lee, 29 June, OP,LC; Lee to Olney, 11 July 1896, microfilmed Dispatches from United States Consuls in Havana, 1783–1906, RG 59 NA (hereafter cited as Dispatches from Havana).

19. Nevins, *Grover Cleveland*, pp. 684, 689–700. For mention of Olney as a candidate, see diary entries, 3, 4, 10 Mar., 18 Apr. 1896, Hamlin Papers.

20. Nevins, *Grover Cleveland*, pp. 701–4.

21. Lee to Olney, 1 July; Lee to Rockhill (two cables), 3 July; Lee to Olney, 4 July 1896, Dispatches from Havana.

22. Lee to Olney, 8 July 1896, Dispatches from Havana.

23. Olney to Herbert, 14 July; Herbert to Olney, 15 July; Cleveland to Olney, 16 July; Olney to Lee, 15 July 1896, OP,LC.

24. Lee to Olney, 22 July 1896, OP,LC.

25. Olney to de Lôme, 18, 20 Apr.; de Lôme to Olney, 20, 22 Apr. 1896, OP,LC.

26. De Lôme to Olney, 11 May 1896, Cleveland Papers, Library of Congress.

27. Wolff to Salisbury, 4 July 1896, Br. Emb. Records, 1021: 170, reported that Spain would request a proclamation based on President Taylor's. See *Messages and Papers*, 5: 7–8.

28. Olney to Cleveland, 18 July 1896, OP,LC.

29. Hannis Taylor to Olney, 18 Aug. 1896, OP,LC.

30. May, *Imperial Democracy*, pp. 107–9; Wolff to Salisbury, 4 July 1896, Br. Emb. Records, 1020: 78.

31. Edmund John Monson, British Ambassador, Vienna, to Salisbury, 9 July 1896, stating the substance of Salisbury's views which he had just delivered to the Austrian government. Br. Emb. Records, 1020: 202.

32. Taylor to Olney, 11 Aug., OP,LC. Wolff to Salisbury, 14 Aug. 1896, Br. Emb. Records, 1020: 250, reported Taylor's comments to the diplomatic corps.

33. Olney to Walter Blandford, 29 May 1897, OP,LC.

34. Wolff to Salisbury, 14 Aug. 1896, Br. Emb. Records, 1020: 250.

35. Drafts dated 9 Nov. and after appear in OP,LC. *Messages and Papers*, 9: 716–22.

36. Draft, 9 Nov. 1896, OP,LC. LaFeber, *The New Empire*, p. 296, incorrectly asserts that Cleveland drafted the Cuban portions of the message and that Olney made corrections. The reverse was the case. Olney prepared various drafts that he and the president discussed. Corrections were made in Cleveland's hand.

37. OP,LC, vol. 65.

38. Grenville and Young, *American Diplomacy*, p. 198.

39. Olney to Clifton R. Breckinridge, U.S. Minister, Russia, 25 Jan.; Olney to Judson Harmon, 3 Nov. 1897, OP,LC.

40. Quoted in James, *Olney*, pp. 168–69.

41. Among those praising Olney were John Russell Young of the Union League of Philadelphia, Robert Bacon, New York financier, Lucius Tuttle, president of the Boston & Maine, and Henry Lee Higginson, Boston banker, 21–29 Dec. 1896, OP,LC.

42. Olney to Straw, 24 Dec. 1896, OP,LC.

43. Atkins to Olney, 16 Dec. 1896, OP,LC.

44. Stillman to Olney, 13 Jan. 1897, OP,LC.

45. Lee to Olney, 15 Jan., Dispatches from Havana; Olney to Lee, 18 Jan. 1897, OP,LC.

46. Olney to Lee, 21 Jan.; Lee to Olney, 27 Jan.; Olney to de Lôme, 30 Jan.; Stillman to Olney, 31 Jan. 1897, OP,LC.

47. Wolff to Salisbury, 20 Nov. 1896, Br. Emb. Records, 1021: 152.

48. Wolff to Salisbury, 14, 17, 21, 26 Jan. 1897, Br. Emb. Records, 1051: 60, 63, 77; 1060: 27, 29. The quotation is from the dispatch of 21 Jan.

49. Olney to Taylor, 22 Jan., Instructions to the Minister to Spain (hereafter cited as Instructions to Spain), 22: 276–77, RG 59 NA; Taylor to Olney, 26 Jan. 1897, OP,LC.

50. Olney to Taylor, 27 Jan. 1897, Instructions to Spain 22: 283.

51. Wolff to Salisbury, 27, 28, 30, 31 Jan. 1897, Br. Emb. Records, 1051: 122–29.

52. Wolff to Salisbury, 19 Feb. 1897, Br. Emb. Records, 1051: 174.

53. Lee to Olney, 9 Feb.; Lee to Rockhill, 13 Feb. 1897, Dispatches from Havana. See also James, *Olney*, p. 167.

54. Lee to Olney, 18 Feb., OP,LC; Stillman to Lee, 18 Feb.; Lee to Olney, 27 Feb. 1897, Cleveland Papers, Library of Congress.

55. De Lôme quoted, *New York Tribune*, 9 Feb.; Olney to Cleveland, 19 Feb. 1898, OP,LC.

56. Lee to Lamont, 3 Feb. 1897, Lamont Papers.

57. Lee to Rockhill, 15 Feb., Dispatches from Havana; Lee to Olney, 18 Feb., OP,LC; Lee to Rockhill (three cables), 18 Feb. 1897, italics added, Dispatches from Havana. For a fuller account, see Eggert, "Our Man in Havana," pp. 471–76.

58. Lee to Rockhill, 18 (two cables), 19 Feb., Dispatches from Havana; 19, 20 (one letter, two cables) Feb. 1897, Cleveland Papers, Library of Congress.

59. Copy, Olney to Lee, 21 Feb. 1897, Cleveland Papers, Library of Congress.

60. Lee to Olney, 22, 23, 24 (one cable, one letter), 25, 26 Feb. 1897, Dispatches from Havana.

61. Copy, Olney to Lee, 24 Feb. 1897, Cleveland Papers, Library of Congress.

62. Lee to Olney, 24 Feb. 1897, Dispatches from Havana.

63. Walter Millis, *The Martial Spirit* (New York, 1931), p. 72; Nevins, *Grover Cleveland*, p. 719.

64. Charles S. Campbell, *Special Business Interests and the Open Door Policy*, pp. 1–18; McCormick, *China Market*, pp. 21–52. David F. Healy, *US Expansionism, The Imperialist Urge in the 1890's* (Madison, 1970), gives insights into the complex motivation of government officials at the time. A thorough study of the degree to which government officials led rather than followed the business community in the quest for commercial expansion would be extremely useful. For recent accounts of Chinese-American relations, 1893–97, see Young, *Rhetoric of Empire*, especially pp. 1–92; McCormick, *China Market*, pp. 1–72; LaFeber, *The New Empire*, pp. 300–11.

65. Healy, *US Expansionism*, pp. 178–93, discusses Denby at length. See also Campbell, *Special Business Interests*, pp. 25–28; Young, *Rhetoric of Empire*, pp. 20–21, 31.

66. Young, *Rhetoric of Empire*, pp. 34–52. Bayard's instruction is quoted, Olney to Denby, 22 June 1895, Instructions to China 5: 200–201, RG 59 NA.

67. Young, *Rhetoric of Empire*, pp. 57–58.

68. Olney to Denby, 22 June 1895, Instructions to China 5: 200–1; Young, *Rhetoric of Empire*, p. 58, interpreted Olney's instruction as giving Denby discre-

tion to assist all but the extraordinary cases. See also McCormick, *China Market*, p. 58.

69. Denby to Olney, 25 Nov. 1895, OP,LC.

70. Denby to Olney, 25 Jan. 1896, Dispatches from China, 100.

71. Denby to Olney, 25 May 1896, Dispatches from China, 101.

72. *London Times*, 8 July–22 Aug. 1896.

73. *New York Times*, 16, 29 Aug. 1896. Many newspapers, particularly in cities visited by Li, editorialized on the commercial significance of the trip. See, for example, *New York Times*, 30 Aug. 1896. At the same time the papers reported in their news columns that Li was making no business transactions. Such business-oriented publications as the *Wall Street Journal* and the *New York Commercial & Financial Chronicle* took no notice of Li's visit.

74. Olney to Cleveland, 1, 7 July; Cleveland to Olney, 4 July 1896, Cleveland Papers, Library of Congress.

75. John J. McCook to Olney, 10 July; Olney to McCook, 17 July; McCook (by Alexander Green) to Olney, 17 July; Lamont to Olney, 7 Aug. 1896, OP,LC.

76. Cleveland to Lamont, 9 Aug. 1896, Cleveland Papers, Library of Congress.

77. McAdoo to Olney, 25 Aug., OP,LC; Olney to Cleveland, 26 Aug. 1896, Cleveland Papers, Library of Congress.

78. *New York Times*, 29, 30 Aug. 1896.

79. For a contrary interpretation, see McCormick, *China Market*, pp. 71–74.

80. *New York Times*, 31 Aug.–7 Sept. 1896; *Philadelphia Public Ledger*, 4 Sept. 1896.

81. Denby to Olney, 4, 21 Sept., 5 Nov. 1896, Dispatches from China, 101, 102.

82. Olney to Denby, 19 Dec. 1896, Instructions to China 5: 398–400.

83. Denby to Olney, 10 Jan. 1897, Dispatches from China, 102.

84. Sherman to Denby, 8 Mar. 1897, Instructions to China 5: 424.

85. Young, *Rhetoric of Empire*, pp. 65–68; William R. Braisted, "The United States and the American-China Development Company," *Far Eastern Quarterly*, 11 (Nov. 1951), 149 ff.

86. Olney to Denby, 27 Feb. 1897, Instructions to China 5: 421–23. For an earlier discussion of the same issue, see Denby to Olney, 3 Sept. 1896, Dispatches from China, 101, and Olney's response, 28 Oct. 1896, Instructions to China 5: 379.

87. Higginson to Olney, 3 Mar. 1897, OP,LC.

88. For example, Charles A. Beard, *The Idea of National Interest* (New York, 1934) and *The Open Door at Home* (New York, 1934); William Appleman Williams, *The Great Evasion* and *Contours of American History*; LaFeber, *The New Empire*; McCormick, *China Market*.

89. De Lôme to Olney, 6 Nov. 1897; Atkins to Olney, 4 Apr.; Higginson to Olney, 20 Apr. 1898, OP,LC.

90. Lee to Olney, 4 Apr.; Cameron to Olney, undated; Lodge to Olney, 3 May 1898, OP,LC.

16 Presidential Boomlet

1. Eliot to Olney, 21 Jan.; Olney to Eliot, 23 Jan. 1897, OP,LC.

2. For clients, see Straw to Greenough, 21 Aug. 1917, OP,MHS; Greenough, "Memoir of Richard Olney," *Proceedings of the Massachusetts Historical Society*, 51 (Dec. 1917): 204–5. For Olney's many other positions I used letters scattered throughout OP,LC.

3. Higginson to Olney, 3 Jan.; Olney to Higginson, 6 Jan. 1899, OP,LC.

4. Executor's Inventory of the Estate of Richard Olney, 22 Aug. 1917, Probate Records, Suffolk County Courthouse, Boston.

5. James, *Olney*, pp. 184–85.

6. Richard Abrams, *Conservatism in a Progressive Era* (Cambridge, Mass., 1964), pp. 136–37. For Olney's role, see typewritten copies, remarks before legislative committee, Mar. 1909, and address as chairman of the Committee of 150, 9 Nov. 1909; draft letters appealing for funds, 14 Dec. 1910; 21 Dec. 1911, OP,LC.

7. Unidentified newspaper clipping, 1 Nov. 1910, OP,LC.

8. James, *Olney*, p. 183.

9. Olney's extensive work for the Red Cross can be traced in his correspondence, 5 Feb. 1900–3 Dec. 1903. See also Olney to Boardman, 24 July 1912, OP,LC.

10. Olney to Cleveland, 9 Apr. 1897, OP,LC.

11. Olney to Cleveland, 6 Mar. 1898, OP,LC.

12. Typescript, Philadelphia speech, June 1897, OP,LC, "International Isolation of the United States," *Atlantic Monthly*, 81 (May 1898): 577–88; "Growth of Our Foreign Policy," *Atlantic Monthly*, 85 (Mar. 1900): 289–301.

13. *Atlantic Monthly*, 81: 579, 582.

14. Ibid., 580–81, 584.

15. Typescript, Philadelphia speech, pp. 3–4, OP,LC; *Atlantic Monthly*, 85: 299; 81: 584–85.

16. Typescript, Philadelphia speech, p. 6, OP,LC.

17. *Atlantic Monthly*, 81: 580; 85: 296, 299.

18. Ibid. 81: 587.

19. Typescript, Philadelphia speech, pp. 4–5, OP,LC.

20. *Atlantic Monthly*, 81: 587–88.

21. Ibid. 85: 300.

22. E. S. Cameron to Olney, undated [Apr. 1898]; Alice Lee to Olney, 4 Apr. 1898; Cleveland to Olney, 27 Mar. 1898, OP,LC.

23. Olney to Henry P. Fletcher, 17 May 1898, OP,LC.

24. Olney to Beatrice Chamberlain, 26 May 1898, OP,LC.

25. *Atlantic Monthly*, 85: 291.

26. Ibid., 291–95.

27. Ibid., 293.

28. Ibid., 296, 298.

29. Typescript, OP,LC.

30. Typewritten MSS.: "National Issues" (Nov. 1901; revised June 1902); "Advance Suggestions as to Democratic Issues" (24 Mar. 1902); "Colonial Policy of the United States" (16 May 1902); "Republican National Policies" (Nov.–Dec. 1902); "Some Aspects of National Politics" (June–July 1903, "slightly revised," Aug. 1904), OP,LC.

31. "Colonial Policy of the United States," pp. 2–5, OP,LC.

32. "The Nation's Parting of the Ways," *Harvard Graduates' Magazine*, Sept. 1904, pp. 48–51. Quotes from "Republican National Policies," pp. 9–13, OP,LC.

33. "Recent Phases of the Monroe Doctrine," memorandum sent to John H. Holmes for use in a *Boston Herald* editorial, 1 Mar. 1903, OP,LC.

34. Olney to Daniel, 16 Dec. 1903, OP,LC.

35. Olney to P. B. Olney, 11 Nov. 1903, OP,LC.

36. *Harvard Graduates' Magazine*, Sept. 1904, p. 51.

37. Typescript, remarks at dinner honoring Wu Ting Fang, the Chinese minister Boston, 23 Apr. 1908, OP,LC.

38. Clement A. Griscom, Jr. to Olney, 10, 19, 23 May 1898; Olney to Griscom, 16, 20, 25 May, 1 (telegram) June 1898, OP,LC.

39. Dickinson to Olney, undated, OP,LC.

40. Olney to Cleveland, 22 Mar. 1899, OP,LC.

41. Diary entries, 1–3 Apr. 1900, Hamlin Papers.

42. Olney to S. B. Griffin, 5 Feb. 1900, OP,LC, and in James, *Olney*, pp. 308–12.

43. Olney to Francis, 15 June; Olney to Henry Loomis Nelson, 14 Aug. 1900, OP,LC. The letter to Nelson was published, *New York World*, 6 Sept., and one million copies were printed and distributed as a campaign document.

44. Hay to A. A. Adee, 8 Sept. 1900, Hay Papers, Library of Congress.

45. Cleveland to Wilson S. Bissell, 16 Sept. 1900, Cleveland Papers, Library of Congress.

46. Smith to Olney, 10 Nov.; Olney to Smith, 19 Nov. 1900, OP,LC. See also Olney to R. B. Bowler, 1 July 1901, OP,LC.

47. Diary entry, 25 July 1902, Hamlin Papers.

48. Olney to Hamlin, 24 Oct. 1902; Olney to John W. Gaines, 3 Feb. 1903, OP,LC. See also Olney memorandum to John H. Holmes, in James, *Olney*, pp. 208–10.

49. Olney to Chas. Taylor, 15 Apr. 1903; Olney to C. W. Bunn, 10 May, 11 Apr. 1903, OP,LC. See also C. E. Perkins to James J. Hill, 20 June 1901, Perkins Papers, O-C.

50. Perkins to Hill, 6 May, Perkins Papers, O-C; Lamont to Olney, 28 Oct. 1903, OP,LC.

51. Olney to Lamont, 24 Oct. 1903; Olney to Lewis Cass Ledyard, 18 Jan. 1904; Stetson to Olney, 8 Dec.; Bunn to Olney, 28 Dec. 1903, OP,LC.

52. Ledyard to Olney, 5 Jan.; Olney to Ledyard, 18 Jan. 1904, OP,LC.

53. Taylor to Olney, 14 Apr.; Olney to Taylor, 15 Apr. 1903, OP,LC.

54. For example, see Olney to Henry F. Hallis, 3 July 1902; Olney to Bourke Cochran, 31 Dec. 1903; Olney to John H. Holmes, 31 July 1902; Olney to Holmes Conrad, 10 Jan. 1903, OP,LC.

55. Olney to M. B. Norfleet, 16 June 1902, OP,LC.

56. For position papers, see n. 30, above. The most important paper, which served as the basis for articles in 1906–1907, was "Republican National Policies," prepared in Nov.–Dec. 1902. For a discussion of portions that later appeared in article form, see chap. 17, below.

57. Olney to Roosevelt, 20 Apr. 1897, OP,LC.

58. Olney to Roosevelt, 20 Sept. 1901, OP,LC.

59. Olney to Cleveland, 14 Jan. 1902, OP,LC.

60. Olney to P. B. Olney, 5 May 1903, OP,LC.

61. Address, McClellan Dinner, printed in *Boston Herald*, 5 Jan. 1904.

62. For example, see C. E. Perkins to Hamlin, 2 Apr. 1904, Hamlin Papers.

63. James, *Olney*, pp. 177–78; diary entries, 9, 10 Jan. 1904, Hamlin Papers. For examples of support for Olney, see Perkins to W. W. Baldwin, 13 Feb. 1904, Perkins Papers, O-C; Baldwin to Lamont, 5 Feb. 1904, Lamont Papers; Chas. F. Adams to Hamlin, 1 Apr. 1904, Hamlin Papers.

64. Olney to Edward B. Whitney, 1 Apr., OP,LC; diary entry, 12 Apr. 1904, Hamlin Papers.

65. P. B. Olney to Olney, 14 Apr. 1904, OP,LC.

66. Olney to P. B. Olney, 15 Apr. 1904, OP,LC.

67. Diary entries, 16, 24 Apr. 1904, Hamlin Papers.

68. Olney to Collins, 24 May, OP,LC; diary entries, 6 June, 3 July 1904, Hamlin Papers.

69. *Chicago Tribune*, 9 July. See also *New York Tribune, New York Times*, 7–10 July 1904.

70. Olney to Parker, 13 July; Olney to Cleveland, 25 July, OP,LC. Olney spoke at Cooper Union and at Faneuil Hall in Oct. 1904.

71. Olney to Hugh C. Wallace, 15 June 1908, OP,LC.

72. Olney to Johnson, 5 Feb.; George Fred Williams to Olney, 3 Mar. 1908, OP,LC.

17 Reflections of an Elder Statesman

1. James, *Olney*, pp. 181–83.

2. Olney to "Mrs. O," 28 June 1896; Olney to Chester Guild, 18 Sept. 1907, OP,LC.

3. Olney to T. A. MacKinnon, 20 Sept.; MacKinnon to Olney, 28 Sept. 1898; Olney to New England Telephone Co., 6 Feb. 1899 and 27 Sept. 1901, OP,LC.

4. Straw to R. L. O'Brien, editor, *Boston Herald*, 13 Sept. 1916, OP,LC.

5. Interview with Francis Minot, Sr., 3 Jan. 1958.

6. Olney to Thomas Higgins, 5 Nov. 1906, OP,LC.

7. Olney to Flannery, 8 Apr. 1903; copy, letter press book 18: 82, OP,LC.

8. Interview with Francis Minot, 3 Jan. 1958. Minot's account, fifty-seven years after the event, agreed remarkably with the account in the *Boston Globe*, 18 Sept. 1901.

9. Olney to Horace S. Crowell, 19 Nov. 1901, OP,LC.

10. P. B. Olney to Olney, 24 Dec.; Olney to P. B. Olney, 27 Dec. 1904, OP,LC.

11. "The Development of International Law," *American Journal of International Law,* 1 (Apr. 1907): 423.

12. The argument here comes from typescript, "Views as to a Proposed Treaty with San Domingo," 24 Mar. 1905, OP,LC. Olney used ideas from these notes in his published articles "The Development of International Law" and "Our Latin American Policy."

13. "The Development of International Law," pp. 418–30.

14. Olney to Abbott, 11 Jan. 1915. See also Olney to editor, *Philadelphia Public Ledger,* 24 Feb.; Olney to Ellery Sedgwick, 17 Mar. 1914, OP,LC.

15. "Our Latin American Policy," *North American Review,* 203 (Feb. 1916): 185–193.

16. Olney, "A Tangible Goal," *Independent,* 80 (26 Oct. 1914): 126, in support of that magazine's proposal for an international "League of Peace."

17. "Modern Industrialism," *Inter-Nation,* Jan. 1907, pp. 29–42. Compare with typescript, "Republican National Policies," pp. 16–26, OP,LC.

18. Typescript, "Republican National Policies," pp. 37–38, OP,LC.

19. "National Judiciary and Big Business," *Boston Herald,* 24 Sept. 1911.

20. "Does the Court Exceed Its Power?" *Boston Herald,* 29 Oct. 1911.

21. Olney to McCall, 22 Dec. 1904, OP,LC.

22. Olney to Elkins, 30 Jan. 1902, OP,LC.

23. Olney to Lamont, 17 Dec. 1904, OP,LC.

24. Olney to Ledyard, 5, 7 July 1905, OP,LC. Quote from letter of 7 July.

25. "Some Legal Aspects of Railroad Rate-Making by Congress," *North American Review,* 181 (Oct. 1905): 481–501.

26. Roosevelt to John Allison, 10 Oct. 1905, Theodore Roosevelt Papers, Library of Congress.

27. Henry Lee Staples and Alpheus Thomas Mason, *The Fall of a Railroad Empire, Brandeis and the New Haven Merger Battle* (Syracuse, N.Y., 1947).

28. Olney wrote Howard Elliott, 25 Feb. 1914, that he represented, in trust and otherwise, 2,500 shares of New Haven Stock. OP,LC.

29. Olney to Wilson, 26 May 1914. See also House to Olney, 3 Aug.; W. N. Crane to Olney, 4, 6 Aug.; Olney to Samuel W. McCall, 29 Oct.; Olney to Ledyard, 2 Nov. 1914, OP,LC.

30. "Labor Unions and Politics," *Inter-Nation,* Dec. 1906, pp. 23–29.

31. "Paternalism and Personal Freedom," *Inter-Nation,* Jan. 1908, pp. 3–10.

32. "Modern Industrialism," *Inter-Nation,* Jan. 1907, p. 36.

33. "Discrimination Against Union Labor–Legal?" *American Law Review,* 42 (Mar.–Apr. 1908): 161–67.

34. *Address of Richard Olney Before Merchants Club Boston, 21 January 1913,* OP,LC.

35. Olney to Geo. H. Olney, 16 May 1907; to P. B. Olney, 19 Sept. 1910, OP,LC.

36. Olney to P. B. Olney, 6 Nov.; to Judson Harmon, 7 Nov. 1908; to Hugh

C. Wallace, 4 Dec. 1909; to Geo. H. Olney, 29 Jan.; to Hilary A. Herbert, 18 Apr.; to P. B. Olney, 2 May; and to Harmon, 3 May 1912; quote from Olney to Wallace, 30 June 1911, OP,LC.

37. Olney to Wilson, 3 July; to Henry Morganthau, 30 Aug. (enclosing $250); copy of speech, 27 Sept.; Olney to Robert L. O'Brien, 31 July; to Wilson, 8 Nov. 1912 and 5 Mar. 1913, OP,LC.

38. Olney to Lawrence, 6 Mar. 1913, OP,LC.

39. James, *Olney*, p. 192; Olney to Wilson, 13 Mar. 1913. See also Wilson to Olney, 8, 10 Mar.; Olney to Wilson, 10 Mar. 1913, OP,LC.

40. Olney to S. B. Griffin, 26 Mar. 1913, OP,LC.

41. Olney to Wilson, 4 Apr. 1914, OP,LC.

42. Wilson to Olney, 30 Apr.; Olney to Wilson, 4 May 1914, OP,LC.

43. Olney to George Harvey, 17 Oct. 1914, OP,LC.

44. I do not believe the evidence cited by James, *Olney*, pp. 194–95, or any that I found to support James's statement that Olney was "none too well satisfied with the country's course" during the neutrality period.

45. Straw to Agnes Minot, 4 May 1932, OP,LC. I was unable to find a copy of the draft in the Olney papers.

46. Olney to Alleyne Ireland, 21 Apr. 1916; Olney to *New York World*, 23 Jan. 1917, OP,LC.

47. Olney to Mrs. Grover Cleveland, 25 Jan.; to Joseph H. Choate, 16 Mar.; to Samuel A. Green, 20 Mar.; to P. B. Olney, 24 Mar.; and to Dr. J. D. Dickinson, 5 Apr. 1909, OP,LC.

48. Olney to P. B. Olney, 1 Jan.; to Robert L. O'Brien, 17 Jan.; to Bellamy Storer, 17 Jan.; to Lawrence, 26 Jan.; to P. B. Olney, 28 Feb.; to Nurse Brooker, 18 Mar.; and to Ledyard, 22 Apr. 1910, OP,LC.

49. Quoted in James, *Olney*, p. 196. See also correspondence, July 1916–Jan. 1917, OP,LC.

50. Olney to Theodore Vail, 1 Feb. 1917, OP,LC.

51. Olney to Arthur F. Estrabrook, 9 Mar. 1917, OP,LC.

52. Lawrence, *Memories of a Happy Life*, p. 383.

53. *Address of Richard Olney Before Merchants Club Boston, 21 January 1913*, pp. 22–23, OP,LC.

List of Sources

Abbreviations used in the notes are shown in italic type.

Primary Sources

Manuscript Materials

Thomas F. Bayard Papers. Library of Congress.
Grover Cleveland Papers.
  Burton Historical Collections. Detroit, Mich., Public Library.
  Library of Congress.
William E. Curtis Papers. Library of Congress.
William G. Dearth. "Praeterita: Journal of Acts and Thoughts, 1854–1855."
  Brown University Archives. John Hay Library, Providence.
Don M. Dickinson Papers.
  Library of Congress.
  Michigan Historical Collections. University of Michigan, Ann Arbor.
William C. Endicott Papers. Massachusetts Historical Society. Boston.
John Murray Forbes File. Burlington Archives. Newberry Library, Chicago.
Walter Q. Gresham Papers. Library of Congress.
Charles S. Hamlin Diary and Papers. Library of Congress.
Benjamin Harrison Papers. Library of Congress. Microfilm.
Albert R. Hatch Papers. New Hampshire Historical Society. Concord.
Henry Lee Higginson Collection. Baker Library. Harvard University. *Higginson*
  Collection.
Daniel S. Lamont Papers. Library of Congress.
John Bassett Moore Papers. Library of Congress.
J. Sterling Morton Papers. University of Nebraska Library, Lincoln.
Richard Olney (1770–1841) Papers. Antiquarian Society of America Library.
  Worcester, Mass. *ASA Library.*
Richard Olney Papers.
  Olney File, Burlington Archives. Newberry Library, Chicago.
  Library of Congress. *OP,LC.*
    Incomplete autobiographic memorandum dictated in Feb. 1901,
      covering the period when Olney was attorney general. *Olney Memoir.*

Massachusetts Historical Society. Boston. *OP,MHS.*
Probate Records. Suffolk County Courthouse. Boston.
  Executor's Inventory of the Estate of Richard Olney, 22 Aug. 1917.
  Last Will and Testament of Richard Olney.
Charles E. Perkins Papers.
  Perkins File, Burlington Archives, Newberry Library, Chicago.
  Overton-Cunningham Collection. Microfilm. Formerly in the possession of
    Richard C. Overton and now in Burlington Archives. *Perkins Papers, O-C.*
Joseph Pulitzer Papers. Library of Congress.
John McAllister Schofield Papers. Library of Congress.
William C. Whitney Papers. Library of Congress.

Brown University Archives. John Hay Library. Providence. *Brown Archives.*
  Junior and Senior Exhibition Programmes.
  Library Record Book, 1850–1854.
  Records of Admission, 1827–1856.
  Records of the Philermenian Society, 1842–1859.
  Student Records, Classes of 1848–1859.
Burlington Archives. Newberry Library. Chicago. *BA.*
  Statement of Amounts Charged to Boston Office Expenses, 1891–1903.
National Archives
  General Records of the Justice Department. Record Group 60. *RG 60 NA.*
    Incoming: Source Chronological.
    Outgoing Letter Books: Executive & Congressional. *E&C.* Instructions.
      Judges & Clerks. *J&C.* Miscellaneous.
  General Records of the Post Office Department. Record Group 28.
    Letters of the Postmaster General of the United States. *Letters PMG.*
  General Records of the State Department. Record Group 59. *RG 59 NA*
    Incoming, by country: Dispatches; Notes; Dispatches from Consuls.
    Outgoing Letter Books, by country: Instructions; Notes.
  Early Wars Branch.
    Record Group 94. Chicago Strikes File, Office of the Adjutant General.
    Army Chicago Strikes file.
    Record Group 108. Headquarters of the Army. *Army Headquarters, RG 108*
    NA.
  Labor and Transportation Branch. Record Group 31.
    Letters of the United States Strike Commission, 1894–1895. *Strike Comm.*
    Letters.
    Interstate Commerce Commission Records.
      Case 308. *Free Pass Case file.*
Public Records Office of Great Britain
  Foreign Office Records, 115. British Embassy Records, Washington, D.C. Micro-
    film. *Br. Emb. Records.*

Public Documents

Great Britain.

Correspondence Respecting the Question of the Boundary of British Guiana, London, 1896.

House of Commons. *Sessional Papers,* 97. London, 1896.

United States—States.

Illinois.

Governor John Peter Altgeld. *Biennial Message to the 39th General Assembly.* n.p., n.d.

Massachusetts.

Acts of the Massachusetts General Court, 1876. Boston, 1876.

Massachusetts Reports.

New Hampshire.

Annual Report of the Railroad Commissioners of the State of New Hampshire. 1888, 1889, 1890, 1895.

Proceedings and Testimony . . . in the Investigation of Charges of Bribery of Members of the Legislature. Concord, 1887.

United States—Federal.

A Compilation of the Messages and Papers of the Presidents, 1789–1897. Compiled by James D. Richardson. n.p., 1899. *Messages and Papers.*

Federal Cases.

Federal Reports.

Revised Statutes. Washington, D.C., 1875.

Statutes at Large of the United States of America. Vols. 24–28. Washington, D.C., 1887–95.

United States Reports.

Congress.

Biographical Directory of the American Congress, 1774–1949. Washington, D.C., 1950.

Congressional Record.

Fiftieth Congress, First Session. *Senate Executive Document 226.* " . . . Report of the Secretary of State, with Accompanying Correspondence, Relating to the . . . boundaries between British Guiana and Venezuela." Washington, D.C., 1888.

Fifty-second Congress, First Session. *Senate Executive Document 115.* " . . . Correspondence in Regard to the Claim of Antonio Maximo Mora . . . " Washington, D.C., 1892.

Fifty-third Congress, Second Session. *House Executive Document 194.* "Letter from the Attorney General . . . April 11, 1894." Washington, D.C., 1894.

Fifty-fourth Congress, Second Session. *Senate Document 187.* "Investigation of the Sale of Bonds during the Years 1894, 1895, and 1896." Washington, D.C., 1896.

Department of Commerce. *Historical Statistics of the United States.* Washington, D.C., 1957.

Department of Justice.
  Annual Report of the Attorney General of the United States. Washington,
    D.C., 1893, 1894, 1895, and 1896.
  *Appendix to the Annual Report of the Attorney General of the United
    States for the Year 1896.* [Official correspondence of the Chicago Strike,
    1894.] Washington, D.C., 1896. *Strike Correspondence.*
  Official Opinions of the Attorneys General of the United States. Washington,
    D.C., 1895.
  Register of the Department of Justice. Washington, D.C., 1895.
Department of State.
  Annual Report of the Secretary of State. Washington, D.C., 1896.
  Commercial Relations of the United States with Foreign Countries, 1902.
    Washington, D.C., 1903.
  Foreign Relations of the United States, 1893, 1894, 1895, 1896, 1897. FRUS.
Government Directors of the Union Pacific Railway. *Report to the Secretary
  of the Interior.* Washington, D.C., 1893.
Industrial Commission. *Report of the Industrial Commission on Transportation.*
  Vol. 9. Washington, D.C., 1901.
United States Strike Commission. *Report on the Chicago Strike of June–July,
  1894.* Washington, D.C., 1894. *Strike Comm. Report.*

Newspapers

Richard Olney Scrapbooks. In possession of Catherine Olney, Leicester, Mass.
Richard Olney Newspaper Clippings. Given to author by Agnes A. Abbot,
  Olney's granddaughter. *Olney news clippings.*
For individual items from scattered newspapers and periodicals, see footnotes.
  Those used for extended coverage were, for Boston: *Globe, Herald, Journal,
  Post, Transcript;* for Chicago: *Times, Tribune;* for London: *Times;* for New
  York: *Times, Tribune, World;* for Washington: *Post, Star.* Other periodicals
  included *The Nation* and *Railroad Gazette.*

Other Primary Sources

Adams, Henry. *Letters of Henry Adams.* Edited by Worthington Chauncey
  Ford. Boston, 1938.
Atkins, Edwin F. *Sixty Years in Cuba.* Cambridge, Mass. 1926.
"Attorney-General Olney." *Green Bag,* 5 (June 1893): 257–59.
Barron, Clarence W. *More They Told Barron.* Edited by Arthur Pound and
  Samuel Taylor Moore. New York, 1931.
Batchelder, Samuel F. *Bits of Harvard History.* Cambridge, Mass., 1924.
Boardman, Mabel T. *Under the Red Cross Flag at Home and Abroad.* Philadelphia,
  1915.

Brown, Robert P. et al., eds. *Memories of Brown* [University]. Providence, 1909.

Catalogue of the Officers and Students of Brown University. Providence, 1851–56.

Catalogue of the Trustees, Instructors and Students of Leicester Academy, Massachusetts. Andover, 1848. Worcester, 1849–51.

Cleveland, Grover. *The Letters of Grover Cleveland, 1850–1908.* Edited by Allan Nevins. Boston, New York, 1933. *Cleveland Letters.*

——. *Presidential Problems.* New York, 1904.

Commager, Henry Steele, ed. *Documents of American History.* 8th ed. New York, 1968.

Congdon, Charles T. *Reminiscences of a Journalist.* Boston, 1880.

Darrow, Clarence. *The Story of My Life.* New York, 1931.

General Managers Association [of Chicago]. *Minutes of Meetings.* Chicago, 1894.

Greenough, Charles P. "Memoir of Richard Olney." *Proceedings of the Massachusetts Historical Society*, 51 (December 1917): 204–205.

Herbert, Hilary A. "Grover Cleveland and His Cabinet at Work." *Century Magazine*, 85 (March 1913): 740–44.

Historical Catalogue of Brown University, 1764–1914. Providence, 1914.

Lawrence, William. *Memories of a Happy Life.* Boston, New York, 1926.

Mallet-Prevost, Severo. [Sworn] "Memorandum Left with Judge Schoenrich, Not to Be Made Public Except at His Discretion After My Death" [8 February 1944]. Published in Otto Schoenrich, "The Venezuela, British Guiana Boundary Dispute." *American Journal of International Law*, 43 (July 1949): 528–30.

Memorial Exercises of the Boston Bar Association Before the Supreme Judicial Court in Memory of Richard Olney, Hon. Caleb W. Loring, Presiding. June 28, 1919. Boston, 1919. *Olney Memorial Exercises.*

Miles, Nelson A. *Serving the Republic.* New York, 1911.

Olney, Richard. *Address of Richard Olney Before Merchants Club Boston, 21 January 1913.* Boston, 1913.

——. *Argument . . . in Favor of Ratifying the Lease of the Worcester, Nashua & Rochester Railroad to the Boston & Maine Railroad.* Boston, 1886.

——. *Arguments Against Compelling Foreign Corporations to File Lists of Stockholders with the Tax Commission.* Pamphlet 12, *Taxation in Massachusetts, 1875–1915.* (Vol. 2). State Library, Boston.

——. "The Development of International Law." *American Journal of International Law*, 1 (April 1907): 418–30.

——. "Discrimination Against Union Labor—Legal?" *American Law Review*, 42 (March, April 1908): 161–67.

——. "Does the Court Exceed Its Power?" *Boston Herald.* 29 October 1911.

——. "Fortification of the Panama Canal." *American Journal of International Law*, 5 (April 1911): 298–301.

——. "General Arbitration Treaties." *American Journal of International Law*, 6 (July 1912): 595–600.

——. "Growth of Our Foreign Policy." *Atlantic Monthly*, 85 (March 1900): 289–301.

——. "International Isolation of the United States." *Atlantic Monthly*, 81 (May 1898): 577–88.

——. "Labor Unions and Politics." *Inter-Nation* (December 1906), pp. 23–29.

——. "Modern Industrialism." *Inter-Nation* (January 1907), pp. 29–42.

——. "National Judiciary and Big Business." *Boston Herald*, 24 September 1911.

——. "The Nation's Parting of the Ways." *Harvard Graduates' Magazine* (September 1904), pp. 48–51.

——. "The New Arbitration Treaty with Great Britain." *Independent*, 61 (21 September 1911): 622–24.

——. "Our Latin-American Policy." *North American Review*, 203 (February 1916): 185–93.

——. "Panama Canal Tolls Legislation and the Hay-Pauncefote Treaty," *Proceedings of the American Society of International Law*, 25 April 1913, pp. 81–92.

——. "Paternalism and Personal Freedom." *Inter-Nation* (January 1908), pp. 3–10.

——. "Recent Phases of the Monroe Doctrine." *Boston Herald*, 1 March 1903.

——. "Summation for the Defense." Edited by Gerald G. Eggert. *American Journal of Legal History*, 13 (January 1969): 68–84.

——. "Some Legal Aspects of Railroad Rate-Making by Congress." *North American Review*, 181 (October 1905): 481–501.

——. "A Tangible Goal." *Independent*, 80 (26 October 1914): 126.

——. *Thomas C. Platt v. Philadelphia & Reading Railroad Co., et al., Some Suggestions Submitted by Richard Olney, esq.* n.p., 1894.

——. "To Uphold the Honor of the Profession of Law." *Yale Law Journal*, 19 (March 1910): 342–43.

Parker, George F. "Cleveland's Second Administration as President." *Saturday Evening Post*, 195 (9 June 1923): 40–50.

——. *Recollections of Grover Cleveland*. New York, 1909.

——. "The Return to the White House and the Second Cabinet." *McClure's Magazine*, 32 (March 1909): 457–72.

Report of the Board of Directors of the Chicago, Burlington & Quincy Railroad Company to the Stockholders. Cambridge, Mass., 1885–1901.

Report of the Directors of the Boston & Maine Railroad to the Stockholders. Boston, 1880–1900.

The –th Report of the Eastern Railroad Company. Boston, 1870–84.

Roosevelt, Theodore. *The Letters of Theodore Roosevelt*. Edited by Elting E. Morison and John M. Blum. 8 vols. Cambridge, Mass., 1951–54.

Schofield, John M. *Forty-Six Years in the Army*. New York, 1897.

Scruggs, William L. *British Aggressions in Venezuela, or The Monroe Doctrine on Trial*. Atlanta, 1895.

Smalley, George W. *Anglo-American Memories*. London, 1910.

Torrey, George Arnold. *A Lawyer's Recollections in and out of Court*. Boston, 1910.

Wayland, Francis, and Wayland, H. L. *A Memoir of the Life and Labors of Francis Wayland*. 2 vols. New York, 1867.

White, James E. *A Life Span and Reminiscences of Railway Mail Service*. Philadephia, 1910.

Whitney, Edward B. "The Income Tax and the Constitution." *Harvard Law Review,* 20 (February 1907): 285–96.

Wilson, William L., *The Cabinet Diary of William L. Wilson, 1896–1897.* Festus Summers, ed., Chapel Hill, 1957. *Wilson's Cabinet Diary.*

Secondary Sources

Abrams, Richard. *Conservatism in a Progressive Era.* Cambridge, Mass., 1964.

Allen, Frederick Lewis. *The Great Pierpont Morgan.* New York, 1949.

Amory, Cleveland. *The Proper Bostonians.* New York, 1947.

Babst, Earl D., and Vander Velde, Lewis G., eds. *Michigan and the Cleveland Era. Sketches of University of Michigan Staff Members and Alumni Who Served the Cleveland Administrations 1885–89, 1893–97.* Ann Arbor, 1948.

Bailey, Hollis R. *Attorneys and Their Admission to the Bar in Massachusetts.* Boston, 1907.

Bailey, Thomas A. *A Diplomatic History of the American People.* 6th ed. New York, 1958.

Baker, George Pierce. *The Formation of the New England Railroad Systems.* Cambridge, Mass., 1949.

Barnard, Harry A. *"Eagle Forgotten": The Life of John Peter Altgeld.* Indianapolis, 1938.

Barnes, James A. *John G. Carlisle: Financial Statesman.* New York, 1931.

Barton, William E. *The Life of Clara Barton.* 2 vols. Boston, 1922.

Bell, Charles H. *The Bench and Bar of New Hampshire.* Boston, New York, 1894.

Berman, Edward. *Labor and the Sherman Act.* New York, 1930.

——. *Labor Disputes and the President of the United States.* New York, 1924.

Bland, J. O. P. *Li. Hung-chang.* London, 1917.

Bogen, Jules I. *The Anthracite Railroads.* New York, 1927.

Boudin, Louis B. *Government by Judiciary.* 2 vols. New York, 1932.

Bradlee, Francis B. C. *The Boston & Maine Railroad. A History of the Main Road, with Its Tributary Lines.* Salem, Mass., 1921.

Braisted, William R. "The United States and the American-China Development Company." *Far Eastern Quarterly,* 11 (November 1951): 147–65.

Briggs, John Ely. *William Peters Hepburn.* Iowa City, 1919.

Bronson, Walter C. *The History of Brown University 1764–1914.* Providence, 1914.

Browne, Waldo R. *Altgeld of Illinois: A Record of His Life and Work.* New York, 1925.

Buck, Solon J. *The Granger Movement. A Study of Agricultural Organization and its Political, Economic and Social Manifestations, 1870–1880.* Cambridge, Mass., 1913.

Buder, Stanley. *Pullman: An Experiment in Industrial Order and Community Planning, 1880–1930.* New York, 1967.

Campbell, A. E. *Great Britain and the United States, 1895–1903*. Glasgow, 1960.

Campbell, Edward Gross. *The Reorganization of the American Railroad System, 1893–1900*. New York, 1938.

Campbell, Charles S., Jr. *Special Business Interests and the Open Door Policy*. New Haven, 1951.

Centenary of Leicester Academy. Worcester, 1884.

The Centennial History of the Harvard Law School 1817–1917. Boston, 1918.

Child, Clifton J. "The Venezuela-British Guiana Boundary Arbitration of 1899." *American Journal of International Law*, 44 (October 1950): 682–93.

Cochran, Thomas C. *Railroad Leaders 1845–1890. The Business Mind in Action*. Cambridge, Mass., 1953.

Corey, Lewis. *The House of Morgan. A Social Biography of the Masters of Money*. New York, 1930.

Corwin, Edwin S. "The Antitrust Acts and the Constitution." *Virginia Law Review*, 18 (February 1932): 355–78.

——. *Court over Constitution*. Princeton, 1938.

Curti, Merle, and Nash, Roderick. *Philanthropy in the Shaping of American Higher Education*. New Brunswick, 1965.

Cummings, Homer, and McFarland, Carl. *Federal Justice*. New York, 1937.

Daggett, Stuart. *Chapters on the History of the Southern Pacific*. New York, 1922.

——. *Railroad Reorganization*. Cambridge, Mass., 1924.

Daniels, George Fisher. *History of the Town of Oxford, Massachusetts*. Oxford, Mass., 1892.

Dennett, Tyler. *John Hay: From Poetry to Politics*. New York, 1933.

Dennis, William Cullen. Editorial Comment, "The Venezuela-British Guiana Boundary Arbitration of 1899." *American Journal of International Law*, 44 (October 1950): 720–27.

Dewey, Davis Rich. *Financial History of the United States*. 12th ed. New York, 1934.

Dictionary of American Biography. Edited by Allen Johnson. 22 vols. New York, 1928–37.

Dulles, Foster R. *The American Red Cross: A History*. New York, 1950.

Dunne, Finley Peter. *Mr. Dooley in the Hearts of His Countrymen*. Boston, 1899.

Edmunds, George F. "The Arbitration Treaty." *Independent*, 49 (4 February 1897): 137–38.

Eggert, Gerald G. "Our Man in Havana: Fitzhugh Lee." *Hispanic American Historical Review*, 47 (November 1967): 463–85.

——. *Railway Labor Disputes: The Beginnings of Federal Strike Policy*. Ann Arbor, 1967.

——. "Richard Olney and the Income Tax Cases." *Mississippi Valley Historical Review*, 48 (June 1961): 24–41.

Ellis, Elmer. "Public Opinion and the Income Tax, 1860–1900." *Mississippi Valley Historical Review*, 26 (September 1940): 236–42.

Fairbanks, Edward T. *The Town of St. Johnsbury, Vt*. St. Johnsbury, Vt., 1914.

Faulkner, Harold U. *Politics, Reform and Expansion, 1890–1900.* New York, 1959.

Flexner, Abraham. *Funds and Foundations, Their Policies Past and Present.* New York, 1952.

Frankfurter, Felix, and Landis, James M. *The Business of the Supreme Court.* New York, 1928.

Gardiner, A. C. *The Life of Sir William Harcourt.* 2 vols. London, 1923.

Garraty, John A. *Henry Cabot Lodge: A Biography.* New York, 1953.

Ginger, Ray. *The Bending Cross: A Biography of Eugene Victor Debs.* New Brunswick, 1949.

Gossip, G. H. D. "England in Nicaragua and Venezuela from an American Point of View." *Fortnightly Review,* 58 (December 1895): 829–42.

Grantham, Dewey W., Jr. *Hoke Smith and the Politics of the New South.* Baton Rouge, 1958.

Grenville, J. A. S. *Lord Salisbury and Foreign Policy, the Close of the Nineteenth Century.* London, 1964.

Grenville, John A. S., and Young, George Berkeley. *Politics, Strategy and American Diplomacy: Studies in Foreign Policy, 1873–1917.* New Haven, London, 1966.

Gresham, Matilda. *Life of Walter Quintin Gresham, 1832–1895.* 2 vols. Chicago, 1919.

Grodinsky, Julius. *The Iowa Pool: A Study in Railroad Competition, 1870–1884.* Chicago, 1950.

———. *Jay Gould: His Business Career, 1867–1892.* Philadelphia, 1957.

Guild, Reuben A. *History of Brown University with Illustrative Documents.* Providence, 1867.

Healy, David F. *US Expansionism: The Imperialist Urge in the 1890's.* Madison, 1970.

Hirsch, Mark D. *William C. Whitney, Modern Warwick.* New York, 1948.

Hoffman, Charles. "Depression of the Nineties." *Journal of Economic History,* 16 (June 1956): 137–64.

———. "The Depression of the Nineties—An Economic History." Diss., Columbia University, 1954.

Holbo, Paul S. "A View of [LaFeber's] *The New Empire.*" Read at meeting of the Organization of American Historians. New Orleans, 16 April 1971.

———. "Economics, Emotion, and Expansion: An Emerging Foreign Policy." In *The Gilded Age,* edited by H. Wayne Morgan. Rev. ed. Syracuse, N.Y., 1970, pp. 199–221.

Hollingsworth, J. Rogers. *The Whirligig of Politics: The Democracy of Cleveland and Bryan.* Chicago, London, 1963.

Hovey, Carl. *The Life Story of J. Pierpont Morgan. A Biography.* New York, 1911.

Hurd, D. Hamilton. *History of Worcester County, Massachusetts.* 2 vols. Philadelphia, 1889.

Industrial Chicago. Vol. 6, *The Bench and Bar.* Chicago, 1896.

James, Henry. *Richard Olney and His Public Service.* Boston, New York, 1923.

Jeyes, Samuel Henry. *Mr. Chamberlain: His Life and Public Career*. London, 1903.

Josephson, Matthew. *The Politicos 1865–1896*. New York, 1938.

Kennedy, Charles J. "The Eastern Rail-road Company, 1855–1884." *Business History Review*, 31 (Spring, Summer 1957): 92–123, 179–208.

King, Willard, *Melville Weston Fuller*. New York, 1950.

Kirkland, Edward Chase. *Men, Cities and Transportation*. 2 vols. Cambridge, Mass., 1948.

Kolko, Gabriel. *Railroads and Regulation 1877–1916*. Princeton, 1965.

LaFeber, Walter. "The American Business Community and Cleveland's Venezuela Message." *Business History Review*, 34 (Winter 1960): 393–402.

———. *The New Empire: An Interpretation of American Expansion, 1860–1898*. Ithaca, N.Y., 1963.

Langeluttig, Albert G. *The Department of Justice of the United States*. Baltimore, 1927.

Latané, John H. *A History of American Foreign Policy*. New York, 1927.

Lauck, William Jett. *The Causes of the Panic of 1893*. New York, 1907.

Lecht, Leonard A. *Experience under Railway Labor Legislation*. New York, 1955.

Leech, Margaret. *In the Days of McKinley*. New York, 1959.

Letwin, William. *Law and Economic Policy in America: The Evolution of the Sherman Act*. New York, 1965.

Lewis, Oscar. *The Big Four: The Story of Huntington, Stanford, Hopkins, and Crocker and of the Building of the Central Pacific*. New York, London, 1938.

Lindsey, Almont. *The Pullman Strike: The Story of a Unique Experiment and of a Great Labor Upheaval*. Chicago, 1942.

Link, Arthur S. *Wilson: The New Freedom*. Princeton, 1956.

Mathews, Joseph J. "Informal Diplomacy in the Venezuelan Crisis of 1896." *Mississippi Valley Historical Review*, 50 (September 1963): 195–212.

May, Ernest R. *Imperial Democracy: The Emergence of America as a Great Power*. New York, 1961.

McClellan, Robert. *The Heathen Chinee: A Study of American Attitudes Toward China, 1890–1905*. Columbus, Ohio, 1971.

McCormick, Thomas J. *China Market: America's Quest for Informal Empire, 1893–1901*. Chicago, 1967.

McElroy, Robert. *Grover Cleveland, the Man and the Statesman*. 2 vols. New York, 1923.

McMurry, Donald L. *Coxey's Army*. Boston, 1929.

———. "Labor Policies of the General Managers' Association of Chicago, 1886–1894." *Journal of Economic History*, 13 (Spring 1953): 160–78.

Merrill, Horace Samuel. *Bourbon Leader: Grover Cleveland and the Democratic Party*. Boston, 1957.

Meyer, H. R. "The Settlement with the Pacific Railways." *Quarterly Journal of Economics*, 13 (1899): 427–44.

Miller, C. A. *Lives of the Interstate Commerce Commissioners and the Commission's Secretaries*. n. p., 1946.

Miller, George H. *Railroads and the Granger Laws*. Madison, Milwaukee, London, 1971.

Millis, Walter. *The Martial Spirit*. New York, 1931.

Morgan, James. *The Life Work of Edward A. Moseley in the Service of Humanity*. New York, 1913.

Morison, Samuel Eliot. *Three Centuries of Harvard, 1636–1936*. Cambridge, Mass., 1936.

National Cyclopaedia of American Biography. 50 vols. New York, 1891–1952.

Nevins, Allan. *Grover Cleveland: A Study in Courage*. New York, 1932.

———. *Henry White: Thirty Years of American Diplomacy*. New York, London, 1930.

Noyes, Alexander Dana. *Forty Years of American Finance*. 2nd ed. New York, 1909.

Olney, James H. *A Genealogy of the Descendants of Thomas Olney*. Providence, 1889.

Olson, James C. *J. Sterling Morton*. Lincoln, Neb., 1942.

Paul, Randolph E. *Taxation in the United States*. Boston, 1954.

Perkins, Dexter. *The Monroe Doctrine, 1867–1907*. Baltimore, 1937.

Poor, Henry V., and Poor, H. W., *Poor's Manual of the Railroads of the United States*. New York, 1895.

"The Presidency and Mr. Olney." *Atlantic Monthly*, 77 (May 1896): 676–82.

"The Presidency and Secretary Morton." *Atlantic Monthly*, 77 (March 1896): 388–94.

Ratner, Sidney. *American Taxation*. New York, 1942.

Reid, Wemyss. *Memoirs and Correspondence of Lord Playfair*. London, 1899.

Richardson, Leon Burr. *William E. Chandler, Republican*. New York, 1940.

Ripley, William Z. *Railroads, Finance and Organization*. 1920 ed. New York, 1920.

Ross, Ishbel. *Angel of the Battlefield: The Life of Clara Barton*. New York, 1956.

Russ, William Adam, Jr. *The Hawaiian Revolution (1893–1894)*. Selinsgrove, Pa., 1959.

Satterlee, Herbert Lee. *J. Pierpont Morgan: An Intimate Portrait*. New York, 1919.

Schlote, Werner. *British Overseas Trade from 1700 to the 1930's*. Translated by W. O. Henderson and W. H. Chaloner. Oxford, England, 1952.

Schoenrich, Otto. "The Venezuela, British Guiana Boundary Dispute." *American Journal of International Law*, 43 (July 1949): 523–30.

Schuyler, Montgomery. "Richard Olney." *The American Secretaries of State*. Edited by Samuel Flagg Bemis. 10 vols. New York, 1927–29.

Scott, James Brown. *Robert Bacon: Life and Letters*. Garden City, N.Y., 1923.

Seligman, Edwin R. A. *The Income Tax*. New York, 1911.

Sharfman, I. L. *The Interstate Commerce Commission. A Study in Administrative Law and Procedure*. 4 vols. New York, 1931–37.

Shiras, George, III. *Justice George Shiras, Jr., of Pittsburgh*. Pittsburgh, 1953.

Sloan, Jennie A. "Anglo-American Relations and the Venezuelan Boundary Dispute." *Hispanic American Historical Review*, 18 (November 1938): 486–506.

Smith, Theodore Clarke. "Secretary Olney's Real Credit in the Venezuela Affair." *Proceedings of the Massachusetts Historical Society,* 65 (May 1933): 112–47.

Staples, Henry Lee, and Mason, Alpheus Thomas, *The Fall of a Railroad Empire: Brandeis and the New Haven Merger Battle.* Syracuse, N.Y., 1947.

Stevens, Sylvester K. *American Expansion in Hawaii.* Harrisburg, Pa., 1945.

Strong, Theron G. *Joseph H. Choate.* New York, 1917.

Studenski, Paul, and Krooss, Herman E. *Financial History of the United States.* New York, 1952.

Swaine, Robert T. *The Cravath Firm and Its Predecessors: 1819–1947.* 2 vols. New York, 1946.

Swift, Morrison I. "Why the Boston Experiment Failed." *Independent,* 68 (10 February 1910): 298–300.

Swisher, Carl B. *American Constitutional Development.* Boston, 1943.

———. *Stephen J. Field, Craftsman of the Law.* Washington, 1930.

Taft, William Howard. *The Anti-Trust Act and the Supreme Court.* New York, 1914.

Tansill, Charles Callan. *The Foreign Policy of Thomas F. Bayard, 1885–1897.* New York, 1940.

Tate, Merze. *The United States and the Hawaiian Kingdom: A Political History,* New Haven, London, 1965.

Terrill, Tom E. "David A. Wells, The Democracy, and Tariff Reduction, 1877–1894." *Journal of American History,* 56 (December 1969): 540–55.

Thorelli, Hans. *The Federal Antitrust Policy.* Baltimore, 1955.

Trottman, Nelson. *History of the Union Pacific: A Financial and Economic Survey.* New York, 1923.

Twiss, Benjamin R. *Lawyers and the Constitution: How Laissez Faire Came to the Supreme Court.* Princeton, 1942.

Tyler, Alice Felt. *The Foreign Policy of James G. Blaine.* Minneapolis, 1927.

Warren, Charles. *History of the Harvard Law School and of Early Legal Conditions in America.* 2 vols. New York, 1908.

Washburn, Emory. *Brief Sketch of the History of Leicester Academy.* Boston, 1855.

Weberg, Frank P. *The Background of the Panic of 1893.* Washington, 1929.

Whates, H. *The Third Salisbury Administration, 1895–1900.* Westminster, 1900.

White, Henry Kirke. *History of the Union Pacific Railway.* Chicago, 1895.

Who's Who in America, 1899–1900. Chicago, 1900.

Williams, Blance Colton. *Clara Barton, Daughter of Destiny.* Philadelphia, 1941.

Williams, William Appleman. *The Contours of American History.* Cleveland, 1961.

———. *The Tragedy of American Diplomacy.* Cleveland, 1959.

Woodward, C. Vann. *Origins of the New South, 1877–1913.* Baton Rouge, 1951.

Young, George Berkeley. "Intervention under the Monroe Doctrine: The Olney Corollary." *Political Science Quarterly,* 57 (June 1942): 247–80.

Young, Marilyn Blatt. *Rhetoric of Empire: American China Policy 1895–1901.* Cambridge, Mass., 1968.

Index